Buddhism in the Modern World

Buddhism in the Modern World

Adaptations of an Ancient Tradition

EDITED BY

STEVEN HEINE AND CHARLES S. PREBISH

OXFORD
UNIVERSITY PRESS

2003

OXFORD
UNIVERSITY PRESS

Oxford   New York
Auckland   Bangkok   Buenos Aires   Cape Town   Chennai
Dar es Salaam   Delhi   Hong Kong   Istanbul   Karachi   Kolkata
Kuala Lumpur   Madrid   Melbourne   Mexico City   Mumbai   Nairobi
São Paulo   Shanghai   Taipei   Tokyo   Toronto

Copyright © 2003 by Oxford University Press, Inc.

Published by Oxford University Press, Inc.
198 Madison Avenue, New York, New York, 10016

www.oup.com

Oxford is a registered trademark of Oxford University Press

Library of Congress Cataloging-in-Publication Data
Buddhism in the modern world : adaptations of an ancient tradition/
edited by Steven Heine and Charles S. Prebish.
p. cm.
Includes bibliographical references and index.
ISBN 0-19-514697-2; ISBN 0-19-514698-0 (pbk.)
1. Buddhism—History—20th century.   I. Heine, Steven, 1950–   II.
Prebish, Charles S.
BQ316 .B83 2003
294.3'09'04—dc21   2002015649

9 8 7 6 5 4 3 2

Printed in the United States of America
on acid-free paper

Acknowledgments

The editors thank their respective institutions, Florida International University and Pennsylvania State University, for research support to complete this book, as well as Cynthia Read, the editor at Oxford University Press, for her help in shaping the direction of the project. In addition, we thank Wendy Lo for her diligent work in editing the manuscript.

Contents

Contributors

RAOUL BIRNBAUM is a professor of Buddhist studies at the University of California, Santa Cruz, where he teaches in the Anthropology and Art History departments. He is the author of *The Healing Buddha* (1989), *Studies on the Mysteries of Mañjuśrī*, and *Body of Practice in Buddhist China*, and numerous articles on Buddhist worlds of practice in China.

BONGKIL CHUNG is professor of philosophy at Florida International University. His major area of research is East Asian Mahāyāna Buddhist philosophy and Won Buddhist philosophy. Chung's publications include *An Introduction to Won Buddhism* (1993), *The Dharma Words of Master Chŏngsan* (2000), *The Scriptures of Won Buddhism with an Introduction* (2002), and numerous articles on Won Buddhism in international scholarly journals.

DAN COZORT is an associate professor of religion at Dickinson College in Carlisle, Pennsylvania, where he teaches about the religions of India and Native America. He is the author of several publications, including *Highest Yoga Tantra* (1994), *Sand Mandala of Vajrabhairava* (1996), and *Unique Tenets of the Middle Way Consequence School* (1998), as well as numerous articles and contributions to other books.

TARA DOYLE is a lecturer in religious studies at Emory University and the director of Emory's Tibetan Studies Program in Dharamshala, India. Her research has focused on contested South Asian religious sites, ex-untouchable Buddhist converts, and Asian contemplative traditions. Doyle was the founding co-director of the Antioch Buddhist Studies Program in Bodh Gaya. She is also the author of *Journeys to the Diamond Throne*.

STEVEN HEINE is professor of religious studies and history and director of the Institute for Asian Studies at Florida International University. His specialty is the history of Ch'an and Zen Buddhism in China and Japan. Heine's publications include *Dōgen and the Kōan Tradition* (1994), *Japan in Traditional and Postmodern Perspectives* (1995), *The Zen Poetry of Dōgen* (1997), *Shifting Shape, Shaping Text* (1999), *The Kōan* (2001), and *Opening a Mountain* (2002). He is also editor of the *Japan Studies Review*.

CHARLES B. JONES is associate professor in the Department of Religion and Religious Education at the Catholic University of America in Washington, D.C. He has published *Buddhism in Taiwan: Religion and the State, 1660–1990* (1999), as well as numerous articles and reviews.

NATHAN KATZ is professor and chair of religious studies at Florida International University. Among Katz's twelve books are *Buddhist Images of Human Perfection* (1989), *Conflict in Buddhist Societies: Thailand, Burma, and Sri Lanka* (1988), and *The Last Jews of Cochin: Jewish Identity in Hindu India* (1993).

CHARLES S. PREBISH is professor of religious studies at Pennsylvania State University. He is the author or editor of eleven books and more than fifty articles and chapters, including *American Buddhism* (1979), *A Survey of Vinaya Literature* (1996), *The Faces of Buddhism in America* (1998), *Luminous Passage: The Practice and Study of Buddhism in America* (1999), *The A to Z of Buddhism* (2001), and *Westward Dharma: Buddhism Beyond Asia* (2002). He is also a founding co-editor of the online *Journal of Buddhist Ethics* and the *Journal of Global Buddhism*.

JACQUELINE I. STONE is professor of religion at Princeton University. Her field of specialization is in Japanese Buddhism. She is the author of the award-winning *Original Enlightenment and the Transformation of Medieval Japanese Buddhism* (1999), as well as numerous articles on the Tendai, Nichiren, and Pure Land Buddhist traditions.

DONALD K. SWEARER is the Charles and Harriet Cox McDowell Professor of Religion at Swarthmore College, where he teaches courses in Asian and comparative religions. His research has focused on Theravada Buddhism, especially in Thailand. His published monographs include *Me and Mine: Selected Essays of Bhikkhu Buddhadasa* (1989), *For the Sake of the World: The Spirit of Buddhist and Christian Monasticism* (1989), *Ethics, Wealth, and Salvation: A Study in Buddhist Social Ethics* (1990), *The Buddhist World of Southeast Asia* (1995), and *The Legend of Queen Cama* (1998).

Buddhism in the Modern World

Introduction

Traditions and Transformations in
Modern Buddhism

Aims of the Volume

Several movies that have gained worldwide popularity in recent years
have highlighted a sense of difficulty and dismay in accepting the
inevitable and sometimes radical challenges and changes that
Buddhist institutions and practitioners have undergone in modern
times. The 1980s film *The Funeral,* by the late Itami Juzo, portrays a
Japanese Buddhist priest performing traditional mortuary rites, such
as the bestowing of a posthumous Buddhist name, as an activity that
seems hypocritical and corrupt in a modern world characterized by
avarice, jealousy, greed, and the breakdown of long-standing family
structures. Similarly, *The Cup* (1999), by Khyentse Norbu, a Tibetan
lama who studied filmmaking with famed director Bernardo
Bertolucci, shows a group of young monks who, despite their
monastic robes and shaved heads, are more eager to watch an
important soccer match on television than to adhere to their strict
training program that does not allow for secular distraction. Such
images of Buddhism caught between worlds—one seemingly archaic
and pure and the other fragmented and contaminated by impurity—
are frequently reinforced by other ironic media constructions of
Buddhists. These include a variety of postmodern drawings of
Bodhidharma shown as a kind of corporate samurai that graced the
covers of *Mangajin,* a magazine on Japanese culture that was popular
in the 1990s, as well as television ads for IBM that show monks
secluded in remote mountains mastering the art of high-tech
software.

As with other major world religions, the history of Buddhism has long been characterized by an ongoing tension between attempts to preserve traditional ideals and modes of practice and the need to adapt to changing social and cultural conditions. In other words, there is a conflict between the seemingly timeless, unchanging values of a pure tradition and the continuing imperative to adjust to and accommodate the forces of change. Many developments in Buddhist history, such as the infusion of esoteric rituals, the arising of forms of devotionalism and lay movements, and the assimilation of warrior practices, reflect the impact of widespread yet fundamental social and cultural changes on traditional religious structures. However, for better or worse, Buddhism—or so it seems in the popular consciousness as people imagine what the religion must be like—has enjoyed the ability to maintain its traditional purity to a remarkable degree. In most Buddhist cultures there has endured some form of throwback to the pristine tradition of monks practicing the Vinaya disciplines; studying sūtras and other primary texts according to sectarian hermeneutic methods; performing rites of contemplation, supplication, repentance, or pilgrimage; or engaging in social welfare programs that reflect the ideals of compassion or right action.

At the same time, these monastic, textual, ritual, or social traditions have been inalterably affected by continuing encounters with modernization. The process of modernization, generally considered to have begun in the nineteenth century as a response to the industrial revolution, encompasses a variety of factors. These include intellectual trends such as scientism and rationalism; changes in lifestyle such as secularization and an increasing dependence on technology; the rise of ideologies that present alternative or rival standpoints to traditional religion ranging from Marxism to psychotherapy, as well as the influx of syncretic and new religious movements; and the effect of ethical crises raised by medical and environmental concerns.

In addition to these worldwide factors, there is another set of elements that seems to be distinctive to the Buddhist experience in Asian society. This set of factors encompasses cultural forces, intellectual trends, societal developments, and political factors. The cultural forces include the inseparability and intertwining of industrialization with Westernization, that is, the identity on many levels of becoming modernized with the importing of values and modes of behavior from the West. The intellectual trends include Orientalism or a cultural stereotyping of the East by the West varying between romanticization/idealization and stigmatization/demonization again by the dominant Western forces. Societal developments such as repressive as well as increasingly democratic responses to age-old problems of gender, racial, and social discrimination continue to alter the relation of Buddhism and society. An array of often conflicting political factors that affect Buddhist societies in Asia includes nationalist movements in India, as well as the rise of both Japanese imperialism and communism in China, in the aftermath of colonialism in South and Southeast Asia. Furthermore, the

Tibetan exile and the geopolitical splintering of Korea and Vietnam have greatly affected the practice of traditional Buddhism. In terms of religion, some of the major factors of modernization affecting Buddhist practice include the introduction of monotheism and competition from Christianity as the dominant global religious structure. Also, the incorporation of Western models for historical, scientific, literary critical, and related methodological approaches has compelled a rethinking and revising of the study of traditional sacred texts and rites, including the reediting and reissue of versions of the Buddhist canon.

This volume explores how a variety of traditional Buddhist schools and movements have been affected by encountering the myriad forces of modernization, especially those factors unique to the Asian experience. The ten chapters contributed by leading scholars deal with whether the encounters engender either a return to the sources of the tradition or reform tendencies. The return to sources is evidenced by the cases of iconoclastic, antimaterialistic trends in Thai Buddhist debates about iconography or modern adaptations of the *Vinaya*. Reform tendencies include modifications in Tibetan monasticism or Sōtō Zen textual studies; or a merging of religion and society as in nationalistic appropriations of Sri Lankan cave temples, political developments in recent Nichiren Buddhist lay movements, or new trends in Korean Buddhist thought. The chapters discuss how the respective schools come to define themselves on the world stage in terms of the ways they have been transformed by social forces affecting the Asian religious experience. All of the contributors consider how traditional practices such as precepts, images, meditation, or scriptures respond to the forces of modernization including nationalist or postcolonial movements, the impact of Westernization, rival religions and ideologies, and the influence of diverse cultural trends.

The term "schools" is understood here in a flexible sense that encompasses a stricter meaning of formal sects or denominations, as in the case of Sōtō Zen and Nichiren in Japan, which have long been regulated by the government and threatened by proscription, and Tibetan or Thai Buddhism. The term also covers a more generic sense of schools of thought or practice, including ritual or textual traditions involving meditative, monastic, devotional, or iconographic traditions that may revolve around an individual leader or a smaller band of followers. These include the *nianfo* movement in Taiwan, the role of the modern monk Hongyi in China, or the revitalization of Bodh Gayā. The volume offers a pan-Buddhist approach by covering all major Buddhist regions of South Asia (India, Sri Lanka), Southeast Asia (Thailand), Central Asia (Tibet), and East Asia (China, Taiwan, Japan, Korea). The contributors cover topics that are designed to be representative case studies of a traditional Buddhist school in the context of its cultural background; however, the chapters do not attempt to be comprehensive in the sense of trying to examine an entire cultural tradition.

This volume is unique in several respects. Thematically, it highlights the encounter between traditional Buddhism and modernization understood in its historical and theoretical implications. Conceptually, it covers nearly all the major Buddhist cultures through a focus on representative case studies. Also, academically, it brings together a distinctively qualified group of scholars who address diverse cultural materials from a variety of methodological perspectives. The book will appeal to scholars specializing in Buddhist thought and practice; undergraduate and graduate students studying the relation between Buddhism and its cultural background; and generalists interested in the relation between religion and modern society.

Overview of Chapters

The first chapter, "Aniconism versus Iconism in Thai Buddhism" by Donald K. Swearer, discusses the recent iconoclastic trends in Thai Buddhist approaches to making images of the Buddha, a crucial element of Thai religious life. The chapter focuses on the dispute over the veneration of cult relics, images, icons, and amulets that have increasingly played a major role in Thai Buddhist religious practice. The mounting popularity of these iconoclastic trends are due to several factors, such as the Thai cultural ethos becoming progressively more secular and commercial, global trends, and rapid changes in the Thai economic and political society. Some critics regard these venerated icons as a threat to the integrity of Theravāda Buddhism in Thailand.

The next chapter, "The Modernization of Sinhalese Buddhism as Reflected in the Dambulla Cave Temples" by Nathan Katz, deals with the significance of the Golden Rock cave temples at Dambulla, Sri Lanka, as meditation caves and as a pilgrimage center through the medieval period, and the new meanings they took on due to their encounter with modernity. The essay traces the history of the temples through four stages: (1) their mythical consecration connecting them with the foundations of the Sinhalese state, (2) how they were austere meditation caves during the classical era, (3) how they became a popular pilgrimage site during medieval times, and (4) how they were overtly connected with nationalism during the colonial and contemporary periods.

The following chapter, "Varying the Vinaya: Creative Responses to Modernity" by Charles S. Prebish, explores how modern Buddhist communities have maintained their vitality by varying the portions of the *Vinaya* that deal with living conditions (especially focusing on the rules governing clothing, food, and work) and with training (including considerations of community hierarchy and modes of teaching). As Buddhist monastic communities have begun to proliferate throughout the Western world, new and creative adjustments to the *Vinaya* are being entertained in a wide variety of exciting ways. These changes have been brought about without necessarily compromising the wisdom, rigor, or intent of the ancient code.

"Master Hongyi Looks Back: A Modern Man Becomes Monk in Twentieth-Century China" by Raoul Birnbaum examines the reasons that this modern man named Li Shutong became a Buddhist monk, the famous Hongyi. This chapter contains an autobiographical account specifically about his years of transition in Hangzhou, coupled with the direct reminiscences of several persons who were close to him at that time. Further, it considers Hongyi's response to modernity from his Buddhist position. Finally, the chapter discusses some Chinese responses to his example, which range from absolute horror that a man of his talents and background would "throw it all away" to unreserved admiration for a man who established a moral position and fully lived within its frame.

The fifth chapter, "Transition in the Practice and Defense of Chinese Pure Land Buddhism" by Charles B. Jones, examines issues arising from both the practice and defense of Pure Land Buddhism in China from classical times to the modern period. Beginning in the late nineteenth and early twentieth centuries, new challenges to Pure Land thought and practice arose from nascent modern consciousness. The first course led to a conservative reaction against modernism, exemplified by the vigorous defense mounted by the master Yinguang (1861–1940). The second course reoriented Pure Land practice away from the search for rebirth in the Pure Land after death and toward the idea of "building a Pure Land on Earth," as advocated by the modern masters Taixu (1890–1947) and Yinshun (1906–) and their many followers. The chapter will conclude with an overview of proponents of these two tendencies within modern Chinese Buddhism on the island of Taiwan.

The next chapter, "Won Buddhism: The Historical Context of Sot'aesan's Reformation of Buddhism for the Modern World" by Bongkil Chung, depicts the nature of Won Buddhism, founded by Sot'aesan (1891–1943), by describing its historical context and the elements of renovation and reformation of Buddhist faith and practice. Won Buddhism is one of the three Korean indigenous religions that arose at the turn of the twentieth century, the other two being *Ch'ŏndogyo* (the religion of the Heavenly Way) and *Chŭngsan'gyo* (the religion of Chŭngsan). Some of the central religious tenets of the two Korean indigenous religions can be identified in the doctrine of Won Buddhism. Included in this chapter is an analysis of salient features of its central doctrine, which is a synthesis of Confucian ethical tenets and Mahāyāna Buddhist metaphysics, a synthesis that characterizes Sot'aesan's way toward the realization of the Mahayana Buddhist ideal to experience the Buddha land in the modern world.

The following chapter, "Abbreviation or Aberration? The Role of the *Shushōgi* in Modern Sōtō Zen Buddhism" by Steven Heine, analyzes the transition from the *Shōbōgenzō* to the *Shushōgi* in light of a number of developments in modern Japanese religion and society. These include the decline of and official discrimination against Buddhism accompanied by a rise in lay Buddhist movements and the refashioning of the Sōtō institutional structure and hierarchy, as well as the influence of Christianity and efforts to create a Buddhist self-identity in a universal context. The *Shōbōgenzō*, is a collection of sermons and other writings by the founder of the sect, Dōgen Zenji (1200–1253). The *Shushōgi* is a highly condensed or abbreviated version of the *Shōbōgenzō*, which consists of selected passages from the source text. The *Shushōgi* has become the primary scripture cited by priests and lay followers in modern Japan and used in a variety of Sōtō rituals. However, the main tenets of this text are quite different from the *Shōbōgenzō*, especially concerning the roles of meditation and repentance.

"By Imperial Edict and Shogunal Decree: Politics and the Issue of the Ordination Platform in Modern Lay Nichiren Buddhism" by Jacqueline I. Stone considers aspects of how the teaching of the Japanese Buddhist master Nichiren (1222–1282) has been transformed and appropriated by some of his modern followers. It focuses on how his teaching of the earthly Buddha land has been interpreted in terms of nationalism, socialism, and postwar peace movements; and how his understanding of Japan's place in the medieval Buddhist cosmos has been redefined in light of modern national concerns. It also examines the challenge posed to his contemporary followers by the need to balance Nichiren's exclusive truth claim against modern pluralistic sensibilities.

The ninth chapter, "The Making of the Western Lama" by Dan Cozort, examines two organizations, the Foundation for the Preservation of the Mahayana Tradition (FPMT) and the New Kadampa Tradition (NKT) and their formal training programs for Westerners and how these programs differ from the Tibetan curriculum that is their model. This chapter describes the paths the new lamas have taken. This inquiry involves the raising of several questions, such as what it means both to the teachers and to their students that they be a "lama" and the extent to which the traditional role of a lama as teacher and object of devotion is being transformed into a new model that includes being a therapist, "life-coach," and discussion leader. The new model is compared to the traditional Tibetan pathway to designation as a lama.

The final chapter, "Liberate the Mahabodhi Temple! Socially Engaged Buddhism, Dalit-Style" by Tara N. Doyle, discusses Mahabodhi Temple, the main Buddhist temple in Bodh Gayā, India, which has become the center of a religious and power struggle between several Buddhist and Hindu activist groups. During the last 150 years, this religious landscape has been radically transformed. The transformation process can be characterized as having remained relatively peaceful, especially when compared to such shared religious sites as Ayodhya or Jerusalem. However, the transformation of Bodh Gayā into a Buddhist center from a long period of Hindu domination and the religious strife involving the Mahabodhi Temple has nonetheless entailed a great deal of negotiation and contest and conflict at the narrative, economic, legal, and political levels.

I

Aniconism Versus Iconism in Thai Buddhism

Donald K. Swearer

Introduction

Westerners whose knowledge of Buddhism comes primarily from textbooks, even those with relatively expansive descriptions of Buddhist practices, are often startled upon observing temple rituals in Thailand or other Asian Buddhist countries. Usually they see devotees prostrating themselves before large Buddha images and performing other devotional acts such as lighting incense, making flower offerings, and praying. These devotional activities appear to be far removed from a common preconception of the Buddha's rejection of Brahmanical ritualism and the singular dedication of Buddhist monks to the path of meditation. Did not the Buddha teach his disciples to be "lamps unto themselves"; to pursue their own inner journey to enlightenment without relying on external rituals? Was not the Buddha a religious philosopher, the teacher of the Noble Eightfold Path to awakening, rather than a divine being to be venerated? The temple practices that the Western student of Buddhism observes in Buddhist Thailand are at odds with a commonly held view of Buddhism as a nonritualistic, nontheistic religion of mystics, meditators, and philosophers. The contradiction becomes even more acute with the realization that the Buddha image, toward which ritual offerings are directed, is considered by many devotees as the living presence of the Buddha himself.

The cognitive dissonance a contemporary Western student of Buddhism may experience upon entering a Thai temple reverberating with the sounds of chanting monks and filled with clouds of incense while devotees lie prostrate before a Buddha image mirrors a long-standing, ongoing dispute within the Buddhist tradition regarding the nature of signs of the Buddha. Is a sign of the Buddha—whether a bodily relic, a relic of association such as the Buddha's alms bowl, or a relic of indication such as a Buddha image or footprint—merely a reminder of the Buddha or is it, in some way or other, the Buddha's real presence? In other words, does the sign merely symbolize or point to the Buddha; is the Buddha miraculously present in some substantive sense; or, is the relationship between the image or another material sign and the person of the Buddha something between symbol and substantive identification? These questions continue to spark contentious debate within the Buddhist tradition, not unlike similar controversies in Christianity regarding the nature of the eucharistic bread and wine, or the iconoclastic controversy that led to the split between Eastern Orthodoxy and Roman Catholicism.

In this chapter I will focus on the dispute over the veneration of signs of the Buddha in the context of contemporary Thailand. The cult of relics, images, icons, and amulets plays a major role in Thai Buddhist religious practice.[1] The prominence of this cult has prompted critical reactions ranging from strident rejection to reasoned censure. Although icon veneration and aniconic dissent has been one of the defining tensions throughout the history of Buddhism, its contemporary Thai version reflects broader global trends that challenge traditional religious worldviews and institutions. In the last five decades, the pervasiveness of Buddhist influence in the Thai social order has eroded as the cultural ethos has become increasingly more secular and commercial. The role of the monastery in public education has been superseded by government and private schools; respect for the monkhood has declined in the face of more highly regarded vocations; the perceived value of monastic learning has deteriorated; the authority of mainstream *nikāyas* (denominations) has been challenged by various splinter movements; and the role of the monk has become more narrowly confined to one of ritualist and merit-making officiant. These developments, in addition to the increasing commodification of Thai Buddhism, have contributed to the efflorescence of the cult of images, icons, and amulets of the Buddha and Thai Buddhist saints past and present, a cult that has achieved a great current popularity. Thus, although the veneration of icons in Thailand reflects an ancient practice rather than a departure from an "original" monastic Buddhism, its contemporary form reflects the forces of modern globalized commercial culture and is seen by some critics as a threat to the integrity of Theravāda Buddhism in Thailand.

Making the Absent Buddha Present: Image and
Relic Veneration in the Buddhist Tradition

One of the most vexing problems faced by the early followers of the Buddha resulted from his death or *parinibbāna*. On the experiential level, the Buddha's devotees, both monastic and lay, felt a great sense of loss, akin to that experienced at the death of an important, highly respected figure in any community or nation. George Washington, Thomas Jefferson, and Abraham Lincoln are memorialized as national founders and great leaders with statues and monuments in the nation's capital. We do so not only to honor them but in a concrete, material sense to make them present. They become part of our physical space and celebratory time. These material representations do more than merely evoke the past; they bring the past into the present. Similarly, the Buddha was memorialized after his death not only to honor him as a great religious leader but to make his person, his life, and his teachings present in space and time.

Initially the strategy for making the parinibbaned Buddha present took the form of venerating his bodily relics. The Sutta of the Great Passsing or the Final Nibbāna (*Mahāparinibbāna Sutta*/MPNS) relates the story of the Buddha Gotama's death and cremation, and the enshrinement of his remains in Jambudīpa. This Pāli discourse reveals a great deal about how the followers of the Buddha coped with the founder's death, the nature of Buddhist devotionalism, and the dispute over material signs of the Buddha.[2] The Pāli *apadānas* represent a later development of belief in the buddha-field, and the functional equivalent of the *stūpa*/relic to the living Buddha for the purposes of making the type of merit that leads to awakening. Indian epigraphic evidence from about the same period as the *apadānas* shows that early Indian Buddhists felt that the Buddha's virtues somehow spread from his mind to his bodily relics, a belief also manifested in the Buddha image consecration ritual discussed later.

The MPNS embeds the cult of Buddha relics in a multiplex network of belief and practice. It is an episodic, disjointed narrative that serves as a travelogue of the Buddha's last days as he toured from Rājagaha to Kusinārā; a summary of the Buddha's essential teachings; a reflection on the nature of the Buddha, the *dhamma,* and the *sangha;* a justification of the cult of Buddha relics and Buddha devotionalism more generally; and a juxtaposition of the "disparities between temporal power . . . and the ascetic quest for the timeless."[3] The essential teachings include repeated litanies on the universality of impermanence ("it is the nature of all conditioned things to change"), the three trainings (*sīla, samādhi, paññā*) leading to liberation, and a list that has come to be known as the "wings to awakening" (*bodhipakkhiyā-dhammā*) consisting of seven sets of teachings: the four foundations of mindfulness (*satipaṭṭhānā*), the four right exertions (*sammappadhānā*), the four bases of attainment (*iddhipāda*), the five strengths (*balāni*), the five faculties (*indriyāna*), the seven factors of awakening (*sattabhojjaṅga*), and the Noble Eightfold Path.[4] The Buddha's travels from place to place could be regarded as dispersing these teachings (*dhamma*) throughout the region in a manner that reflects the subsequent division of the Buddha's cremated remains that brings the Sutta to a close—bodily relics, urn, and ashes—and their enshrinement in *stūpas* in ten locations throughout India. According to *avadāna* legend, King Asoka later reassembled the relics and redistributed them in 84,000 different places throughout Jambudīpa, a number synonymous with the totality of the Buddha's *dhamma*. This discorporated body of the Buddha is to be reincorporated during the age of the future Buddha, Metteyya, a time when the *dhamma* also will be renewed.

Seen from this perspective, the MPNS constructs the body of the Buddha (*buddhakāya*) and the body of the Dhamma (*dhammakāya*) in a parallel, over-lapping fashion. While the Buddha's body is one, through the distribution of his relics it is also many. Through the cult of *stūpas* the person of the Buddha, made absent by his *parinibbāna*, is made present in time and space. The uni-versal *dhamma* likewise is distributed throughout space and time, by the agency of the *sangha*. For this reason, one of the Sutta's subtexts is the Buddha's con-cern that the *sangha* be adequately prepared to perpetuate the *dhamma*. The theme of honoring the Buddha, in particular venerating his bone relics—"who-ever lays wreaths or puts sweet perfumes and colors . . . [at a *stūpa* for the Tathāgata] with a devout heart, will reap benefit and happiness for a long time" (ii.142)—is matched by passages advocating dedication to the *dhamma*—"what-ever monk, nun, male or female lay-follower dwells practicing the *dhamma* prop-erly, and perfectly fulfills the way of the *dhamma*, he or she honors the Tathāgata, reveres and esteems him and pays him supreme homage" (ii.138). Practicing the *dhamma* and venerating the Buddha complement each other and fuse in the Sutta's powerful image of the Mirror of the Dhamma: "Ānanda, I will teach you a way of knowing the *dhamma* called the Mirror of the Dhamma . . . And, what is the Mirror of the Dhamma? Confidence in the Buddha, that: 'This Blessed Lord is an *arahant*, a fully enlightened Buddha, perfected in wisdom and con-duct, the well-gone one, knower of the worlds, incomparable trainer of men to be tamed, teacher of gods and humans, enlightened, the Lord'" (ii.93). In Buddhaghosa's *Visuddhimagga* these epithets become the focus of mediation on the Buddha (*buddhānussati*). In Thai, Lao, and Khmer ritual practice, the Mirror of Dhamma in its Pāli form—*iti pi so bhagavā arahaṃ sammāsam-buddho*—consists of 108 syllables representing the qualities (*guṇa*) of the Bud-dha (56), the *dhamma* (38), and the *sangha* (14). Reciting or visualizing the formula, a practice that occurs in many ritual contexts including the consecra-tion of Buddha images, invokes the power of the triple gem and is also one of the supreme evocations of devotion to the Buddha.[5]

Although *stūpa*-enshrined relics preceded the appearance of Buddha im-ages in the development of Buddhist devotionalism, anthropomorphic forms followed soon thereafter. It has even been suggested that images of the Buddha may have been fabricated within the lifetime of those who had known the Bud-dha. The Chinese Buddhist monk-pilgrims Faxian (fifth century) and Xuangzang (seventh century) recorded two different versions of the paradigmatic legend of the building of the sandalwood Buddha image; however, similar accounts are found in other traditions, including northern Thailand. As related in the *Vaṭṭaṅgulirāja Jātaka* (VJ) written in Chiang Mai in the thirteenth or fourteenth century, the image (*bimba*) functions as the Buddha's surrogate when the Blessed One is absent and, in this sense, parallels the depiction of the role of the Buddha relic in the *apadānas*. Although in the narrative the Buddha is only temporarily away from the Jetavana monastery, the story prefigures the dilemma of the Buddha's absence brought about by the Buddha's decease.

> Once upon a time the Lord journeyed to Sāvatthi to a distant place to preach the Dhamma. At that time King Pasenadi of Kosala surrounded by a great number of people carrying perfume, garlands, and other means of worship went to the great monastery in Jetavana. Not seeing the Enlightened One, the king was filled with disappointment and saying, "Alas, alas, this Jetavana is empty without the Lord," he returned home greatly dejected. The citizens, filled with agitation, said to one another, "Alas, O sirs, this world without the Enlightened One is indeed empty, without a refuge and without a protector." After some time, the Lord returned to Jetavana. Hearing the news, the king returned with the citizens to pay his respects to the Buddha. Having worshipped the Master he said, "O Lord, even while you are still alive, whenever you go away and people can't see your form [*rūpaṃ apassanato*] they become full of misery [*atidukkhito*] [thinking] they have no protector [*nātho*]. How could they ever be happy and not feel bereaved when you will have entered *parinibbāna*? Therefore, O lord, please allow me to make an image of you to be worshipped by both human beings and gods." Hearing the king's words, the teacher—perceiving that it would bring welfare to the entire world, and to ensure that his teaching endure forever—gave permission to the king to make an image.[6]

The king then has an image carved from sandalwood, covered with robes, and placed on a platform in his palace. When the Buddha enters the room, the image arises to pay respects as if animated by the power of the Buddha. The Blessed One then speaks to the image, charging it to sustain the *sāsana* (religion) for the welfare and benefit of the world for five thousand years. Much of the remainder of the text recounts the great merit acquired from making Buddha images.

The story contextualizes the making of the Buddha image within a ritual, merit-making setting. Here the image compensates for the effects of the Buddha's absence on the well-being of the *sāsana*, in particular, its impact on lay support of the monastic order. Devoid of the actual presence or form (*rūpa*) of the Buddha, the Jetavana monastery seems empty (*suññaṃ*). Therefore, when the Buddha is absent, King Pasenadi and his retinue are unable to present their scented water, flowers, and other offerings (*pūjābaṇḍāni*). Consequently, their opportunity for making merit is forfeited. Furthermore, they are deprived of the protective power of the Buddha and other saints (*arahants*). Today, virtually all rituals in Buddhist

Thailand begin with the assembled congregants "taking refuge" in the Buddha (*Buddhaṃ saraṇaṃ gacchāmi*). Although taking refuge has various meanings, as the VJ suggests, the presence of the Buddha in the person of his image gives the devotees the confidence of his protection after his *parinibbāna* because the image represents the real presence of the Blessed One.

The story makes quite clear that the image is essential to Buddha-*pūjā* and Buddha-*bhakti*. But is the image portrayed as alive or in some substantive sense the Buddha himself? It might seem so, for in the narrative the image rises to greet the Buddha; the Blessed One speaks to it and entrusts his teaching to the image for the welfare of the world. The assembled crowd, as well, seems to regard the miraculous image as though it were alive, for they are so filled with joy upon seeing it that "their hair stood on end." However, the writer continues," a *lifeless* image honors the best among the Buddhas. Who [among you], endowed with life and seeking his own happiness, will not worship the Teacher?"[7] And at another point the author remarks that the image shines "*as if* it were endowed with life."[8] Clearly, the image is not alive in the sense of being the historical Buddha in some literal or substantive sense. The image functions as the Buddha's surrogate and in this capacity represents the Buddha as the head of the *sangha* and the locus of devotional ritual; more than that, however, a superlative image (*seṭṭharūpaṃ*) embodies a verisimilitude that makes it the Buddha's double. The image is enlivened because a nonsentient object is perceived as the real presence of the Buddha, a transformative enactment that occurs at the image's consecration (*buddhābhiseka*) when its eyes are opened (Thai, *phitī bōek phranāet*).

The Ritual of Image Consecration and the Veneration of Sacred Objects in Thailand

Buddha image consecrations in northern Thailand ritualize the act of enlivening a Buddha image as portrayed in the *Vaṭṭaṅgulirāja Jātaka*. They provide a venue for understanding the image as the real presence of the Buddha. In recent years the ceremony has become more prevalent due to the increasing popularity of the cult of images and amulets and the relative decline of other merit-making ceremonies that produce donatory income for the *wat* (temple-monastery), such as ordinations and the preaching of the complete Thai version of the *Vessantara Jātaka* (Thai, *thāet mahāchāt*), observances that in an earlier day played a more central role in village and town life. It is becoming common for monasteries to sponsor a *buddhābhiseka* in order to raise funds for temple construction. Money is generated by donations at the event itself and by the subsequent sale of images and amulets. The value of these icons increases if the monk being honored by the event is highly revered for the perfections (*pāramī*) and powers achieved in *samatha* meditation or if the monks invited to lead the ritual have similar reputations. Thus, paradoxical as it may seem, the increasing popularity of image consecration rites in recent years reflects not a strengthening of Buddhist institutions in Thai society but their weakening as a consequence of the impact of the decline of the *sangha* in other areas, for example, education.

In northern Thailand the ritual to consecrate new Buddha images (*buddhābhiseka*) reenacts the night of the Buddha's enlightenment.[9] Consequently, the ceremony begins at dusk and continues until sunrise. Ordinarily the ceremony will take place in the main hall of a monastery in a specially constructed space that replicates the *bodhimaṇḍa*, the site of the Buddha's enlightenment. After an opening *paritta* recitation, the evening's main activities include monastic chant unique to the *buddhābhiseka*, the preaching of sermons describing the Buddha's journey to enlightenment, extended periods of meditation, and *dāna* presentations given by lay patrons to the participating monks. These activities take place around the *bodhimaṇḍa*, a sacred space encircled by a protective fence (*rājavati*) within which rest the images and amulets to be consecrated and over which spreads a web of consecrated string (Thai, *sai siñcana*) arranged into 108 squares. This web symbolizes the cosmic significance of the Buddha's awakening with its numerical construction matching the supernal qualities of the Buddha, *dhamma*, and *sangha*. Following a reenactment of Sujātā's offering of sweetened milk-rice to the future Buddha, when the morning sun breaks over the horizon, the monk ritualists preach the *Dhammacakkappavattana Sutta* symbolizing the Buddha's awakening and first teaching on the cause and cessation of suffering. Meanwhile, white cloth head coverings that shrouded the Buddha images throughout the evening are removed, marking the successful completion of the enlivening empowerment of the image.[10]

The consecrated image is now infused with the qualities of the Buddha (*buddha-guṇa*). The northern Thai *buddhābhiseka* ceremony, like eye-opening rituals in other Buddhist cultures, makes the Buddha present in the image. Although the precise meaning of the claim that the *parinibbān*ed Buddha is present in any material form has been debated from the time of the Buddha's decease to the present, the *buddhābhiseka* ritual suggests practical strategies by which this happens. As a mimetic reenactment of the night of the Buddha's enlightenment, the ritual brings into time a timeless truth. Just as the abstract, eternal *dhamma* is instantiated by Gotama Buddha, the *buddhābhiseka* brings the absent Buddha into a particular time and place. The means by which this takes place are chant-recitation, sermon-story, dramatic reenactment, and focused recollection. Power is transmitted through chant recitation and the mental qualities meditating monks infuse into the objects of the *buddhābhiseka*.[11] Rehearsing the future Buddha's quest for awakening programs the image with the story that it embodies. Monks noted for *jhānic* attainments achieved by the Buddha infuse these qualities into the image by means of intensive meditation.[12] An *abhiseka* cord connects the previously consecrated Buddha image with the *bodhimaṇḍa*, thereby incorporating the newly consecrated image into a lineage going back to the Buddha's sanctification of the original image. These multiple strategies have a performative signification that infuses, enlivens, and empowers the image with the Buddha's qualities. As Guiseppi Tucci observed of the equivalent Tibetan ritual: "The divine image, whatever it be, has no liturgical value if it has not been consecrated; it is not a holy thing, no spiritual force issues from it, it remains a lifeless object which will never be able to establish any living and direct relation with those who pray."[13]

The current popularity of the *buddhābhiseka* ritual can be seen as one measure of the cult of material signs of the Buddha in Thailand, but there are others, not the least of which is their commercial significance. Stanley Tambiah characterizes the cult of amulets (Thai, *phrakru'ang rāng*) in Thailand as the objectification and transmission of the charisma of Buddhist saints.[14] He observes that there is a huge trade in amulets, votive tablets, images, and other sacralized material icons, as well as a vast popular literature replete with stories of supernormal feats ascribed to revered monks and miraculous powers associated with objects that objectify and transmit their charisma. Glossy magazines such as *Lān-bodhi* (The Realm of Awakening), *Phutho* (Buddha), and *Sūn Phrakru'ang: Nityasānsamrapbuangkānphrakru'ang* (The Journal of the Center for the Cult of Amulets) have become part of the sacred objects industry and often carry ads for images valued at thousands of baht. It is said that commerce in images, amulets, charms, and talismans rivals commerce in real estate. Temple-monasteries (*wats*), especially pilgrimage centers, sell consecrated images, amulets, and other icons either from a separate building or in the main image hall, but shops in downtown business areas and shopping malls also specialize in the sale of such objects.

Most Thai Buddhists wear gold, silver, or bronze neck chains to which several amulets are attached, since specific protective powers may be ascribed to a particular *phrakru'ang rāng* or the type it represents, which is determined by such factors as the historical period, the monastery where it was cast, the figure it represents, and its miraculous history. Tambiah interviewed a successful businessman who ascribed amulets with the power to confer protection and prosperity if one is morally virtuous. He also interviewed a thirty-year-old Bangkok graduate student who wore three amulets: a copper medallion commemorating Phra Ājān Fan, a widely venerated northeastern forest monk; an antique clay amulet from the ancient central Thai city of Pitsanulōk called Phra Sīthit (the Buddha of the four directions); and a bronzed amulet with the impression of Phra Rōt (the Buddha who frees from danger) from northern Thailand. Such evidence led Tambiah to find in the widespread veneration of such sacrala a kind of national cult in which "many contemporary Thai of diverse social and regional origins carry on their persons material signs and mental images of national identity and history."[15] Further, he also sees the Thai obsession with sacralized

material objects as a response to Thailand's rapid economic development beginning in the 1950s and 1960s, "a function . . . of hopeful aspirations for social mobility; for making money in an expanding, though stilted, urban economy;
and for achieving career success through education [despite] . . . vast disparities
of wealth and power, and uncertainties of international politics."[16] Finally, in
the urban ruling elite's ardent pursuit of amulets sanctified by highly revered
forest monks, Tambiah sees a crisis of legitimacy among the privileged sectors
of society confronting a situation of rapid social, political, and economic change.[17]
To be sure, the modern-day cult of amulets reflects premodern belief and practice. However, contrary to what one might expect, with the increasing dominance
of Western rationalism and the influences of modern technology, the cult has
not weakened but has flourished. The destabilization of Thai society did not
create the cult but gave it new fuel by putting people in a position where they
feel the need to rely on supernatural powers to help them negotiate the uncertainties of the new situation.

The following brief translations from popular Buddhist magazines sold at
newsstands in cities, towns, and villages throughout Thailand illustrate several
facets of the cult of images, amulets and similar sacred objects. The first is a
letter written by an editor of *The Realm of Awakening*:

> Before this issue of *Lān Bodhi* went to press, I traveled to pay my
> respects to two old images [of the revered saint] Luang Pū Thuad at
> Wat Chānghai, Pattani Province and Wat Phakho, Songkhlā Prov-
> ince [in south Thailand] venerated by devotees in the area. On the
> day of my visit, crowds of the faithful continuously paid their
> respects [to the images]. The smell of incense and candle smoke
> permeated the atmosphere. Buses of tourists from Bangkok and
> other distant provinces including Thai and Chinese from Malaysia
> and Singapore were parked in front of the *wat*. When one bus left,
> another took its place without letup. The only possible reason for
> this kind of devoted attention is the faith of the people in the effica-
> cious power [Thai, *khwamsaksit*] of the image of Luang Pū Thuad
> that radiates from this place to all who go there to pay their respects,
> make offerings, and ask for the blessing and protection that Luang
> Pū Thuad bestows through the perfection [*pāramī*] of his loving-
> kindness [*mettā*].[18]

> To raise money to build a hospital, the abbot of Wat
> Sīnawalathammawimon, Nongkhāem, arranged a three-day image
> consecration ritual. Luang Pho [the venerable father] has arranged
> for a fulsome ritual as stipulated by traditional learned scholars so
> that the auspicious objects to be consecrated will be especially

efficacious and filled with the power of the Buddha, thereby enabling the objects to protect those who wear them from danger and bring them good fortune in everything they desire.[19]

Christians, Muslims, and Chinese animists continuously come in large numbers to the shrine at Wat Khanlat because they believe in the miraculous power of the marvelous objects that Luang Pho [the venerable father] at Wat Khan Lat has consecrated there following all of the correct procedures. These auspicious objects have gained a considerable reputation among those who have used them. . . . [They include amulets, images, and loving-kindness holy water.] The Venerable Father of Wat Khanlat has gathered [and consecrated] these miraculous, powerful objects representing different religious traditions. Therefore it's no wonder that adherents of various religions come [to purchase] these marvelous objects, which have proven to be efficacious in all circumstances. In addition to all of the miraculous benefits received from using these powerful objects, those who purchase them also achieve another good, for the money will be used to build a new, large hall for religious instruction.[20]

Buddhist Modernism and the Critique of the Cult of Images, Amulets, and Relics

Tambiah suggests that the cult of amulets and other iconic forms of the Buddha and Buddhist saints, so ubiquitous a feature of contemporary Thai popular religion, may function as a marker by which people from diverse social classes and regions construct a shared identity. His more cogent assessment, however, is that this pervasive practice is a means of coping with the impact of the global marketplace on Thai society, the commercialization of Thai culture, and the uncertainties these changes have brought to people's lives with its attendant crisis of legitimation. Whatever explanations one might adduce, both monastic and lay reformers condemn these practices.[21] The critics range from some Thammayut monks of the Ājān Man lineage whose observance of a strict meditation regime is at odds with the magical ritualism of relic veneration[22] to urban-based reformers who assault its blatant commercialism and seeming departure from authentic Buddhist teachings. Prominent media commentators include Sanitsuda Ekachai, assistant editor of the *Bangkok Post*, who attacks the cult of amulets as commercial exploitation of Buddhism by outside economic interests: "Monks used to monopolize amulet-making, but with big money available in the amulet business, they are being edged out. They are used only as ritual performers and thus receive only the crumbs of profits."[23] Included among the major aniconic dissenters in the culture wars over the popular cult of relics, images, and amulets are the prominent Thai monks Phra Prayudh and Buddha-dāsa Bhikkhu, who bring a modernist, rationalist perspective to the debate, and the Santi Asok movement's broad-based assault on culture-Buddhism as a de-basement of the authentic tradition. Phra Prayudh and Buddhadāsa Bhikkhu stand on the shoulders of Prince Patriarch Vajirañāṇavororasa, the early twen-tieth-century reformist *sangharāja*, who wrote textbooks with a rationalist stance and was a promoter of what has been termed "protestant Buddhism."

Phra Prayudh was ordained a novice monk in 1950 at the age of eleven and by 1961 had passed the ninth and highest level of Pāli studies in the Thai *sangha* as well as the three levels of Buddhist studies in the monastic curriculum.[24] He has served as the deputy secretary-general of Mahāchulālongkorn monastic university and the abbot of Wat Phra Phirain monastery in Bangkok, but is best known for his intellectual acumen and scholarly publications that include two Pāli dictionaries of enduring value, editorial leadership in the newest edition of the Thai Pāli *tipiṭaka* and the Mahidol University CD-ROM Pāli canon, and a standard-setting, seminal treatise on Buddhist thought. The corpus of his pub-lished work includes numerous monographs, essays, and talks on a wide vari-ety of topics including criticisms of magical practices in popular Thai Buddhism.

Phra Prayudh, like Tambiah, attributes the increase in the cult of sacred objects (Thai, *sing saksit*) and other beliefs that he considers supernaturalistic, miraculous, and magical to be a consequence of the disruptions and uncertain-ties created by rapid economic and social change related to modernization and Thailand's participation in the global economy.[25] He does not summarily reject the veneration of monks to whom are ascribed supernatural powers or the use of sacred objects sanctified by them. For Phra Prayudh their only legitimate place, however, is as a means by which educated, skillful monks can direct devotees to the *dhamma* rather than to exploit these practices for their own gain. Although the veneration of sacred persons, divine beings, and objects believed to have numinous power may be preferable to no belief at all and might be appropriate in specific settings or circumstances, Phra Prayudh sees the tremendous prolif-eration of such cults as a threat not only to Buddhism but to Thai society in a broader sense.[26] He considers them to be childish and, even worse, to promote the *kilesas* (defilements)—delusion, aversion, and lust. Drawing a sharp distinc-tion between authentic Buddhist teachings and what he considers to be magi-cal practices (Thai, *saiyasāt*), Phra Prayudh characterizes Buddhism as a religion based on reasoned experience and thoughtful attention (*yoniso-manasikāra*). To protect against the threat posed by magical cults, the *sangha*, in particular, must uphold and teach the fundamental principles of Buddhism.

Buddhism promotes the development of virtue (*sīla*), concentration (*samādhi*), and knowledge (*paññā*). In contrast, magical practices champion an intoxication with the benefits of the propitiation of fearful supernatural powers rather than a way of life based on the universal truth of cause and effect. In-stead of advocating the worship of sacred objects, monks must teach purity of intention, loving-kindness and compassion, and the three basic fundamentals of Buddhism regarding action, education, and the sacred. The principle behind all action is the law of *kamma*, that good results come from good actions and bad results from bad actions. This is a rational principle and quite different from the belief in the miraculous power of deities or sacred objects. Closely connected to it is the emphasis in Buddhism on education, training, and the development of one's self. To the degree that preoccupation with sacred powers diverts one from trying to improve oneself in body and mind, then magical cults have a detrimental impact on Buddhism as an institution and also stifle human growth and development. Finally, for Phra Prayudh Buddhism transforms the meaning of the sacred (Thai, *saksit*) from faith in the intervention of outside powers wherever they might be located—in the gods, amulets, images, or even the Buddha—into an ethico-spiritual path that leads to the destruction of delusion, aversion, and lust. In Buddhism the highest form of the "supernatural" refers to purity, wisdom, and virtue.

We find a similar rationalist critique of iconic cults in the teachings of Buddhadāsa Bhikkhu, one of the most influential Thai monks of the twentieth century. Born in Chaiya, south Thailand, on 21 May 1906, as Nguam Panich, he was ordained in 1926. In 1928 he passed the third and final level of the monastic *dhamma* curriculum; however, two years of study in Bangkok, 1930–1932, left him disenchanted with traditional monastic learning, the distractions of the city, and what he saw as the lax behavior of Bangkok monks. Eschewing a conventional monastic career, he returned to Chaiya where he established a forest monastery, Suan Mokkhabalārāma (The Garden of Empowering Liberation), known simply as Suan Mokkh and a prolific publishing career. Buddhadāsa attracted a large following over the years, initially in Thailand but increasingly from other lands including North America, England, and Europe. By the time he died in 1993, Suan Mokkh had become a widely known center for meditation and *dhamma* teaching.

Like Phra Prayudh, Buddhadāsa sees the cult of sacred objects as antithetical to the true *dhamma*, the universal principle of conditionality (*idapaccayatā*), primarily because it promotes blind attachment (*upādāna*). The truly sacred (Thai, *saksit*) in Buddhism is not found in amulets or images but the *dhamma*: "You ought to know that there is nothing more sacred than the laws of *idappaccayatā* [the law of conditionality], the supreme holiness higher than all things. Everything else is holy by assumption or by what people concoct themselves which is holy through *upādāna* [attachment, grasping]."[27] Like Phra Prayudh, Buddhadāsa makes a sharp distinction between magic (Thai, *saiyasāt*) and the perception of the way things are in their true conditioned, interdependent nature: "All superstitious formalities and beliefs are *saiyasāt* [magic]. The more ignorance there is, the more one lacks correct knowledge, then the more trapped one is in superstitious prisons."[28]

Buddhadāsa brings to his critique of the cult of Buddha images and amulets a Buddhological argument. To venerate a Buddha image as though the historical Buddha were actually present misconstrues the true nature of the Buddha. Only when we have attained the same understanding of reality that the Buddha achieved do we truly see the Buddha. In this regard, the Buddha is within us.[29] Buddhadāsa directs his most scathing remarks at those who pray to Buddha images solely for material benefits such as a new car or luck in business as through the image were possessed by the Buddha's spirit or ghost (Thai, *phī*), and at those who invoke the Buddha's presence at seances: "It's laughable if they say that they invite the spirit of the Buddha from Tāvatiṃsa heaven, and even more ludicrous if they claim that the spirit of the Buddha returned from *parinibbāna!*"[30]

In more philosophical terms, Buddhadāsa criticizes attachment to Buddha images and even the person of the Buddha himself, on epistemological grounds. His distinction between two types of knowledge, or, as Buddhadāsa puts it, two types of language—everyday language (Thai, *phassā khon*) and truth language (*phassā dhamma*)—echoes the Mādhyamika distinction between ultimate and conventional levels of truth:

> As you know, the Buddha in everyday language refers to the histori-
> cal Enlightened Being, Gotama Buddha. It refers to a physical man
> of flesh and bone who was born in India more than two thousand
> years ago, died, and was cremated. This is the meaning of the
> Buddha in everyday language. Considered in terms of *dhamma*
> language, however, the word Buddha refers to the Truth that the
> historical Buddha realized and taught, the *dhamma* itself.[31]

And in even more provocatively iconoclastic language:

> We can forget about the birth, enlightenment and death of the
> Buddha!—or that he was someone's child, nephew or lived in such
> and such a city. The *dhamma* in the deepest sense is the truth of
> nature. . . . Indeed, the *dhamma* of "who sees me sees the *dhamma*"
> is nothing other than the law of nature, and [to perceive] the funda-
> mental law of nature is the extinction of suffering. This is the true
> *dhamma*, so to truly see the Buddha is [nothing other than] to see the
> arising and cessation of suffering.[32]

Santi Asok is my third example of iconoclastic dissent in modern Thailand. Founded in the mid-1970s by Phra Bodhiraksa, it is a utopian, communalistic movement on the margins of the Thai Buddhist mainstream.[33] From the outset Santi Asok has been controversial for several reasons: its involvement in Thai politics in the 1970s; its outspoken criticism of the Buddhist establishment and of Thai social mores; and Phra Bodhiraksa's actions in blatant disregard for mo-

nastic regulations that led to his expulsion from the Thai *sangha* in 1989. Despite
being defrocked, Phra Bodhiraksa continues to lead a monastic lifestyle at the
largest continuing Santi Asok center in Sisaket Province in northeast Thailand.

Santi Asok's attack on the cult of images and amulets is part of its broader
iconoclastic stance toward Thai Buddhism and its moralistic critique of Thai
culture. It has taken an uncompromising stand against drinking, smoking, gam-
bling, prostitution, and the promotion of a hedonistic lifestyle disseminated
through film, television, advertising, and other media.[34] The movement criticizes many commonly accepted devotional practices; does not use Buddha images at its centers; and rejects the conventional Thai custom of wearing amulets.
The *abhiseka* ritual that is at the very core of the cult of images and amulets has
been transformed by Santi Asok from a ritual empowering sacred objects to the
moral empowerment of the Santi Asok community. The thirteenth "consecration" retreat held in 1989 involved nearly 2,500 participants.[35] The main activities were group meditation and extemporaneous *dhamma* talks rather than the
usual *paritta* and *abhiseka* chanting and standard sermons. The transformation
of the *abhiseka* from the ritual empowerment of objects to the moral empowerment of persons is well illustrated by the following "Genuine Buddha Image
Consecration":

> *Pluk* (arouse). My life inscribed on a new path
>
> *Sāek* (consecrate). My heart aflame with the truth of the Dhamma
>
> *Phra* (image). Polished with self-knowledge
>
> *Thāe* (genuine). Seeing the truth of the path and its fruit.[36]

The contemporary aniconic dissent regarding the popular cult of icons has
both doctrinal and practical dimensions. It reflects a critique of what is perceived
as an overly acculturated Buddhist religion; a philosophical debate over the nature of the Buddha; a dispute over the meaning of the material signs of the Buddha; and differing views regarding authentic Buddhist practice. Although the
iconic/aniconic argument has a long history in the Buddhist tradition, what we
see now in Thailand is how the forces of modernization, instead of resolving it,
have cast it in a new form with some ironic twists. On the one hand, the destabilization of Thai society resulting from globalization has given new fuel to the desire
for protection that has been funneled into the cult of amulets. Thus, the increased
exposure to modern technology has, ironically, fueled a very nonmodern cult. On
the other hand, Buddhists educated in Western patterns of thought in general and
"protestant" Buddhism in particular, have used the notions of Buddhism derived
from their education and training to attack the cult. These dynamics represent a
particular historical and cultural configuration of an ancient debate within Buddhism and one encountered in other religious traditions, as well. The contemporary Thai case, while not a repeat of history, opens up a window into one of the
defining issues at the very core of the Buddhist tradition.

NOTES

1. See Stanley J. Tambiah, *The Buddhist Saints of the Forest and Cult of Amulets: A Study in Charisma, Hagiography, Sectarianism and Millennial Buddhism*, Cambridge Studies in Social Anthropology, no. 49 (Cambridge: Cambridge University Press, 1984), especially part 3.

2. See Gregory Schopen, "Monks and the Relic Cult in the Mahāparinibbānasutta: An Old Misunderstanding in Regard to Monastic Buddhism," in *From Benares to Beijing: Essays on Buddhism and Chinese Religion in Honour of Professor Jan Yün-hua*, ed. Koichi Shinohara and Gregory Schopen (Oakville, N.Y.: Mosaic Press, 1991), pp. 187–201.

3. Steven Collins, *Nirvana and Other Buddhist Felicities: Utopias of the Pali Imaginaire* (Cambridge: Cambridge University Press, 1998), p. 445.

4. See Thanissaro Bhikkhu, *The Wings to Awakening* (Valley Center, Calif.: Metta Forest Monastery, 1996).

5. For a study of the mantric use of the *iti pi so* formula see F. Bizot and O. von Hinüber, *La guirlande de Joyaux* (Paris: École française d'Extrême-Orient, 1994).

6. Adapted from I. B. Horner and Padmanabh S. Jaini, trans., *Apocryphal Birth-Stories (Paññjsa Jātaka)*, vol. 2, Sacred Books of the Buddhists 39 (London: Pali Text Society, 1986), pp. 103–104, and Padmanabh S. Jaini, "On the Buddha Image," in *Studies in Pāli Buddhism*, ed. A. K. Narain (Delhi: B. R. Publishing Corp., 1979), p. 185.

7. Horner and Jaina, *Apocryphal Birth-Stories*, p. 116. Italics mine.

8. Ibid., p. 115. Italics mine.

9. I discuss the *buddhābhiseka* in "Hypostasizing the Buddha: Buddha Image Consecration in Northern Thailand," *History of Religions* 34, no. 3 (February, 1995): 263–280; "In the Presence of the Buddha," in Anne Blackburn and Jeffrey Samuels, eds., *Essays in Honor of Godwin Samararatne* (Seattle: Pariyatti Books, 2002); and *Becoming the Buddha: Image Consecration in Northern Thailand, Sources and Interpretation*, forthcoming.

10. Bernard Faure, "The Buddhist Icon and the Modern Gaze," *Critical Inquiry* 24, no. 3 (Spring 1998): 768.

11. The power of sacred words to sacralize/transform the mere appearance of the Buddha into the Buddha's real presence resonates with Brahmanical/Tantric notions of language as being the source of power (*saktī*). The Thai term, *saksit* (=sacred power), comes from a combination of *saktā* and *siddhi*.

12. Thanissaro Bhikkhu (Geoff DeGraff), the abbot of Metta Forest Monastery, Valley Center, California, and a monk ordained in the Thammayut tradition of Thai forest monks, observes, "There's a whole set of beliefs around objects containing power which show that they [i. e., Thais] have a concept of power as originating in a mind and then transferred to the object, even though the identity of the person making the transference is not also transferred. In some cases, the power itself is not personal, but quite impersonal." Personal communication, 5 August, 2001.

13. Guiseppi Tucci, *Tibetan Painted Scrolls* (Kyoto: Rinsen Books, 1949; Rome: La liberia dello stato, 1980), 1: 309.

14. Tambiah, *The Buddhist Saints of the Forest and the Cult of Amulets*, part 3. The cult of sacred objects is not limited to those associated with Buddhism; it

includes statues of Thai royalty, Hindu deities, and a wide variety of talismen and charms. The generic terms for amulet, talisman, medallion (*phrakru'ang, phrakru'ang rāng, rian*), do not have a specifically Buddhist connotation. The eclectic nature of the cult of sacred objects reflects the syncretic nature of popular devotional Buddhism.

15. Ibid., pp. 197–199, 263.

16. Ibid., p. 229.

17. Ibid., p. 345.

18. *Lān Bodhi* 16, no. 549 (February 28, B. E. 2533 [C. E. 1990]): 2. Translation mine.

19. *Phutho* [Buddha] 7, no. 10 (March, B. E. 2534 [C. E. 1991]): 2. Translation mine.

20. Ibid., p. 55. Translation mine.

21. For a discussion of modern urban-based movements in Thai Buddhism, see Peter A. Jackson, *Buddhism, Legitimation, and Conflict: The Political Functions of Urban Thai Buddhism* (Singapore: Institute of Southeast Asian Studies, 1989).

22. One of the paradoxes of the forest monk movement in the twentieth century is that several monks, highly regarded as advanced meditators, have become the object of cultic veneration. See Tambiah, *The Buddhist Saints of the Forest*, and James Taylor, *Forest Monks and the Nation-State: An Anthropological and Historical Study in Northeastern Thailand* (Singapore: Institute of Southeast Asian Studies, 1993). Thanissaro Bhikkhu points out that while the Ājān Mun tradition has been critical of magical ritualism, it has included a strong strand of relic veneration. Personal communication, 5 August, 2001.

23. Sanitsuda Ekachai, "Sale of Amulets Is Not So Charming," *Bangkok Post*, November 26, 1997, p. 11.

24. During his long and distinguished monastic career, Phra (Venerable) Prayudh has advanced through several ecclesastical ranks in the Thai *sangha* with different titles. His current title, Phra Dhammapiṭaka, was formally conferred by the king of Thailand in 1993. In this chapter I follow the convention used by Grant A. Olson, the translator of the first edition of Phra Prayudh's *Buddhadhamma*, who refers to him as Phra (Venerable) Prayudh. Recent English translations of his work published in Thailand by the Buddhadhamma Foundation use P. A. Payutto as his nom de plume (P. A. stands for his given and family names, Prayudh Arayangkun). The Thai term, *phra* (Pāli, *vara*), carries the general sense of worthy or venerable.

25. My discussion of Phra Prayudh's critique of the cult of sacred objects and related phenomena is based primarily on Phra Dhammapiṭaka (P. A. Payutto), "Sing Saksit, Devakrœt, Pāthihān" (Sacred objects, efficacious deities, and miracles) in *Chīwit Nu'ng Thaw Thaw Nī Sang Khwamd Dai Anan* (In this single lifetime one can create endless good) (Bangkok: Sahathammika, B. E. 2537 [C. E. 1994]), pp. 157–161. Also consulted were the following relevant essays by Phra Dhammapiṭaka (P. A. Payutto): *Thāyākphonwikru't Tong L'uk Khit Saiyasāt* (To be free from unnatural powers, give up magical thought) (Bangkok: Thammasịn, B. E. 2540 [C. E. 1997]); *Sing Saksit, Devakrœt, Pāthihān* (Sacred objects, efficacious deities, and miracles) (Bangkok: The Buddhadhamma Foundation, B. E. 2538 [C. E. 1994]); " Mu'angthai Ja Wikrit Thā Khonthai Mī Satthị Wiparit" (Thailand Will Reform if the Thai People

Have the Faith to Change)," in *Chīwit Nu'ng Thaw Nī: Sang Khwamd™ Dai Anan* (In this single lifetime one can create endless good), pp. 83–162.

26. Phra Dhammapiṭaka (P. A. Payutto), "Sing Saksit, Devakrœt, Pāthihān" [Sacred objects, efficacious deities, and miracles], p. 157.

27. Buddhadāsa Bhikkhu, *The Prison of Life* (Khuk Khong Chwit), trans. Santikaro Bhikkhu (Bangkok: The Dhamma Study and Practice Group, 1988), p. 21.

28. Ibid., p. 17.

29. For a more extensive analysis of Buddhadāsa's Buddhology, see Donald K. Swearer, "Bhikkhu Buddhadāsa's Interpretation of the Buddha," *Journal of the American Academy of Religion* 64, no. 2 (Summer 1996): 313–336.

30. Buddhadāsa Bhikkhu, *Phra Phuttha Jao Thī Yū Kap Raw Kai Talot Welā* (The Buddha is with us all the time) (Bangkok: Healthy Mind Press, 1990), p. 21. Translation mine.

31. Buddhadāsa Bhikkhu, "Everyday Language and Truth Language," in *Me and Mine: Selected Essays of Bhikkhu Buddhadasa*, ed. Donald K. Swearer (Albany: State University of New York Press, 1989), p. 127.

32. Buddhadāsa Bhikkhu, *Chut Mu'n Lo* (Turning the wheel), 48 (Bangkok: Healthy Mind Press, 1989), pp. 51–52. Translation mine.

33. See Marja-Leena Heikkilä-Horn, *Buddhism with Open Eyes: Belief and Practice of Santi Asoke* (Bangkok: Fah Apai, 1997), and Donald K. Swearer, "Fundamentalistic Movements in Theravada Buddhism," in *Fundamentalisms Observed*, ed. Martin E. Marty and R. Scott Appleby (Chicago: University of Chicago Press, 1991), pp. 628–690. See also Jackson, *Buddhism, Legitimation and Conflict*.

34. Swearer, "Fundamentalistic Movements in Theravada Buddhism," p. 671.

35. "Pluksek Phrathāe Khong Phuttha Khrang Thī 13," (The 13th authentic Buddhist consecration retreat), *Sānasok* 9, nos. 7–8: 19.

36. Ibid., p. 27. Translation mine.

2

The Modernization of Sinhalese Buddhism as Reflected in the Dambulla Cave Temples

Nathan Katz

This chapter will argue that modern Sinhalese Buddhism begins not with the arrival of the British, much less with the 1957 watershed elections, but during Kandyan times (1649–1815), especially during the reign of Kīrti Śrī Rājasinha (1747–1780). As John C. Holt has shown in his masterful book *The Religious World of Kīrti Śrī*, a close examination of Kīrti Śrī's renovations of the Dambulla cave temples, among several other sites, reveals themes, concerns, and motifs typically associated with modern Buddhism.[1]

Holt sees Kīrti Śrī as a transitional figure, a revivalist rooted in his late medieval era. Of his meaning for modern Sinhalese Buddhism, Holt writes, "Yet his response remains relevant in modern Sri Lanka, despite the fact that it is a late medieval, revived form of classical religion and, as such, is not completely synchronized (in fact, is often at odds) with the emphases and orientations of twentieth-century, urban Buddhist modernism."[2] While obviously Sinhalese Buddhism has changed over the past two and a half centuries, it is in precisely this revival of classical themes that Kīrti Śrī so closely resembles the nation's Buddhism modernists.

Among the distinctive characteristics of modern Sinhalese Buddhism are: (1) a response to foreign political, cultural, and economic incursions into Sri Lanka; (2) attempts to respond to these incursions by revitalizing classical themes and institutions; and (3) a redefinition of the interactions between the *Sangha* and the laity, largely enhancing the laity's role in religious institutions as well as its religious aspirations. These trends, taken together, have been called "Protestant Buddhism."[3] I will argue that all three of these characteristics can be found in Kīrti Śrī's eighteenth-century revival. I shall also argue that the Dambulla cave temples have been a venue for expressing Kīrti Śrī's innovations and therefore have remained a significant site in modern Sinhalese Buddhism.

The Dambulla Cave Temples

The history of the cave temples of Dambulla intersects repeatedly with that of the Sinhalese nation.[4] In classical, medieval, colonial, and contemporary times, the temples have both reflected and shaped the development of the island. Dambulla is in the center of a triangle formed by the country's three precolonial capitals: Anurādhapura, Polonnoruwa, and Kandy. Located on the side of a massive rock some 500 feet above the highway, the temple complex is surrounded by flowering trees and the ever-encroaching lush jungle (fig. 2.1). After marveling at the vast panorama of the Kurunegala plains and the Riṭigala Mountains from atop the temples' hillside perch, the visitor is inevitably drawn to the

FIGURE 2.1. Exterior of the Golden Rock Temples at Dambulla. Photo by Ellen S. Goldberg.

FIGURE 2.2. Buddha image. Photo by Ellen S. Goldberg.

caves' darkened interiors. The effect of such a profusion of visual imagery is overwhelming.

Historical records counted seventy-three seated, standing, and reclining Buddha statues in the twelfth century (fig. 2.2). When the modern period was emerging six hundred years later, some 2,300 paintings were said to adorn the caves' walls and ceilings. Since that time, changes and development have occurred to such an extent that today we see easily twice that number.

Although not naturalistic statues, most of the Buddha images in the cave temples are human-size or slightly larger (fig. 2.3). They seem all the more alive for this, an effect further enhanced by the dim light. The murals, which completely cover the ceilings and walls, follow the rock's contours so perfectly as to appear like tapestries (fig. 2.4). A predominance of reds and yellows adds an aura of warmth and vibrancy. The overall impression is that the cold hardness of the caves has been made alive and feeling.

Origin Legends

According to the *Mahāvaṃsa*, the famous fifth-century Pāli chronicle of Sinhalese history, a magical bamboo tree sprouted at Dambulla at the very moment of King Devānaṃpiya Tissa's conversion to Buddhism in the third century BCE,

FIGURE 2.3. Seated Buddha image, cave no. 3. Note intricate dragon-arch. Photo by
Ellen S. Goldberg.

linking the caves with the sacred time when the *Dharma* was brought to
Sinhaladvīpa, fulfilling a prophecy of the Buddha.[5] While hunting deer in one
of his parks at nearby Mahintale, the king encountered the missionary *arahant*
Mahinda, son or nephew of Emperor Aśoka of India. Preaching about the Buddhist virtue of nonharmfulness (*ahiṃsā*), Mahinda opened the king's heart to
the *Dharma* and the king opened his capital, Anurādhapura, to Aśoka's missionary envoys. Led by Mahinda and his sister, Sanghamittā Therī, who brought
a sapling of the famous Bodhi tree from Bodh Gayā, India, the inauguration of
the orders of monks and nuns and the coming of Buddhism to Sri Lanka were
mythically connected with Dambulla.

These sacred events are not only recorded in the Pāli chronicles but are
motifs dominating the remarkable murals that cover Dambulla's five caves today.
Indeed, it could be said that the Dambulla cave paintings are a visual version of
the *Mahāvaṃsa* mythology. The sacred history, in turn, is the basis both for the
transition into modern times during the eighteenth century and for contemporary Sri Lankan Buddhist religio-nationalism.

The importance of the caves predates even the advent of Buddhism, according to the late Senarat Paranavitana, Sri Lanka's acclaimed archaeologist. The
Dambulla caves, he wrote, "occupied an important place in the religious beliefs
and the political ideology of the Sinhalese people in the period before Buddhism
became their religion."[6]

FIGURE 2.4. The "legions of Mara," the Evil One, trying to frighten the Buddha just after his enlightenment. Ceiling mural, cave no. 2. Photo by Ellen S. Goldberg.

Classical Period

The cave temples enter the historical stage during the reign of King Vaṭṭhagāmaṇī Abhaya (137–119 BCE). Forced to flee Anurādhapura due to invasions from south India, the king spent several years hiding in the Dambulla caves before political and military circumstances allowed for his return to the capital. He left Brahmi epigraphs, still visible on the drip-ledges above the cave entrances, donating the temples to the *Sangha*, the order of Buddhist monks and nuns.

It was during this ancient time that caves became extremely popular among monks and nuns as meditation abodes, and the island is studded with these sacred caves, many of which are in use to this day.[7] It was also during this politically turbulent century that the Pāli *Tipiṭaka* (canon) was first committed to writing at the nearby rock temple, Alu Vihāraya, in Matale. Before this time, the discourses and discipline of the Buddha were passed on from memory.

Medieval Period

During the eleventh and twelfth centuries CE, the austere meditation caves were converted into magnificent temples. Following another period of unrest due to invasions by the Cola dynasty of south India, King Vijayabāhu I of Polonnoruwa (1055–1110) restored the caves. But it was his successor, King Nissankamalla (1187–1196), who had the statues gilded and murals painted, naming the site "Swarna Giriguhara," or "Golden Rock Caves." The *Cūḷavaṃsa*, a succession of Pāli texts that continue the narrative of the *Mahāvaṃsa*, describes Dambulla as "resplendent with walls and pillars shimmering in gold and silver, where the floor was of red lead and the bricks of the roof were of gold and the wise (monarch Nissankamalla) had rebuilt and placed therein seventy-three golden statues of the Master (Buddha)."[8] Statues of Kings Nissankamalla and Vaṭṭhagāmaṇī Abhaya still stand, proudly surveying their devout work, in the second and largest of the five cave temples, the "Mahārājalena," or "cave of the great kings" (fig. 2.5).

From Late Medieval to Modern Times

As we move toward the modern period, during Kandyan times (1649–1815) the caves took on their present appearance. The last dynasty of Sinhalese kings regularly constructed and renovated temples in a manner remarkable for its independent development and quite uninfluenced by European painting, which, by this time, had modified indigenous art forms in most of south Asia. This independent style, however, masks its indirect relationship to the encroachment of

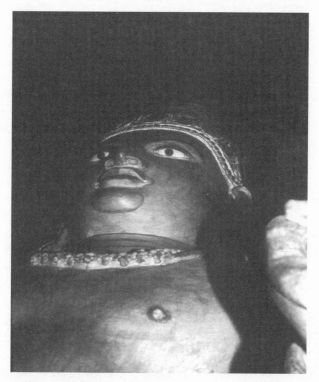

FIGURE 2.5. King Vaṭṭhagāmaṇī Abhaya, who dedicated the Dambulla Cave Temples to the *Sangha* in the second century BCE. Note the crown and garland, emblems of the "bodhisattva-king," the concept used to sacralize kingship in Sinhalese Buddhism ever since the classical period. Cave no. 2. Photo by Ellen S. Goldberg.

colonial powers, already established on the island's western and southern littoral, into the upcountry cultural preserve known as the Kandyan kingdom.

The greatest of the Kandyan kings was Kīrti Śrī Rājasinha (1747–1780), and his statue dominates the fourth cave at Dambulla. Himself a Tamil, Kīrti Śrī was piously both Hindu and Buddhist, and a great patron of religion. It was during his reign that the lineage of Buddhist monastic ordination was reintroduced to Sinhaladvīpa from Thailand. The *Cūlavaṃsa* says that the monarch "made himself one with the religion and the people,"[9] the highest praise possible from the viewpoint of Sri Lanka's chronicles. The vast work undertaken at Dambulla is just one example of the religious and artistic renaissance generated by the Kandyan ruler.

Holt views him as a late medieval figure who was a "classicist"; that is, in response to challenges from the Dutch and from elite and monastic Kandyan factions, both opposed to the rule of the South Indian-origin Nayakkars although for different reasons, Kīrti Śrī reverted to the classical Sinhalese Buddhism of the Anurādhapura period as depicted in the *Mahāvaṃsa*.[10] Holt's study focuses on the Kandyan temple wall paintings refurbished by Kīrti Śrī, of which the Dambulla cave temples are the finest example, "to understand that they are, on the whole, a revitalized form of a classical style appropriated to express paradigmatic themes of religious meaning deemed significant or wholly relevant for their contemporary milieu. They signal a late medieval attempt to express what Buddhism has meant in the past and what it can mean to its masses of adherents in the present."[11]

In just these senses, Kīrti Śrī was also a modern figure, or at least a precursor to modernity. One reason is that Kīrti Śrī's neoclassicism was articulated in response to colonialism, and in this sense his neoclassicism is modern. Another reason is that the Buddhism of Kīrti Śrī has deep resonances with the Sinhalese Buddhism of the twentieth century, such as the centrality of the *Mahāvaṃsa* narrative, the application of the Aśokan model of Buddhist leadership, the subjugation of local gods in a Buddha-dominated cosmology, and the defensive stance of the nation vis-à-vis invaders. It also has very important differences, especially regarding the role of the laity in religious leadership and in the practice of meditation and the pursuit of *nirvāṇa*. But his overall tactic of responding to an external threat by reclaiming and refashioning the symbols, rituals, and polity of a classical period, is a typically modern religious response.

To return to the Dambulla temples themselves, two types of sculptures adorn the cave temples: religious and secular. Of the religious motifs, the vast majority are Buddha figures of varying sizes and attitudes. One also finds statues of gods and bodhisattvas, such as Vishnu (fig. 2.6), appointed by the Buddha to be the guardian of Sinhaladvīpa,[12] and Maitreya, the future Buddha around whom many medieval devotional cults emerged throughout the Buddhist world,[13] as well as a variety of *devas* (deities) (fig. 2.7). Richly ornamented with crowns and jewels, they are easily distinguishable by their stance and color. Secular images include those of Kings Vaṭṭhagāmaṇī Abhaya, Nissankamalla, and Kīrti Śrī Rājasinha, great patrons of the rock temples.

There is debate among scholars as to some of the statues' origins. A number of images resemble stylistically those of the flourishing Anurādhapura period, from the third century BCE to the eighth century CE. One such example is the colossal Buddha standing in the *abhaya-mudrā*, or fearless gesture, facing the main entrance of the second cave (fig. 2.8). It bears a striking resemblance to stone and bronze Buddha figures from the second and third centuries, respectively, now found in the Anurādhapura Museum. However, attempts to accurately date many of these images are frustrated by the subsequent repainting and plastering of them over centuries. During the eighteenth century, in particular, the caves underwent massive renovation as part of Kīrti Śrī's revitalization of Sinhalese Buddhism. Although well intended, the result has been a distortion of the original forms.

FIGURE 2.6. Vishnu statue, cave no. 2. In Sinhalese Buddhism, Vishnu is the protector of the nation. Legend has it that Vishnu originally excavated the Dambulla caves. Photo by Ellen S. Goldberg.

Despite their origin, religious statues of this region are believed to adhere to the artistic canons of proportion found in the *Śāriputra*, a north Indian Sanskrit text. The bulk of the *Śāriputra* is devoted to the creation of Buddha figures in every imaginable pose, and provides the artist with meticulous dimensions and stylistic instructions. The translated text is on permanent display in the Colombo Museum in the nation's capital. It makes fascinating reading and sheds valuable insight as to how Buddhist images were created. When rendering the Buddha in the meditation pose, for example, the canons stipulate "the image must exemplify a person with an unfettered, quiescent and absolutely pure mind, preeminent from head to foot" (fig. 2.9). But let the sculptor beware if his pro-

FIGURE 2.7. A *deva* (deity) observing the enlightenment of the Buddha. Mural ceiling painting, cave no. 2. Photo by Ellen S. Goldberg.

portions are not up to standard: "If the measurements be (off) . . . by . . . (even) a barleycorn, it will result in loss of wealth, and death."[14] Performance aside, the canons provided an invaluable rule of thumb for artists, relieving them of part of the technical worries, while at the same time allowing them to concentrate on the message or burden of the work.

The statues of Dambulla are fashioned from either rock, brick, or wood and then plastered over and painted. Some of the giant Buddha figures have cotton robes over the plaster, on which paint was applied directly. Almost all are painted a vibrant yellow.

The *siraspata*, or circle of light, is a consistent feature in all of the Buddha statues. The hand expressions most commonly depicted are those of the *abhaya-mudra*, or fearless gesture, and *dhyāna-mudrā*, or meditative gesture. Seated

FIGURE 2.8. Standing Buddha in *abhaya-mudrā* (fearlessness gesture), cave
no. 2. Constructed by King Nissankamalla. Photo by Ellen S. Goldberg.

Buddhas are portrayed in a *vīrāsana*, or heroic attitude, while the standing or
reclining Buddhas rest on a *padmāsana*, or lotus base. The reverence the sculp-
tors must have felt for their subject matter is obvious. The Buddha figures, in
particular, fill the dank, dark caves with sublime spiritual radiance.

    Covering an area of roughly 20,000 square feet, the Dambulla temples boast
one of the largest collections of wall and ceiling paintings in all of Asia, and have
been called "the most spectacular examples of extant Sri Lankan temple wall

FIGURE 2.9. The Buddha attaining enlightenment under the Bo-tree. Ceiling mural, cave no. 2. Photo by Ellen S. Goldberg.

paintings."[15] The murals encompass a wide range of themes. The vast majority conveys *Jātaka* scenes, or stories of the Buddha's previous births, incidents connected with the Buddha's present life (fig. 2.10), and the advent of Buddhism in Sri Lanka. Vivid tales of the country's early sacred history are also portrayed. In the second cave, for example, a large portion of the ceiling space shows the Sinhalese ruler Duṭṭhagāminī's resounding victory over the Cola King Eḷāra's armies, so important in the contemporary period and as chronicled in the *Mahāvaṃsa*. In addition, pictures of popular gods, plants, wildlife, and geometric designs are woven into intricate patterns.

Because of the caves' massive renovations two centuries ago, all of the murals—despite their date of execution—are consummate examples of eighteenth-

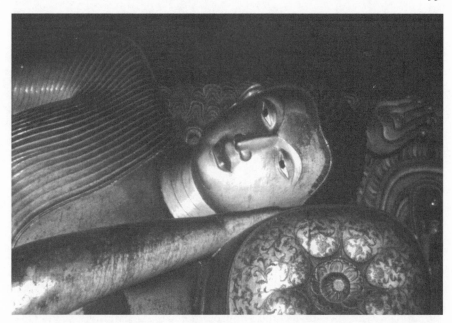

FIGURE 2.10. The Buddha in *parinibbāna* (dying) posture. Cave no. 3. Photo by Ellen S. Goldberg.

century Kandyan art. Scholars commonly peg the work as folk art, rather than the highly evolved local art forms found in the early Anurādhapura or Polonnoruwa periods. "A great and beautiful peasant decoration . . . in many ways primitive," is how the late Ananda Coomaraswamy, the country's most renowned art historian, describes the style.[16] Most contemporary scholars tend to shy away from such labels when depicting indigenous art forms. Yet these terms are apt for Dambulla and are by no means derogatory. With their bold stories, vivid colors, and whimsical designs, the murals are more concerned with portraying the country's rich religious and cultural history than with mimicking nature. Their simplicity gives them a universal appeal that can be appreciated by all strata of society. As local scholar Anuradha Seneviratne aptly notes, "the frescoes depict the aspirations of the common man."[17]

Holt makes this point more forcefully. He sees in the folk quality of the murals an intent to structure and reflect a layperson's understanding of *Dharma*. He wrote, "Modest and simple in terms of style and design, and usually categorized as folk art, the paintings discussed here functioned preeminently as the most important didactic devices to instill the classical Buddhist world view in the vast majority of Sinhalese Buddhist religious adherents. My argument here is very simple: that more than any other form of cultic religious expression, these paintings clearly illustrate, through their obvious accessibility, not only the fundamental mythic history of Theravāda Buddhist tradition but also the basic behavioral actions and cognitive tenets that explain what it meant to be Buddhist during this time."[18]

The characteristics of Kandyan art are distinct. Features of this style, which are readily apparent at Dambulla, are narrations of stories, particularly *Jātaka* scenes in epic format; the total absence of perspective and shading; figures represented in full, three-quarter, or profile views, but never from behind; characters portrayed in a vivacious, proud manner; and idealization of all subject matter. Episodes, whether from *Jātaka* scenes or historical events, are all depicted in panels of continuous narration, reflecting a didactic intent. The wall surfaces are divided into horizontal strips. Each strip portrays a major scene that moves sequentially either left to right, right to left, or up to down. At times, the scenes are accompanied by captions painted beneath the strip itself.

Although the canons of proportion were utilized in paintings of the Buddha, it is not apparent in most *Jātaka* or secular scenes. Characters are flat, two-dimensional. In many ways, the Dambulla murals resemble wall paintings of ancient Egypt; the work is more epic in scope than artistic in the modern sense. Certainly we can envision technical improvements in the paintings, such as the use of perspective and division of the picture into several planes. However, to alter the work would not necessarily constitute an improvement, Coomaraswamy argues.[19] Indeed, it could no longer be called Kandyan painting.

Idealization is the most essential aspect of Kandyan art. Artists, as mentioned, were more concerned with representing forms as they saw fit rather than merely imitating them. Plants, wildlife, even gods and men, take on an abstract, interpretive quality. "We are not told and do not want to be told what (an) animal itself was like," Coomaraswamy says, "but what it meant to the men who painted it, what it was like for them and, so, what they were like."[20] Indeed, the Dambulla paintings are a gateway to the imagination. Their value may not lie in their artistic expertise but in the rendering of subjects readily accessible to all. Moreover, visitors can gaze upon these dreamlike images and, like the Sinhalese masters, conjure up their own visions of the world.

Colonial Period

During the colonial period, the Dambulla caves played a vital, symbolic role in the emergence of Sinhalese nationalism, a hallmark of the modern period. When the Kandyan kingdom was ceded to Britain in 1815, the terms of the treaty called for the sovereign of England to assume the traditional monarchical duties as protector of Buddhism. As some zealous Christians came to dominate the Foreign Office in London, however, this role was rejected and the empire pursued as official policy the evangelizing of colonized peoples. As colonial privilege came

to require conversion, the situation for Buddhists became more and more in-
tolerable in Sri Lanka. In 1848, an insurrection was centered at the Dambulla
cave temples. The chief incumbent of the shrine, the Venerable Girangama
Thera, officiated at a rebellious coronation ceremony for Gongalegoda Banda, a
pretender to the throne of Kandy.[21] The British promptly squelched the insurrection, but the national and religious importance of Dambulla was evidently
as vital as it had been ever since perhaps pre-Buddhist times more than two
millennia earlier.

Contemporary Period

The symbolic power of the Dambulla caves has not been lost to contemporary
Sri Lankan society either. The center-right government of President Junius R.
Jayewardene during the early 1980s planned to construct a sixth cave temple,
one hundred yards beyond the current temple complex. They envisioned murals commemorating the Mahaweli Development Scheme, the government's
ambitious project for irrigation and hydroelectric power, as an expression of
the *Dharma* in the twentieth century. Recalling kingship as portrayed in the
chronicles, as did Kīrti Śrī, contemporary Sinhalese Buddhism portrays the
island's ancient kings as being as prolific in constructing tanks (reservoirs) for
irrigation as *stūpas* for veneration. Ever since the twentieth century's fully modernist Buddhist Revival, especially as articulated by the Vidyālanaka Group of
bhikkhus in the 1950s, indigenous interpretations of Buddhism have stressed
its relevance for polity and development equally with its spiritual teachings.[22]

Jayewardene's government engaged artist Kushan Manjusri for consulta-
tions about the design of the proposed cave temple. Son of the late L. T. P.
Manjusri, the greatest documenter and preserver of Sinhalese temple art and
one of the nation's most creative painters,[23] the younger Manjusri proposed
relating *Jātaka* stories of the Buddha's previous births to contemporary development projects and issues. A Buddhist monk for six years, Manjusri left the
order, as did his father, to pursue his love of art. He and his two sisters began
by documenting the murals and statues of the cave temples. Threatened by soot
from pilgrims' votive lamps, along with dripping water, termites, and assorted
blights and fungi, the remote Dambulla temples became a center of activity that
is a far cry from the traditional solitude and meditative atmosphere. The
government's Ministry of Cultural Affairs and UNESCO included the documentation and some restoration of the cave temples in the massive Cultural Triangle
Project, designed to preserve and upgrade conditions at Sri Lanka's most renowned cultural sites. In addition to local and foreign tourists, workmen and
scaffolding have become familiar sights at the ancient capitals at Anurādhapura
and Polonnoruwa; at Sigiriya, the inspiring rock fortress of King Kāśyapa; at

Kandy, the last independent capital; and, of course, at Dambulla itself. Besides conservation, documentation, and restoration work, the Cultural Triangle Project brought to Dambulla better lighting and humidity control, the construction of a museum near the temples, and landscaping.

Conclusion

Other features of Sinhalese Buddhism of the Revival era (which I date from the compilation of Buddhist responses to Christian missionaries, which began as early as 1828, through the 1957 watershed elections) are unique developments, such as its emphasis on Buddhism's "rationalism" and the use of debates and pamphlets to champion its view. Similarly, the Revival was led by both laity (which began with Anagarika Dharmapala, and was expressed through such lay organizations as the All-Ceylon Buddhist Congress and the Young Men's Buddhist Association) and monks (especially the Vidyālaṅkara Group), whereas King Kīrti Śrī's innovations sought to expand the role of the laity and the expense of the *Sangha*, whom he saw as a political rival. While Kīrti Śrī sought to diminish the power of the *Sangha*, the Vidyālaṅkara Group in particular saw the interests of the *Sangha* and of the state as identical. Their paradigm was the monastic involvement of monks in Prince Duṭṭagāmaṇī's war against the Colas, a paradigm that, when applied in the modern world, heralded the decline of Sinhalese Buddhism into what might be called postmodernism.

During the 1980s, technology began to catch up with ideology, at least at Dambulla. The renovations were sidetracked, as has been the nation itself, by ongoing strife. If it is the case that the postmodern period is characterized by ethnic fragmentation and violence, then one might sadly anticipate a new reconfiguration of Sinhalese Buddhism. The modern period was heralded by Kīrti Śrī at Dambulla at the very intersection of the late medieval and colonial eras. Its vision was of a Buddhist polity of generosity, inclusiveness, and ethically guided development. That understanding of *Dharma* may be replaced with a postmodern Buddhism of a combative, ethnic-based warrior creed. But postmodern developments are, thankfully, beyond the scope of this chapter.

NOTES

This essay has its origin in Nathan Katz and Ellen S. Goldberg, "The Golden Rock Temples of Dambulla: Their Role in Sinhalese Buddhism and Nationalism," *Southeast Conference Association for Asian Studies Annals* 7 (1986): 85–93. It has been thoroughly revised, expanded, and refocused.

1. John Clifford Holt, *The Religious World of Kīrti Śrī: Buddhism, Art, and Politics in Late Medieval Sri Lanka* (New York: Oxford University Press, 1996).

2. Ibid., p. 13.

3. Indeed "Protestant Buddhism" is the title of the seventh chapter in Richard Gombrich's influential work *Theravada Buddhism: A Social History from Ancient Benares to Modern Colombo* (London: Routledge, 1991 [1988]). Gananath Obeyesekere coined the term.

4. In this chapter, the term Sinhalese will be used for the Sinhala-speaking majority of contemporary Sri Lanka, most of whom are Theravāda Buddhists. To refer to the island nation prior to 1972, when its name was changed from the colonial Ceylon (itself an Anglicization of the Arabic Sailoon) to Sri Lanka, Sinhaladvīpa ("the island of the Sinhalese") will be employed.

5. *Mahāvaṃsa*, 11: 10–13, Wilhelm Geiger, ed. (London: Pali Text Society, 1958), p. 90. Senarat Paranavitana identifies Chatapabbata as an ancient name of Dambulla, but Anuradha Seneviratna disagrees. See his *Golden Rock Temple of Dambulla: Cave of Infinite Buddhas* (Colombo: Central Cultural Fund, Ministry of Cultural Affairs, 1983), p. 23.

6. Quoted by Seneviratna, *Golden Rock Temple of Dambulla*, p. 25.

7. Sparse Dambulla meditation abodes are featured in "Footprint of the Buddha," a popular early-1970s BBC television program (now available in The Long Search video series). about Sinhalese Buddhism.

8. *Cūlavaṃsa*, 80: 22–23, Wilhelm Geiger, ed. (London: Pali Text Society, 1980).

9. *Cūḷavaṃsa*, 99:172.

10. Holt, *The Religious World of Kīrti Śrī*, p. 16.

11. Ibid., p. 47.

12. On Vishnu, known as Upulvan in Sinhalese Buddhism, as protector of Buddhism and patron of Sinhaladvīpa, see Senarat Paranavitana, *The Shrine of Upulvan at Devundara* (Colombo: Ceylon Government Archaeological Department, 1953).

13. Alan Sponberg and Helen Hardacre, eds., *Maitreya, the Future Buddha* (New York: Cambridge University Press, 1988).

14. Quoted by Ananda Coomaraswamy, *Mediaeval Sinhalese Art*, 2nd ed. (New York: Pantheon Books, 1856), p. 154. A translation of the entire text is given on pages 150–163.

15. Holt, *The Religious World of Kīrti Śrī*, p. 52.

16. Coomaraswamy, *Mediaeval Sinhalese Art*, p. 170.

17. Seneviratna, *Golden Rock Temple of Dambulla*, p. 84.

18. Holt, *The Religious World of Kīrti Śrī*, p. 93.

19. Coomaraswamy, *Mediaeval Sinhalese Art*, p. 169.

20. Ibid., p. 171.

21. See K. M. de Silva, "The Government and Religion: Problems and Policies c. 1832 to c. 1910," in *History of Ceylon, Vol. 3: From the Beginnings of the nineteenth Century to 1948*, ed. K. M. de Silva (Peradeniya: University of Ceylon, 1973), pp. 187–212.

22. On the Sri Lankan Buddhist Revival, see Nathan Katz, "Buddhism and Politics in Sri Lanka and Other Theravada Nations Since 1945," in *Movements and Issues in World Religions: A Sourcebook of Developments Since 1945*, ed. Charles Wei-hsun Fu and Gerhard E. Spiegler (Westport, Conn.: Greenwood Press, 1987),

pp. 157–175. On the continuing appeal of this view within the *Sangha* through the 1980s, see Nathan Katz and F. Robert Stiglicz, "Social and Political Attitudes of Sri Lankan Monks: An Empirical Study," *South Asia Research* 6, no. 2 (November 1986): 159–180. For the unofficial manifesto of the Vidyalankara Group in particular, see the work by its preeminent spokesman, Walpola Rahula, *The Heritage of the Bhikkhu* (New York: Grove Press, 1974).

    23. On the elder Manjusri, see David L. Umemoto, "The Quiet Achievers of Asia's 'Nobel Prizes,'" *Asia* 6, no. 3 (September–October 1983): 24–27; 40–45.

3

Varying the Vinaya

Creative Responses to Modernity

Charles S. Prebish

In an interesting article published in the first issue of the online
Journal of Buddhist Ethics, Paul Numrich recounts the famous
dialogue, included in a variety of Theravāda sources, between the
Buddhist monk Mahinda and King Devānampiya Tissa of Ceylon
(now Sri Lanka) concerning Buddhism's establishment in Sri Lanka.
The king, properly concerned, wants to know precisely when this
new religion's roots may be considered to be firmly established on
the island. Mahinda's reply: "When a young man, born of Ceylonese
parents on the island of Ceylon, having gone forth on the island of
Ceylon and learned the monastic discipline in this same island of
Ceylon, when he will recite that discipline on the island of Ceylon—
then, Great king, will the roots of the religion indeed be deep."[1] In
other words, as Numrich points out, recitation of the precepts of the
Prātimokṣa by indigenous monks is a requisite for the establishment
of Buddhism. Numrich then cites Michael Carrithers's often quoted
remark: "No Buddhism without the *Sangha* and no *Sangha* without
the Discipline."[2] As such, the growth of Buddhism into countries
beyond its Indian birthplace, and its survival in those countries,
required and was predicated upon the establishment of the monastic
sangha and the fortnightly recitation of the monastic code. This
chapter explores the meaning of the term *sangha*, focusing on the
application of its original, restricted meaning. It then explains the
structure and contents of Buddhist *Vinaya* literature, including its
commentarial tradition, and makes a careful distinction between the
terms *Vinaya* and *śīla*, demonstrating how the monastic code known
as *Vinaya* embodies the ethical conduct presumed by *śīla*. Finally,

the chapter examines the way in which modern Theravāda monastic communities, including some located in the West, have adjusted the traditional *Vinaya*
code in an attempt to accommodate modernity.

The Buddhist *Sangha*

Although the term *sangha* is used today to refer to almost any community or
group loosely associated with Buddhism, in the time of the Buddha the term
was used in a radically different fashion. The Sanskrit word *sangha* simply con-
notes a society or company or a number of people living together for a certain
purpose. Akira Hirakawa points out that political groups and trade guilds, as
well as religious orders, were called *sanghas*.[3] As such, in the midst of many
religious *sanghas* in the general wanderers' (parivrājaka) community, the
Buddha's followers appropriated the term in a rather distinct fashion, one that
gave their fledgling community a clear and unique identity. While outsiders may
have referred to the Buddha's first disciples as *śākyaputrīya-śramaṇas* or "men-
dicants who follow the Buddha," the original community referred to itself as
the *bhikṣu-sangha*, or community of monks. Later, when the order of nuns was
founded, they became known as the *bhikṣuṇī-sangha*, and the two units were
collectively known as the *ubhayato-sangha*, the "twofold community." In
Theravāda countries, this quite narrow usage of the term *sangha* has remained
the predominant meaning of the word, as is pointed out by most modern scholars writing on the Buddhist community. Richard Gombrich, for example, says:

> The *Sangha* consists of all those ordained, both monks and nuns. In
> fact in the Theravāda Buddhist countries (Sri Lanka and most of
> continental Southeast Asia) the Order of nuns in the strict sense has
> died out. There are women in those countries who lead cloistered
> lives and behave like nuns, but for lack of a valid ordination tradition
> they remain outside the *Sangha* in the usual, strict sense. In those
> countries, therefore, the term *Sangha* is generally understood to refer
> only to monks and male novices.[4]

Occasionally, in the early literature, the Buddha uses the term *cāturdisa-sangha*
or the "*sangha* of the four quarters,"[5] but it seems clear from his usage that he
means the *monastic sangha*. Sukumar Dutt says as much, suggesting, "The exact import and implication of the phrase is somewhat obscure, but is indicative
of the growth of a sense of unity in the scattered body of the Lord's Bhikkhu
followers—a unity of ideal and purpose, though perhaps no union of corporate
life and activity yet. The expression, '*Sangha* of the Four Quarters,' became canonical; it is taken in donatory inscriptions of later ages to connote a conceptual and ideal confraternity."[6]

Eventually, however, as the erememetical lifestyle deteriorated in favor of settled monasticism, the term "*sangha* of the four quarters" took on a new meaning. As Akira Hirakawa explains,

> A present order was governed by the precepts of the *vinaya*, but did not have the right to alter those precepts. The *vinaya* transcended the rights and interests of any single order. Moreover, although a present order had the right to use the monastery and its buildings, it did not have the right to sell them. To explain this situation, the existence of a higher level of the *sangha* was posited. It was called "the order of the four quarters" or the "universal order" (*cāturdisa-sangha*) and consisted of all the disciples of the Buddha. It transcended time and place and included all the monks of the past, present, and future; it encompassed all geographical areas; it continued forever.[7]

Despite the fact that Hirakawa's statement greatly expands the temporal and geographic scope of the phrase *cāturdisa-sangha*, it is clear enough that only the Buddhist monastic assemblies are its constituent members.

Yet early Buddhist history records that the Buddha also admitted lay members into his community, and that they eventually became a vital, symbiotic part of that community. Nevertheless, the lay community was initially considered distinct from, and even autonomous in relation to, the monastic community. Thus, "the four groups of Buddhists were not referred to collectively as a single order (*sangha*)."[8] How did this transformation from two distinct and autonomous groups (i.e., monastic and lay members) to a "fourfold *sangha*" of *bhikṣus, bhikṣunīs, upāsakas, and upāsikās* evolve? Reginald Ray, in his explanation of the so-called two-tiered model of Buddhist practitioners, is quite clear about the role of the laity in the early Buddhist tradition:

> On the one hand is the Buddhism of the founder, the Buddhism of the monks, marked by renunciation of the world and entry into the monastic *sangha*, decorous behavior as defined by the *vinaya*, the pursuit of the vocation of texts and scholarship, and the goal of nirvāṇa. On the other hand is the Buddhism of the laity, characterized by virtuous behavior and generosity toward monastics as well as by participation in the cults of the stūpa and of local deities. The laity practiced a compromised Buddhism and, in so doing, acted as a kind of buffer between the authentic Buddhism of the monks and the non-Buddhist environment of larger India.[9]

The importance of this role for the laity, or what Ray calls "the second normative lifestyle"[10] of Indian Buddhism, cannot be minimized. Although the goal of the lay Buddhist is *puṇya* or "merit," while the monastic's goal is arhantship

or "liberation," the two communities are clearly interdependent. To think otherwise, and especially so in the West, would be incorrect, as Gombrich notes:
"Buddhism is sometimes presented in the West as if the religion of the laity on
the one hand and of the clergy on the other were discontinuous, completely
separate. That is wrong."[11] It is not hard to see, then, how the fourfold *sangha* of
monks, nuns, laymen, and laywomen came to interpenetrate and become coin-
cident with the *sangha* of the four quarters. In other words, it is possible to use
the word *sangha*, in the broadest sense, to include all Buddhists. Étienne Lamotte
summarizes both the result and process:

> The *sangha* or Buddhist community consists of four assemblies
> (*pariṣad*): mendicant monks (*bhikṣu*), nuns (*bhikṣuṇī*), laymen
> (*upāsaka*), and laywomen (*upāsikā*). The religious are distinguishable
> from the lay followers through their robes, discipline, and ideal and
> religious prerogatives. At the risk of being misunderstood . . .
> Although both the sons of the Śākya, the monks and the layman
> represent divergent tendencies which, without coming into direct
> opposition, were to be asserted with increasing explicitness: on the
> one hand the ideal of renunciation and personal holiness and, on the
> other, active virtues and altruistic preoccupations.[12]

Without minimizing the important role of the laity in Buddhism, this chapter focuses on the monastic *sangha*, and the way in which modern Buddhist
communities have maintained their vitality by varying the *Vinaya* without compromising the wisdom, rigor, or intent of the ancient code. Although changing
times and cultures dictated the necessity for updating the specifics of the *Vinaya*
regulations through commentaries, until recently this practice obviously had no
relevance for monastic communities outside Asia, since there were none. Now,
however, as Buddhist monastic communities have begun to proliferate throughout the Western world, new and creative adjustments to the *Vinaya* are being
entertained in a wide variety of exciting ways.

In his consequential article "The Problem of the *Saṅgha* in the West,"
Walpola Rahula has noted,

> As the Order of the *Bhikkhu-saṅgha* is constituted and conducted
> according to the *Vinaya*, it should be made clear, even briefly, what
> the *Vinaya* is. First of all, it must be clearly understood that the
> *Vinaya* is different from the *Dhamma*. The *Vinaya* is not Ultimate
> Truth which does not and cannot change; it is only a convention
> established and accepted for the smooth and orderly conduct of a
> particular community. As such, it is bound to be changed and
> modified in different places at different times according to need.
> Thus, the Buddha himself amended and modified some *Vinaya* rules
> several times.[13]

In other words, because the internal governance of the monastic Buddhist *sangha*, for both the individual monastics and the collective community, is controlled by the canonical regulations contained in the *Vinaya Piṭaka*, and since it was codified so early in Buddhist religious history, it is important to elucidate its structure. In so doing, we will get a clear picture of precisely how comprehensive the disciplinary code was, thus foreshadowing the need for varying the *Vinaya* in modern times.

Vinaya Literature

Properly speaking, the *Vinaya Piṭaka*, or that portion of the Buddhist canon regulating the monastic life of the monks and nuns, is composed of three parts: the (1) *Sūtravibhaṅga*, (2) *Skandhaka*, and (3) Appendices. However, a consideration of the monastic disciplinary tradition must be taken in broad perspective, focusing not only on that portion of monastic law which was canonized but on *Vinaya* literature in general, thus affording us an opportunity to view the developmental process going on within the early Buddhist community in the first few centuries following Buddha's death. Consequently, we can include the *Prātimokṣa* and the *Karmavācanās*, although not considered to be canonical in the strictest sense, under the heading of Paracanonical *Vinaya* Literature,[14] and the commentaries and miscellaneous texts under the heading of Non-Canonical *Vinaya* Literature. Thus we arrive at the following arrangement:

> Paracanonical *Vinaya* Literature
> > *Prātimokṣa*
> > *Karmavācanā*
> Canonical *Vinaya* Literature
> > *Sūtravibhaṅga*
> > *Skandhaka*
> > Appendices
> Non-Canonical *Vinaya* Literature
> > Commentaries
> > Miscellaneous Texts

We can now proceed to an examination of these categories.

Paracanonical Vinaya Literature

Prātimokṣa

The *Prātimokṣa* is an inventory of offenses, being primarily "a collection of liturgical formularies governing the conduct of the *Bhikṣus* and *Bhikṣuṇīs*."[15] The *Prātimokṣa* was recited at each *Poṣadha* day, and regarding its function, I. B.

Horner candidly observes, "This recitation served the double purpose of keep-ing the rules fresh in the minds of the monks and nuns, and of giving each member of the monastic community the opportunity, while the rules were being repeated or recited, to avow any offences that he or she had committed."[16] For each breach of the rules, appropriate punitive measures are indicated. Since the *Prātimokṣa* concerns both monks and nuns, it is twofold (i.e., *Bhikṣu Prātimokṣa* and *Bhikṣuṇī Prātimokṣa*). The monks' *Prātimokṣa* contains eight categories of offenses, classified according to the degree of gravity. The nuns' *Prātimokṣa* covers the same categories with the third (or *Aniyata* offenses) being omitted.[17] The eight categories of offenses can now be listed and explained (with reference to the monks' text).

PĀRĀJIKA-DHARMAS. These four offenses are the most serious that can be com-mitted by the monks. They include (1) sexual intercourse, (2) theft, (3) depriva-tion of life (of a human), and (4) false proclamation of superhuman faculties. Violation of any one of the *pārājika-dharmas* results in permanent expulsion from the *sangha*.

SAMGHĀVAŚEṢA-DHARMAS. These thirteen offenses represent, following the *pārājika-dharmas*, the most severe breach of monastic discipline. Five offenses deal with sexual transgressions, two with dwelling places, two with false accu-sation, two with schisms, one with a monk who is difficult to speak to, and one with monks who corrupt families. The section of the *samghāvaśeṣa-dharmas* is unique in that it represents the only class of *Prātimokṣa* offenses, which con-tains specific provisions for disciplinary action. When a monk is culpable of a *samghāvaśeṣa* offense, he is subjected to a probationary period (*parivāsa*) for as many days as the offense was concealed. If the offense was confessed at once, the *parivāsa* period is reduced to nil. When the *parivāsa* is completed, a further period called *mānatva* must also be spent.

ANIYATA-DHARMAS. These two offenses include cases whereby a monk may be accused by a trustworthy female lay follower, and dealt with according to her dictate. In case 1, if a monk should sit together with a woman in a secret place convenient for sexual intercourse, he may be charged with either a *pārājika*, *samghāvaśeṣa*, or *pāyantika* (see later) offense, according to what actually tran-spired. In case 2, if a monk should sit together with a woman in a place unfit for indulging in sexual intercourse, but suitable for speaking to her in lewd words, he may be charged with a *samghāvaśeṣa* or *pāyantika* offense, the *pārājika* offense of unchastity having been ruled out.

NIHSARGIKA-PĀYANTIKA-DHARMAS. There are thirty offenses in this class, violation of which require expiation and forfeiture, as can be seen from the class title. Horner notes, "From internal evidence, *pācittiya* [Skt. *pāyantika*] is a (minor) offence to be confessed, *āpatti desetabbā* [Skt. *āpatti deśayitavyā*], a state common to all the *Nissagiyas* [Skt. *Niḥsargikas*]."[18] The *niḥsargika-pāyantika-dharmas* are arranged in three *vargas*, or sections, of ten rules each, with ten rules concerning robes, ten rules concerning rugs and the use of money, and ten rules concerning alms bowls, medicine, and the like.

PĀYANTIKA-DHARMAS. There are ninety offenses in this category,[19] violation of which require expiation. Although the number pattern in this class of rules is widely divergent in the various *nikāyas*, an examination of the contents of the rules yields surprising results. The vast majority of rules (74) may be grouped under five major headings:[20]

  1. Moral rules — 23 rules
  2. Conduct with women — 14 rules
  3. Food and drink — 16 rules
  4. *Dharma, Vinaya*, and their application — 11 rules
  5. Use of requisites — 10 rules.

The remaining sixteen rules may be grouped under three further rubrics, each containing a lesser number of items:

  1. Behavior in the *vihāra* — 6 rules
  2. Travel regulations — 5 rules
  3. Various types of destruction — 5 rules.

PRATIDEŚANĪYA-DHARMAS. The *Pratideśanīya* section contains four straightforward offenses, which are to be confessed. They include (1) partaking of food obtained through the intervention of a nun, (2) not reproving a nun for giving orders (pertaining to a meal) while a meal is being served, (3) accepting food from a family that is undergoing training, and (4) obtaining food while living in a dangerous setting, without having announced it being so beforehand (unless the monk is ill).

ŚAIKṢA-DHARMAS. This group of rules is the most disparate in the entire *Prātimokṣa*. The number of *śaikṣa-dharmas* varies in number from 66 in the Chinese Mahāsāṃghika version to 113 in the Chinese Sarvāstivādin version. Pachow describes the section in the following manner:

> The nature of these rules is essentially concerned with the daily
> conduct and decorum of the Bhikṣus such as: walking, moving to
> and fro, looking, dressing, contracting, and stretching and so forth.
> They do not come under any penal section inasmuch as there will
> not be any sanction or punishment for their breaches of violations.
> The violation of any of them by a Bhikṣu is not considered to be a
> criminal act but simply bad manners.[21]

This section of the *Prātimokṣa* is perhaps the most revealing with regard to delineating the particular customs of individual Buddhist sects in the earliest sectarian movement.[22]

ADHIKARAṆA-ŚAMATHA-DHARMAS. These seven rules represent a system by which the preceding offenses catalogued in the *Prātimokṣa* may be resolved. The *adhikaraṇa-śamatha-dharmas* are discussed at length in Sukumar Dutt's volume *Early Buddhist Monachism* (chapter 6, "The Internal Polity of a Buddhist *Sangha*," pp. 113–145 in the revised edition).

These eight classes of rules comprise the monks' *Prātimokṣa-sūtra*. The texts are prefaced by a series of verses praising the disciplined life, and also by a ritual formulary. A series of verses, often concurring with similar passages in the *Dhammapada* or *Udānavarga*, also follow the text proper, uniformly mentioning the six Buddhas immediately antecedent to Śākyamuni Gautama and Gautama himself.[23]

The nuns' *Prātimokṣa-sūtra* consists of the same classes of rules as the monks' text, but with the omission of the *aniyata-dharmas* as noted earlier. The number of rules in the nuns' *Prātimokṣa-sūtra* is considerably larger than in the monks' version, many rules having been inserted specifically for females.[24] A comparative study of the nuns' *Prātimokṣa-sūtra*, quite similar in structure and format to Pachow's study of the monks' text, was published by Chatsumarn Kabilsingh.[25] Kabilsingh's volume presents a number of extremely useful charts and tables as well as a helpful bibliography.

Karmavācanā

All the transactions pertaining to the communal life of a *sangha* were settled by acts referred to as *sanghakarmas*. *Sanghakarmas* could arise in either of two ways:[26]

1. By a general requisition
2. By a dispute.

Regarding the term *Karmavācanā*, Dr. B. Jinananda notes, "A formula, styled karmavācanā (Pāli kammavācā), was resorted to for performing sanghakarmas. There are two forms of arriving at a resolution (i) a summary decision (Jñaptidvitīyakarma) in which a resolution is arrived at by the first reading and (ii) a decision by the third reading (Jñapticaturthakarma)."[27]

Jinananda cites fourteen *Karmavācanās*:[28]

1. Admission into the order (*pravrajyā*)
2. Ordination of monks (*upasaṃpadā*)
3. Holding the confession ceremony (*poṣadha*)
4. Holding the ceremony of invitation (*pravāraṇā*)
5. Residence obligation during the rainy season (*varṣopagamana*)
6. Use of leather objects (*carman*)

7. Use and preparation of medicines (*bhaiṣajya*)
8. Robe-giving ceremony (*kaṭhina*)
9. Discipline
10. Daily life of monks
11. Beds and seats, that is, dwellings (*śayanāsana*)
12. Schisms in the order (*sanghabheda*)
13. Duties of a student and teacher to one another
14. Rules for nuns.

A valid *sanghakarma* consists of the following requisites:[29]

1. The presence of the proper number of competent monks[30]
2. The conveyance of all absentee ballots
3. The motion (*jñapti*) being proposed
4. The proper proclamation of *karmavācanā*.

Having recounted the structure of the Paracanonical *Vinaya* literature, and having examined the administration of the *Vinaya* system of monastic discipline, we can consider the structure and contents of the Canonical *Vinaya* Literature.

Canonical *Vinaya* Literature

Sūtravibhaṅga

The term *Sūtravibhaṅga* is literally translated as "analysis of a sūtra." Thus, the *Sūtravibhaṅga* is a detailed analysis concerning the offenses recorded in the *Prātimokṣa-sūtra*. As we should expect, the *Sūtravibhaṅga* has the same eight sections as the *Prātimokṣa-sūtra*. Regarding each of the *Prātimokṣa* rules, the *Sūtravibhaṅga* has a fourfold structure:

1. A story (or stories) explaining the circumstances under which the rule was pronounced
2. The actual *Prātimokṣa* rule
3. A word-for-word commentary on the rule[31]
4. Stories indicating mitigating circumstances in which exceptions to the rule or deviations in punishment might be made.

In addition to the *Prātimokṣa* offenses, several new disciplinary terms are found in the text of the *Sūtravibhaṅga*. These include *duṣkṛta* (light offense), *sthūlātyaya* (grave offense), and *durbhāṣita* (offense of improper speech). Horner describes the nature of these offenses: "One or other of these offences is said to be incurred if behaviour has approximated to that which a particular Pātimokkha rule has been designated to restrain, but which is, so far as can be judged, not so grave in nature as a breach of the rule itself, because of certain differences in its execution, or because of certain extenuating circumstances."[32]

As with the *Prātimokṣa*, there is both a *Bhikṣu Sūtravibhaṅga* (referred to as the *Mahāvibhaṅga*) and a *Bhikṣuṇī Sūtravibhaṅga*.

Skandhaka

The *Skandhaka* contains the regulations pertaining to the organization of the *sangha*. The *Skandhaka* functions on the basis of the acts and ceremonies dictated by the *Karmavācanās*. Two statements can be made in the way of analogy:[33]

1. The *Skandhaka* represents to the *sangha* what the *Sūtravibhaṅga* represents to the individual monk or nun.
2. The *Karmavācanās* are to the *Skandhaka* what the *Prātimokṣa* is to the *Sūtravibhaṅga*.

There are twenty chapters in the *Skandhaka*, each referred to as a *vastu*, which shall now be listed with a brief summary of the main features of each.

PRAVRAJYĀVASTU. This *vastu* discusses, at length, admission into the order (*pravrajyā*), ordination to full monkhood (*upasaṃpadā*), admission of novices (*śrāmaṇeras*), regulations regarding behavior of a monk toward his master (*upadhyāya*) or teacher (*ācārya*), and a summary of the cases disqualifying one from admission into the order.

POṢADHAVASTU. The *Poṣadhavastu* discusses the monthly confession ceremony from its inception to its final form and also outlines the rules connected with the *Poṣadha* ceremony. At first, the ceremony was held on the eighth, fourteenth, and fifteenth of every fortnight, but later, observance on the eighth was eliminated, and Buddha declared that the *Prātimokṣa-sūtra* should be recited at the *Poṣadha* ceremony.

VARṢĀVASTU. The third *vastu* sets forth the rules for the observance of the rainy season. The period for rainy season residence is fixed at three months, and a discussion of when to enter the rain residence, acceptable and forbidden dwellings, and room and furniture distribution is also included.

PRAVĀRAṆĀVASTU. This chapter treats the invitation (*Pravāraṇā*) ceremony that comes at the end of the rainy season. The ceremony is designed to prevent disharmony in the monastic community, and involves each monk inviting other monks to state whether there is anything for which he should be reproved, being prepared, of course, to make the proper reparation.

CARMAVASTU. The *Carmavastu* deals with the usage of leather (and shoes in particular).

BHAIṢAJYAVASTU. This chapter discusses the rules concerning foods and medicines allowed to the monks. Several stories are utilized to outline a definition of medicinal drugs and an explanation of how and when they are to be used. With regard to food, the rules are severe, stating which alms foods may be accepted, how an invitation should be dealt with, how alms foods are to be prepared, and how the storeroom is to be used. Relaxation of these rules is allowed in hard times.

CĪVARAVASTU. The *Cīvaravastu* treats the rules regarding monks' clothing. The legend of the physician Jīvaka is recounted, at length, culminating with the Buddha allowing monks to accept robes from the laity. Rules concerning which robes may and may not be worn, the cutting and sewing of robes, the disfiguring of robes, and the number of robes are set forth.

KAṬHINAVASTU. This *vastu* sets forth rules concerning the manufacture and distribution of robes for the monks, initiated because of the poor condition of the clothing of the monks after the period of rainy season residence.

KOŚĀMBAKAVASTU. The *Kośāmbakavastu* is a short chapter relating a dispute that develops between two groups of monks in Kauśāmbī concerning the expulsion of a monk. Elaborate instructions on proper conduct are given to the community by the Buddha. Finally, the excluded monk confesses his guilt, is readmitted, and harmony is restored.

KARMAVASTU. This chapter discusses acts carried out by the monastic community, emphasizing the various sorts of assemblies in the *sangha* and in which acts they are competent to function. Valid and invalid procedures are also outlined.

PĀṆḌULOHITAKAVASTU. This *vastu* outlines monastic disciplinary measures. Five cases are mentioned, the first two of which refer to the individuals for whom the chapter is named.

PUDGALAVASTU. The *Pudgalavastu* discusses the treatment of *saṃghāvaśeṣa* offenses, precipitated by the conduct of a monk named Udāyī. The *parivāsa* and *mānatva* probations are outlined, in detail, as well as formal enactment of the reinstatement ceremony (*āvarhaṇa*).

PĀRIVĀSIKAVASTU. This chapter discusses the standards of behavior to be observed during the *parivāsa* and *mānatva* periods.

POṢADHASTHĀPANAVASTU. This *vastu* discusses the prohibiting of a monk from participating in the *Poṣadha* ceremony. The chapter commences with the Buddha refusing to recite the *Prātimokṣa*, despite Ānanda's several requests, because there is an impure monk in the assemblage. When the monk is removed, the Buddha announces that in the future the *sangha* itself (and not the Buddha) must hold *Poṣadha* and recite the *Prātimokṣa*. Moreover, monks guilty of offenses are excluded from the ceremony.

ŚAMATHAVASTU. The *śamathavastu* is divided into two parts, the first of which outlines the procedures for the resolution of legal questions (*adhikaraṇas*). The seven *adhikaraṇa-śamatha-dharmas* are discussed, as well as the four classes of disputes. The second part is concerned with motives for the various conciliation procedures.

SANGHABHEDAVASTU. This chapter discusses schisms in the *sangha*. The Devadatta legend occupies a large portion of the *vastu*. Following the Devadatta legend, there is a general discussion of schisms in the *sangha*.

ŚAYANĀSANAVASTU. The *śayanāsanavastu* concerns the dwellings of the *sangha*.

ĀCĀRAVASTU. This chapter is a miscellany concerning rules of conduct. Behavior with regard to alms begging, meals among the laity, attitudes toward newly arrived monks, and forest-dwelling monks are also issues of discussion.

KṢUDRAKAVASTU. The *Kṣudrakavastu* is an inventory of rules that are of minor importance and, by their nature, could not be appropriately placed elsewhere. Such topics as toothpicks and bathroom furniture are discussed.

BHIKṢUṆĪVASTU. As is obvious from the title, this chapter treats rules designed specifically for nuns. At the beginning of the *vastu*, the story leading up to the admission of women into the *sangha* is related. The nuns' admission, confession, and invitation ceremonies are discussed, as well as rules for conduct toward the male *sangha* members. Minor regulations conclude the chapter.

In addition to the twenty *vastus* in the *Skandhaka*, there is an introductory section discussing the Buddha's genealogy, birth, and life history up to the conversion of Śāriputra and Maudgalyāyana, and also a concluding section covering Buddha's death, the council of Rājagṛha, the history of the patriarchs, and the council of Vaiśālī. We may thus outline the following schema for the structure of the *Skandhaka*:[34]

1. Introduction: Buddha's early life and career
2. Buddhist monastic institutions (chapters 1–4)
3. Daily needs of the monks (chapters 5–8)
4. Monastic law (chapters 9–10)

5. Disciplinary proceedings (chapters 11–13)
6. Miscellaneous (chapters 14–20)
7. Conclusion: Buddha's death and afterward.

Appendices

Appendices are attached to several *Vinayas* as a supplement. They serve two basic functions:[35]

1. Providing summaries of the rules found in the *Sūtravibhaṅga* and *Skandhaka*
2. Providing interesting bits of monastic history.

Non-Canonical *Vinaya* Literature

Commentaries

Fortunately, a wide variety of *Vinaya* commentaries have been preserved, and their importance for the student of *Vinaya* literature need not be stressed here. The most complete commentarial traditions have been preserved in the Theravādin and Mūlasarvāstivādin nikāyas (in Pāli and Tibetan, respectively). A useful summary of some of the Theravādin commentaries can be found in *The Buddhist Monastic Code,* by Thanissaro Bhikkhu.[36] We also possess Chinese translations for *Vinaya* commentaries in many of the Indian Buddhist *nikāyas,* lacking only modern texts.

Miscellaneous Texts

In this category, we can place two types of texts. First, we must list those texts, existing only in translation, which can no longer be identified with a particular *nikāya.* Second, we have a rather amorphous group of texts that, although not being classified as *Vinaya* literature in the strictest sense, are clearly *Vinaya*-related and that influence the *Vinaya* traditions of several *nikāyas.*

Vinaya and *Śīla*: The Foundation of the Sangha

In trying to understand the nature and function of the Theravada *sangha*, Michael Carrithers has remarked, "In fact, if one were to seek one theme, one idea, which could be said to underlie the Theravāda Sangha, it would be Discipline: a word that applied both to the monastic code and to the moral purity embodied in the code."[37] Clearly, if one is to exercise precision in the application of Carrithers's

comprehension of the word "discipline," it is necessary to have a solid understanding of the distinction between the words *Vinaya* and *śīla*, each of which is
consequential in the Buddhist disciplinary tradition.

Venerable Sheng-Yen, in the prologue to *Buddhist Ethics and Modern Society*, says, "The precepts (Vinaya) form the basis of Buddhist ethics." He goes on
to say that "Buddhist lay members need obey only 5, or at the most 8, Buddhist
novices must obey 10, while adult monks and nuns have to obey anywhere from
250 to more than 300."[38] Although Sheng-Yen is wrong in not distinguishing
the basis of ethical conduct for the laity as separate from the monastic code of
the *Vinaya*, a traditional association in East Asian Buddhism where the terms
śīla and *Vinaya* are compounded, his mistake is rather commonly made even in
the Indian tradition where the terms are indeed separate and never compounded.
Akira Hirakawa has offered considerable insight on the need to separate the
traditional compound *śīla/vinaya* into its component parts for a proper understanding of each term,[39] but it is rather common, I think, for scholars to associate *Vinaya* rather than *śīla* with ethics.

As noted earlier, it is important to understand why the distinction between
these terms is so important, and precisely how the distinction affects my original topic. The technical term *Vinaya*, derived from the Sanskrit prefix vi + √nī,
is often rendered as (some variant of) training, education, discipline, or control.
John Holt, utilizing another etymologically valid approach suggests, "Vinaya,
the reified noun form of the verb vi + √nī therefore leads us to the general meaning of 'that which separates,' or 'that which removes.'"[40] Holt goes on:

> Our translation of the term vinaya begs the question: what is being
> removed? To answer that question in the simplest terms, that which
> is being removed are wrong states of mind, the conditions of
> grasping, desire and ignorance which stem from the delusion that
> we have a "self" that can be satiated. The discipline of the
> *Vinayapiṭaka* represents a systematic assault on the idea of "ego-
> consciousness."[41]

Charles Wei-hsun Fu, utilizing Hirakawa's etymological analysis, which captures the essence of both meanings cited here, comes to the same conclusion:
"*Vinaya* referred to the established norms of the *Sangha* that all members were
expected to observe to maintain the monastic order and insure its continuation."[42] In other words, the *Vinaya* was as much concerned with the *pariśuddhi*
or complete purity of the community, individually and organizationally, as it
was with the specifics of ethical conduct.[43] Under no circumstances should we
presume that ethical concerns were superseded in the *Vinaya*; rather, they were
included in a series of tiered concerns that focused on institutional, but not
exclusively ethical conduct. *Śīla*, more difficult etymologically than *Vinaya*, is
probably derived from the verb √śīl and generally translated as virtue, moral
conduct, morality, or some similar variant (although Buddhaghosa in the

Visuddhimagga traces it to a different verb root, associated with "cooling" and Vasubandhu in the *Abhidharmakośa* suggests it derives from the verb √śī, which he too associates with cooling).[44] As such, it is a highly ethical term, almost exclusively applied to the individual and referenced to his or her self-discipline. Additionally, one finds such references continually in the literature.[45] Unlike the *Vinaya*, which is externally enforced, *śīla* refers to the internally enforced ethical framework by which the monk or nun structures his or her life.[46] Taken in this light, we can see that *śīla* is an incredibly rich concept for understanding individual ethical conduct. Thus, as Fu points out, with respect to *śīla* and *Vinaya*:

> Hirakawa's analysis of the two words seems to have enormous significance for Buddhist ethics. Our present inquiry into the essential meaning of Buddhist ethics and morality, to address the task of its constructive modernization, demands that we give serious consideration to the means for maintaining a balance between autonomy (*śīla*) [*sic*], expressing the inner spirit of Dharma, and the heteronomous norms or precepts (*vinaya*) of the Buddhist order.[47]

If we could establish that the canonical *Vinaya* texts, of which the *Sūtravibhaṅga* is a critical part, have their basis in the precepts of *śīla*, then such an argument might be well taken. In this regard, one of the pioneers of comparative *Prātimokṣa* study, W. Pachow, argues for precisely that position in asserting that the Buddhist disciplinary code was little more than an embellishment of the traditional, widely known, and quite early *pañcaśīla* or five ethical precepts. Pachow says,

> It would not be unreasonable to say that the code of discipline of the *sangha* is but an enlarged edition of the *Pañcaśīla* which have been adopted by the Buddhists and the Jains from the Brāhmaṇical ascetics. And under various circumstances, they have developed subsidiary rules in order to meet various requirements on various occasions. This appears to us to be the line of development through which the growth of these rules could be explained.[48]

He then attempts to identify a clear developmental relationship between the individual precepts of the *pañcaśīla* and the lesser, secondary rules of the *Prātimokṣa*. Pachow's interesting approach is cited by most scholars researching the problem. Holt, for example, says, "If this hypothesis were absolutely sound, we could somehow relate all of the disciplinary rules in some way to the four *pārājikas* or to the *pañcaśīla*. Unfortunately, we are not able to do this."[49] Using the Pāli text as the benchmark, 139 of the 227 *Pātimokkha* rules can be explained. Nonetheless, 88 rules cannot be reconciled. Undaunted, Pachow simply creates new categories to accommodate them.[50] The problem is further exacerbated by the fact that the *pañcaśīla* largely mirror the rules for Brāhmaṇical ascetics and Jain monks. Holt summarizes well: "Thus, if we are to argue that the fundamental basis of Buddhist discipline consists of the primary concerns of śīla, we would have to admit that the basis of Buddhist discipline is not exclusively Buddhist, nor śramaṇic, not even monastic for that matter: not a very satisfying finding."[51]

In the beginning of his important chapter "Aspects of Sīla" in *The Nature of Buddhist Ethics*, Damien Keown echoes Holt, and clearly identifies the impact of Holt's argument: "Overall, there seems to be no reason to assume that the *Vinaya* is either derived from a simpler set of moral principles or founded upon a single underlying principle or rationale."[52] The remarks of Holt and Keown mirror what I said rather directly in 1980: the "*Prātimokṣa* is not just monastic 'glue' holding the *saṃgha* together, but the common ground on which the internally enforced life of *śīla* is manifested externally in the community."[53] Richard Gombrich and Mohan Wijayaratna say as much, with Gombrich referring to the twice-monthly *Prātimokṣa* as a "solidarity ritual," and Wijayaratna calling it "a kind of 'quality control.'"[54] More recently, and aggressively, Lambert Schmithausen has made the same point. He notes, "The *Vinaya* is not concerned, primarily, with morality proper but rather with the internal harmony and external reputation of the Order."[55] He goes on to say, "One of the main purposes of the *Pātimokkha* (though some of its prohibitions do also refer to orality proper) is no doubt, besides internal harmony, the correct and decorous behaviour of the Order and its members in society."[56] Although the *Sūtravibhaṅga* and its paracanonical precursor, the *Prātimokṣa* (that portion of the *Vinaya Piṭaka* devoted to precepts for the individual monks and nuns), contain many rules reflective of significant ethical awareness and concern, is it appropriate to identify the *Sūtravibhaṅga* as an exclusively ethical document? Probably not.

Modernizing the Vinaya

Walpola Rahula was remarkably insightful when he wrote, in 1978:

> It is the members of the "Institutional *Saṅgha*," the *bhikkhus*, who have been the custodians of the *Dhamma*, and have transmitted it throughout these twenty-five centuries for the perpetuation of the *Sāsana* (Buddhism). It is this "Institutional *Saṅgha*" that can be established in a country as an organized, visible, representative body of the *Saṅgha* of the Three Jewels. So those interested in the establishment and perpetuation of the *Sāsana* in the West must be concerned with the establishment of the *Bhikkhu-saṅgha* there.[57]

If the establishment of the monastic community in each country into which Buddhism is introduced is critical for the ongoing history and development of the *Sāsana* in that country, then nothing is more significant to the achievement of that end than firmly establishing the rules of the discipline. As the *Vinaya* itself notes—and Wijayaratna points out[58]—the rules of discipline for the monastic community have ten intentions:

1. Protecting the community
2. Insuring the community's comfort
3. Warding off ill-meaning people
4. Helping well-behaved monks and nuns
5. Destroying present defilements
6. Preventing future defilements
7. Benefiting non-followers
8. Increasing the number of followers
9. Establishing the discipline
10. Observing the rules of restraint.

How these intentions, and the specific rules of the *Vinaya*, are applied to modern Buddhist communities in Asia and the West is no simple matter, as times and circumstances have changed enormously since the *Vinaya Piṭaka* was codified in the first centuries following Buddha's demise.

Prior to his death, and as recorded in the proceedings of the first Buddhist council at Rājagṛha, the Buddha was reputed to have given his consent for the monks to abolish the lesser and minor disciplinary precepts. Despite reproving Ānanda for not ascertaining precisely *which* rules the Buddha considered lesser and minor, the council's participants were nevertheless faced with an obviously difficult decision on this matter, prompting Mahākāśyapa, as president of the council, to put forth a motion—unanimously accepted by the *sangha*—that rules would be neither added nor deleted from those recited by Upāli, the master of the *Vinaya*. It did not take long for the *sangha* to face the grim reality that the decision made at the first council was profoundly impractical, as Rahula points out:

> But as time went on *bhikkhus* had to face the realities of life under newly developed circumstances, and realize the impracticality and difficulty of following some rules in their original form. Therefore, without changing the letter of the law, monks discovered ways and means of overcoming the difficulty by interpreting the law without compromising themselves. These interpretations and decisions, concluded first at the Mahāvihāra at Anurādhapura in Śrī Laṅkā and later accepted by all Theravāda countries, are known under the term *pālimuttaka-vinicchaya*, i.e. decisions not found in the original canonical texts. These are tantamount to amendments or new rules, though they are not considered as such.[59]

These decisions were eventually collected in a book titled *Pālimuttaka-vinayavincchaya*, written by the thirteenth-century Śrī Laṅkān monk Sāriputta Thera. Despite the fact that *pālimuttaka-vinicchaya* resolutions, or "decisions standing outside the canonical texts," could only be arrived at by a consensual agreement of the monks (called *katikāvata*), Paul Numrich describes the process as a "paradoxical hermeneutic."[60] Numrich goes on to report that although the *katikāvata* hermeneutical principle has not been utilized in Theravāda countries since the thirteenth or fourteenth century, it is currently being discussed in American Theravāda communities.[61]

In July 1987, a "Conference on World Buddhism in North America" was sponsored by the Zen Lotus Society in Ann Arbor, Michigan, conceived by Ven. Samu Sunim, and co-coordinated by Professor Luis Gómez. Amidst the many panel discussions, meetings, and talks, no individual topic seemed more critical than that of how Theravāda *bhikkhus*–both Asian immigrants and American converts–might successfully observe the precepts of the *Vinaya* in Western countries. Venerable Havanpola Ratanasara of the Dharma Vijaya Buddhist Vihara in Los Angeles, who was eventually named executive president of the American Buddhist Congress, noted (as reported by Paul Numrich and captured on the video documentary of the conference): "[Vinaya] is not a static thing because it concerns a living group of persons. Living persons will have to adjust to the changing conditions of the society. Monks are not like stones . . . they are living creatures, they have to face changing conditions in the society. So according to certain conditions, things are changing."[62]

Ven. Ratanasara's comments clearly echo those of Walpola Rahula's voiced a decade earlier:

> The reality has to be faced that *bhikkhus* living in the West cannot follow the way of life as practised in Buddhist countries in Asia. Certain changes and modifications should be made to suit social and economic conditions in the West, and this is quite in keeping with the tradition of Buddhist history, as has been shown already. Certain practices will have to be modified or abandoned. The Buddha himself accepted some practices and customs of other religions in India at the time, and prescribed them for *bhikkhus*, such as the observance of *vassa* during the rainy season and the *uposatha* ceremony. In this liberal spirit of the Buddha, it is nothing but proper to adopt some customs and practices of other religions there, so long as they do not interfere with the fundamental tenets of Buddhism.[63]

Nonetheless, other Theravāda monks at the conference, including the abbot of Dharma Vijaya (Ven. Walpola Piyananda), disagreed, citing the ruling of the first Buddhist council as their precedent. One participant, Samaneri Sunanda, even postulated that the current alteration or elimination of minor rules would eventually lead to the disappearance of all precepts. Trapped between the proverbial rock and the hard place with regard to *Vinaya* observance, modern *bhikkhus* have clearly taken up the challenge and begun to engage in a creative dialogue concerning the issue. Moreover, the activities of some of these Theravāda Buddhist communities in North America and Europe have been recently studied. A very brief examination of at least a few of these communities is extremely constructive.

It is beyond the scope of this chapter to examine the process by which Buddhist monastics moved from an eremetical to a settled lifestyle. Nonetheless, it is clear that in doing so, the establishment of boundaries, or sīmā, for their monasteries became critical because it denoted the geographic space in which ritual activities—including the Prātimokṣa-sūtra recitation—could properly take place. Sīmā establishment is strictly regulated by the Vinaya and almost always coincided with natural boundaries (such as a mountain, a rock, or a river). Where none could be found, boundaries were often marked by a village or town.[64] Eventually, after Buddha's death, as the sangha grew and expanded, a new kind of boundary regulation was established—authorized in the Vinaya commentary known as the Samantapāsādikā—and dealing with monasteries (i.e., vihāras) built by kings or ministers. This boundary, referred to as lābha-sīmā, denoted the "income-boundary" of the monastery, and acknowledged that monks made use of the property of the monastery, but now religionized, to generate income. It would seem that this process of establishing lābha-sīmā is critical for understanding the development of monastic life, and the Vinaya that governs its conduct, in the modern world. Corollary to the establishment of settled monastic life was the continued, ongoing requirement of the sangha to engage in the twice-monthly poṣadha ceremony in which the offenses of the Prātimokṣa-sūtra were recited. In the early monastic settlements, four monks were required to hold a valid Prātimokṣa ceremony—a requirement that would be difficult to establish in many Western monasteries—but even that requirement can be waived in certain circumstances.[65] In other words, while it was readily imaginable, and even likely, to adjust the geographic requirements, as well as the requisite number of monastics for a valid recitation ceremony, it was not acceptable to alter the rules and precepts of the Vinaya, as Rahula points out: "From that day to this, as far as is known, not a single Vinaya rule was officially changed nor were new rules introduced into the body of the Vinaya by the Saṅgha of the Theravāda."[66] As such, the application of the process of pālimuttaka-vinicchaya became increasingly important, both in ancient times and modern.

Recently, the Canadian bhikkhu Ajahn Tiradhammo has written about the challenge of living a Theravāda monk's life in the West, with special reference to the Dhammapala Buddhistisches Kloster he established in Switzerland in 1988.[67] His focus throughout is on the Thai Forest Tradition in the lineage of Ven. Ajahn Chah. This tradition currently refers primarily to the disciples of Phra Ajahn Mun Buridatto (d. 1949), who established a very strict observance of the precepts of Vinaya in his community. Ajahn Chah established his first monastery, Wat Pah Pong, in 1954. By 1999, his disciples had established over 150 monasteries in Thailand, and 11 in the West. According to Tiradhammo:

He maintained one of the strictest forms of Vinaya in Thailand, but not rigid (i.e., one of the few teachers who does not allow disciples to have personal funds). He sees Vinaya as a support for spiritual practice, most particularly to help increase mindfulness and encourage communal harmony. For example, it requires a fair degree of wisdom and much awareness of body, speech and mind in order to keep Vinaya in a relaxed and skilful way rather than through fear or repression.[68]

Nonetheless, Ajahn Chah—like other modern Buddhists cited earlier—was keenly aware that the *Vinaya* did not cover every situation and circumstance facing Buddhist communities and the individual monastic who inhabit them. To deal with new issues not explicitly covered in the canonical text, he relied on the precedent established in the sixth chapter of the *Mahāvagga* (concerning medicines). It can be summarized by two basic principles:[69]

1. Whatever has not been mentioned as allowable or unallowable, which agrees with what is allowable and not with what is unallowable, that is allowable.
2. Whatever has not been mentioned as allowable or unallowable, which agrees with what is unallowable and not with what is allowable, that is unallowable.

By 1975, when Ajahn Chah established Wat Pah Nanachat (or "International Forest Monastery") in Thailand for training Western monks, and in 1977, when he traveled to England (along with the American monk Ven. Sumedho and the British monk Ven. Khantipalo) to lead a small community of monastics at the Hampstead Vihara in England, it was the above formula that guided their *Vinaya* observance.

Tiradhammo organizes the challenges facing Theravāda monks in the West into three categories: cultural challenges, psychological challenges, and the challenge of spiritual teachings. It is the first of these which is critical to my topic, for it spotlights not only attitudes and teachings but more importantly, the adjustment to living conditions and training customs operative in a new setting. In other words, how might the mendicant, and perhaps even ascetic, lifestyle cultivated in seclusion of the Thai forest monastery adjust to the less-than-secluded environment of the modern West? Even a couple of examples demonstrate the difficulty of the issue.

Initially, the key *Vinaya*-related factors to be considered involved clothing, food, and work. In Theravāda countries, three robes (inner, upper, and outer) were prescribed. Clearly, in Europe and North America, the traditional robes of the *bhikkhu* were insufficient in the generally colder climate. The first experiments, utilizing thicker robes, were unsatisfactory, for these robes proved too hot in the summer months. This eventually led to the current practice of wear-

ing several layers of underclothing with a light outer robe. But it was also necessary to make sure that the outer robe covered the undergarments thoroughly,
as these varied greatly in color and size. In Thailand, the standard of this monastic tradition was to eat one meal per day, usually as early as 8:30 A.M. In the
West, this time frame proved too early for food donors, so the morning meal
was moved to 10:30 A.M., preceded by a hot drink earlier. However, for those
walking extended distances on their almstour, or who were engaged in various
forms of work, some accommodation needed to be made to provide added ca-
loric intake. Eventually, a milk drink and some light porridge was allowed in
the afternoon, as were some of the foods considered to be "medicinal" in the
Vinaya. While most Asian Theravāda monks do not work, in Thailand some work
was added to the monks' regimen as what Tiradhammo calls "active meditation." This form was continued in Western monasteries where some amount
of work was required to establish and maintain the monasteries. It would be
possible to continue outlining the various *Vinaya* adjustments made in these
monasteries, but it is certainly obvious that each of the items outlined above fits
well within the description of the *pālimuttaka-vinicchaya* principle, and affirmed
by the *katikāvata* process.

Paul Numrich's work with Wat Dhammaran in Chicago and Dharma Vijaya
in Los Angeles mirrors Ven. Tiradhammo's experience in Europe. Numrich
focuses on four major areas of *Vinaya* adaptation, presented in detail in his
volume *Old Wisdom in the New World: Americanization in Two Immigrant
Theravada Buddhist Temples*: (1) dress code, (2) meals, (3) urban transportation,
and (4) celibacy. According to Numrich, the most discussed problem involved
the three traditional robes required in the Theravāda tradition. In rather dramatic fashion, he relates an incident when, on Christmas Day 1976, Ven.
Piyananda deplaned at O'Hare Airport in Chicago wearing only his three robes
and sandals. Fearing the very real possibility of the monk's experiencing hypo-
thermia, Robert Fodde, the director of security for a Thai temple in the midwest,
"wrote a letter to the Council of Thai Bhikkhus suggesting adoption of a 'proper
winter uniform for Monks,' with yellow clerical collar and Buddhist lapel pin to
identify the wearers as legitimate clergy."[70] While Fodde's request was not honored as requested, additional clothing was sanctioned by the supreme patriarch
of Thailand. Monks at Dharma Vijaya thus wear yellow (or saffron) T-shirts under
their upper robe, while *bhikkhus* at Wat Dhammaram wear socks, sweaters, and
stocking hats during the harsh Chicago winters.[71] At this point, there seems little
likelihood that Theravāda monks will eschew traditional robes for civilian clothing, except at ceremonial functions, as some Zen groups have done.

Traditionally, Theravāda monks in Asia eat no solid food after noon. Most
investigators of ethnic Theravāda temples in North America have noted the
difficulty in adapting this practice to everyday life, and especially so as the
bhikkhus interact with a laity that has embraced American customs. As Numrich
tells us,

Foregoing an evening meal seems to present little difficulty as long as monks in America limit their activities and contacts with laity to temple confines, but as monks enter more and more into the orbit of the lives of typical Americans, conflicts do arise, or at least opportunities can be lost. Americans typically work during the day, and their main meal is dinner, at which they often entertain guests and even conduct business. As Ven. Dr. Ratanasara told me, relations with American laity may suffer severe limitations if monks cannot take advantage of such evening interaction. The complication here became evident as I accompanied some Dharma Vijaya monks on an early evening visit to a temple family's home. The husband and wife disagreed over whether to serve us any food at all, even soup, and their quandary led to a pointed discussion among all of us about the right thing to do in the light of both ancient *vinaya* and modern America. This particular *vinaya* dilemma will take on larger proportions in coming years.[72]

Equally, transportation has become a thorny issue. The Pāli *Mahāvagga* (V.9.1–4; V.10.1–3) prohibits the use of vehicles by monks except in the case of illness. As such, riding in vehicles in North America, or driving them, would be prohibited, despite the gross impracticality of the observance of this aspect of the *Vinaya*. By strictly adhering to the prohibition of vehicular use, monks in North American temples would seriously truncate the range and scope of their Dhamma activities, limiting visits to lay community members, visiting other temples, and engaging in outreach activities only to those within walking distance. Eventually, Dharma Vijaya broke new ground in this area, allowing its monks to drive automobiles, some of which were owned by the monastery. Ven. Dr. Ratanasara informed Paul Numrich that Wat Thai of Los Angeles had also adopted the practice of allowing monks to drive, and that he expected the practice to spread. It seems that the defining characteristic in adopting this *pālimuttaka-vinicchaya* practice was whether the monks was engaged in *Dhamma* activity rather than personal service.

The monastic requirement of celibacy is the first precept listed in the Theravāda monastic code known as the *Pātimokkha*. Violation of one of the *pārājika dhammas*—as this category is titled—requires immediate expulsion from the *sangha*.[74] In addition, virtually every aspect of the monks' relationship with women is regulated. Monks cannot travel with women, touch women, or even preach the *Dhamma* to women in more than five or six words (unless a wise man is present).[75] The dilemma is twofold: "First, there is the relatively simple issue of decorum in their interactions with women. Should monks shake hands or exchange a friendly embrace with women in a society that sees such expressions as perfectly acceptable and where refusal to do so can be interpreted as a person affront? Second, there is the more complex issue of celibacy per se."[76]

Apparently, Ven. Dr. Ratanasara thinks many of the traditional issues defining the relationship of monks to women are senseless in the American context. As Numrich reports,

> He thinks monks will inevitably begin to shake hands and keep
> casual company with women as part of their normal pastoral
> relationships in America. But, he notes, the celibacy issue remains a
> stickler in the development of a native Theravada *bhikkhu-sangha* in
> America, for Americans generally seem to view sex as a human
> necessity, like food and water. Yet celibacy is the most dramatic
> symbol of the "set apart" character of the *bhikkhu-sangha* in the
> Theravada tradition.[77]

A variety of non-Theravāda groups in the West have explored alternatives to the insistence on celibacy required in the *Vinaya*. The Friends of the Western Buddhist Order have developed a three-stage pattern for renunciation that establishes lifestyle categories without emphasizing celibacy: (1) "friend," (2) "spiritual friend" (or mitra), and (3) ordination (as an expression of lifelong commitment to Buddhism). Some Zen groups allow married priests, of both genders, who pursue the complete career of a Zen monastic while maintaining traditional American families and vocations. Dharma Vijaya itself even presented a novel ordination scheme that allowed an intermediate bridge between the full monastic lifestyle and traditional lay life. In its February 1982 newsletter it proposed:

> Now in this country, the lay person–monk gap might be bridged in
> part through a system of several types ordinations of formal disci-
> plines. There could *perhaps be three levels:*
>   i. *Bhikkhu: A monk who follows virtually [?] all the* Vinaya rules.
>   ii. *Anagārika*: The full minister who follows ten precepts and devotes all
>   his efforts to religious practice and teachings.
>   iii. *Ajivasila*: A lay minister who follows eight precepts, leads a lay life,
>   may marry and give much attention to religious activities.[78]

The so-called ordination was never instituted. Other experimental ordination schemes were considered at Dharma Vijaya over the next decade.

During a July 1989 visit to North America, the Dalai Lama met with the Buddhist *Sangha* Council of Southern California. At that time, he noted, "Therefore, in certain vinaya rules, when it comes to [a] clash between existing situations, sometimes a change can be undertaken. But these things depend upon particular circumstances in a particular individual. We cannot change the rule."[79] The very next year, as reported by Numrich, Ven. Piyananda, the abbot of Dharma Vijaya, noted in his keynote address at the Tenth Annual Vaisakha Celebration in Los Angeles that, although it was permissible to make some minor changes in accommodating Theravāda Buddhism to the West, these changes should not be allowed to damage "the original structure of the monk-lay devotee relationship." He went on to explain to Numrich: "In my experience, it will be difficult for us as Theravada monks if we try to survive in this country, even within our immigrant communities. There is no future here if we very strictly try to stay as Theravada monks."[80] That same year, Ven. Dr. Chuen Phangcham of Wat Dhammaram told the 1990 Conference on Buddhism in Canada, "Some Thai tradition[s] will not be accepted in American society. The seasons are different, climate is different, rules and regulations should be adapted."[81]

As a result of his work with immigrant Theravāda communities in the United States, Paul Numrich distinguishes three operative hermeneutical principles of *Vinaya* adaptation.[82] The first he calls "minor modification." More precisely, this means that only minor *Vinaya* rules have been modified, and all regulations that involve distinguishing features of Theravāda monastic life have been preserved intact. The second principle is "practicality" and addresses only those precepts—such as the ones involving transportation—that are impractical in an American context. The third principle is "consensus." It is here that the formal revival of *katikāvata* is employed to allow Theravāda communities to add new rules that fall outside the *Vinaya* texts (or *pālimuttaka-vinicchaya*). There is little doubt that the Buddhist *Vinaya* tradition has already begun to creatively respond to the challenges of Buddhist globalization. Nonetheless, the current results are at best ambiguous. How the process of "varying the *Vinaya*" continues in the early decades of the new century remains a critical factor in determining the new shape and character of Buddhism as a truly global religion.

NOTES

1. See Paul David Numrich, "Vinaya in Theravāda Temples in the United States," *Journal of Buddhist Ethics* 1 (1994): 23. The passage appears in the *Samantapāsādikā* 1, p. 102; *Mahāvaṃsa* p. 126; *Dīpavaṃsa*, chapter 14, verses 20–24; and *Vinaya-nidāna* p. 103.

2. See Michael B. Carrithers, "'They Will Be Lords Upon the Island': Buddhism in Sri Lanka," in *The World of Buddhism: Buddhist Monks and Nuns in Society and Culture*, ed. Heinz Bechert and Richard Gombrich (New York: Facts on File, 1984), p. 133.

3. Akira Hirakawa, *A History of Indian Buddhism: From Śākyamuni to Early Mahāyāna*, translated and edited by Paul Groner (Honolulu: University of Hawaii Press, 1990), p. 62.

4. Richard Gombrich, "Introduction: The Buddhist Way," in Bechert and Gombrich, *The World of Buddhism: Buddhist Monks and Nuns in Society and Culture*, p. 13.

5. See, for example, Hermann Oldenberg, ed., *The Vinaya Piṭakaṃ*, 5 vols. (rpt. London: Luzac and Company, Ltd., 1964), 1: 305; or 2: 147.

6. Sukumar Dutt, *The Buddha and Five After Centuries* (London: Luzac and Company, Ltd., 1957), pp. 60–61. Also see the discussion in Sukumar Dutt, *Early*

Buddhist Monachism (London: Kegan Paul, Trench, Trübner and Company, 1924), pp. 83ff.

7. Hirakawa, *A History of Indian Buddhism*, p. 64.

8. Ibid., p. 60.

9. Reginald Ray, *Buddhist Saints in India: A Study in Buddhist Values and Orientations* (New York: Oxford University Press, 1994), p. 21.

10. Ibid., p. 19.

11. Gombrich, "Introduction," p. 14.

12. Étienne Lamotte, *History of Indian Buddhism: From the Origins to the Śaka Era*, translated by Sara Webb-Boin (Louvain: Institute Orientaliste de l'Université, Catholique de Louvain, 1988), p. 54.

13. Walpola Rahula, "The Problem of the Saṅgha in the West," in *Zen and the Taming of the Bull: Towards the Definition of Buddhist Thought*, ed. Walpola Rahula (London: Gordon Fraser, 1978), p. 61.

14. On this point, see, for example, Dutt, *The Buddha and Five After Centuries*, p. 76. Dutt notes, "The Pātimokkha forms no part of the Pāli canon, even though the bulk of the Vinaya-piṭaka is based upon it; it is embedded, however, in the ancient commentary called Sutta-vibhaṅga on the canon." In using the term paracanonical, I am following Louis Renou and Jean Filliozat, *L'Inde Classique*, Tome 2 (Paris: Imprimerie Nationale, 1953), p. 351 (par. 1980).

15. W. Pachow, *A Comparative Study of the Prātimokṣa*, in *Sino-Indian Studies* (vol. 4. parts 1–4 and 5, part 1 [1951–1955]), 4. 1:19.

16. I. B. Horner, *The Book of the Discipline*, 6 vols. (London: Luzac and Company Ltd, 1938–1966), 1: xii.

17. See, for example, Ernst Waldschmidt, ed. and trans., *Bruchstücke des BhikṣuṇīPrātimokṣa der Sarvāstivādins*, volume 3 of Kleinere Sanskrittexte (Leipzig: Deutsche Morgenländischen Gesellschaft in Kommission bei F. A. Brockhaus, 1926).

18. Horner, *The Book of the Discipline*, 2: vii. I have added the Sanskrit equivalents in brackets for the Pāli terms employed by Horner, here and throughout.

19. Pachow, *A Comparative Study of the Prātimokṣa*, 4: 1, 27, notes that the Pāli version and the Chinese Mahāsāṃghika text each have ninety-two rules, while the Chinese Mahīśāsaka version has ninety-one rules. The Sanskrit Mahāsāṃghika and Mūlasarvāstivādin texts have ninety-two and ninety rules, respectively. See Charles S. Prebish, *Buddhist Monastic Discipline: The Sanskrit Prātimokṣa Sūtras of the Mahāsāṃghikas and Mūlasarvāstivādins* (University Park: Pennsylvania State University Press, 1975), pp. 142–144.

20. These headings have been outlined by Thomas, *The History of Buddhist Thought*, p. 20. However, I deviate considerably from his placement of the rules into the various categories.

21. Pachow, *A Comparative Study of the Prātimokṣa*, 4. 2: 69.

22. On this latter point, refer to Charles S. Prebish, "Vinaya and Prātimokṣa: The Foundation of Buddhist Ethics," in *Studies in the History of Buddhism*, ed. A. K. Narain (Delhi: B. R. Publishing Corporation, 1980), pp. 249–253, Charles S. Prebish and Janice J. Nattier, "Mahāsāṃghika Origins: The Beginnings of Buddhist Sectarianism," *History of Religions* 16, no. 3 (February 1977): 267–270, and Charles S.

Prebish, "Śaikṣa-dharmas Revisited: Further Considerations of Mahāsāṃghika Origins," *History of Religions* 35, no. 3 (February 1996): 258–270.

23. The verses preceding and following the *Prātimokṣa-sūtra* are absent in the Theravādin version, and the ritual formulary is found not only before the text but also in the *Skandhaka*. See Oldenberg, *The Vinaya Piṭakaṃ*, 1: 102–104 (Mahāvagga 2.3: 1–8).

24. See Gustav Roth, "Bhikṣuṇīvinaya and Bhikṣu-Prakīrṇaka and Notes on the Language," *Journal of the Bihar Research Society* 52, 1–4 (January–December 1966): 32, and Waldschmidt, *Bruchstücke des Bhikṣuṇī-Prātimokṣa der Sarvāstivādins*, pp. 2–3.

25. See Chatsumarn Kabilsingh, *A Comparative Study of the Bhikkunī Pātimokkha* (Varanasi: Chaukhambha Orientalia, 1984), but also consult her translation *The Bhikkunī Pātimokkha of the Six Schools* (Bangkok: Chatsumarn Kabilsingh, 1991).

26. Sukumar Dutt, *Early Buddhist Monachism*, rev. ed. (Bombay: Asian Publishing House, 1960), p. 125.

27. B. Jinananda, ed., *Upasaṃpadājñaptiḥ*, Volume 4 of the Tibetan Sanskrit Works Series (Patna: Kashi Prasad Jayaswal Research Institute, 1961), p. 3. In fact, the procedure is somewhat more complicated than Jinananda indicates. In the *Mahāvyutpatti* we find mention of *jñaptikarman, jñaptidvitīyakarman*, and *jñapticaturthakarman* (nos. 8660–8662 in Sakaki's edition), as well as *prathamā karmavācanā, dvitīyā karmavācanā*, and *tṛtīyā karmavācanā* (nos. 8664–8666 in Sakaki's edition). Also, in Anukul Chandra Banerjee, ed., "*Bhikṣukarmavakya*," *Indian Historical Quarterly* 25, no. 1 (March 1949): 20, note: [*iyaṃ prathamā karmavācanā / evaṃ dvirapi trirapi /*]. These terms are discussed in Herbert Härtel, ed. and tr., *Karmavācanā* (Berlin: Deutsche Akademie der Wissenschaften zu Berlin, Institut für Orientforschung, 1956), pp. 13–16. It appears that the following conclusions are possible: *jñaptikarman* is the bare resolution, *jñaptidvitīyakarman* is the resolution plus the first *karmavācanā*, and *jñapticaturthakarman* is the resolution plus the third karmavācanā. It is not clear why there is no *jñaptitṛtīyakarman*.

28. Jinananda, *Upasaṃpadājñaptiḥ*, p. 3.

29. See Oldenberg, *The Vinaya Piṭakaṃ*, 1: 319 (*Mahāvagga* 9.3.9), and Dutt, *Early Buddhist Monachism*, p. 125.

30. Oldenberg, The *Vinaya Piṭakaṃ*, 1: 319–320 (*Mahāvagga* 9.4.1–2) designates the proper number of monks as follows:

(1) Four for all acts excepting ordination (*upasaṃpadā*), invitation (*pravāraṇā*), and rehabilitation (*āvarhaṇa*).
(2) Five for all acts excepting ordination in the middle country and the rehabilitation ceremony.
(3) Ten for all acts excepting the rehabilitation ceremony.
(4) Twenty for all acts.

A list of twenty-four persons not eligible to be counted in constituting this assembly is also listed. On this point, see also Dutt, *Early Buddhist Monachism*, p. 121 and p. 123. For more concerning the completeness of the *sangha*, see Heinz Bechert, "Asoka's 'Schismedikt' under der Begriff Sanghabheda," *Wiener Zeitschrift für die Kunde Süd und Ostasiens*, 5 (1961): 21 ff.

31. In the Theravādin tradition, this commentary is referred to as the *Padabhājan-iya* commentary. See, for example, Horner, *The Book of the Discipline*, 1: xi.

32. Ibid., p. xxxv.

33. See Renou and Filliozat, *L'Inde Classique*, Tome 2, p. 332 (par. 1949).

34. The suggestions for groupings 2, 3, 4, and 5 may be found on pages 70, 89, 104, and 107, respectively, in Erich Frauwallner, *The Earliest Vinaya and the Beginnings of Buddhist Literature* (Rome: Instituto per il Medio ed Estremo Oriente, 1956). I have added 1, 6, and 7 so as to set forth a reasonable outline (which Frauwallner does not provide).

35. See Lamotte, *History of Indian Buddhism*, p. 167.

36. See Thanissaro Bhikkhu, *The Buddhist Monastic Code*, private ed. (Valley Center, Calif.: Metta Forest Monastery, 1994), pp. 8–9.

37. Carrithers, "'They Will Be Lords Upon the Island,'" p. 133.

38. See Charles Wei-hsun Fu and Sandra A. Wawryto, eds., *Buddhist Ethics and Modern Society* (Westport, Conn.: Greenwood Press, 1991), p. 4.

39. Akira Hirakawa, *Studies in Primal Buddhism: The Original Model of the Organization of the Buddhist Order* (Tokyo: Shunshusha Press, 1964), pp. 107–108.

40. John Holt, *Discipline: The Canonical Buddhism of the Vinayapiṭaka* (Delhi: Motilal Banarsidass, 1981), p. 3.

41. Ibid., p. 4.

42. Charles Wei-hsun Fu, "From Paramārtha-satya to Samvṛti-satya: An Attempt at Constructive Modernization of (Mahāyāna) Buddhist Ethics," in Fu and Wawrytko, *Buddhist Ethics and Modern Society*, p. 315.

43. See, for example, Charles S. Prebish, "The Prātimokṣa Puzzle: Fact Versus Fantasy," *Journal of the American Oriental Society* 94, no. 2 (April–June, 1974), pp. 168–176. Holt, *Discipline: The Canonical Buddhism of the Vinayapiṭaka*, p. 125, makes the same point.

44. See Henry Clarke Warren and Dharmananda Kosambi, eds., *Visuddhimagga of Buddhaghosācariya* (Cambridge, Mass.: Harvard University Press, 1950), p. 7 (chapter 1.19), and Louis de La Vallée Poussin, tr., *L'Abhidharmakośa de Vasubandhu* (Paris: Paul Geuthner, 1924), vol. 3 (chapter 4.16a-b).

45. For example, see Charles S. Prebish, *Buddhist Monastic Discipline*, p. 42. The text reads:

> śīlena yukto śramaṇo tireti śīlena yukto brāhmaṇo tireti /
> śīlena yukto naradevapūjyo śīlena yuktasya hi prātimokṣaṃ //

46. See Charles S. Prebish, *American Buddhism* (North Scituate, Mass.: Duxbury Press, 1979), p. 45.

47. Fu, "From Paramārtha-satya to Samvṛti-satya: An Attempt at Constructive Modernization of (Mahāyāna) Buddhist Ethics," p. 315.

48. W. Pachow, *A Comparative Study of the Prātimokṣa* (Santiniketan: Sino-Indian Cultural Society, 1955), p. 37.

49. Holt, *Discipline: The Canonical Buddhism of the Vinayapiṭaka*, p. 64. Damien Keown, in *The Nature of Buddhist Ethics* (New York: St. Martin's Press, 1992), p. 33, notices the same dilemma.

50. Pachow, *A Comparative Study of the Prātimokṣa*, appendix 1, pp. 1–2.

51. Holt, *Discipline: The Canonical Buddhism of the Vinayapiṭaka*, p. 65.

52. Damien Keown, *The Nature of Buddhist Ethics*, p. 34.

53. Charles S. Prebish, "Vinaya and Prātimokṣa: The Foundation of Buddhist Ethics," p. 248.

54. See Richard Gombrich, *Theravāda Buddhism: A Social History from Ancient Benares to Modern Columbo* (New York: RKP, 1988), p. 108; and Mohan Wijayaratna, *Buddhist Monastic Life, According to the Texts of the Theravāda Tradition*, trans. Claude Grangier and Steven Collins (New York: Cambridge University Press, 1990), p. 124.

55. Lambert Schmithausen, *Buddhism and Nature* (Tokyo: International Institute for Buddhist Studies, 1991), *Studia Philologica Buddhica* Occasional Paper Series 7, p. 43.

56. Lambert Schmithausen, *The Problem of the Sentience of Plants in Earliest Buddhism* (Tokyo: International Institute for Buddhist Studies, 1991), *Studia Philologica Buddhica* Monograph Series 6, p. 16.

57. Rahula, "The Problem of the Saṅgha in the West," p. 61.

58. See Wijayaratna, *Buddhist Monastic Life*, p. 122 (and *Vinaya* 3. 21; 4. 91, 120, 182, 299).

59. Rahula, "The Problem of the Saṅgha in the West," pp. 62–63.

60. Numrich, "Vinaya in Theravāda Temples in the United States," p. 25.

61. Paul David Numrich, *Old Wisdom in the New World: Americanization in Two Immigrant Theravada Buddhist Temples* (Knoxville: University of Tennessee Press, 1996), p. 52.

62. See Numrich, "Vinaya in Theravāda Temples in the United States," p. 25; and the video documentary "World Buddhism in North America" (Ann Arbor, Michigan, Zen Lotus Society, 1989).

63. Rahula, "The Problem of the Saṅgha in the West," p. 65.

64. These regulations are discussed in great detail in the second chapter of the *Mahāvagga* of the Pāli *Vinaya* or the *Poṣadhavastu* of the Sanskrit versions of sects other than the Theravāda.

65. Ibid. Also see Numrich, *Old Wisdom in the New World*, pp. 40, 159, who points out that both Dharma Vijaya and Wat Dhammaram carry monastic staffs exceeding the required four fully ordained *bhikkhus* requisite for proper *Pātimokkha* recitation, but that Dharma Vijaya performs the ceremony only once yearly (before the rain retreat), and Wat Dhammaram performs the ceremony once monthly.

66. Rahula, "The Problem of the Saṅgha in the West," p. 62.

67. See Ajahn Tiradhammo, "The Challenges of Community," in *Westward Dharma: Buddhism Beyond Asia*, ed. Martin Baumann and Charles Prebish (Berkeley: University of California Press, 2002), pp. 245–254.

68. Ibid.

69. Ibid. Tiradhammo is summarizing *Mahāvagga* 6.40.1.

70. Numrich, *Old Wisdom in the New World*, pp. 46–47.

71. Ibid., p. 47.

72. Ibid., p. 48.

73. Ibid., p. 49.

74. See Prebish, *Buddhist Monastic Discipline*, p. 11.

75. Ibid, pp. 42–113.

76. Numrich, *Old Wisdom in the New World*, p. 50.

77. Ibid.

78. Dharma Vijaya Newsletter, February 1992, p. 3.

79. *Changing Faces of Buddhism in America: The Dalai Lama Meets the Buddhist Sangha Council of Southern California* (Los Angeles, Buddhist Sangha Council of Southern California, n.d.), p. 21.

80. Numrich, *Old Wisdom in the New World*, p. 52.

81. Ibid.

82. Ibid., pp. 52–55.

4

Master Hongyi Looks Back

*A Modern Man Becomes a Monk in
Twentieth-Century China*

Raoul Birnbaum

The story that I have to tell concerns the quiet dramas of one man's life. This particular man was born in 1880, in the waning decades of the Qing dynasty, and he came of age as tremendous forces of change swept across China. Li Shutong—a stunningly talented and influential artist, writer, musician, actor, and educator—became famous in China as a "modern man," but in 1918 at the height of this fame he altered his course to become a Buddhist monk, re-named Hongyi.[1] By the time of his death in 1942, Chinese Bud-dhists considered Hongyi a towering figure in their modern history (fig. 4.1). Among Buddhists, he was well known for his profound scholarship on *Vinaya* (monastic rules), but he was honored most especially for the depth of his religious practice. His artistic talents found particular expression in a unique style of brush writing, developed in his mature years, that ever since has been identified as quintessentially "Buddhist."

The center of my narrative focuses on Hongyi's recollections of the pivotal years at midlife when he decided to "leave home" (be-come a monk). Since this chapter looks at his recollections, its subject also is self-representation—reflections on one man's experi-ences and the ways that he chose to express them.

Hongyi's story is neither typical nor representative. He was an extraordinary person in many ways, which is why memories of him linger sixty years after his death. Indeed, he remains well known in China far beyond Buddhist circles as an enigmatic and romantic figure of the near past. In presenting his tale, what I want to do here above all else is gain a deeper understanding of this one man as an

FIGURE 4.1. Formal portrait in his last year: Hongyi at age sixty-two (1940), Quanzhou.

individual, and try to think through what it is that he sought to communicate when he composed an autobiographical statement late in his life.

From a Buddhist point of view, perhaps his most astonishing accomplishment rests in the harnessing of a ferociously courageous willpower to effect profound internal change. This is a tale of a man intent on changing his course. Such tales of self-transformation form a very old kind of narrative in Buddhist communities, but the details differ for each individual. The key points of each of these tales are expressed in a language of references and literary gestures intrinsic to a particular cultural environment. This matter is fundamental to any reading of Hongyi's work.

Caught in time's web, Hongyi tried to negotiate his way through the challenges of his era. These challenges were interwoven with Hongyi's personal complexities and contradictions. His tale is highly inflected by the forces of modernity, for the details of his experiences naturally were shaped by the age in which he lived, and some of the ways in which he expressed himself reflect the modernizing currents of that era. In keeping with the subject of this volume, Buddhism and modernity, I will highlight these particular facets of his experience.

Li Shutong was an active participant in the intellectual-artistic-revolutionary project of modernization that was instrumental in toppling the Qing and creating a new republic in the first decades of the twentieth century. The modernizing activities of that time were a response to a general perception of stagnation and decline in China, made more evident and pressing by a succession of foreign interventions—military and commercial—on Chinese soil that revealed the deep weaknesses of late Qing rule. Li Shutong and many others looked beyond China's cultural borders for new approaches. It is important to bear in mind, though, that the modernizing process in China in that era was not simply an uncritical "Westernization," even as many leading figures turned outward for answers to the problems of their age.

From his teenage years on, Li Shutong joined revolutionary political groups, and as he matured, his desire to bring about change in China increasingly was channeled into the world of the arts. Li Shutong went abroad to Japan—at that time a key site of modernity in the Chinese imagination—and studied art and music there from 1905 to 1910. He was among the very earliest Chinese artists to receive a thorough training in Western-style oil painting, which he then systematically taught after his return to China. His teaching methods included such innovations in China as *plein air* painting and life-drawing. The wood-cut traditions that he revived in China later became the quintessential visual art medium of the Communist revolution. In addition, Li Shutong studied European and American folk music, as well as works of Romantic masters such as Beethoven. Under these influences he composed numerous songs—some intensely patriotic, others about love or various moods—that still are sung or performed today. He was a literary editor, and became a founding member in 1912 of the revolutionary literary society *Nanshe*.

This list can go on. Li Shutong was a man full of talent and energy. He achieved notable success in almost every endeavor to which he turned his attention. In surveying Li Shutong's accomplishments, it is important to bear in mind that in his era many artistic activities were framed as integral elements of an attempt at conscious transformation of Chinese society. Such activities were at the core of the modernizing project in the first decades of the twentieth century. And Li Shutong was one of the pioneers in this project. His decision to become a Buddhist monk, then, may seem an abrupt turnabout, in which this man simply steps out of the modern world. But Li Shutong was not a simple

man, and we need to consider his tale with care in order to engage with it beyond a superficial reading.

There are several voices that speak in the telling of his story, but the central
voice is that of Hongyi himself, in the form of a remarkable document in which
he reminisces about his years in Hangzhou and his transformation from layman to monk. I would like to begin there, with Hongyi's voice, heard at length.

His autobiographical essay was prepared in 1937 in response to an invitation to contribute to a special supplement of the regional journal *Yuefeng* on the
subject of Hangzhou's famed West Lake.[2] By this time, Hongyi was widely recognized as a preeminent Buddhist teacher of his era, honored and respected in
the monastic world for his teachings and personal example. He also was a renowned literary and cultural figure, and his influence extended to (and through)
many prominent and talented lay disciples, such as the painter and essayist Feng
Zikai (1898–1975).

Hongyi composed his autobiographical essay while living at Nanputuo
Monastery in the Fujian coastal port of Xiamen. Nanputuo is located directly
next to Xiamen University, and he chose to collaborate with his disciple Gao
Wenxian (1912–1991, also known as Gao Shengjin), a Fujian native and young
Buddhist layman and scholar affiliated with the university, who also was lodging at the monastery.[3] The text is an oral recounting, as set down by Gao. In
contrast to the substantial body of his many formal writings, Hongyi's style here
is relatively informal and highly accessible, similar in tone to many of the lectures from this period that were recorded by disciples and subsequently published (indeed, Gao Wenxian recorded a number of these lectures).[4]

Hongyi was only fifty-seven at this time, but his health was never robust.
The text was composed while he slowly recovered from a near-fatal illness. This
might be borne in mind as one reads through his brief essay, in which he casts
his gaze—sometimes obliquely—on a turbulent and pivotal time in his life.
Hongyi died only five years after completing the essay, at the age of sixty-two.

I would like to present the autobiographical document whole, as we have
received it, rather than interrupt the narrative flow by stopping for discussion
after each paragraph, or simply presenting a few dislocated excerpts for comment and analysis. Discussion of several issues raised by the text will follow.
This method leads to a certain amount of disjuncture and clumsiness, but it
does not fracture the voice of the protagonist and permits him to set forth his
tale in the way originally intended.

In the translation, I have preserved parenthetical explanations found in the
original text, while all items in brackets are my own explanatory additions. Some
essential explanatory notes have been included with the translation, while in the
discussion that follows, notes have been reserved primarily for bibliographic and
technical matters. (Also, I should explain here two common terms that appear
in the text. A *li* is a measurement of distance, roughly equivalent to a third of a
mile. *Sui* refers to age according to traditional count; a child is one *sui* at birth,

two *sui* at the following New Year's celebration. Li Shutong was born on 23 October 1880, so he already was two *sui* before he was a half-year old by Western reckoning.)

"My Experiences in 'Leaving Home' at West Lake"
Oral transmission by Great Master Hongyi
Recorded by the brush of Gao Shengjin

Hangzhou truly can be called a Buddha-land. There have been more than two thousand monasteries and temples within its bounds, so one can readily imagine the flourishing state of the Buddha's teachings in Hangzhou.

Most recently the Yuefeng Society has sought to publish a "West Lake Supplement." Layman Huang[5] wrote to me with a request that I write on the topic of "West Lake and Its Buddhist Connections." I felt that the scope of this title was too broad, and moreover I do not have the necessary reference books at hand, so I cannot complete such a work within the short time period. I thought therefore that it might be worthwhile to reflect on some of the various matters related to the period when I lived by West Lake and discuss them informally. One could say that this essay commemorates my experiences of "leaving home."[6]

I first went to Hangzhou in the seventh month of Guangxu 28 [1902] (the dates of years and months in this article are recorded following the old calendar). At that time, I probably stayed in Hangzhou for nearly a month, but I didn't go into any monasteries. I only remember going once to drink tea outside the Yongjin Gate. At that time I gazed for a bit at the West Lake scenery.

The second time I went to Hangzhou was in the seventh month of Minguo 1 [1912]. This time I lived in Hangzhou for quite awhile, nearly ten years. One can say that is a very long time.

The place where I lived was within Qiantang Gate, quite near West Lake, a distance of only two *li*. Outside Qiantang Gate there was a small teahouse named Bright Spring Gardens that adjoined the West Lake shores. I often went out the gate alone and went by myself to the upper story of Bright Spring Gardens to drink tea. In those first years of the Republic, the condition of the shores of West Lake was entirely different from today. At that time the city wall was still standing, as well as many willow trees, all very attractive. Aside from those who gathered to offer incense on the two spring and autumn holidays,[7] people along the West Lake shores generally were quite sparse, and it was even more placid outside the Qiantang Gate.

There always were many customers on the ground floor of Bright Spring Gardens. They all were laborers who worked as boatmen and sedan-chair carriers, quite a few sitting there. As to the tea drinkers on the floor above—there was only me. Therefore I often sat alone on the upper floor drinking tea, and at the same time I would lean on the railing and look out at the West Lake scenery. There was a well-known monastery near the teahouse—Chaoqing si, Bright Blessings Monastery. After drinking tea, often I also would stroll there to look around.

In the summer of Minguo 2 [1913], I lived for quite a few days at West Lake's Guanghua si, Broad Transformation Monastery, but the place where I stayed really was not within the monks' sphere. It was beside that monastery, in the upper story of a place called Toushen ci, Smallpox God Shrine. Smallpox God Shrine was a place used to board Guanghua Monastery's lay guests. During the time that I stayed there, when I went to the area of the monks' quarters to look around, in my heart I felt it was significant!

I remember that in those days I also often took a boat to drink tea at Lake's Heart Pavilion. Once a well-known person came to lecture at our school. On that occasion Layman Xia Mianzun[8] and I—the two of us—withdrew through the gate and escaped to Lake's Heart Pavilion for some tea. Xia Mianzun said to me on that occasion: "For persons of our sort, it is good to leave home and become monks." When I heard this sentence, I felt it was very significant. You could say that this was a distant cause in the past that led to my becoming a monk.

In the summer of Minguo 5 [1916], I saw in a Japanese magazine some discussion of a method for fasting, which stated that fasting can cure various diseases. That immediately aroused my curiosity, and I thought to try out this fast. Because at that time I had come down with *shenjing shuairuo* [lit. "nerve weakness"], I thought to actually practice the fast in order to see if it could cure this disease. This fast should be carried out at the end of the cold season, so I then planned the fasting period for the eleventh month.

But where could I go to carry out this fast? I needed first to think it over, and after some consideration it seemed that a pure and secluded place would be essential. At that time I talked it over with Mr. Ye Pinsan of the Xiling Seal Society.[9] The end result was that he recommended a place near West Lake—the Hupao Monastery—that could serve as a fasting site.[10]

In that case, I then asked him, if I were to go to Hupao, it would be most appropriate for someone to provide an introduction. Whom should I ask? He said that a Mr. Ding Fuzhi was a great Dharma-protector [i.e., lay patron] of Hupao Monastery, and he could ask him to go talk it over with them. And at this he immediately wrote a letter to Ding Fuzhi to provide an introduction. Hupao in those days did not resemble its present lively state. Visitors were few, so it was an utterly tranquil place. If that were to be the site for my practice of this fast, one could say that it would be a most appropriate one.

By the eleventh month, I still had not gone to Hupao Monastery myself, and I had another person pay a visit to see if there were a suitable room where I could stay. That person returned to say that the ground floor of the Abbot's Hall was particularly secluded and quiet. Although there were many rooms, ordinarily they were closed up and visitors were unable to enter. And only a single monk lived on the upper floor of the Abbot's Hall. Aside from him, no one else lived there. I waited to the end of the eleventh month, and then arrived at Hupao Monastery, where I lived in a room on the ground floor of the Abbot's Hall.

After I entered [the monastery] to live there, I often saw a monk pass by my window. This was the man who lived on the upper story of the hall. I saw that he was entirely happy! From this time on, I often chatted with him, and he frequently brought Buddhist scriptures for me to look at.

Although from the age of five *sui* onward I often met monks, on those occasions I often saw monks who came to our home to chant scriptures and carry out worship and repentance rites. I even studied the *fang yankou* at age twelve or thirteen *sui*. But I never lived together with "having the Way" monks, and I didn't know what it was like inside a monastery, nor what monks' lives were like.[11] When I went to stay at Hupao Monastery, I saw their sort of lives. I not only was very glad, but moreover I came to admire their way of life.

Even though I only lived within the monastery precincts for a bit more than a half-month, my heart was utterly joyful. And I enjoyed eating their vegetarian food. After I returned to school, I asked the workers to prepare dishes in that style for me to eat.

It can be said that the near cause for my becoming a monk was this time in which I went to Hupao to fast. By the second half of Minguo 6 [1917], I had decided to eat [only] vegetarian food. Then during that winter I sought out many scriptures, such as the "Chapter on Puxian's Acts and Vows" [from the *Huayan Sūtra*], the *Lengyan Sūtra*, the *Treatise on Arising Faith in Mahāyāna*—many Buddhist scriptures—and in my room I also gathered together images of Buddhist figures such as the bodhisattvas Dizang and Guanshiyin, and burned incense before them every day.

When it came time for New Year's vacation, I did not return home. Instead, I went to Hupao Monastery to pass the New Year. As before, I lived on the ground floor of the Abbot's Hall. At that time I felt even more joyful. It was then that I raised the thought of leaving home. And at that same time I wanted to honor as my master the monk who lived in the upper story of the Abbot's Hall. His name was Master Hongxiang. But he would not permit me to honor him in this way, and instead sought to introduce me to his own master.[12] His master at that time was living at Huguo si, Protect the Nation Monastery, at Songmuchang. He asked his master to return to Hupao Monastery, and I then accepted the Triple Refuge on the fifteenth day of the first month of Minguo 7 [1918].[13]

I planned to "enter the mountain" [i.e., enter the monastery] during this year's summer vacation, live in the monastery for a year, and then actually become a monk. At this time I had a *haiqing* (monk's robe) made, and studied the daily liturgies. The fifth day of the second month is my mother's memorial day, and in this year I went to Hupao Monastery two days beforehand. There at the monastery I recited the *Dizang Sūtra* for three days and transferred the merit to my mother.[14] At the end of the fifth month I gave precedence to school examinations, and when they were completed, I went to Hupao and entered the mountain.

The day after I arrived at the monastery, I began wearing monks' clothes, and I prepared to have my head shaved in the coming year. At the beginning of the seventh month Layman Xia Mianzun came. When he saw that I wore the clothes of a "left-home person" but had not yet left home, he said to me: "You live in a monastery and what's more you wear monks' clothes, but you have not yet left home. This doesn't make sense. It would be better for you to have your head shaved at once."

I originally thought to leave home in the next year, but at his urging I then quickly left home. Conveniently, the thirteenth day of the seventh month traditionally is Dashizhi Bodhisattva's birthday celebration [and thus a very auspicious date], so I had my head shaved on that day.[15]

After the head-shaving ceremony, I still needed to receive the [full] precepts. With Mr. Lin Tongzhang's introduction, I went to Lingyin Monastery to receive the precepts.

Lingyin Monastery is Hangzhou's largest model monastery,[16] and I had always been very fond of that place. After leaving home, I went to all the various large monasteries [in the region] to have a look, but there were none as fine as Lingyin Monastery. I went to Lingyin Monastery at the end of the eighth month. The monastery's abbot was very polite, and told me to live on the upper story of the Yunxiang ge, the Rue Pavilion, behind the Guest Hall.[17]

The eminent teacher there at that time was Dharma Master Huiming. One day I met that Dharma Master at the Guest Hall. When he saw me, he asked—since I had come to receive precepts, why had I not entered the Precepts Hall? Although you were a scholar in lay life—he said—even so are scholars able to be so casual? He said that I was being treated just as if I were a worldly emperor. At that time the abbot still wanted me to live in the Guest Hall upper story, but when there were important ceremonies in the Precept Hall he then had me participate once or twice.

Although I was not able to meet with Dharma Master Huiming on a regular basis, yet observing his honest and sincere demeanor caused me to have endless respect for him.

After receiving the precepts, I returned to live at Hupao Monastery. Then at the end of the twelfth month, I moved to Yuquan si, Jade Spring Monastery. And after this, I was ever going to different places and did not live for long at West Lake.

I remember that in the summer of Minguo 12 [1923], I went to Hangzhou for a time. That was precisely when Dharma Master Huiming was lecturing on the *Lengyan Sūtra* at Lingyin Monastery. On the day when the lectures began, I went to listen to him speak the Dharma. Because I had not seen him in quite a few years, I felt that he had aged quite a bit. His hair had turned gray, and most of his teeth had fallen out. I was considerably moved, and when I bowed in respect to him I couldn't stop tears from flowing. I heard not a few years later that Dharma Master Huiming had passed away.

Regarding Dharma Master Huiming's life history, a good bit is known amongst monks. Here I would like to raise a few matters for discussion. Dharma Master Huiming was a native of Tingzhou in Fujian province. He was not at all particular about his clothing, and he certainly did not impress one as having the manner of a great monastery's Dharma Master, but he treated all persons equally. Whether you were a "venerable sir" or a downtrodden one, he looked upon all persons alike. Therefore amongst all the monks and laypersons of all sorts and kinds, there wasn't a single one who did not respect him.

This old gentleman truly did much in his lifetime, but he was most unusual in his ability to teach and transform *maliuzi*. (This is a term for vagrant monks.)[18] *Maliuzi* were not permitted to live inside monasteries, and during the season when they could live in open pavilions, they were plentiful.[19] Whenever they heard that someone was sponsoring a *zhai*[20] at one of the monasteries, then they gathered together and went to attend that *zhai* (to eat the white rice).

Maliuzi were especially numerous in Hangzhou. People generally did not treat them as equals, yet *maliuzi* also did injury to themselves, for there is nothing that they would not do. But Dharma Master Huiming was able to teach and transform *maliuzi*. These *maliuzi* often went to Lingyin Monastery to visit Master Huiming. The old gentleman treated them very courteously, and moreover he gave them all sorts of good food, good clothes, and so on. Whatever they sought, he would give it to them. Sometimes the Dharma Master also would speak a few sentences of Buddhist teachings and in this way aid and influence them.

Dharma Master Huiming had problems with his legs, and there were many times that he left and returned to the monastery by sedan-chair. Once when he returned to Lingyin Monastery on a sedan-chair, bystanders noticed when he got down from the chair that the Dharma Master wasn't wearing trousers. They all felt it quite odd, and so they questioned him: "Dharma Master, why aren't you wearing trousers?" He said that he ran into a *maliuzi* outside the monastery and because the *maliuzi* begged for trousers from him, he immediately took his off and gave them away. There are many, many stories besides this that have circulated regarding Dharma Master Huiming's activities teaching and transforming *maliuzi*. I have only summarily raised the matter in this way. Not only did the *maliuzi* hold Dharma Master Huiming in very deep respect and trust, but also amongst the other monks there were none who did not respect him.

I haven't visited Hangzhou in many years. The paved roads and foreign-style buildings on West Lake's shores gradually have been built up to a considerable extent, and automobiles increase daily. Therefore when I recall the former time when I lived by West Lake's shores, that type of quiet and secluded life truly seems like a far-off world, which now can only appear in a dream.

Why Did Hongyi Leave Home?

Hongyi's text is entitled "My Experiences in 'Leaving Home' at West Lake." A key question raised by the text, if not in the text, is *why* he became a monk. Actually, while monks sometimes address this matter in their autobiographies and may discuss it in private with close friends, the question of why one has "left home" is not commonly raised within Chinese Buddhist monastic circles, at least in contemporary times. This question is considered rude, intrusive, and also perhaps not very interesting. But Hongyi was such an extraordinary man, and such a prominent person, that his leaving is wrapped in a kind of mystique.

Here he opens a door briefly so that we can have a sense of what happened. The view provided is revealing, but there is much that is left in the shadows, so the appearance of openness simultaneously is concealing. Still, Hongyi provides enough hints for a good bit to have been communicated.

He highlights two events. First, there is the "distant cause," a stray remark of Xia Mianzun as the two men sat drinking tea on an island in the middle of West Lake, having successfully escaped from a tedious event at their school. That remark—perhaps just a conversational gesture—somehow sat in Li Shutong's memory, working slowly within his mind. Second, there is the "nearby cause," the fast at Hupao. This is the precipitating event.

I also should add Xia Mianzun's verbal reaction when he visited his friend at Hupao and saw that he no longer was a layman in appearance or attitude, but still not yet a monk. And it was Xia who originally brought the fasting method to Li Shutong's attention and loaned him the magazine. Thus, Xia Mianzun played a pivotal role in these key events that had such a profound influence on the course of Li Shutong's life. [21]

Xia Mianzun's own account of these matters makes clear that in those days he did not have a high opinion of monastic life. He was dismayed and embarrassed at the turn his friend was taking, and felt rather bad that he had influenced it. This view of monastic life appears also to have been shared at first by Li Shutong. We see this in the rhetoric of surprise Hongyi employs when he discusses the evident happiness of Master Hongxiang, as well as when he relates how much he admired the way of life at Hupao. Indeed, while Xia Mianzun and Li Shutong could idly chat over a pot of tea, in those days it was not at all common for men of their sort—sophisticated, talented, highly educated men of the world, already at midlife—to become monks. [22]

Now these three matters—the remarks, the fasting, and the further remarks—are outer causes; they are external matters and can be discussed easily enough. But what of the inner causes, what of the state of mind, the internal flux that responded to these stimuli? After all, a thousand men might hear it said casually that they ought to live a monastic life, but most would laugh in response. Very few decide to completely overturn their lives.

I will not presume to explain Hongyi, as if I could read his mind. He was extraordinarily complex, which is one reason that so many find him fascinating. Here I will try to set forth some of the circumstances of his life at the time of this transformation. While still confined to the "outer," this discussion may impinge on, or put pressure on, some of what Hongyi has not put into words. He has left out quite a lot.

At this point it is essential to provide an outline of his life up to the time when he begins his narrative, in order to establish some contexts for this pivotal period in his life. Li Shutong's background and his activities until age thirty-eight were richly complicated, so much so that one would be hard pressed to create such a character for a realistic novel: few would find him believable.

Li Shutong was born into a large and wealthy family in 1880. Although the family's origins were in the Hangzhou area, they were settled at this time in the northern city of Tianjin, where his father was a banker. At the time of the child's birth, his father was sixty-seven years old, his mother nineteen. She was the fourth wife in this extended family, all of whom lived together in a large four-courtyard domestic complex. Many in the family were lay Buddhists. His father was so famed for his extensive charitable activities that he commonly was known as Li Shanren, Good Man Li. His father had passed the *jinshi* examination, the *summa* of the Qing civil service exams, in his early fifties, and his traditional literary learning was considerable.

His father died at age seventy-two. There were several mothers and other relatives, as well as a brother twelve years his senior, to look after the small boy, and Shutong received the extensive classical training appropriate to his privileged birth. Early on, he displayed exceptional intellectual and artistic talents, which were furthered by special tutors.

At age seventeen an arranged marriage was completed to the daughter of a family friend née Yu, who was two years his senior. Two boys were born of this union, which otherwise appears to have been barren. Shutong remained closer to his mother. He was involved in anti-Qing revolutionary activities while still quite young, and when he had to flee to the safety of the French Concession in Shanghai during the suppression of the Hundred Days Reform of 1898, his mother accompanied him. His wife remained in Tianjin.

He stayed in Shanghai for about six years where, as a young man of talent, he found his literary and artistic activities flourishing in association with the great figures of the day (fig. 4.2). By his twentieth year, his first two books were published, collections of his poetry and seal-carvings. He also was active in calligraphy, painting, music, and amateur performances of traditional opera. During this period he also had much contact with figures of Shanghai's "flowery world," including a notable romance in 1901 with Yang Cuixi, a beauty famed for her singing voice and tiny feet.[23]

In these years Shutong developed a fascination for the "West" and the "modern," as understood by those of his class in the early twentieth century. In 1905, after his mother suddenly died, he prepared to leave for Japan, at that time a principal source for modernism.[24] He studied oil painting and other European-derived art techniques at the Tokyo School of Fine Arts (Tokyo Bijutsu Gakko) for four years, graduating in 1910. At the same time, he also made intensive studies of European and American music forms, and created a music magazine to disseminate new knowledge and new music in China. He joined Sun Yatsen's Revolutionary Alliance (Tongmen hui) and composed patriotic songs that many still sing today.

He also was a cofounder of the Spring Willow Drama Society, in which fellow Chinese students in Tokyo experimented with the newly discovered world of Western drama by staging translations of a variety of works, such as Dumas's

La Dame aux camélias and Harriet Beecher Stowe's *Uncle Tom's Cabin.*[25] The choice of works such as these melodramas—one on the evils of slavery—suggests that even as these men explored new possibilities, their vision of modernity did not encompass an uncritical embrace of Western values.

During this period abroad, Li Shutong appears to have been especially fascinated by Western constructions of femininity. These explorations are recorded in some of his surviving artwork of the period, and also most strikingly in posed photographs of his roles as "leading lady" in the two Spring Willow productions mentioned earlier (he was famously effective in the role of Marguérite, the heroine of *La Dame aux camélias*). Multitalented and possessed of seemingly limitless energy, Li Shutong also created many of the gowns that he wore on stage at the time (fig. 4.3).

Upon return to China in 1910, he took up a series of positions as editor, illustrator, art and music teacher, and played a prominent role as a revolutionary and modernizer in all the fields of the arts. His life was somewhat peripatetic (and indeed later as a monk he was famous for not having a fixed place of abode). Finally, by 1912 he had become established in Hangzhou, eventually taking a position as teacher of art and music at the Zhejiang First Normal College. There he specialized in European traditions, and among his many daring innovations, in 1913 he set up China's first life-drawing studio with nude models (memorialized with a photo of its first occurrence).[26]

This brief summary sketch only hints at Li Shutong's complex personality and his extraordinary creative drives and accomplishments. He clearly was a daring figure who followed his own mind and was committed to the "modern," to new approaches to life in twentieth-century China. With this background in mind, I can return to the question raised earlier: why did Li Shutong become a monk?

Li Shutong's illness and his attempt to cure it are central to his narrative. They form a pivotal point in his reflections on why and how he became a monk. In his day the disease—*shenjing shuairuo*—was widely considered a manifestation of modernity, a disease that stemmed most especially from modern problems and afflicted modern persons. In addition, the source of the experimental cure was derived from a Japanese magazine, a relatively new form of knowledge dissemination, rather than from traditional Chinese practices.

I would like to inquire into the matter of his illness from several angles. An extensive literature, clinical and historical, opens up possibilities of approach to how this disease was understood in early twentieth-century China. *Shenjing shuairuo*, literally "weak nerves" or perhaps more properly "nerve weakness," is the Chinese term given to "neurasthenia," a new disease of the modern age, which spread from America and Europe to Japan, and then to China as part of the transmission of modernity. In the United States and Europe, it was considered a disease of "brain workers," an affliction due to overwork and overstress to which those at the intellectual forefront of modernity were especially suscep-

FIGURE 4.2. Li Shutong at nineteen (1899), Shanghai (*above*) and Li Shutong at twenty (1900), Tianjin (*opposite*).

tible. It spread not as an infection, of course, but as a peculiarly congenial category or concept.

Neurasthenia was known as "the American disease" in the late nineteenth century, especially through the efforts beginning in 1869 of New York physician George M. Beard (1839–1883) to define the term and then popularize its description. He described neurasthenia as a "chronic, functional disease of the nervous system," a condition of "nerve deficiency" or "nerve weakness" suffered by those whose tiring, reckless, or sexually profligate behavior had exhausted their store of "nerve energy." This condition of physical and mental exhaustion manifests in a wide variety of symptoms through the body, which may appear in different constellations. Consider this brief extract from a two-page summary

of typical neurasthenic symptoms, as described in Beard's 1881 text *American Nervousness*:

> [i]nsomnia, drowsiness, bad dreams, cerebral irritation, dilated pupils, pain, pressure and heaviness in the head, tenderness of the scalp, changes in the expression of the eye, increased blushing, desire for stimulants and narcotics, sweating hands and feet with redness, impotence, hopelessness, ticklishness, writer's cramp, fear of lightning, or fear of responsibility, of open places or of closed places, fear of society, fear of being alone, fear of fears, fear of contamination, fear of everything.[27]

FIGURE 4.3. Li Shutong (left) and Zeng Yannian (right) in "Uncle Tom's Cabin" (1907), Tokyo.

A prominent French physician of the time, Jean-Martin Charcot, described the neurasthenic as *"l'homme de petit papier,"* because literate patients tended to write down all their symptoms prior to a physician's office visit[28] (here I might point out Li Shutong's daily observations of his mental, physical, and emotional states, carefully recorded in a diary during his fast at Hupao, to be discussed later).

Li Shutong may first have learned about neurasthenia in Japan, where at that time it was understood, following Beard, as a physical disorder of the nervous system. Medical response included various drugs and physical treatments.[29] The term came to China in the early twentieth century and first appeared in a Chinese medical publication in the 1930s. As Zhang Mingyuan describes:

> The term and concept of neurasthenia found ready acceptance
> among the Chinese medical practitioners who were then dominating
> the medical world in China. The literal translation of neurasthenia
> was nerves-weakness, which fit in neatly with the concept of *"shu"*
> (deficiency or weakness) in traditional Chinese medicine. To be

more specific, the main symptoms of neurasthenia such as insomnia, poor concentration and poor memory correspond to the main symptoms of "*shenshu*" (*shenkui*) in traditional Chinese medicine, which means kidney weakness, or *xinshu* (heart weakness).[30]

We do not know which particular constellation of symptoms Li Shutong presented, such that he would complain of *shenjing shuairuo*. Some patients register concern over fatigue and the inability to get work done, but we know that Li Shutong was tremendously productive during this period. His complaints in the Hupao diary about the sound of footsteps overhead at night suggests that he may have suffered from insomnia and general restlessness in sleep.

Tea drinking, especially in the context of teahouse culture, can be an intensely social phenomenon,[31] yet Li Shutong had the habit in Hangzhou of going alone to a teahouse frequented by laborers. That is, of all the many teahouses by West Lake, he deliberately chose to go to one where the customers were of an entirely different social class. There he would sit apart from them in an entirely separate room, indeed on a separate floor above the other patrons. In a Chinese context, that behavior may be considered strange. Is this part of his "*shenjing shuairuo*," or is it just the behavior of a tired artist and teacher who enjoys an hour of quiet with his own thoughts, as he gazes at the lake scenery?

When Hongyi says that he suffered from *shenjing shuairuo*, which he sought to cure through a physical treatment involving fasting, rest, and quiet, just what is it that he is saying? It might be useful to look at traditional conceptions of kidney deficiency (*shenshu* or *shenkui*) for some further explication, since *shenjing shuairuo* sometimes was used as a modern label for a complaint rooted in a less modern conception of essential vitality. According to Keh-ming Lin:

> The importance of the kidney in psychological functioning was probably further enhanced when Chinese began to understand the psychological relevance of the spinal cord and the brain. A theory was developed to connect the kidney, sexual function (regarded as belonging to the kidney), and the central nervous system. It was asserted that sperm (which is also called *jing*, the essence of *qi*), optimally conserved, is sifted into the spinal cord to nourish both the cord and the brain. A condition called *shenkui* ("kidney insufficiency") is regarded as resulting from excessive loss of sperm (*jing*), and thus, also the essence of *qi*, which produces psychological, psychosomatic and sexual symptoms such as difficulty in concentration, forgetfulness, weakness, back pain, tiredness, dizziness, nocturnal ejaculation and impotence.[32]

In thinking about his anxiety and fatigue, there are three related matters that he does not address in his autobiographical essay. First, he experienced considerable strain in his home life due to the fact that he had two households, in addition to his residence at school in Hangzhou. Not only did he have a wife and two sons, whom he rarely visited, but also he had a Japanese lover who is said to have come to China with him in 1910. She lived in Shanghai. Second, in part as a result of the 1911 revolution, his family fortune had gravely diminished by 1912, thus substantially altering his possibilities. And third, because of these financial pressures, he took on an additional teaching position in Nanjing. To fulfill his commitments required long railroad trips back and forth. By the time of his fast, it is not surprising that he felt considerably frayed.

Li Shutong sought to cure his disease by a graduated fast, which he carried out over a twenty-day period in a quiet, nearly isolated place. He arrived at Hupao on the last day of the eleventh month (14 December 1916), and left on the nineteenth of the twelfth month. Some materials have survived from this pivotal moment: his special diary of the fasting period ("*Duanshi rizhi*" or "Daily Record of the Fast"),[33] a photo taken at the end of the fast, and calligraphy made to commemorate the experience. These materials are helpful in gaining a sense of the strangeness and intensity of the moment.

The diary has a brief introduction and then records certain types of information for each of the twenty days he lived at Hupao. He records the time he wakes up, the weather, the particular food and drink consumed, the quality of his bowel movements, his calligraphic or painting work of the day (including a precise total of how many characters written, their style and size), as well as an assessment of his physical, mental, and emotional states. Also, there are occasional comments on his dreams and quality of sleep (as mentioned earlier, he slept poorly on his first night, for example, due to the footfalls of the monk living above his room).

While one must acknowledge that the diary may be construed as a careful and detailed record of an experiment, its tenor also suggests a level of obsessive self-involvement that well supports Li Shutong's concerns about *shenjing shuairou*. The introduction makes clear that he has put a certain kind of pressure on this experience, or on himself, for even before he commences the practice Li Shutong has decided to give himself a comprehensive set of new names, which he will begin to use at the completion of the twenty days. (Indeed, he does use these names, at least briefly. We see them in correspondence immediately following the fast, and in his calligraphic souvenir.)

His calligraphy, a gift to his student Zhu Sudian, consists of two bold characters, using richly dark ink, in a style strongly influenced by his studies of *Weibei*, stone-carved inscriptions of the fifth and sixth centuries. It says: *linghua*, "spiritual transformation." He appends a brief explanation, in which he provides the date he entered the monastery for the fast and an eight-character description of its result ("body and mind spiritually transformed, joyful at improved health"). He indicates that this work is a souvenir of the experience, and signs it with several of his new names (fig. 4.4).

The third item in this group is a photograph that records a dramatic pose. Wearing a dark robe or high-collared shirt, Li Shutong sits with eyes downcast, his diary held open to face the viewer. It is a consciously "spiritual" pose that captures a certain kind of self-display (fig. 4.4).

We will turn back to these three artifacts in the following section, on "a performance of self." Here the key issue is the extraordinary importance that Li Shutong placed on this experience, most especially the manifest desire he had for significant change in his life. This is a man who is looking for an answer to a question that he has not yet fully articulated. But he knows that he needs *something*.

At this point there is another important matter that Hongyi does not mention. One has the sense from his narrative that there was a smooth transition from his experiences at Hupao to becoming a Buddhist. In fact, according to Xia Mianzun, at this time Li Shutong studied Confucian texts of the Song and Yuan periods, and also Daoist texts and views as he attempted to grapple with his internal transformation. [34] He quickly changed his name again, now to Li Ying (Infant Li), drawn from a sense of rebirth and also in specific reference to Laozi's injunction for the sage to become as a child. This is not a "Buddhist" name.

But slowly something tugged at him, and the Daoist materials were discarded for Buddhist texts and images, with incense offerings burnt every day. What influence can we see in his own account that led him to this position? Let us turn to the Hupao fast for another look at the circumstances of the experience.

Li Shutong went to Hupao not for religious practice, not to attain "awakening" or "enlightenment," not to consult with wise and learned monks, nor to partake of their life for a few weeks, but because he felt sick and needed a quiet place for a diet-and-rest cure. What he did not know at the time is that traditional Buddhist practice is founded on the notion that all humans are profoundly ill and require a cure. This sickness—living in a deluded, unawakened state—is viewed as both metaphor and reality. Later on, after he became a monk, Hongyi became a great devotee of the buddha known as Master of Medicines (Yaoshi rulai), a powerful celestial figure in the Chinese Buddhist pantheon. He copied out this buddha's famous scripture on several occasions, and he gave numerous lectures on it. [35] But before that, he went to the Buddhist monastery for the sake of his health, and there he met a monk whose countenance and bearing—which he first observed from afar, and then later close up—really affected him. Perhaps this monk, named Hongxiang, recognized some of Li Shutong's needs for healing and thus spoke the right words to him, and gave him the right books to read. But mainly it was the overall impression of the monk that so affected this visitor in need of change. Shutong's own profound discomfort and unhappiness is made more vivid by his response to this sight. The man he saw was a

FIGURE 4.4. Li Shutong after the Hupao fast, holding his diary (*top*); his calligraphy commemorating the experience, "Spiritual Transformation" (*below*).

monk, so he began to look to the source of the monk's happiness as part of the process of curing his deep unease.

Let us step out of Li Shutong's world for an instant to recall the story of how Sakyamuni left the home life. It is said that the young prince set out from his palace on four excursions. On the first three occasions he encountered signs of suffering: an old person, a sick person, a corpse. In a state of turmoil, the prince went out one more time and saw something else: a man in simple garb walking through the streets, utterly calm and detached—a renunciant. The prince returned home. He then observed the last of the four sufferings that all beings experience, the pain of birth—for his son was born that night. The impact of the sight of the calm renunciant took hold. It suggested the way out of his dilemma, the dilemma of a man acutely aware of suffering. He acted on it.

I do not propose to say that Li Shutong "imitated" Śākyamuni in the way that Christians may consciously imitate Christ. His experience, though, is not far distant from that of Śākyamuni. It seems that something came into his sight lines at a charged moment in his life, and this something that he observed—a man free of worldly cares—constituted the gateway into a new world of practice and meaning.

There are many monks and nuns who enter the order in flight from poverty or violence, or as a means for education, power, and respect, or even for want of any other prospects. But the story I have just told is also one I have heard a good many times, related in individual ways by monks and nuns engaged in serious practice: they joined the order because of the personal example of a monastic whose peaceful, self-contained bearing inspired them to follow this path. In this sense, Li Shutong's experience was not unusual. It is striking only because he appears to have given up so much, and because in the act of "leaving home" this "modern man" appears to have stepped out of the world of modernity.

A Performance of Self

What traces remain of the experiences of a monk of the Tang or Song, a man who lived some thousand years ago? For those rare individuals who have not yet altogether vanished, there may be a few bits of text to piece together: a funerary inscription, some comments in another monk's biography, a brief mention in historical records. It is difficult to see the once-vibrant human behind such materials, for often these meager remains are built mainly of stock phrases that suggest a certain type of accomplishment or place in a carefully defined world. What is left, most often, is a memory in the form of a caricature.

With Hongyi we have quite the opposite. There are masses of surviving documents, many in his own hand—letters, diaries, literary compositions, treatises, prayers and vows, collections of aphorisms. The bulk of these works have been gathered together in the collected works published in 1991, but more documents surface every year.[36] In addition to his own writings, there is a great pile of material composed by friends, acquaintances, and disciples, some of whom are still alive and can be interviewed. And there are Hongyi's artistic works: drawings, paintings, calligraphy, seal carvings, as well as musical compositions (still performed and recorded). Hongyi was a man of recent times, and many of his possessions also have been saved: spectacles, reading stand, shoes, robes, umbrella, even a chamber pot.[37] He was a modern man, so also there are quintessentially modern items. Amongst these, very importantly, there are numerous photos, ranging from his childhood in Tianjin all across his life to his deathbed in Quanzhou. These photos and documents of many sorts give us a textured picture of a complex individual. As we have seen already, it is not a thoroughly sanitized or idealized picture, but one of stress and strain, contradictions, and accomplishment.

Using some of these materials, in this section I would like to reflect on how Hongyi, or Li Shutong, presented himself to the world. Surviving materials suggest that he had an acute sense of self-presentation, especially from his youth through the period covered by the autobiographical essay. He was concerned with presentation to the public (however small or large that became), and I think that he also was concerned with what might be thought of as the presentation of self to self. That is, his own identity was often in flux, and he used various methods to continually redefine or reconstruct this self and fix it in place. I think of these acts and related productions (to be discussed later) as a kind of "performance of self."

Some distinctive aspects of his performance of self were played out through the new technologies or customs of modernity, such as carefully posed photographs, certain types of changes to his body surface (especially clothing and hairstyle), and the opportunity to engage in amateur dramatic performance. His writing sent his insights, his poetic talents, and also his personality out into a public gaze, and this was accomplished in part through the new publication technologies and channels of the twentieth century. In addition to these conspicuously modern elements, Li Shutong's ongoing performance of self was carried out through such traditional means as name changes and calligraphic practices. The composition of an autobiographical essay constitutes a reflection back on those old shifting selves, as well as the self-presentation of a mature individual nearing the end of his life.

This is not a small matter. Buddhist teachings specifically address the futility of constructing an enduring self. Works such as the *Lengyan Sūtra*, which Hongyi studied so closely in his early years as a monk, consider from all manner of angles how the seemingly irresistible urge to construct a self and hang on to it is both a natural reaction to the truth of emptiness and a principal impediment to full liberation. One of the most remarkable aspects of Hongyi's accomplishment, in my view, is how a man so habituated to self-construction and self-presentation—indeed, so dramatically and fascinatingly expert in these endeavors—was able to set that process aside.

Hongyi's changeability, his very fluid sense of self, is nowhere more apparent than in his self-naming process. Men of his era and class background, especially artists, took on multiple names. Some were used as pen names, others for paintings, and some were adopted for public or private use as an individual crossed new stages of life. This use of multiple names was part of an expansive projection of self into the world, a kind of flowering or blossoming forth. Li Shutong, a man of many talents, also was a man of many names. By the time he was thirty-eight, he is known to have used at least thirty-five names. These include two new sets of names adopted in quick succession after the Hupao fast, names that he used in his correspondence and calligraphy of the period.

While his use of multiple names during lay life in part simply was social custom, the very large number and rapid succession suggests something more. This may have been of a piece with the restlessness and anxiety that characterized a good bit of his early adult years. And while he took on many names in lay life, after he became a monk this process was amplified. By the time he died twenty-four years later, he was known to have used at least 251 different monastic names.[38]

This activity simply is extraordinary within the monastic world. What are we to make of it? From a Buddhist point of view, it is not clear whether this constant renaming is a sign of deep and even obsessive attachment to a sense of self, or instead signified at this stage of his life something quite the opposite—a playful expression of no attachment to the false notion of an enduring and stable identity, in contrast to his earlier self-concerns.

Li Shutong grew up just as the medium of photography was becoming established in China. As an urban elite—first as a child born into a wealthy family, then later as an adult who had a directive say in his own activities—he found photo opportunities a customary part of his life. One might think of the spread of this technology as "Westernization," but the principal "Western" aspect was the site of the original technological innovations. Portrait photography spread early to China, as part of a global phenomenon, and posing for the photographer around the turn of the century was a regular element in the lives of those who could afford it. As a particular type of technological innovation, photography is an expression of modernity, a constituent part of this new age.[39]

Photography provided a new means of defining the self, especially through the posing process and the opportunity then to repeatedly scrutinize an image, an image that could be circulated readily. Fortunately, a wonderful range of photographs of Li Shutong has been preserved. He had accumulated a large collection by the time he was thirty-eight, and when he dispersed his possessions prior to becoming a monk, he gave the photos to his young student Feng Zikai. Feng had the presence of mind to safeguard them, so today we can look more closely at Li Shutong's life. The progression of images of Li Shutong through the years, this photographic record, presents a dramatic display of his changes. And after he became a monk, Hongyi continued to be the subject of many photos. Many of these have been published and now are well-known.[40]

The range of photos makes clear that Li Shutong grew up having his picture taken. A generation later, his son Li Duan recorded his memories of family photos taken regularly at the compound in Tianjin;[41] from the evidence of Li Shutong's collection, this custom apparently was long-established. Beyond the standard obligations, there is every appearance from the number and differing aspects of the surviving photos that Li Shutong enjoyed posing for pictures and arranged to do so on special occasions. The variety of consciously held poses and of strikingly different costumes provides some sense of his youthful response to the world.

These photos record Li Shutong's conscious alteration of his body surface, especially his sartorial presentation, as he moves through various periods of his life. As a boy and then a young man, he appears in the traditional male attire and hairstyle of the late Qing elite, but he breaks with this dramatically with his departure for schooling in Japan, when he becomes a modern man, with cropped hair and three-piece western suit. The photos show that this is one of his personae in Japan. But then after some time back in China, teaching music and art, he poses with a fan and partially sinicized clothes. The last of his photos from worldly life shows him at age thirty-eight wearing a Buddhist ritual vestment, even before he became a monk, with his two young students Feng Zikai and Liu Zhiping seated below him as if they were disciples. This is the last identity, the last costume that Li Shutong tries on, but it needs to be modified to fit properly. The assertive pose Li Shutong takes here—that of a great monk—is premature and jarring, even shocking in its self-pretensions. It is this expansive self, a bloated, inflated self, that Master Huiming soon will slap down.

Additional photos record some of Li Shutong's dramatic activities. In Shanghai in the years before he left for Japan, he played some traditional male roles in Chinese opera. What is not traditional is that a man of his background might engage in what earlier were considered "low" activities.[42] This breakdown of certain types of class barriers was a characteristic of urban modernity at the time.

In Japan, the envisioned site of modernity for Chinese "moderns" of the period, Li Shutong had the opportunity to engage in a wide range of new experiences and perhaps explore new modes of behavior. He studied piano and classical Western music, as well as his primary studies of oil painting and drawing in specifically Western modes. Earlier in this essay I discussed his activities with the Spring Willow Drama Society in Tokyo. A 1907 stage photo from "Uncle Tom's Cabin" shows Li Shutong in a Victorian gown arm-in-arm with his fellow painting student Zeng Yannian, and gives some sense of his ability to take the role of a leading lady in a convincing manner see (fig. 4.3).

If nothing else, we can sense from the sheer variety of these posed photographs that Li Shutong liked to dress up. His posing and dressing up is of a piece with other elements of his self-presentation: there is a playful quality to this, but also a lack of fixity and a sense of constant process, a sense of being within dynamic change.

In contrast to these many dramatic changes, it is remarkable, I think, that within a few years after he became a monk the photos become strikingly consistent in appearance and affect. The photographs do not register any further significant changes to Hongyi's body surface. One significant change, though, is hidden from the lens and our eyes. Hongyi engaged in ascetic practices and made a set of ten vows, together with a layman named Wu Jiandong (who later became a monk), at Yuquan Monastery in Hangzhou at the end of the year in which he was ordained. In accordance with Chinese Buddhist custom, he sealed these vows with an offering of his body, done by affixing bits of incense sticks to his inner arm and letting them burn down to their ends. The scars remain and are visible if revealed, but more importantly the memory remains. One purpose of this intense physical practice is the symbolic act of giving over the self by offering the physical object that is most dear to one, one's own body.[43]

Returning to what is visible in the photographic record, Hongyi wears the same very simple monastic garments in photo after photo, only varying his clothes by donning warmer outer layers in cold weather. At times his robes look distinctly worn, with large visible patches and mending. The Tiantai master Tanxu provides an extremely amusing inventory of the ragged and threadbare contents of Hongyi's scant luggage when he came in 1937 to Tanxu's monastery in Qingdao to lecture for several months.[44] This certainly contrasts with the stylish appearance of Li Shutong, unless we read his monastic presentation simply as the other side to that coin. Significantly, while many senior monks will pose for formal photographs wearing the dignified multistripped red *jiasha* outer cloak, which indicates high station in the monastic world, I am not aware of any photo in which the monk Hongyi establishes this kind of emblematic authority. He just wears his simple, patched clothing.

He liked to dress up, and then he wore rags. One could consider Hongyi's sartorial choices of the latter period of his life as a change that is no change at all, simply another highly constructed way of projecting his self into the world. This view is easily argued, but I also would like to propose a different reading. After he became a monk, Hongyi became acutely aware of a wide range of habits that had ruled his life, and he sought through conscious and systematic effort to set them down. This was part of his spiritual discipline, aimed in a very traditional Buddhist sense at reducing and eventually conquering the constructed self. He described this in a lecture given to monks in Quanzhou in 1933, entitled "Changing Habits," where he proposed a set of very basic guidelines for daily behavior. These guidelines for daily activity are aimed at assisting in setting a stable foundation for interior transformation. Among the points listed in "Changing Habits," Hongyi advises that monks wear clothing that is plain and simple, and orderly.[45] In this context, one can read the pattern of the later photos as evidence that Hongyi followed his own precept, that he lost interest in dressing up, that he recognized clothing as a means to cover up and keep warm, that he took seriously the symbolic value of monastic clothing as a visible sign of separation from a world that places value in external appearance (fig. 4.5).

One more point. Li Shutong was a talented painter whose formal training extended to Western media and idioms, including figure painting and portraits. All graduates of the Tokyo art school produce a final project, which remains at the school in its permanent collection. Li Shutong's oil painting, on any subject he might choose, was a self-portrait.[46] It is a haunting image, mysterious and inexpressibly complex, of a man looking out (at whom? at what?), yet still looking in. Here he has created a representation of a moment, knowing that it will be preserved in the art school's collection. His posed photos, especially those taken in Tokyo and later, should be viewed with this context in mind: he was trained to produce self-representations, and he chose to do so. When we look at the post-Hupao photo, for example, it should be understood as another very carefully produced self-portrait, here employing the modern technology of photography.

Before turning to discussion of the autobiographical essay in the contexts set out here, I would like briefly to raise the topic of Li Shutong's calligraphy.

FIGURE 4.5. Hongyi at age fifty-eight (1938), with his disciple Xingchang.

Since medieval times, brush writing has been the king of traditional Chinese arts (I use gendered language deliberately here, since almost all the famed practitioners were men), and Li Shutong was a prodigiously capable calligrapher.

He was a man of his age, and the sophisticated modern style since the late Qing was based on studies of archaeological materials: the engraved writings, often anonymous, of early medieval stone monuments from northern China; writings cast or engraved on even earlier bronze ritual vessels; medieval manuscripts newly discovered in the caves of Dunhuang. These ancient, foundational styles were absorbed and processed by calligraphers of the late nineteenth and early twentieth centuries. The best artists transformed these influences into graphic visions of their own, whose calligraphy thus had deep roots in the past but lived in the present.

This matter is profoundly important in seeking to understand elements of China's modernity, especially for elites such as Li Shutong. For some, modernity did not consist of abandoning a Chinese past, so much as finding different roots in tradition and eventually combining this with the new currents of the age. It is this particular combination of the very ancient with a new vision that for them is precisely the center of modernity.[47]

Li Shutong's enormously capable calligraphy shows a wide range of influences. His writing often is infused with vibrant "personality." It is again, I think, an expression of this performance of self, in which a self is constituted and fixed on the paper, to endure as long as that paper is preserved. In this context, what is most striking is the mature work of Hongyi, in which all his influences finally have been digested and incorporated into a coherent hand. The overwhelming impression is what Buddhists describe as *"qingliang,"* a coolness and clarity that seems entirely free. There is no "personality" here, no assertion, no "spirituality," nothing to prove. One senses that Hongyi has gone beyond that (fig. 4.6).

This mature presence, expressed in calligraphy, is relevant to how we might view the autobiographical essay. That matter will become more clear in the final section of this chapter, when we consider the form and structure of Hongyi's recollections. Here, we need to examine several contexts of the autobiography.

It has been conventional for some scholars to say that autobiographies of Chinese Buddhist monks are rare, but in fact that is not at all true, especially for the twentieth century. Hongyi's autobiographical essay most decidedly is not an isolated phenomenon. It rests within several contexts that give it shape and meaning.

In the discussion that follows, I will look at two different realms of production. First, I provide a sketch of Chinese Buddhist autobiographical writing (a sector of the larger world of Chinese autobiographical writing), with some focus on works that may have been Hongyi's specific inspirations. Then I look at the text within Hongyi's personal world, as one element of his "performance of self." (The concluding section of this chapter will consider Hongyi's text from a different angle to examine how the contents have been structured to produce

FIGURE 4.6. Hongyi's mature calligraphy (1940), collection of Ven. Guanyan, Chengtian Monastery, Quanzhou.

a certain kind of meaning.) I provide an initial survey of some of the principal sources here, based on research in progress, because—beyond the limits of Chinese Buddhist circles—very little is known about these materials, the worlds that produced them, and the worlds in which they have freely circulated.

As Donald J. Winslow succinctly wrote, autobiography is "a cluster of genres, varying greatly in form and in style."[48] One might define autobiography strictly as "the writing of one's own history; the story of one's life written by oneself,"[49] but I would like to take a somewhat wider view here and think in terms of "written testimony about oneself."

In this context, the practice of autobiography has a very long tradition in China.[50] One can find extended reflective accounts of one's self in the world as early as the Han period, such as the fascinating self-account by the prominent poet and moral thinker Yang Xiong (53 BCE–18 CE). One paragraph from this long work quickly conveys a sense of the man, at least as he wants to be perceived and remembered:

When I was young, I was fond of study. I did not engage in the
chapters and sections method, but limited myself to an understanding of the glosses and explanations. I read widely, and there is
nothing that I have not seen. In conduct, I am easygoing and
relaxed. I stutter and cannot speak quickly. Of a taciturn nature, I am
fond of deep contemplation. I am calm and unassertive, have few
desires, do not scurry after wealth and honor, and am not troubled
by poverty and low position. I do not cultivate a punctilious manner
in order to seek fame in my time. Although my family wealth is no
more than ten catties of gold, and I lack reserves of even a bushel or
half bushel of grain, I am content. I have my own grand scheme of
things. I do not like writings that are not by the sage and wise, and I
will not devote myself to anything against my beliefs even though it
may bring wealth and honor. However, I have been fond of the
rhapsody.[51]

Chinese Buddhist autobiographies, which vary in length and type, may be
considered as a coherent category, for once such textual practices became established within this social group, certain specific issues have tended to dominate their narratives. The great stumbling block in the composition and
dissemination of these works is that Buddhist practitioners aim to reduce and
eventually annihilate a sense of personal self. Even if they could not or would
not do so, this remains a powerful value within their world of experience. The
creation of an autobiography appears to strike against this principle.

Some prefaces to scripture translations, which may provide an account of
the circumstances of the translation work, bring individuals to the foreground
in their own words, though very briefly. Perhaps more significantly, some of
the earliest surviving first-person accounts where a distinctive self is revealed
or projected onto the page are found in Tang period records of visionary experience. In these texts, an assertive "I" testifies to what was seen, heard, experienced. For example, the eminent *Vinaya* master and historian Daoxuan
(596–667) reveals an unexpected side to his personality in his discussion of the
many late-night visitations of the spirit-general Weituo during the last year of
his life.[52] One of the longest of the medieval visionary accounts associated with
the pilgrimage site of the Wutai Mountains was composed by the Pure Land
teacher Fazhao (d. ca. 820).[53] In his written statement, Fazhao makes clear his
aversion to communicating the details of his experiences. The impasse is resolved by his capitulation to the repeated insistence of various spirits that he
must share this newly bequeathed knowledge with others. Here then is an "I"
that presents itself as backing onto the stage of self-revelation, pushed out from
the wings by compelling force.

Importantly, some Buddhists created extended self-accounts, works whose
narratives stretch over some period of time and describe interior movement

through that period by changes in personality or levels of understanding. The earliest of these works may first have been produced within circles of Chan practitioners. For example, there is the famous *Platform Sūtra*, whose long initial section constitutes a self-account by Huineng (638–713), the "sixth patriarch." Recent scholarship suggests that the text may well have been composed a good while after Huineng's death by members of the Oxhead lineage.[54] If the *Platform Sūtra* is not genuinely autobiographical, still the text attests to the power already established by the Tang of this type of articulated voice, for what we then have is the production of written teachings whose authority is encased in their mode of presentation, an autobiography. Because Huineng was illiterate (according to the narrative), the text is presented as a record of verbal activity, as a verbatim record of what has been heard.

Many spiritual autobiographies of this type were produced by eminent Chan masters of the Song and Yuan periods.[55] A good number of these classic testimonies were collected at the beginning of the seventeenth century by the famed monk Yunqi Zhuhong in his *Changuan cijin* (*Forging Through the Chan Barriers*). Zhuhong's work consists of apt quotes on Chan practice compiled from his wide reading, together with his comments. It is organized into three sections: testimony on Chan practice by well-known teachers (including some autobiographical accounts), brief tales about the practice matters of some eminent teachers, and relevant excerpts from scriptural texts. *Forging Through the Chan Barriers* most specifically is a practical text for Chan adherents. The tenor of its contents, as well as the title, suggests that its intended audience consists of practitioners who have achieved some attainment but are stalled or stymied in their practice. Aside from the fact that Zhuhong's text brings together a wide variety of fascinating materials, it is absolutely significant to see that the autobiographies are understood to have a function for Buddhist practitioners. They point out a path of attainment, and provide encouragement—a fortifying courage— to those who seek accomplishment in this tradition.[56]

It seems that for many highly accomplished Buddhist masters of that time, the production of such texts became one element within their expected sphere of activities. These accounts suggest an attempt to define one's sense of self (even when this self has been "killed" or "annihilated"), and an attempt to map out a trajectory of events as a way to bring coherence to one's experiences. They make visible an interest in explaining and representing one's life to oneself and others. Also, the composition of an autobiographical account is a method by which one can attempt to control the discourse about oneself, rather than trusting solely to the bare facts of a memorial inscription or judgments that may be found in official historical records, all recorded posthumously. And because such works are printed and circulated, their growing numbers suggest a more widespread interest in reading other persons' self-accounts and reflecting on what it means to be a human.

The relatively brief spiritual autobiographies collected by Zhuhong date especially from the Song through early Ming. By his own era, the seventeenth century (late Ming), this textual practice had experienced a sea change. Pei-yi Wu identifies this moment as "the golden age of Chinese autobiography."[57] As was the case for other eminent men of the time, autobiographical accounts by notable Buddhist monks appeared with regularity and extended even to book-length. Filled with rich detail, some of them were highly textured and revealing. The personal "I" was insistently present. One of the most famous of these long autobiographies is the *nianpu* (year-by-year account) of Chan master Hanshan Deqing (1546–1623), preserved within the *Record of the Dream Wanderings of Old Man Hanshan*, his collected works. It traces the full course of his life, including inner and outer experiences.[58]

By setting forth these very brief comments on Chinese Buddhist autobiographical traditions, I want to make clear that Hongyi's twentieth-century self-account has a place within a long-established practice. In addition, if we seek to understand Hongyi in his own context, then we need to consider specific works by individuals who provided him with inspiration and served as models.

One man often cited in Hongyi's writings throughout his monastic career is Ouyi Zhixu (1599–1655), a master of the late Ming. He is quoted frequently in Hongyi's letters and calligraphic manuscripts, and Hongyi eventually prepared a *nianpu* summary of the master's life.[59] Ouyi was a remarkable teacher whose writings are so voluminous as to suggest obsession (the modern edition of his collected works extends to twenty-two volumes).[60] This quality also played a role in his body practices, for Ouyi again and again made burnt offerings of his body through multiple branding acts.[61] Hongyi may have found a kind of personal kinship with the driving energy to set matters down in writing that Master Ouyi demonstrated. Ouyi, whose work was central to Hongyi's studies, wrote an autobiographical statement that is included as the first item in his substantial collection of "literary" pieces.[62]

There is one more work of this period that without doubt influenced Hongyi. This is *Comments on a Singular Dream*, the long autobiography of the prominent *Vinaya* master Jianyue Duti, composed in 1674 when he was seventy-three *sui*. Hongyi studied this work intensively and prepared an annotated edition, with preface, that was published in 1934. According to Hongyi's diary notes from this period in Fujian, he lectured on Jianyue's autobiography at Cao'an (in Jinjiang) for more than a fortnight in 1934, and then did so again at Quanzhou's Kaiyuan Monastery in 1935 (where a map is still preserved that traces Jianyue's ten-year-long journey by foot across China, meticulously drawn by Hongyi).[63] Like Hongyi, Jianyue had been an artist in lay life, became a monk relatively late, in his mid-thirties, carried out ascetic practices including extended retreats in caves, and focused on *Vinaya* as a subject of intensive study. I have no doubt that Jianyue's work influenced Hongyi to produce his own self-account in 1937.[64]

If we look to Hongyi's contemporaries and peers—the most influential monks of the Republican era, most especially those best known for their practice achievements—we can see that he was not alone in composing an autobiographical statement. For example, the highly influential Chan abbot Jing'an (1851–1913), perhaps better known by his alternate name of Bazhi toutuo (Eight-Fingered Ascetic), composed a self-statement that surveys his life; this is appended to his collected poems. The two most prominent Chan masters of the age, Xuyun (1840–1959) and Laiguo (1881–1953), each produced book-length works. There is no autobiography found among the collected writings of the eminent Tiantai teacher Dixian (1858–1932), but Dixian's very influential disciple and lineage successor Tanxu (1875–1963) produced a substantial two-volume self-account entitled *Recollections of Shadows and Dust* (that is, recollections of the insubstantial vagaries of this transient world). The energetic reformer Taixu (1890–1947) passed the New Year with Hongyi in 1928 at Lingfeng Monastery in Nan'an (Fujian), where they jointly composed the "Song of the Three Jewels," an anthem that still may be heard at Buddhist meetings. Taixu wrote a book-length autobiography at age fifty, a few years after Hongyi's essay was composed.[65]

This list by no means is complete, surveying only the best-known works. However, it should make clear that the composition of Hongyi's autobiographical essay is not in itself strange. Many of his peers did quite the same. They wrote not only as eminent Buddhist monks but as men of their modern times whose autobiographical impulses resulted in an outpouring of work that now, in Peiyi Wu's apt description, has reached "torrential proportions in the present age."[66]

Importantly, in contrast to the monks' autobiographies from Ming to the present, Hongyi's work presents a significant difference: it does not cover his life span. It focuses on a discrete period. Indeed, its length and tone align it with the type of rather informal personal essay made popular in his time (his disciples Feng Zikai and Xia Mianzun were among the foremost exponents of this form). And unlike many of the monks' autobiographies, Hongyi does not dwell on his accomplishments, nor does he mention any of the serious religious practices he embarked on in the Hangzhou area after ordination: meditation studies; more fasting and ascetic practice; formal vow-taking, which included the traditional incense burns on his arm to seal the vows and make an offering to the buddhas of the ten directions; copying out of scriptures as offerings; intense textual study; and other activities.

If we think of some of his earlier works as part of a performance of self in which the self is writ large, even grandiose, here we see some Buddhist progress. His self-portrayal presents not a natural saint, predestined from birth to achieve spiritual greatness, but a troubled man who seeks answers, who struggles along and makes both discoveries and mistakes.

In his career, Hongyi wrote numerous posthumous biographies of monks and laypersons. Twenty of these works (some intended for inscription on memorial stones) are gathered together in his collected writings. He also wrote a very brief biography of Beethoven. And he prepared four separate *nianpu*, year-by-year accounts of Master Ouyi and three major figures of the *Vinaya* tradition in China: Daoxuan, Lingzhi, and Jianyue.[67] Thus, Hongyi was well aware of how lives are constructed in writing, and how memory of an individual is created and transmitted for posterity. Therefore, we need to attend with care to the form and contents (and, indeed, the contents of the form) of Hongyi's autobiographical essay in order to approach an understanding of what he sought to communicate.

On Form, Structure, and Meaning in Hongyi's "Experiences"

Some questions remain regarding the composition of Hongyi's narrative. While these questions address matters of form and structure, they arise from the issue of presentation of self, and they move us toward the heart of accomplishment, as Hongyi sought to express it.

As we have received it, the text appears not in classical Chinese but in *baihua*, the new form of writing stemming from everyday speech that gained currency in the initial decades of the twentieth century. The narrative in this way is established as a deliberately modern work, especially when set against the backdrop of Hongyi's substantial body of elegantly composed classical writings.

Not only does this particular *baihua* composition maintain a conversational tone, to a certain extent it preserves an oral transmission rather than a written original. Why did Hongyi "speak" the text to Gao Wenxian, rather than write it out? Was this essay understood by him as a "lesser" text, a kind of offhand creation, or was it perhaps a text from which he wanted to maintain some distance?

The presentation of oral transcripts in polished form has a long tradition in the history of Chinese Buddhist literature. To cite some widely disparate examples, these range from extensive teachings on practice set forth by the sixth-century Tiantai master Zhiyi, such as his famous long treatise on meditation entitled *Mohe zhiguan*, which originally was presented as a series of lectures during an annual three-month summer retreat; to the *yulu*, or "discourse records"—conversations (or compositions presented as conversations) of a variety of Tang and Song Chan masters (this genre has continued to the present day); to more recent works by Hongyi's contemporaries, such as instructions given in the meditation hall by Chan masters Laiguo and Xuyun, as well as Yuanying's famous line-by-line oral commentary on the *Lengyan Sūtra*, as recorded by his close disciple Mingyang.[68] A collection of Hongyi's lectures from 1932 to 1940 were transcribed and subsequently published—some in polished form, others retaining the distinctive flavor of somewhat informal oral discourse.[69]

But Hongyi's autobiographical narrative was not a lecture, nor was it a recorded conversation. And in contrast to certain illiterate monks, such as Hongyi's astonishingly accomplished contemporary Guangqin, whose pithy teachings were set down by attentive disciples, Hongyi was ferociously literate and famously was a tremendously productive writer. [70]

When we look to Buddhist autobiographies, we find that two of Hongyi's contemporaries also produced their works in the "as told to" manner. Xuyun's autobiography was compiled at the request of disciples and consists of a polishing of his verbal recounting. There appears to have been enough editorial involvement such that the composition of the elderly master's work, which was released posthumously, was also credited to his lay disciple Cen Xuelu. Tanxu's substantial two-volume memoirs similarly were produced in concert with his disciple Daguang, although Tanxu appears to have retained more direct control over the finished product. Again, he told his tales in response to requests from disciples.

Part of the explanation for the oral composition of Hongyi's essay is simple, and it is revealed in two documents: a letter to the publisher from Hongyi and an essay written by Gao Wenxian. Hongyi's letter makes clear that his health was bad at this time, and he was having trouble with his right arm. Indeed, this work was composed while Hongyi was recovering in Xiamen from a debilitating and near-fatal illness, one element of which included very painful ulcers on his arm. (He was so sick in that previous year that he provided his attendant with written instructions to be carried out upon his death, such as how to dispose of his body, etc.) Gao Wenxian, in an essay written a year after he collaborated with Hongyi, also remarks on the master's health problems at that time.[71]

Still, Hongyi rejected the invitation to write in general about Buddhist life in Hangzhou, and instead volunteered to write about himself. What is more, in contrast to peers who explicitly state that their autobiographies are recorded at the urging of disciples, Hongyi makes no such rhetorical moves. This is the only time in his career—a career that involved extensive writing for publication—that Hongyi chose to compose such a work. Thus, within the context of his writing career Hongyi employed an anomalous method to produce a document on an anomalous topic. We might also recognize, then, that this particular method of composition provided a certain seemly distance from the decidedly self-involved process of constructing an autobiography. Even if autobiographical practice for monks had become uncontroversial by this time, the tension between a stance of detachment from self and disregard for name and fame— a critical position in Chinese Buddhist views of what it means to be a truly cultivated person—and the obvious focus on one's own life causes an uneasiness with these works.

I would like to raise a final question, one that relates to Hongyi's self-representation in his text. This question focuses on what may be the strangest and most endearing element of Hongyi's narrative. Although the text specifically is framed as a reminiscence of the time when he became a monk, Hongyi devotes almost a third of his autobiographical account to tales of someone else. And he met this someone else, Master Huiming, only once during the period in question; then some years later he heard the elderly teacher give a lecture. What is Hongyi doing here?

Before attempting to answer this question, we need to know a bit about Huiming. Huiming was born into a poor peasant family in Fujian province in 1859. He became a monk at nine *sui* and was ordained at nineteen *sui*. He did not receive an education in his youth and so was illiterate. Huiming served as a laborer in monastic kitchens, with duties such as carrying water and firewood, cutting vegetables, and so on. Apparently, he looked the part: very short, face darkened by the sun, raggedy clothes.

Huiming may not have been literate, but he was fond of meditative practice, which of course depends on mental cultivation and focus, rather than book learning. In the midst of chores in the kitchen at Tiantong Monastery—at that time one of the great meditation centers in China—he first had an awakening experience. Although he was a laborer and could not read texts, Huiming made sure to attend lectures given by eminent visiting monks, and during one such talk on the *Yuanjue jing* (*Complete Awakening Sūtra*) he had another profound experience. Following this opening, Huiming wanted to give sutra lectures himself, based on his personal understanding, but he was loudly derided by his fellow laborers for attempting to rise above his station. Huiming immediately left Tiantong Monastery to wander for three years, visiting mountain practice centers. When he returned, it was to lecture from the high seat of Tiantong's Dharma Hall. This is an astonishing rise in station. Huiming then was in his early thirties.

From that time on, Huiming was famed as a compelling lecturer, with a resounding bell-like voice that could fill a hall (here "bell-like" is not the sharp, clear, high pitch of Western imagining, but the deep and expansively penetrating sound of a massive bronze temple bell, full of rich overtones). He spoke on the *Lotus Sūtra*, the *Huayan Sūtra*, the *Complete Awakening Sūtra*, and on general topics of instruction. His activities were centered most especially in Zhejiang province: at the Fayu Monastery on Putuo Island, at Tiantong Monastery outside of Ningbo, and at Lingyin Monastery near Hangzhou, where in the latter part of his life he served as abbot for over eleven years.

His lectures were known neither for scholarly content nor for their recitation of other persons' views, but for their basis in his own realizations. In his recollections, Huiming's disciple Leguan emphasizes that although the master was illiterate, his lectures at times were notably poetic. The set of transcripts collected as the *Huiming fashi kaishi lu* (*Record of Instructions of Dharma Master Huiming*) presents a series of fifteen talks on Buddhist practice. They reveal—in his systematic and multiangled examination of key issues in religious life—a secure and confident brilliance. Huiming's language is basic, his thoughts are deep, and his instruction is practical.[72]

Despite his eminence as a lecturer, he remained a modest and unassuming figure whom others often mistook as an ordinary monk-laborer. Any money that came his way, or gifts of new clothes, or any other items that he did not immediately need—these all were passed along quickly to those who could make use of them.

Around 1911, Hangzhou's Lingyin Monastery underwent significant reforms, and over a period of six months Huiming was invited repeatedly to become the new abbot. Lingyin Monastery was (and remains) the largest and wealthiest monastic establishment of the region. Huiming did his best to stay clear of what for some would be a great honor and even greater economic opportunity, but for him would be an onerous responsibility. Finally, the monks invited Huiming to Lingyin si for a meal, and under this ruse essentially forced him to give in to their request. Huiming famously sat on the ground and wept, but they would not relent.

Although Huiming now was head of one of the greatest monasteries of the land, he did not stray far from his very humble origins. According to reports, a steady stream of impoverished monks would visit him at Lingyin si and receive his support. It was in this period that Hongyi came to the monastery for ordination. Twelve years later, in 1930, Huiming passed away at age seventy-one.

With this brief background in mind, we can turn back to Hongyi's recollections and think through his rhetorical moves. Of course, one could say that Hongyi's discussion of Master Huiming simply stemmed from a kind of uninhibited mind-wandering, which included ruminations on the venerable cleric under the general heading of experiences at West Lake. Presented in this way, Huiming might be considered one of the notable Buddhist sights of the region in the first decades of the twentieth century. However, Hongyi's other writings and preserved lectures, including those of the period in question, do not have this mind-wandering quality. Indeed, an outstanding characteristic of his written work is a sense of extraordinary clarity and focus. I think it is reasonable, then, to attempt to understand his comments as structurally determined, as strategically formed.

Hongyi was a skillful composer of texts. His writings are characterized by structure and balance. One major goal of his larger project was to set things into effective and comprehensible order. Thus, he produced a concise and powerfully influential essay on how to read the *Huayan Sūtra*, in which he sets forth a considered and logical path by which one can make one's way through this immense text collection.[73] His studies on monastic rule (*Vinaya*), for which he is most famous in monastic circles, take masses of scattered materials and set them forth into a practical and useful system. One particularly accessible example of this is found in a series of lectures given in Quanzhou about a year before he composed the autobiographical essay. In these lectures, Hongyi lays out all the sets of precepts that Buddhist lay and monastic practitioners may accept, and he shows with exceptional clarity the logic of progression from one stage to the next.[74] As a calligrapher, Hongyi produced countless *duilian* (paired phrases), many of them culled from his extensive readings and study of the

Huayan Sūtra. One can see these paired phrases carved on monastery pillars all across Fujian, the region where Hongyi spent most of his later years.[75] One can see (or hear) this same concern for balance and structure in his musical compositions; and this also is a characteristic feature of his seal-carvings. These concerns, in my view, are elements integral to the mental stance of his mature years.

Hongyi begins his narrative with an introduction and a few brief comments about early visits to Hangzhou. After the introduction, he moves quickly to the heart of the matter: the circumstances in Hangzhou that led to his "leaving home." He expands the body of this essay with tales of Master Huiming, and then balances the introductory lines with a brief conclusion. My sense is that this narrative is structured as an example of "path literature."

Hongyi's narrative looks at his transformation from lay life to absorption in the monastic tradition. This was a period when he was intensely self-involved, and the tale accordingly is one of self-involvement. Hongyi depicts his first, faltering steps on the path. But then he sets his own story in relief by introducing Master Huiming, who immediately gives the newly tonsured monk a hearty Chan slap during the ordination training process: "New monk, what's so special about you?" The narrative veers away from Hongyi to make clear what is genuinely special about Huiming: he treats all persons equally; he lectures on a sophisticated core text for practitioners, the *Lengyan Sūtra*; he makes a special project of teaching *maliuzi*, and never hesitates to give them necessities, going so far as to take the clothes off his own body even though he was aged and ailing. Hongyi begins his tale with a confused and troubled young man who seeks to forge a new path, and ends with an example of a man for whom the path has led to significant accomplishment. Hongyi at the time of ordination had potential; Huiming was a living example of the development of this potential. That forms a kind of paired phrase that would adorn any temple entrance.

There is one final point to raise in relation to Hongyi's discussion of Master Huiming. Hongyi reinserts his presence in the narrative when he returns to Hangzhou in 1923 and goes to Lingyin Monastery to hear Huiming lecture. What does this forty-five-year old man do? He bows before the old master and tears flow from his eyes.

There is no particular reason to doubt that this happened, to doubt that tears really did course down his cheeks. But we should not ignore that such tears are both a literary trope and a category of performed behavior with deep roots in Chinese history, as Hongyi—an extraordinarily well educated man—certainly was aware.

In the Tang period, for example, elite gentlemen were expected to weep before their teachers or patrons, this act thus representing or even creating a deep and "sincere" emotional pledge within a hierarchical relationship. Successful candidates in the civil service exams performed this act before their examiners within a formally established ritual context. As Oliver Moore wrote in his study of this rite: "The intimacy of this teacher-student relationship is evident in the graduands' weeping at the ceremony of gratitude. In the late Tang weeping was, with little exaggeration, tantamount to an art form, and some men even associated it with the behavior of a sage." Indeed, Moore notes, some individuals were famously adept at weeping.[76]

There is much that may be expressed in Hongyi's tears. Beyond spontaneous feeling, they may well represent an assertion of a special bond between the elderly master and the younger man. After all, as the accomplished teacher of Lingyin Monastery, Huiming surely presided at the ordination ceremonies where Hongyi received the complete monastic precepts that conferred upon him the full rights and responsibilities of life as a Buddhist monk. Although scarcely discussed in Buddhist scholarship outside East Asia, the ordination master can play a powerful symbolic role in one's monastic career. This most especially was important in the case of Hongyi, who was deeply concerned with the living qualities of precepts throughout his career, and whose ordination master was esteemed as a rare man who fully embodied those rules and showed by his accomplishments the logic of their practice.

Conclusion

Li Shutong was a man who stepped out of the vanguard of modernity to turn back to a very old tradition. And he was known especially for *Vinaya* studies—studies of the ancient rules by which monks and nuns guide their daily lives. What could be more conservative? Sometimes people look at the contours of his life, especially the turn from talent and fame at midlife, and they suggest that he was, well, "crazy." He had "everything," yet he set it all down and walked away.

But he recognized that modern life—at least as he was living it—made him sick. The cure for his disease involved setting down old habits and desires, and deflating an over-expansive self. This alternative that Hongyi found and embraced, Buddhist monastic life, could be understood as a retreat back in time, a step out of modernity, but that would trivialize or misconstrue the acts of an unusually thoughtful man. The ways in which he went about being a monk, while perhaps framed by some as a return to old traditions, in fact were unmistakably characteristic of this particular age. His reformer's zeal, originally applied to politics, art, and music, now found practical expression in Buddhist studies, as he made sense for his and following generations of an accretion of unsystematized *Vinaya* traditions. Beyond the specific contributions and achievements, Hongyi is honored as a model monk who was unswayed by conditions, who lost the need for worldly achievement. This model that he presents still remains powerful in the living traditions of the Chinese Buddhist world and beyond.

The man who composed the autobiographical essay was very different from the person described within, that fellow afflicted by *shenjing shuairuo*. The author was an ascetic monk in his late fifties who regularly carried out three-month or half-year retreats for intensive practice; who not only wrote about vows and lectured extensively on Vinaya but in fact embodied those vows in his daily life; who in the face of war (Japanese invasions of China) spoke about peace and did not flee; who in the face of honors such as high monastic appointments famously would simply move on to live in the barest of accommodations; who taught not only by lecturing, writing, and by personal example but also—even when desperately ill—by a seemingly tireless production of calligraphic gifts of pithy Buddhist teachings. The gentle and self-effacing recollections of his essay, in which his faults are displayed and his rigorous activities of spiritual cultivation are kept private, are not far from the example of Master Huiming, whom he held with such respect.

The Chinese Buddhist world has never been separate from Chinese society. It is a constituent element, and the drive for reform took hold there as well as elsewhere in the late Qing and Republican periods. Some reformers of this era, such as Taixu, took their cues from a Westernizing approach. They sought to bring Buddhist activities closer to a Christian model, and monastic education closer to a university curriculum. This tack remains a powerful one in the contemporary Chinese world, and it conventionally is framed as a "modern" response.

The other principal approach was set forth by practitioners such as Chan masters Xuyun and Laiguo, Pure Land master Yinguang, and Hongyi. They were profoundly concerned with monastic reform, but they did not couch their rhetoric in terms of the "new." They looked back for inspiration, especially to teachers of the late Ming, but most important they looked inward to personal experience and realization as a basis for their teachings. First and foremost, they urged a return to concentrated religious practice, including a return to life guided strictly by the *Vinaya*. But their articulation of the bounds of religious practice, although drawn in part from masters of past centuries, was distinctively new. It both mirrored and contributed to the wider changes underway in China. These matters, though, begin to turn us away from focus on Hongyi's autobiographical essay, which is the center of this present study. They make clear that Hongyi's remarkable story does not end here.

NOTES

1. Actually, he used many names, as will be discussed later. In this chapter I will refer to him as Li Shutong when discussing events or activities before he became a monk in 1918; thereafter, he is known as Hongyi.

2. For the early publishing history of this text, see Chen Xing, *Hongyi dashi yu wenhua mingliu* (Gaoxiong: Foguangshan chubanshe, 1992), pp. 192–195. On changing representations of West Lake in the early twentieth century, see Eugene Y. Wang, "Perceptions of Change, Changes in Perception—West Lake as Contested Site/Sight in the Wake of the 1911 Revolution," in *Modern Chinese Literature and Culture* 12 (2000): 73–122.

3. The two men were long acquainted by the time of this collaboration. Hongyi's surviving correspondence with Gao spans the years 1933–1941. (These thirty-five letters are collected in Lin Ziqing, ed., *Hongyi dashi quanji* [Fuzhou: Fujian renmin chubanshe, 1991], vol. 8, pp. 224a–233a.) Also, in 1936 Hongyi wrote a foreword and provided the title calligraphy for Gao's first book, a study of the tenth-century scholar Han Wo (*Han Wo* [Taibei: Xinwenfeng, rpt. 1984]), who settled in southern Fujian after the fall of the Tang. A photo taken with Hongyi and others in 1938 makes clear Gao's relative youth (see Chen Xing and Zhao Changqun, *Hongyi dashi yingji* [Ji'nan: Shandong huabao chubanshe, 1999], p. 138). Gao recalls the circumstances of the collaboration in his "Hongyi fashi di shengping," in *Hongyi dashi yonghuai lu*, ed. Xia Mianzun (Taibei: Longshu pusa zengjing hui, rpt. 1991), p. 36. Traces of Gao Wenxian remain in Fujian, such as his forceful calligraphy on the entrance signboard at Shuangling Monastery in Nan'an, which I was able to see in May 2001.

4. For a collection from the period 1932–1940 of twenty-seven lectures and an additional document, see *Hongyi dashi yanjiang lu* (Gaoxiong: Gaoxiong jingzong xuehui, rpt. 1992). On Hongyi's entire body of writings, see Lin Ziqing, ed., *Hongyi dashi quanji*, in ten substantial volumes of small print and double registers (the first nine volumes are compiled from Hongyi's works, while volume 10 collects supplementary biographical materials). For the autobiographical essay, see *Hongyi dashi quanji*, vol. 8, pp. 16b–18b.

5. Huang Pingsun. Hongyi very politely refers to him and several others in this essay as *jushi*, or lay Buddhist. (This term is both a title, as used here, and a category.) Even when writing notes to his closest friends, some of whom he had known for several decades, Hongyi always retained a meticulously formal and respectful propriety by addressing them as *"jushi."*

6. The term here is *chujia*, to leave home or leave the home-life, thus to become a monk (a *chujia ren*, or left-home person).

7. In the spring of 1949, Henri Cartier-Bresson made an extensive series of photographs of the Qingming festival, in which pilgrims walk from West Lake to Lingyin Monastery and beyond; for twenty-two of these images, see the plate pages bound between pages 131 and 132 in Holmes Welch, *The Buddhist Revival of China* (Cambridge: Harvard University Press, 1968).

8. Xia Mianzun (1886–1946), who taught literature, was a colleague for seven years and became one of Li Shutong's closest friends during this period. The two men remained lifelong friends. Xia eventually became a lay disciple of Hongyi, and he took responsibility to make sure that the master always had appropriate brushes, inks, and paper for his calligraphic work. Xia Mianzun became a prominent essayist, and he also was an editor in Shanghai at the important Kaiming publishing house (together with several other disciples of Hongyi, including Feng Zikai). For a brief biography, see Yu Lingbo, *Zhongguo jindai famen renwu zhi*, vol. 2 (Taibei: Huideng chubanshe, 1993), pp. 207–213. One can gain a brief glimpse of the man through two brief essays translated in David Pollard, *The Chinese Essay* (London: Hurst, 2000), pp. 160–165.

9. Li Shutong became a member of this society of distinguished seal-carvers and calligraphers in 1914. Some members achieved national renown, such as Wu

Changshuo (1844–1927), with whom he studied briefly. Founded in 1904, the society still maintains a presence at West Lake in its complex of buildings and gardens. Ye Pinsan, also known as Ye Ming, was a founder of the society. An undated leaflet produced by the society (entitled *Xiling yinshe*, obtained at the West Lake compound in 2000) provides a number of historical photos, including an early portrait of Ye. A 1913 group photo of members at the site shows them all wearing long scholar's gowns.

10. More properly, Dinghui Monastery, at the site known as Hupao, or Tiger's Run. This site was named after a large spring (Hupao quan) that was uncovered in the ninth century—according to legend—by tigers, who scraped away the dirt with their paws to aid a sage-hermit. The spring on the hillside still flows with abundant water, which remains famous for its excellent qualities for brewing tea. For a comprehensive account of Dinghui Monastery, see Shengguang, *Hupao Dinghuisi zhi* (1900), reprinted in *Zhongguo fosi zhi huikan*, ser. 1, vol. 28 (Taibei: Mingwen, 1980); see also the brief remarks in Leng Xiao, *Hangzhou fojiao shi* (Hangzhou: Hangzhoushi fojiao xiehui, 1993), pp. 61–62. Hupao also is associated with the early thirteenth-century monk known as Daiji or Jigong, an eccentric miracle worker who has been the protagonist of many tales, novels, operas, and—more recently—comics, movies, and television shows. It is at Hupao that the burial remains of Jigong are enshrined, with a small memorial hall and monument, in short walking distance from a memorial hall for Hongyi and a stūpa containing some of the *Vinaya* master's relics. Thus we have the strange and even provocative juxtaposition of a wild rule-breaker and a mild precept-holder. On Jigong, see Meir Shahar, *Crazy Ji: Chinese Religion and Popular Literature* (Cambridge: Harvard University Asia Center, 1998); for Jigong's relations to Hupao, see esp. pp. 172–174.

11. The *fang yankou*, or Releasing the Burning Mouths, is a complex and highly theatrical rite to bring relief to hungry ghosts. Thus, the rite generates merit, which then may be dedicated to the benefit of others, such as deceased relatives. The rite takes about three hours to perform (including a brief rest break), and includes group chanting, solo "arias" recited by crowned officiants seated behind special daises, the shifting and subtle rhythms of wonderfully vibrant two-handed drumming, and recitation of long mantras to the accompaniment of ringing handbells and flashing ritual hand gestures, as well as the burning of various paper materials (and is thus very dramatic in the darkness of night, when it customarily is performed). The rite ordinarily is carried out by fully ordained monks on behalf of lay sponsors, who may witness the actual performance. Usually these monks are ritual specialists, whose work primarily consists of such performances, from which they (and their monastery) may receive considerable income. These ritual specialists may travel within a defined region as a team to perform rites at sponsors' homes. Here Hongyi contrasts these men, more easily encountered by those outside the monastic system, with monks whose lives are devoted to quiet study and practice within the monastery.

12. Dharma Master Liaowu.

13. That is, he went through the ceremony by which one formally becomes a Buddhist in Chinese traditions. The rite was held on one of the auspicious days of the Chinese calendar (see 15 for further discussion).

14. Dizang Bodhisattva (Skt. Kṣitigarbha) is especially honored for his pledge to

rescue all beings from the hell realms, and he often is invoked to aid one's deceased relatives. The practice of reading, reciting, or copying out scriptures in order to generate merit has been widespread in China (as well as other Buddhist locales). This accumulated merit usually is dedicated to the benefit of someone else, in a sense shifted from one account to another. After becoming a monk, Hongyi copied this scripture a number of times, as well as many other texts. For an important study of his scripture-copying practices and philosophy, see Yixin, "Hongyi dashi di xiejing," in *Hongyi dashi yishu lun*, ed. Cao Bula (Hangzhou: Xiling yinshe, 2000), pp. 216–225.

15. In China at this time important acts ordinarily were carried out on auspicious days, either those noted as such in an almanac or also for Buddhists on one of the annual holidays associated with the various figures of the pantheon. The widely distributed Buddhist ritual handbook *Chanmen risong* provides specific information on which days of the month are most appropriate for the head-shaving ceremony; it is included on p. 144b of my blockprint edition, which dates to 1900. Dashizhi Bodhisattva (Skt. Mahāsthāmaprāpta), together with Guanyin Bodhisattva, serves as Amitābha Buddha's attendant. He also is especially well known in China for his practice method of mindfulness of the Buddha, as he describes in the *Lengyan Sūtra*. Hongyi felt a special affinity with this bodhisattva. When Xia Mianzun visited him on the day following the head-shaving ceremony, he copied out the first half of that particular chapter and inscribed it to commemorate the moment. For a reproduction of this document, see *Xia Mianzun jiuzang Hongyi fashi moji* (Hangzhou: Huabao zhaishu she, 2000), p. 32.

16. Reforms were carried out at Lingyin Monastery in 1911, when it was converted to "public monastery" status, which included strict observance of standard regulations. Dharma Master Huiming (1859–1930), whom Hongyi introduces later, was named its first abbot after the reforms were achieved. I suspect that the man to whom Hongyi refers as "abbot" (*fangzhang heshang*) was the principal administrator, as counterpart to Huiming's position as eminent teacher. More extensive discussion of Huiming follows in the section "On Form, Structure, and Meaning."

17. As a man of high status, Hongyi was given special guest quarters rather than assigned lodging in the Precepts Hall with the other novice monks gathered for ordination training and rites. Most novices would have been half his age and likely from peasant backgrounds, thus perhaps very different in their living habits from those of our upper-class, artistic, highly educated narrator. Regarding the name "Rue Pavilion": rue, or *ruta graveola*, also known as "herb of grace," is a strong-scented perennial herb with woody bark, yellow flowers, and decompound leaves.

18. The term *maliuzi* appears to be monastic slang. It is not found in any dictionaries I have consulted, but I have noticed the term in at least two additional Buddhist memoirs of the period. In his early years as an impoverished young monk the eminent Chan master Laiguo (1881–1953, thus Hongyi's contemporary) was unfamiliar with proper monastic etiquette. He wandered about applying for ordination, but was taken for a *maliuzi*—here understood as a kind of young tough disguised as a monk—and was treated very harshly at monasteries where he sought food and shelter. (See his 1949 work, *Laiguo chanshi zixing lu* [Taibei: Tianhua chubanshe, rpt. 1981], pp. 6–7.) Such figures still are found in the Chinese Buddhist

world. Zhenhua's (b. 1922) reminiscences of the early stages of his monastic career at the end of the Republican period provide a somewhat different explanation, which perhaps reflects the use of the term several decades later: "*Maliuzi* are con artists, but their abilities go far beyond your ordinary con artists. They can tell what you're worth and whether you're an easy mark just by looking at you and hearing you talk. . . . They can dress up like monks or change into Taoist priests. They can cry and laugh at will. They know jargon from all walks of life and can speak any dialect. They hang around at train stations and docks—any place there are lots of people. When they discover their prey, they latch onto it and don't let it out of sight. When the time is right, they set their schemes in motion and, easy as a snap, the game is theirs." See Chen-hua, *In Search of the Dharma: Memoirs of a Modern Chinese Buddhist Pilgrim*, tr. Denis C. Mair (Albany: State University of New York Press, 1992), p. 39.

19. *Liangting*, lit. "cool pavilion" or summer house. At present there are quite a few open pavilions in the vicinity of Lingyin Monastery, where visitors may rest on their uphill walk along a small river and gaze at the scenery.

20. A *zhai* is a vegetarian feast preceded by merit-producing ceremonies, ordinarily sponsored by laypersons.

21. Xia Mianzun's role is pointed out forcefully in Yixin, "Hongyi dashi chujia, chilu honglu yinyuan zhi si kao," in *Hongyi dashi xinlun*, ed. Fang Ailung (Hangzhou: Xiling yinshe, 2000), pp. 31–34.

22. Xia presents his account of Hongyi's leaving home, "Hongyi fashi zhi chujia," in the memorial volume he edited entitled *Hongyi dashi yonghuai lu* (Taibei: Longshu pusa zengjing hui, rpt. 1991), pp. 26–31; also included in *Hongyi dashi quanji*, vol. 10, pp. 38b–40b (for his views on Buddhist monastic life at the time Hongyi left home, see pp. 38b–39a). Xia's family donated his substantial collection of Hongyi's calligraphy to the Shanghai Museum, and the introductory materials to a recent catalog of these works include some discussion of his relation to Hongyi; see *Xia Mianzun jiuzang Hongyi fashi moji* (Hangzhou: Huabao zhaishu she, 2000), pp. 1–26.

23. Yang Cuixi has made a recent and fortuitous appearance in a Yale University Press publication, where her photo illustrates an essay on shoes; see *China Chic: East Meets West*, ed. Valerie Steele and John S. Major (New Haven: Yale University Press, 1999), p.140 (identified by inscription on the face of the photo). Such portrait photos—which served a variety of purposes personal and commercial—were not unusual for courtesans of the period in Shanghai. For some brief discussion of this practice, as well as similar examples, see Christian Henriot, *Prostitution and Sexuality in Shanghai: A Social History, 1849–1949* (Cambridge: Cambridge University Press, 2001), pp. 48–49; and Gail Hershatter, *Dangerous Pleasures: Prostitution and Modernity in Twentieth-Century Shanghai* (Berkeley: University of California, 1997), pp. 83–84 and figures 5–14.

24. On modernity in Japan in that era, see most recently Elise K. Tipton and John Clark, *Being Modern in Japan: Culture and Society from the 1910s to the 1930s* (Honolulu: University of Hawaii Press, 2000).

25. For some context on *Uncle Tom's Cabin* (translated as *Heinu yutian lu*, or *Black Slaves Appeal to Heaven*) and the Spring Willow troupe, see Yue Meng, *The*

Invention of Shanghai: Cultural Passages and their Transformation, 1860–1920 (unpublished Ph.D. dissertation, UCLA, 2000), chapter 7, most esp. pp. 420–435. See also two important essays by Ouyang Yuqian, a principal figure in the Spring Willow troupe: "Huiyi Chunliu," in *Ouyang Yuqian xiju lunwen ji* (Shanghai: Shanghai wenyi chubanshe, 1984), pp. 142–174; and "Ji Chunliushe di Li Shutong," in *Hongyi Dashi quanji*, vol. 10, pp. 31b–32a. I thank Professor Yue Meng for providing me with relevant sections of her dissertation, as well as the first of the two essays listed here.

26. For more extensive discussion of Li's considerable pioneering accomplishments in the arts, see Mayching Kao, "Reforms in Education and the Beginning of the Western-style Painting Movement in China," in *A Century in Crisis: Modernity and Tradition in the Art of Twentieth-Century China*, ed. Julia F. Andrews and Kuiyi Shen (New York: Abrams, 1998), pp. 155–157; in that same volume, see also Andrews and Shen, "The Modern Woodcut Movement," esp. p. 214.

27. Cited in Barbara Will, "Nervous Systems, 1880–1915," in *American Bodies: Cultural Histories of the Physique*, ed. Tim Armstrong (New York: New York University Press, 1996), p. 89. Material in the preceding paragraph is drawn from her work, pp. 86–89, as well as from Tsung-yi Lin, "Neurasthenia Revisited: Its Place in Modern Psychiatry," *Culture, Medicine, and Psychiatry* 13 (1989): 105. Lin's article is found in a special issue of *Culture, Medicine, and Psychiatry* that he edited entitled *Neurasthenia in Asian Culture*. See also the foundational works by George M. Beard: "Neurasthenia or Nervous Exhaustion," *Boston Medical and Surgical Journal* 3 (1869): 217–220; *American Nervousness, Its Causes and Consequences: A Supplement to Nervous Exhaustion (Neurasthenia)* (New York: Putnam, 1881); *A Practical Treatise on Nervous Exhaustion (Neurasthenia), Its Symptoms, Nature, Sequences, Treatment* (New York: E. B. Treat, 2nd ed. 1888), and *Sexual Neurasthenia (Nervous Exhaustion), Its Hygiene, Causes, Symptoms and Treatment, with a chapter on Diet for the Nervous*, ed., with notes and additions, by A. D. Rockwell (New York: E. B. Treat, 5th ed., 1898).

28. Will, "Nervous Systems," p. 89.

29. Tomonori Suzuki, "The Concept of Neurasthenia and Its Treatment in Japan," *Culture, Medicine, and Psychiatry* 13 (1989): 188. Suzuki notes that in Japan fasting remains a treatment for certain types of psychosomatic conditions, carried out under medical supervision (although rarely) or at privately run fasting centers (p. 200).

30. Zhang Ming-yuan, "The Diagnosis and Phenomenology of Neurasthenia: A Shanghai Study," *Culture, Medicine, and Psychiatry* 13 (1989): 156–157. Liu Shixie suggests five major patterns of neurasthenia from the point of view of traditional Chinese medicine; see his "Neurasthenia in China: Modern and Traditional Criteria for Its Diagnosis," *Culture, Medicine, and Psychiatry* 13 (1989): 172–173.

31. For one look at teahouse culture in the early Republican period, see Qin Shao, "Tempest over Teapots: The Vilification of Teahouse Culture in Early Republican China," *Journal of Asian Studies* 57 (1998): 1009–1041.

32. Keh-ming Lin, "Traditional Medical Beliefs and Their Relevance for Mental Illness and Psychiatry," in *Normal and Abnormal Behavior in Chinese Culture*, ed. Arthur Kleinman and Tsung-yi Lin (Dordrecht: D. Reidel, 1981), p. 103. For additional discussion of *shenkui, shenjing shuairuo*, and related problems, see Jung-kwang Wen and Ching-lung Wang, "*Shen-k'uei* Syndrome: A Culture-Specific Sexual

Neurosis in Taiwan," in *Normal and Abnormal Behavior in China*, pp. 357–370; Hugh Shapiro,"The Puzzle of Spermatorrhea in Republican China," *positions* 6.3 (Winter 1998): 551–596; and Frank Dikotter, *Sex, Culture, and Modernity in China: Medical Science and the Construction of Sexual Identities in the Early Republican Period* (Hong Kong: Hong Kong University Press, 1995), esp. pp. 162–164. Informal inquiries at several pharmacies in Luoyang in spring 2001 confirmed that traditional tonics to alleviate kidney deficiency also are specifically marked as treatment for *shenjing shuairuo*.

33. *Hongyi dashi quanji*, vol. 8, pp. 13a–16b.

34. "Hongyi fashi zhi chujia," in *Hongyi dashi quanji*, vol. 10, p. 40a.

35. On the traditions surrounding this figure, see Raoul Birnbaum, *The Healing Buddha* (Boston: Shambhala, 2nd ed., 1989). For three of Hongyi's lectures on the *Yaoshi jing*, see *Hongyi dashi yanjiang lu*, pp. 122–134. At present I am completing a new translation of the *Yaoshi jing* based on Hongyi's commentaries and his hand-written, punctuated text. This translation reflects a twentieth-century Chinese context of meaning and thus differs from the earlier translation included in *The Healing Buddha*.

36. For example, Ven. Guanyan, retired head of Chengtian Monastery in Quanzhou and a disciple of Hongyi, kindly let me study his large collection of Hongyi's unpublished letters, documents, and sutra copies in June 2001.

37. Many objects (and important documents) are preserved in various memorial halls established at sites in southeast China where Hongyi lived. The largest of these is at Quanzhou's Kaiyuan Monastery.

38. Chen Huijian provides a list of all these names and sorts them out in "Hongyi dashi minghao kaoshi," in his *Hongyi dashi lun* (Taibei: Dongda, 1995), pp. 249–368.

39. These views are an extension of Andrew F. Jones's arguments regarding the use of sound recording technologies in early twentieth-century China; see his *Yellow Music: Media Culture and Colonial Modernity in the Chinese Jazz Age* (Durham: Duke University Press, 2001).

40. Feng Zikai wrote a brief essay about Li Shutong's gift of the photos; see his "Baiguan Hongyi fashi sheying ji houji," in his *Yuanyuan tang suibi* (Hangzhou: Zhejiang wenyi chubanshe, 2000), pp. 116–120. There are many sources for a wide range of relevant images. Two recent compilations include Chen Xing and Zhao Changqun, *Hongyi dashi yingji* (Ji'nan: Shandong huabao chubanshe, 1999), and Jin Mei and Guo Fengqi, *Li Shutong Hongyi dashi yingzhi* (Tianjin: Tianjin renmin chubanshe, 2000).

41. Li Duan, "Jiashi suoji," in *Hongyi dashi quanji*, vol. 10, p. 190b.

42. On the problematic legal status and gendered position of male actors within Qing legal practices, particularly those who played female roles, see Matthew Sommer, "Dangerous Males, Vulnerable Males, and Polluted Males: The Regulation of Masculinity in Qing Dynasty Law," in *Chinese Femininities/Chinese Masculinities*, ed. Susan Brownell and Jeffrey N. Wasserstrom (Berkeley: University of California Press, 2002), pp. 67–88, esp. pp. 78–79.

43. This act is commemorated in his memorial inscription for Wu Jiandong, entitled "Yuquan jushi mu zhiming," *Hongyi dashi quanji*, vol. 7, pp. 400b–401a.

44. Tanxu, *Yingchen huiyi lu*, vol. 2 (Taizhong: Taizhong lianshe, 2000), p. 210.

45. See "Gai xiguan," in *Hongyi dashi yanjiang lu*, pp. 143–146, esp. p. 144.

46. I have not yet been able to obtain a proper reproduction of this painting. As part of an exhibition on the history of oil painting by Chinese artists, a life-size photographic reproduction was displayed at the Shanghai Art Museum in 2000. There one could see Li Shutong's (exceptional) work in the context of his peers. For a color image of the painting, slightly cropped, see the cover of Fang Ailong, ed., *Hongyi dashi xinlun* (Hangzhou: Xiling yinshe, 2000).

47. For some approaches to this matter, see two related works by Lothar Ledderose: "Calligraphy at the Close of the Chinese Empire," in *Art at the Close of the Chinese Empire*, ed. Ju-hsi Chou (Tempe: Arizona State University Press, 1998), pp. 189–207; and "Aesthetic Appropriation of Ancient Calligraphy in Modern China," in *Chinese Art: Modern Expressions*, ed. Maxwell K. Hearn and Judith G. Smith (New York: Metropolitan Museum of Art, 2001), pp. 212–245. See also Hua Rende, "The History and Revival of Northern Wei Stele-Style Calligraphy," in *Character and Context in Chinese Calligraphy*, ed. Cary Y. Liu, Dora C. Y. Ching, and Judith G. Smith (Princeton: Princeton University Art Museum, 1999), pp. 104–131.

48. Donald J. Winslow, *Life-Writing: A Glossary of Terms in Biography, Autobiography, and Related Forms* (Honolulu: University of Hawaii Press, 2nd ed., 1995), p. 60.

49. Winslow, *Life-Writing*, p. 3.

50. See Pei-yi Wu's pioneering study of Chinese traditions, *The Confucian's Progress: Autobiographical Writings in Traditional China* (Princeton: Princeton University Press, 1990).

51. The autobiography was incorporated in Ban Gu's biography of Yang Xiong, found in the *Han shu* (*History of the Former Han Dynasty*); the excerpt is taken from David R. Knechtges, tr., *The Han shu Biography of Yang Xiong* (Tempe: Arizona State University, Center for Asian Studies Occasional Paper 14, 1982), pp. 12–13, where also extensive annotation not included here may be found. On the form of the Han period *zixu*, or "account of oneself," as well as issues pertinent to this particular account, see pp. 1–7. I thank Michael Nylan for pointing me to this reference.

52. See his *Luxiang gantong zhuan*, T. 1898: 45, 874c–882a; and discussion in "Weituo, Protector of Practice," chapter 5 of my forthcoming *Body and Practice in Buddhist China*.

53. For a translation and study of this work and related materials, see Daniel B. Stevenson, "Visions of Mañjuśrī on Mount Wutai," in *Religions of China in Practice*, ed. Donald S. Lopez, Jr. (Princeton: Princeton University Press, 1996), pp. 203–222.

54. See Carl Bielefeldt and Lewis Lancaster, "T'an Ching (Platform Scripture)," *Philosophy East and West* 25 (1975): 197–212; and John R. McRae, *The Northern School and the Formation of Early Chan Buddhism* (Honolulu: University of Hawaii Press, 1986).

55. For a study of one of these works, see Miriam Levering, "Was There Religious Autobiography in China before the Thirteenth Century? The Ch'an Master Ta-hui Tsung-kao (1089–1163) as Autobiographer," forthcoming in *Journal of Chinese Religions*.

56. The *Changuan cijin* is conveniently found in *Lianchi dashi quanji*, vol. 2 (Tainan: Heyu chubanshe, 1999), pp. 1999–2092 (photographic reprint of a

woodblock edition of the *Yunqi fahui* [Nanjing: Jinling kejing chu, 1898]). Zhuhong's preface dates to 1600 (p. 2000). This text had a powerful influence on the Japanese Rinzai master Hakuin (1689–1769), who encountered it at a crucial moment of his development, when he was at an impasse. According to Hakuin's autobiography, he regarded it as a key text throughout his life. See Norman Waddell, tr., *Wild Ivy* (Boston: Shambhala, 1999). The *Changuan cijin* is an advanced practice text. One element of Zhuhong's particular genius was the ability to compose works with immediate practical use for well-defined audiences. His *Shami luyi yaolue*, which draws extensively from Tang and Song sources to set forth and explain basic vows and essential rules of deportment, remains to this day a principal training text for novices in the Chinese Buddhist monastic system (see *Lianchi dashi quanji*, vol. 2, pp. 1917–1958; nowadays, Zhuhong's text often is studied with the commentary of the contemporary *Vinaya* master Guanghua [1924–1996]).

57. Wu, *The Confucian's Progress*, p. xii.

58. Hanshan Deqing, "Zishu nianpu," in *Hanshan dashi mengyu ji* (Gaoxiong: Gaoxiong jingzong xuehui, 1998), pp. 2873–2986. (This is a photographic reprint of an 1879 blockprint edition.) For translations and studies in English, see: Lu K'uan Yu, *Practical Buddhism* (Wheaton, Ill.: Theosophical Publishing House, 1973), pp. 57–162; Sung-peng Hsu, *A Buddhist Leader in China: The Life and Thought of Han-shan Te-ch'ing, 1546–1623* (University Park: Pennsylvania State University Press, 1979); and Pei-yi Wu, *The Confucian's Progress*, pp. 142–162.

59. "Ouyi dashi nianpu," in *Hongyi dashi quanji*, vol. 7, pp. 406b–414a.

60. See *Ouyi dashi quanji* (Taibei: Fojiao shuju, 1989).

61. For an important study of Ouyi's life and thought, see Shi Shengyan, *Mingmo zhongguo fojiao zhi yanjiu* (Taibei: Xuesheng shuzhu, 1988). On obsession as a characteristic of late Ming culture, see Judith T. Zeitlin, *Historian of the Strange: Pu Songling and the Chinese Classical Tale* (Stanford: Stanford University Press, 1993), esp. pp. 61–97. For discussion of "incense scars" (*xiangba*), see chapter 3, "Offerings of Blood and Flesh," in my forthcoming *Body and Practice in Buddhist China*.

62. "Lingfeng Ouyi dashi zizhuan," in *Lingfeng zonglun* (Nanjing: Jinling kejing chu, n.d.), vol. 1, pp. 14a–21a.

63. For this text with Hongyi's annotation, see Jianyue, *Yimeng manyan* (Taibei: Xinwenfeng, rpt. 1990). For the relevant diary entries, see "Renbing Nanmin hongfa luezhi," in *Hongyi dashi quanji*, vol. 8, p. 22b. See also Hongyi's *nianpu* for Jianyue, "Jianyue lushi nianpu," in *Hongyi dashi quanji*, vol. 7, pp. 414a–415b.

64. In contrast to the two late Ming/early Qing works just mentioned, I have found no record that establishes Hongyi's specific familiarity with Hanshan Deqing's well-known autobiography. Several points, though, suggest that likelihood. First, Hongyi's hero Master Ouyi considered himself a disciple of Hanshan Deqing, although they never met. Ouyi wrote a number of works about his predecessor, including a poem in praise of the relic-body famously preserved at Nanhua Monastery in Guangdong. As Hongyi was intimately familiar with Ouyi's writings and was himself a prodigiously thorough scholar (as seen in his Vinaya studies), it seems likely that he would at least have read through Deqing's *nianpu*. This of course is merely a supposition. Second, while the text is found within the larger context of

Deqing's collected works, it also circulated as an independent work. An annotated edition of the autobiography (orig. 1651) was reprinted a few years before Hongyi composed his autobiographical essay. It includes not only Master Ouyi's poem but also very importantly a preface dated to 1934 in which the Pure Land master Yinguang (1861–1940) speaks to the significance of Hanshan Deqing and his autobiography. Hongyi considered Yinguang his master. Although they spent only one week together, they had an important correspondence in which Yinguang gave Hongyi instruction. Given the respect with which he held Yinguang, if Hongyi came into contact with this edition I would be surprised if he then did not study it. These suppositions are relevant since it was precisely in the period when the new edition was printed and circulated that Hongyi decided to compose his own autobiographical essay. (The edition in question is Fuzheng's *Hanshan dashi nianpu shu*. My copy is a recent photographic reprint [Taibei: Xinwenfeng, 1987]. Ouyi's poem is found on pp. 3–4; Yinguang's 1934 preface [most likely the date of publication] is found on p. 6. For Hongyi's personal account of Yinguang after that master's death, see his "Lueshu Yinguang dashi zhi shengde," in his *Hongyi dashi yanjiang lu*, pp. 86–89.) One further point in support of the likelihood of Hongyi's familiarity with Deqing's autobiography: Hongyi compiled several works during periodic retreats that might be termed "commonplace books" or, more elegantly, "florilegia." They include apt quotes drawn from his wide reading and thus give some sense of the types of works he studied at particular points in his life. While Yinguang figures importantly in these works, the four best-known monks of the late Ming—Deqing, Zibo, Zhuhong, and Ouyi—all are cited prominently, suggesting wide reading in their works. Hongyi's commonplace books have been collected as a single volume under the title *Hongyi dashi geyan bieji* (Taibei: Tianhua, 1998).

65. For Jing'an, see his *Bazhi toutuo shiji*, 2 vols. (Beijing: Fayuan si, 1919), supplement following *juan* 10, pp. 1a–4a. For Xuyun, see Cen Xuelu, ed., *Xuyun heshang nianpu*, in *Xuyun heshang fahui nianpu ji*, vol. 2 (Taizhong: Puli Zhongtai chansi, 1999); and Charles Luk, tr., *Empty Cloud; The Autobiography of the Chinese Zen Master Xu Yun* (Shaftesbury: Element, 1988). For the other works mentioned, see Laiguo, *Laiguo chanshi zixing lu* (Taibei: Tianhua, 1981); Tanxu, *Yingchen huiyi lu*, 2 vols. (Taizhong: Taizhong lianshe, 2000); and Taixu, *Taixu dashi zizhuan* (Taibei: Fuzhi zhi sheng chuban she, 1996).

66. Wu, *The Confucian's Progress*, p. xii.

67. These all may be found in *Hongyi dashi quanji*, vol. 7, pp. 393a–415b.

68. On the *Mohe zhiguan*, see Neal Donner and Daniel B. Stevenson, *The Great Calming and Contemplation: A Study and Annotated Translation of the First Chapter of Chih-i's Mo-ho chih-kuan* (Honolulu: University of Hawaii, 1993). On the *yulu* genre, see Yanagida Seizan (tr. John R. MacRae), "The 'Recorded Sayings' Texts of Chinese Ch'an Buddhism," in *Early Ch'an in China and Tibet*, ed. Whalen Lai and Lewis R. Lancaster (Berkeley: Berkeley Buddhist Studies Series, 1983), pp. 185–205. For meditation hall teachings, see Laiguo, *Laiguo chanshi chanqi kaishi lu*, 2 vols. (Hong Kong: Xianggang fojing liutong chu, 1970), and Xuyun, *Xuyun heshang fahui nianpu ji*, vol. 1 (Taizhong: Puli Zhongtai chansi, 1999), pp. 122–182. For Mingyang's record of his teacher's lectures on the *Lengyan jing*, see Yuanying, *Da foding shou leng yan jing jiangyi* (Taibei: Fotuo jiaoyou jijin hui, repr. 1999). New technologies now make

it considerably easier to produce such works, and indeed the contemporary Chinese Buddhist world is flooded not only with published transcripts but increasingly with audio and video recordings, many in digital formats.

69. For Hongyi's lectures, see 4. In addition, an important lecture on calligraphy given in 1937 to young student monks at Xiamen's Nanputuo Monastery, "Tan xiezi di fangfa," was transcribed by Gao Wenxian and has been published separately in Ke Wenhui and Liu Xueyang, compilers, *Ershhi shiji shufa jingdian: Li Shutong* (Shijiazhuan and Guangzhou: Hebei jiaoyou chubanshe and Guangdong jiaoyou chubanshe, 1996), pp. 112–115; see also *Hongyi dashi hanmo yinyuan*, pp. 198–201.

70. For records of Guangqin's teachings, see *Yidai gaoseng: Guangqin shangren* (Gaoxiong: Heyu chubanshe, 1997); and *Guangqin shangren shiji xupian* (Taibei: Fotuo jiaoyou jijin hui, 1999). On his life, which at least by legend memorably intersected with that of Hongyi, see Chen Huijian, *Dangdai fomen renwu* (Taibei: Dongda, 1994), pp. 299–328; and Kan Zhengzong, *Taiwan gaoseng* (Taibei: Puti changqing chubanshe, 1996), pp. 21–46.

71. For Hongyi's letter to Huang Pingsun, see Chen Xing, *Hongyi dashi yu wenhua mingliu*, pp. 193–194. For Gao's comments, see his "Hongyi fashi di shengping," in *Hongyi dashi yonghuai lu*, ed. Xia Mianzun (Taibei: Longshu pusa zenghui yinshe, 1990), p. 36. For the text of Hongyi's instructions, see "Yihai Cao'an yizhu," in *Hongyi dashi quanji*, vol. 8, p. 24b.

72. This work has been reprinted several times (I have at hand editions from Tiantai shan: Guoqing si, 1991; and Gaoxiong: Puzhao fotang, 1999). The original preface by Chen Raozhi dates to 1936. These editions both include a long biographical essay on Huiming by his disciple Leguan ("*Ji Huiming fashi*"), which originally was published separately in 1966. Leguan's essay is the principal source for my brief biographical sketch here. In addition to the *Huiming fashi kaishi lu*, Leguan refers to a *Huiming fashi yulu* in one volume, recorded and collected by Dharma Master Tanxuan of Hunan; I have not yet been able to obtain this work. A few brief biographical notes are found in the online version (but not the seven-volume printed edition) of the *Foguang da cidian*, which can be accessed at <http://sql.fgs.org.tw/webfgd>. Huiming's biography is not included in any of the key sources for this period, and further information has been gleaned in a random fashion by stumbling upon references in works by Buddhists of that era. For example, according to the prominent Beijing-based Pure Land practitioner Huang Nianzu (1913–1992), his learned teacher Xia Lianju (1884–1965) was a lay disciple of Huiming; see Huang's undated preface to *Lian'gong dashi jingyu* (Tainan: Jingzong xuehui, 1993), p. 1.

73. "Huayan jing dusong jiuxi rumen cidi," in *Hongyi dashi quanji*, vol. 1, pp. 259b–260a.

74. "Luxue yaolue," in *Hongyi dashi yanjiang lu*, pp. 13–29.

75. On the phenomenon of *duilian*, see Cary Liu, "Calligraphic Couplets as Manifestations of Deities and Markers of Buildings," in *The Embodied Image: Chinese Calligraphy from the John B. Elliott Collection*, ed. Robert E. Harris, Jr. and Wen C. Fong (Princeton: Princeton University Art Museum, 1999), pp. 360–379. For a good number (but not all) of Hongyi's inscriptions in monasteries located in the Quanzhou region, see He Jianrui, et al., compilers, *Quanzhou shi simiao gongguan yinglian xuanji* (Beijing: Zongjiao wenhua chubanshe, 1999).

76. See Oliver Moore, "The Ceremony of Gratitude," in *State and Court Ritual in China*, ed. Joseph P. McDermott (Cambridge: Cambridge University Press, 1999), pp. 197–236, esp. pp. 216–217. Thanks to James A. Benn for suggesting this reference (as well as for his thoughtful reading of the draft manuscript of this essay). For a somewhat different approach, see T. H. Barrett, "Exploratory Observations on Some Weeping Pilgrims," in *The Buddhist Forum*, ed. Tadeusz Skorupski (London: School of Oriental and African Studies, 1990), pp. 99–110.

5

Transitions in the Practice and Defense of Chinese Pure Land Buddhism

Charles B. Jones

Once upon a time, nearly two thousand five hundred years ago, the world was quite different from the way it is today. When Siddhārtha Gautama attained enlightenment and became the Buddha, the Awakened One, he turned his newly omniscient eye to view the world and see if there were beings around of sharp faculties and advanced religious practice who would be able to comprehend the fullness of his vision. When he had found such people, he went to them, preached to them, trained them, and led them to escape from the world of defilement and suffering into the peace of Nirvāṇa.

Sadly, however, the world has changed and grown turbid since that time. Human lifespans have shortened, so that people who wish to practice do not have sufficient time to achieve enlightenment. Violence is rampant, virtuous teachers are scarce, and the chance of escape has all but disappeared. Traditional means of Buddhist practice—meditation, moral conduct, philosophical reflection, and so on—no longer provide a realistic hope for the vast majority of suffering beings. The Age of the Decline of the Dharma (Ch.: mo fa) has arrived.

Nevertheless, hope still remains for those trapped in the burning house of *saṃsāra*. Long ago, in an age separated from our own by countless eons, a monk named Dharmākara made a series of vows before a fully enlightened Buddha named Lokeśvararāja. He would do whatever it takes, for however long it takes, to achieve a level of enlightenment so perfect that his pure karma would create a buddha-land of utmost purity. Beings who dwelt in it would want nothing; their every need for food, clothing, and long life would be fulfilled simply by willing it. The buddha that Dharmākara would become would be ever-present, along with celestial bodhisattvas who would assist him, to provide training and instruction to all the inhabitants of this land. They could dwell in it for a time without limit, so that all would be assured of attaining buddhahood themselves. Best of all, beings would not need to achieve perfect purity themselves before they could enter this land. In fact, all they would have to do is think of this buddha, and call out his name, and he would come to meet them at the time of their deaths and escort them to this Pure Land. They needed only faith in him to attain rebirth there.

After the passage of an unimaginable span of time, Dharmākara achieved his goal. He became a Buddha named Amitābha (Immeasurable Light), or Amitāyus (Immeasurable Life), and in so doing, satisfied all of the conditions of his vows. He indeed created a Pure Land, called Sukhāvatī, the Land of Utmost Bliss. Even now, beings that have no other hope of finding release from suffering in this Saha world, this World of Endurance, are calling upon his name and finding their way upon death to that land, from which they will never again fall into the trap of *saṃsāra*.

So runs the story that forms the basis of the most widespread school of Buddhist practice throughout East Asia. The myth formed in India, and in fifth-century China began to take shape as an "easy path" of practice that could potentially be open to all people, regardless of their inclinations, intelligence, virtue, or circumstance. While many Chinese, Japanese, and Korean Buddhists regarded the practices based on this story as an aberration, an abdication of traditional Buddhist values and practices in favor of some fairy-tale heaven, the majority accepted it. To this day, throughout China, one may see people chanting the name of Amitābha using the traditional formula *namo Amituo fo* ("homage to the Buddha Amitābha") in all manner of settings, from grand liturgies in magnificent temples to spare moments of free time in the midst of daily activities. This is all done in the hope of being prepared to meet Amitābha on their deathbeds and accompany him back to Sukhāvatī.

While Pure Land Buddhism has always had its detractors, the modern world has presented it with new challenges that have prompted some to change the tactics by which they frame both their theology and their apologetic, and caused others to rethink the meaning and purpose of belief in Pure Land Buddhism. In this chapter, we will look at both of these developments as they have evolved from the late nineteenth century to the present day.

Conditions of Modernity in Chinese Buddhism

Cultures, societies, nations, and religions do not march united into modernity. There is always contention within the group over the extent to which it will embrace both the outer trappings of modern times, and the inner logic and worldview of those times. In a 1989 study of fundamentalism in Islam, Judaism, and Christianity, Bruce Lawrence made a very useful distinction between "modernity" and "modernism," a distinction which will serve here as well.

"Modernity," he said, was nothing more than the paraphernalia of the modern world: it is the emergence of a new index of human life shaped, above all, by increasing bureaucratization and rationalization as well as technical capacities and global exchanges unthinkable in the premodern era. "Modernism" is more complex; it is the mindset of the modern world, the ethos and worldview that generally accompany "modernity." It is (at least in the West) the search for individual autonomy driven by a set of socially encoded values emphasizing change over continuity; quantity over quality; and efficient production, power, and profit over sympathy for traditional values or vocations, in both the public and private spheres.[1] Modernism thus values quantifiable results over less tangible improvements in quality, pragmatism ("what will work?") over truth ("what is true?"), and efficiency over aesthetics.[2]

While Lawrence's characterization of the modernist mindset is valuable, it is not exhaustive. To this list we may add Michel Foucault's identification of historicism—the view that time moves forward and changes all things in such a way that they are intelligible only when seen in their historical context—as an element of the modernist view, opposed to the traditional search for timeless truths.[3] In addition, we should also attend to Joseph Kitagawa's representation of modern religion and Don A. Pittman's more specific list of factors at work in the modern transformation of Chinese Buddhism. According to the former, three factors have emerged as hallmarks of modern religion. The first factor is a search for the meaning of human life in and of itself as a quest more urgent than the search for ultimate and universal truths. Second, modern religion tends to emphasize a this-worldly soteriology, affirming that salvation (however conceived) is to be sought and found within this world, and not in an escape from it to a better realm. The third factor is that modern religion emphasizes freedom over order; that is, it no longer accepts the present natural and social orders as divinely mandated or given in the nature of reality, but sees them as mutable, and, above all, improvable through human efforts undertaken in freedom.[4]

Pittman offers five further factors specific to the situation of Buddhism in the modern world. Modern Buddhism (1) entails an "inner-worldly asceticism," a concept that he takes from the writings of Max Weber, which signifies the impulse to remake the world; (2) is marked by rationalism, or the attempt to present Buddhism as reasonable and consistent with the findings of modern sciences (though not coextensive with it); (3) sees itself as part of a restoration, by which he means a denial of innovation on the part of modernizers, preferring instead to consider itself as recovering Buddhism's original intent and spirit so as to face the future more faithfully; (4) is ecumenical and global in scope, seeking to embrace all of humanity and transcend any provincialism or sectarianism; and (5) reveals a dynamic interplay between Buddhism as a religion and Buddhism as a means to an end that, once achieved, obviates the need for Buddhism itself.[5]

If we adopt Lawrence's analytical scheme, then, to reject both "modernity" and "modernism" is to embrace a traditional lifestyle that makes no use at all of new technological capabilities and that also rejects all (or most) of the ideas or values listed here. The Old Order Amish (at least as popularly stereotyped) would be an example of such a double rejection. However, a person or group may choose to embrace *modernity* but reject *modernism*, and one may certainly see examples of this among Chinese Pure Land Buddhists in contemporary Taiwan. During my own fieldwork there between 1992 and 1994, I saw copious use of mass media to promote the version of Pure Land thought and practice outlined in the introduction. Television shows preached this story and exhorted viewers to practice assiduously, cassette tapes and compact discs provided models for reciting the name of the buddha, and factories used modern production materials and methods to turn out rosaries and other aids for cultivation. The Xilian Temple outside the town of Sanxia had a computer laboratory where devotees constructed their own media players in order to tell the story of the thirteenth "patriarch" (Ch: *zu*) of Pure Land, Ven. Yinguang (1861–1940), a tireless denouncer of modernist interpretations of Pure Land. They were also in the process of preparing for the passing of their founding abbot and his traditional style of governing by charisma by mapping out a new, bureaucratized structure of governance using standards and procedures.

Alternatively, persons or groups may embrace both modernity and modernism. In many instances they will reject traditional religion altogether as a result, but they may also attempt to reinterpret their religious beliefs and practices in a modernist light. Those in Chinese Pure Land who took this route will be the subject of the next section.

Redefining the Pure Land

Taixu

Holmes Welch, in the second book in his trilogy on Buddhism in modern China called *The Buddhist Revival in China*, detailed many ways in which certain reformers within Republican-era Buddhism (1911–1949) attempted to modernize Buddhism and fit it for the new conditions of the twentieth century.[6] Unlike the traditionalists, who, as we have seen, unwillingly adapted their message and practices to the conditions of *modernity* without ever embracing *modernism*, these reformers familiarized themselves with new currents of thought such as Marxism, science, and democracy, and predicted that Buddhism would have to absorb elements from them actively, even enthusiastically, or it would perish. The most well-known example of this is the monk Taixu (1890–1947), who expended tremendous energy in modernizing and rationalizing Buddhist education, monastic organization, and Buddhist doctrine.[7] As we shall see, Taixu's disciple Yinshun (1906–) paid more specific attention to transforming Pure Land teachings, and other leaders more indirectly indebted to Taixu also tried to adapt Pure Land for modern conditions.

The specific innovation Taixu left to his followers that has had the greatest impact on Pure Land thought is that of "Buddhism for Human Life" (Ch: *rensheng is fojiao*), the practice of which would lead to the establishment of a "Pure Land on Earth" (*renjian jingtu*). One of Taixu's dissatisfactions with the Buddhist tradition that had come from the late Qing dynasty period was that it made much of its livelihood from the performance of funerals, and so invested much of its time and energy in learning and performing ceremonies for the dead and dying, to the detriment of teachings and ministries for the living. Thus, his catchphrase "Buddhism for Human Life" conveyed his hope that Buddhism might turn from its focus on death rituals to the needs of the living. In this way, he hoped to blunt criticism from secular modernizers such as Liang Shuming (1893–1977), himself a relatively mild and conservative voice, who charged that Buddhism was useless and wasteful because of its otherworldly focus. He also recommended that its properties and resources be confiscated so that the government could use them for more obviously beneficial purposes in society, for instance, by turning temples into schools.[8]

This had direct implications for the practice of Pure Land Buddhism, since its mythological narrative centered on the postmortem salvation of the devotee and it traditionally regarded the moment of death as the most critical in terms of determining whether the devotee made it to the Pure Land or not. Its literature and practice did indeed display a focus on deathbed and funeral practices designed to keep the devotee's mind focused on Amitābha and the Pure Land right at that pivotal moment. One of the most distinctive forms of Pure Land literature, in fact, consisted of deathbed narratives that recounted a devotee's long fervor in Pure Land practice and the signs and wonders that manifested at the moment of death to prove that he had indeed gained rebirth in Sukhāvatī. Taixu sought to change the focus radically from the next world to this world.

He mounted his challenge using tools both old and new. One perennial dissent from the Pure Land myth of Amitābha had to do with the very issue of whether the Pure Land could be manifested in the present world, or if devotees had to await their time of death to gain entrance, a question that had obvious connection with the modern critique of Pure Land as otherworldly. One side stated that the Pure Land manifests when the mind itself is purified. Taking their cue from the second chapter of the *Vimalakīrti-nirdeśa sūtra* called "On Buddha Lands," they asserted that the Pure Land is nothing but this present defiled world seen correctly by an enlightened mind.[9] For this group, Pure Land thought was a call to action, goading Buddhists to work assiduously in mental cultivation through meditation and study so that they could see the world aright.

Taixu was certainly familiar with this strain of thought, and it fitted well with his efforts (along with those of the layman Ouyang Jingwu 1871–1943) to reintroduce the highly psychological scheme of Consciousness-Only thought (Ch: *weishi*) as a system more suited to the modern scientific temperament.

But Taixu also had a less metaphysical and more literal meaning for the term "Pure Land," one that involved human striving at the social and political levels. He used the term "the Pure Land in the Human Realm" (Ch: *renjian jingtu*) to describe a literal geographical zone in which, with governmental backing, the teachings of Buddhism would be put into effect in erecting both environmental and social structures. Industry, educational institutions, and public morals would all be modeled on Buddhist visions of the good, so that the idealized society that would emerge would be a Buddhist Pure Land.[10] This went well beyond the traditional vision derived from the *Vimalakīrti-nirdeśa sūtra*, in which the individual's mental cultivation and purification would lead to the appearance of the Pure Land *for that individual only*. Rather, Taixu envisioned a social-political-cultural reformation that would bring about an idealized Buddhist society for all its members, regardless of their individual level of attainment, and he captured the essence of this vision in his slogan "the Pure Land in the Human Realm."

Don A. Pittman summarizes Taixu's modernism under the three headings proposed by Joseph Kitagawa: "He understood the significance of human existence, emphasized the attainment of buddhahood within the world, and rejected the given-ness of the social order in favor of building a pure land on earth."[11] As an "ethical pietist," his own religion sought expression and found validation in concrete reforms within the social realm. He rejected Pure Land thought and practice as articulated by staunch traditionalists such as Yinguang, who accepted the social and natural orders as unsalvageable, rejected the possibility of any reform or change, and counseled belief in the Pure Land mythos given at the beginning of this chapter. Taixu's disciple Yinshun was to tackle Pure Land traditionalism in much more direct manner under the same motto of "building a Pure Land on Earth," but for the moment we will turn our attention to a figure in Taiwan Buddhism whose efforts to reform Pure Land teachings predated Yinshun's.

Lin Qiuwu

During the first thirty years of the twentieth century, the monk Lin Qiuwu (or Ven. Zhengfeng, 1903–1934) worked to harmonize Buddhist thought and practice with the newly imported Marxist teachings of social action and historical materialism. Like Taixu, he wanted to meet the modernist critique of Buddhism by adapting the religion to the times, and in a move that has been emulated by later generations of Taiwan's Buddhists, he began to redirect the focus of Pure Land devotionalism away from the afterlife and toward conditions of the world at hand. The point of Pure Land teaching, he said, was not to abandon this world and attempt to gain rebirth in an idealized world after death. Instead, it constituted a call to make efforts to transform the present world into a Pure Land. In one place, he wrote: "From each according to his ability, to each according to his need, without a trace of selfish intention, each and every person strives to produce in common. In this kind of society, everyone will have enough, and thievery will disappear all by itself. Buddhism has a name for this kind of world: the Pure Land of Utmost Bliss."[12]

This was a sentiment he repeated in several places, emphasizing his belief that Pure Land ought not to be a passive rejection of this world but an active embrace of it and an attempt to purify it by working for justice and peace.

It is important to note here that Lin was not the first Chinese Buddhist to criticize Pure Land teaching for abandoning this world. In fact, a major component of the long-standing Chan critique of Pure Land lay in this assertion. However, the Chan critique had more to do with a disagreement over the nature of enlightenment. According to Chan Buddhists, the world as it is was already pure, and Pure Land followers were drawing an illegitimate distinction between "purity" and "impurity" by wanting to abandon this world to gain the Pure Land after death. Following the *Vimalakīrti-nirdeśa sūtra* as well as sayings of venerable Chan masters, they claimed that, to an enlightened Buddha, all distinctions prove illusory, and this world is just as pure as any other. Lin's point was different, and turned on the notion that this present world was not already pure, except perhaps in the most abstract philosophical sense. At the conventional level, it had impurities and problems in plenty, and he wanted Taiwan's Buddhists to take as their task the rectification of these problems so that it could become a Pure Land on earth, not so that practitioners could realize its already-perfected purity. If one did gain some apprehension of the philosophical issues, it would serve to spur the believer on to greater efforts in this direction; it would not (or ideally should not) become an accomplishment that marks the end of the religious path.

As I have pointed out elsewhere, Lin's criticisms of traditional conceptions of Pure Land practice were fairly mild. He wanted to recruit others for his social-reform efforts, not alienate them, so his use of Pure Land ideas and terms seems to have been more rhetorical than theological—he simply used terms and concepts with which his audience would already be familiar and to which they would already be favorably disposed, and redirected them to new referents within his own social thought.[13]

Yinshun

The case of Yinshun reveals a much more hostile and trenchant attitude toward Pure Land, one worth extended consideration because of Yinshun's standing as one of the most formidable and influential intellectuals in the modern Chinese Buddhist world.[14] The attitude he displays toward Pure Land in his writings on Chinese Buddhist history and practice appears to be connected with his generally critical attitude toward the kind of debased, folk Buddhism that he witnessed during his early years. In an autobiographical essay published in 1985, he reports that he developed an intellectual curiosity about Buddhism in his late teens and early twenties, and began reading all of the books on the topic he could acquire, books that mostly dealt with Sanlun and Weishi philosophical thought. At the same time, he noticed that the kind of Buddhism he saw in practice in rural Zhejiang province did not seem connected in any way to the highly subtle and inspiring metaphysics he was reading. Indeed, the monks he met in local temples were largely uneducated and made a living performing funerals. The laity, for their part, participated in rituals for purely secular gains, and many were members of various lay Buddhist sects that generally go by the name "vegetarian religions" (Ch: *zhaijiao*).[15] This disjunction between the textual tradition and the actual practice of Chinese Buddhism set up a fundamental problem for which he spent much of his subsequent life seeking a remedy: What had happened to Buddhism between the time of its transmission from India and its modern, seemingly corrupted, form, and how might it be renovated?[16]

Taking the tonsure in 1930, Yinshun went to the Minnan Buddhist Seminary in 1931, and so spent time studying in one of the institutions for the reform of Buddhist education founded by Taixu. Despite differences in their interpretation of Buddhism, Yinshun has affirmed that he always considered himself a follower of Taixu, and shared his vision of a reformed and modernized Buddhism.[17] Specifically, he followed Taixu in seeing Indian Mahāyāna thought, particularly the Madhyamika thought of Nāgārjuna (2nd century), as the apex of Buddhism. This, for Yinshun, represented the most ideal form of Buddhism because it engaged in an uncompromising critique of reality at the metaphysical level, but never let its intellectual disparagement of the categories that humans use to understand it (such as good and evil) to invalidate the need for concrete works of compassion. However, Buddhism entered China soon after arriving at this synthesis, and there went through a process of debasement, becoming too focused on the worship of buddhas and bodhisattvas, misconstrued by the average Buddhist as godlike savior figures rather than as models of perfected humanity to be emulated.

Because of this misapprehension, Buddhism had lost the message of human striving in intellectual and moral self-cultivation and had become preoccupied with gods and saviors (Ch: *shenhua* or *guihua*, literally "god-ification" or "ghost-ification"). He saw this, rather than the overreliance on funerals and its consequent concern for the dead, as the main problem that had beset Buddhism in China for over a millennium. Thus, he made a conscious decision not to use Taixu's catchphrase "Buddhism for Human Life" and chose instead "Buddhism in the Human Realm" (Ch: *renjian fojiao*, often rendered "Humanistic Buddhism"), a slogan he parsed out in detail in a highly influential book entitled *The Buddha is in the Human Realm* (*Fo zai ren jian*). In this book he demonstrated in various ways that the message of Buddhism had always been aimed at an audience of human beings, and that, as an early Buddhist scripture put it, "All Buddhas and World-Honored Ones emerge from the human realm; they do not attain buddhahood somewhere above the heavens."[18] Buddhas were not gods nor were they superhuman; to become a buddha, he said, was simply to attain a perfected humanity. The virtues of the buddha—(1) superior mental faculties; (2) ethics for building upon human relationships; (3) determination or heroism—are specifically human qualities, which even traditional Buddhist scriptures claim are not shared by other types of beings.[19]

This implied that the proper sphere of Buddhist activity was the human realm. When the historical Buddha left home to seek enlightenment, according to Yinshun, he did not take leave of the world of human society altogether. Instead, he left the narrow confines of family and clan and made his way into the world of humanity as a whole with its troubles and travails.[20] While this holds true throughout all of Buddhist history, Yinshun observes that this emphasis on human concerns and compassionate activity within the human sphere best suited the needs of the modern world. It allowed modern historical consciousness room to interpret different forms of Buddhism by analyzing their historical and cultural contexts. Thus, whereas the traditionalist teaching of Pure Land (which Yinshun identifies specifically with the master Yinguang) remains stuck in a premodern mode, teaching about a layered reality with Pure Lands off to the west, seemingly invisible to astronomical instruments, a modernized Buddhism can modify its views to take into account the findings of astronomy, as well as psychology, history, sociology, and so on.[21] However, Yinshun rested his recommendation of a historicized Buddhism not strictly on the exigencies of modernism but on traditional Buddhist grounds: Buddhism has always recognized the necessity of applying expedient means in order to communicate its message to the audience at hand. If the audience is a modern(ist) audience, then the terms of modernism must be employed and a traditionalist presentation eschewed as counterproductive. His efforts to adapt Buddhism were no innovation, but a restoration of Buddhism's original adaptability.[22]

While his book *The Buddha Is in the Human Realm* laid out his general call for a modernized Buddhism and only incidentally touched on Pure Land, another book produced soon after his flight to Taiwan with the Nationalist government confronted Pure Land directly and led to a clash with the traditionalists. The book, called *A New Treatise on the Pure Land* (*Jingtu xin lun*), consisted of notes taken during a series of lectures Yinshun delivered on the mainland, which some students edited and published. Whether Yinshun himself intended it or not, the *New Treatise* has an unmistakably disparaging tone as it relentlessly subjects traditional Pure Land thought and practice to a highly modern social, scientific, and historical critique.[23]

I have detailed the contents of the *New Treatise* elsewhere,[24] and so I will only briefly indicate some of the results of Yinshun's research and analysis here.

On the cultural level, he criticizes the Pure Land as unsuitable for China. Sukhāvatī is described in terms of geometrical perfection, with broad avenues that form a grid, perfectly flat ground covered with golden sand, trees standing in straight lines, and so on. One look at a typical Chinese landscape painting will reveal that it represents a foreign, not a Chinese, ideal.[25] Historically, one may easily observe that Pure Land cosmology and practice do not display any simple or univocal teaching that the Pure Land lies off to the west, that Amitābha Buddha presides over it, and that the way to get there consists in reciting or chanting his name. In fact, the complex ideas and practices that can be placed under the broad rubric "Pure Land" throughout Chinese history—that is, teachings about any buddha-land whatever and the means by which beings may come to dwell in one—are extremely diverse, positing many buddha-lands, many other buddhas, many different means of attaining rebirth in an existing buddha's land, many means of attaining birth in one's own land as a result of the attainment of buddhahood for oneself, esoteric practices requiring initiation by a *guru*, difficult and complex meditations, simple invocation of the buddha's name, and so on.[26] Textual-critical studies reveal that the foundational scriptures of Pure Land are not "sutras" in the technical sense of "word of the [historical] buddha" but are later compositions. Comparative mythology reveals that the savior figure, Amitābha Buddha, could be derived from an Indo-Iranian solar deity imported into Buddhism.[27] Scientifically, the Pure Land itself represents an idealized psychological state rather than a literally existent heaven.[28]

As unwelcome as such academic assertions might be to a traditional Pure Land devotee, Yinshun makes matters worse by making these findings the basis for a highly critical assessment of traditional Pure Land thought and practice. To him, it represented a debasement, oversimplified and dumbed-down to the lowest common denominator, of a set of ideas and practices that could be quite complex, challenging, and conducive to the betterment of life in the present world. As it is, the most vulgar version of it, which simply states that all people are incapable of real progress on the Buddhist path and recommends the easiest practice for an escapist goal, has edged out all other kinds of Buddhist practice for the vast majority of Chinese followers. As if to ensure his book's hostile reception, he even went so far as to refer to the Pure Land as "Marxist utopia,"[29] something that, in the staunchly anti-Communist atmosphere of Chiang Kai-shek's Taiwan, led to his ouster as head of the Shandao Temple in Taipei and the public burning of his book (although, as we saw earlier, Lin Qiuwu made the same comparison in a less polarized atmosphere and was not mistreated as a result).

Does Yinshun's plan of reforming Buddhism and his attack on traditional Pure Land in favor of a more socially engaged reading make him a modernizer, or a "modernist" in Lawrence's sense? Yes and no. His historical consciousness led him to understand Buddhism in terms of the various contexts, both historical and geographical, within which it thrived, and this empowered him to recommend changes in its teaching and practice to suit the present context, but at the same time his justification for this reformist attitude was based in the traditional Buddhist doctrine of *upāya*, or expedient means. He was also more than willing to apply many academic research methodologies to Buddhism—textual-critical, historical, scientific, cultural—without worrying that he might be undermining a certain practice or the authority of scriptural texts, but at the same time he was no secularist. He still maintains that the goal of Buddhism is to enable people to attain buddhahood, purify their minds, which will situate them in Pure Lands of their own. His quibble with Pure Land is not really in its conceptions or its goals but with the ways in which it is taught and put into practice. For example, when dismissing the simplification of Pure Land practice into the single, simple act of reciting Amitābha's name, he is not saying Amitābha does not exist or that buddhahood is an illusory goal. He is simply saying that it does not work very well: "It's hard to become a buddha by taking the easy path, and it's easy to become a buddha by taking the difficult path."[30] Like Taixu, he is a mix of the traditional and the modernist, although he clearly leans more to the modernist than did his master.

Modern Progressive Pure Land

Finally, in present-day Taiwan, we find a set of Buddhists who are even more modernist and secularized. If they have taken anything from their predecessors in the early and mid-twentieth century, it is the phrase "Building a Pure Land in the Human Realm" (Ch: *jian renjian jingtu*). However, they break with them in remaining silent on the ostensible goals of traditional Buddhism (e.g., attaining buddhahood) and concentrate their rhetoric on social, political, economic, and environmental activism. Building the "Pure Land in the Human Realm," then, becomes a process not so much of creating a geographical zone in which Buddhist morality and practice prevails as Taixu defined it but of creating a "purity" defined according to the secular agenda created by the individual's main concern: purified of pollution and waste for the environmental activist, purified of patriarchy for the feminist, purified of political oppression for the dissident, and so on.

While several sources exist in which we may look for these interpretations of Pure Land, few are as fruitful as the Taiwan-based Buddhist magazine *Buddhist Culture* (*Fojiao Wenhua*). From its inception in 1989, the editor, Li Zhenglong, took as the magazine's motto "Building the Pure Land in the Human Realm" and selected articles that focused on progressive Buddhist figures from the past such as Taixu, Yinshun, and Lin Qiuwu, and that discussed Buddhist involvement in social movements and street demonstrations. His lead editorials in the first trial issue and in volume one, which appeared the following year, outlined the magazine's stance.[31] Li criticized both sides of the traditional debate over Pure Land, which concentrated on the question of whether the Pure Land manifests here and now through the purification of the individual's mind or whether it is a postmortem attainment achieved through *nianfo*, the recitation of the buddha's name. Both were wrong, he said, because both concentrated on individual practices and rewards, neglecting the social dimension of human existence. The historical Buddha Śākyamuni himself, Li said, entered deeply into human society during his forty-five-year ministry, and worked tirelessly for equality of the sexes and an end to social and racial discrimination. People in contemporary China should strive to emulate these aspects of the Buddha's work, and not content themselves with the search for individual liberation. Much of Li's rhetoric quotes Yinshun closely, even verbatim at times, but goes farther than Yinshun in recommending systemic social action rather than a cultivation of individual charity.

Two articles of particular interest that appeared in early issues of *Buddhist Culture* consisted of transcripts of symposia Li organized, one for laity and another for clergy, during which panelists discussed the meaning of "Building the Pure Land in the Human Realm" (Ch: *jianshe renjian jingtu*).[33] In the course of these symposia, some interesting differences emerged between the lay and clerical perspectives. The lay participants, including an industrialist, a professor of Buddhist philosophy at National Taiwan University, and others, proved much more progressive in stressing the need for direct action in this world and the necessity of systemic (as opposed to individual) transformation in order to realize the Pure Land in the here and now. From their perspective, traditional Buddhist practices for individual purification were too slow, atomized, and uncertain for the needs of the modern nation. Yang Huinan enunciated his position in this way: There are two ways of understanding "universal salvation" (*pudu*). One is "mechanistic," meaning that one gets each person to practice purification individually, and when everyone has done this, then there is universal salvation. But this traditional way of looking at things was influenced by Confucianism, which had always assumed that individual moral cultivation would bring about social reform automatically without any further effort at systemic change. According to Yang, it is not certain that one could induce all individuals to practice and purify their minds, making this a poor starting point. Therefore, one needs the other level of universal salvation: the organic. This takes into account the relationality of sentient beings with one another, and sees one person's attainment as the whole country's, or at least most of its citizens', salvation. For example, the passage of endangered species or environmental protection legislation benefits all of society, not just those who propose and pass laws. This is a "theory of organic salvation," whereby one person's enlightened attitude and action helps to save the many. One who professes to practice "Buddhism in the Human Realm" ought, therefore, to have a care for political affairs.[34]

The clergy in the second symposium tended toward a more traditional construction of Buddhist practice and emphasized the need for individual cultivation and mental purification, going so far at times as to deny Yang's call for systemically oriented political action. For example, in the middle of the symposium moderator Li Zhenglong observed that the discussion so far had centered completely on the need for solitary practice and wondered whether there might be a possibility of working at the social level to bring about change within this world. He asked that the participating clergy comment on this question, and in response, Ven. Yiyu of Fo Kuang Shan rebuffed the request, saying that the individual level of practice is the only one possible. If individual minds have not yet been purified so as to see the world correctly, then social action cannot be of any benefit. When everyone corrects their own perceptions and behavior, the world will quickly transform into a Pure Land of peace.[35] Ven. Jianzheng of the Nongchan Temple in Taipei recalled a trip to India during which time he encountered much poverty and social inequality, but said that he still saw people smiling and enjoying life even in the slums:

> We all felt that the life of the people of India is very difficult, yet at the same time I saw people enjoying themselves out on the street; to look at them they seemed quite content in their adversity. Now why did they not feel *dukkha* [suffering]? Did they not know what *dukkha* is? Or was it that their religious belief gave them something to hold onto, and therefore they did not feel bitter? Did it not thus give them a piece of the Pure Land here in the human realm ... ? I agree with Ven. Yiyu: if I cannot change my own way of looking at things, if I have no true mind to establish, then even if the external world is wonderful, I will have no way to experience its goodness.[36]

Thus, the clergy point back to an older model of Buddhist practice, in which a clear perception of the nature of the self and the world leads to a correct apprehension of reality that reduces suffering to a mere contingent judgment on the world that has no ultimate validity. One might attempt to mount a social or political campaign to help the poor in India, but it would be better to teach them methods of mental purification that will lead them to penetrate the appearance of poverty and see its radical contingency upon their own state of mind. Thus, these two clerics, even though they came from two Taiwan Buddhist institutions that have as their motto "to build the Pure Land in the Human Realm," still exhibited skepticism about the potential of systemic action at the social, cultural, and political levels to alleviate suffering. The Pure Land in the Human Realm comes into being only when each individual sees reality for what it is, and no social program can accomplish this.

I will conclude with a voice from another direction. During a 1997 conference in Taipei, Mei Naiwen of the Chinese Buddhist Studies Academy presented a paper entitled "The Pure Land in the Human Realm from a Feminist Perspective."[37] According to Mei, gender inequality is one of the factors that makes the present world impure. If, in a society or a religion, one gender claims innate superiority over another, it leads to self-aggrandizement on one side and self-loathing on the other, and this obstructs the appearance of the Pure Land. Any kind of discrimination or unequal treatment violates the Mahāyāna spirit of the bodhisattva path. It distorts human development, and is a feature of a male-centered society, not the Pure Land.[38] A historical consideration of Buddhism shows that the religion itself has contributed to this state of affairs. Traditionalists tend to accept the writings of past masters as unassailable witnesses to truth as experienced by enlightened minds, but Mei insists that even these must be judged according to fundamental principles of Mahāyāna Buddhism, including its philosophical position of nondiscrimination and the equality of all beings. Feminist scholarship, therefore, can provide a much-needed critique and corrective measures, which will help reestablish Mahāyāna Buddhism on its original principles, and this reform will help in its own way to eliminate a form of impurity and move the present world one step closer to its transformation into the Pure Land.[39]

While the viewpoints reported show a wide disparity in points of practical application, particularly in the question of whether to esteem individual cultivation over mass action directed at systemic change or vice versa, they all distinguish themselves from the traditionalist views represented by Yinguang and his followers in some crucial aspects. All alike reject the postponement of the Pure Land to the afterlife; their disagreement centers around the question of how to achieve the purification of the present world. They all accept a historical understanding of Buddhist doctrinal development and a willingness to critique past masters as bound by their own contexts. They all stress the need for practices that lead to publicly observable and quantifiable results, in lower poverty levels, improved status for women, amelioration of environmental degradation, and so on. Even when, as in the clerical symposium, advocates of the "Pure Land in the Human Realm" accepted the traditional idea that the purification of the mind leads to a lessening of suffering for the individual, they do not, as Pure Land authors of the past did, accept this as a sufficient goal in and of itself. Rather, it represents a preparation for compassionate action in the world, undertaken with more skill because it is based on a truer view of reality. For all the Buddhists represented in this section, the goal becomes tangible improvements in human society. Whatever impedes these improvements becomes the impurity to be eliminated so that the Pure Land may appear right here on earth.

Conclusions: Persistence, Change, and Modernity

A survey of the situation of Pure Land Buddhism in modern China and Taiwan shows that it is far from monolithic. At the most general level, it divides into the two streams of those who accept modernity without embracing modernism and think of themselves as "traditionalists," and those who accept both but have no desire to abandon religion altogether, and so have sought ways to adapt Pure

Land language, concepts, and practices to the needs of the modern world. This latter group, as we have seen, is quite heterogeneous.

The "traditionalists" represent the numerical majority in Chinese Buddhism. As Buddhist historian Jiang Canteng notes, efforts to reform and modernize Pure Land involved only a handful of elite thinkers and activists, and have never affected the bulk of devotees. In modern Taiwan, as well as on the mainland, Yinguang's Pure Land revival, antimodern in its intent, dominates the scene.[40] Yinguang's spiritual heirs, whom I encountered at the Xilian Temple, fit Lawrence's model quite well as they continued to teach and practice methods for gaining rebirth in Amitābha's Pure Land to the west after death, but showed a willingness to apply the tools of modern technology to further their efforts.

The other side, comprising those who are self-consciously modernist in outlook, was defined by its willingness to subject the past to critique and to attempt programs of change and reform to fashion a Pure Land Buddhism that would suit the needs of contemporary society. In general, they shared the following features:

(1) The figure of Amitābha has become an exemplar of taking and keeping compassionate vows instead of a savior figure for helpless devotees. Yinshun in particular was very vocal in claiming that the real lesson of Pure Land Buddhism was to show all believers how to emulate the path of the monk Dharmākara in becoming the Buddha Amitābha so that they might undertake active work in the world rather than simply await death to begin pursuing buddhahood.

(2) "Purity" has come to stand for the goal of all manner of reforms. For Mei, patriarchy and gender inequality constituted the impurity that had to be addressed; for others, it was poverty, environmental degradation, or other problems. Once these were eliminated by direct individual or mass action, then the Pure Land in the Human Realm could manifest.

(3) Modernizers seek to move the locus of action from individual psychological-moral cultivation to efforts at systemic change. The land does not become pure only for those individuals who perceive it correctly; coordinated action on the part of groups in doing such things as changing the economic system or passing environmental legislation will purify the land in such a way that even the most unenlightened can see the change and benefit from it.

(4) Western influences (especially science and democracy, as analyzed by Tong Shijun)[41] are to be included as ingredients of the program of social reform. Scientific research can provide the means for purifying the evils of the world, and the scientistic attitude demands empirically quantifiable results. Democracy provides a model for the equality of men and women, and of clergy and laity, and, in Mei's case, the kind of peer-review process that enables scholarship to arrive at the truth unimpeded by claims of authority on the part of past masters and classic texts.

Finally, a word or two about modernization theory itself is necessary. One of the great problems that the Western scholar of Chinese religion encounters is the limited extent to which theories of modernization in religion aid in interpreting the data. As Tong Shijun points out, some factors, such as the "disenchantment of the world" and "rationalization" that Weber noted, are certainly present in the history of Chinese religion but cannot always be lined up chronologically with the "modern age." To give two instances, Confucius's dismissive attitude toward spirits as objects of religious rituals, and Zen's insistence that the purpose of meditation was not to acquire supernatural powers but simply to become aware of the ordinary world at hand, can be seen as instances of such disenchantment that happened 2,500 and 1,200 years ago, respectively.[42] The historicist mindset has been part of Buddhism from the outset, with the Buddha's own realization that the possibility for discovery of the truth of things was contingent upon historical circumstances, and that his own teachings would not abide but would change over time either due to adaptation to local understandings or through simple deterioration in transmission. In a sense, the introduction of Buddhism into China at the turn of the first millennium was itself a modernizing influence.[43] Thus, one must exercise caution in seeing the dawning of a modernist outlook based on the presence of these factors.

This chapter, therefore, has looked at changes in Pure Land thought and practice that have surfaced in the late nineteenth century or later. The most fundamental change that has taken place within this time frame, spurred on by exposure to Western science and political democracy beginning in the 1860s, has been in the terms under which debates within the Pure Land camp are framed. In former times, the debate was between two positions called "Mind-Only Pure Land" and "Western-Direction Pure Land" (Ch: *weixin jingtu* and *xifang jingtu*). The first indicated the view contained in the *Vimalakīrti-nirdeśa sūtra* that this very present world could be the Pure Land if only the consciousness that apprehended it were purified and could see it correctly. The second counseled that the present world was indeed unsalvageable, humanity was helpless to overcome its turbidity and engage in effective religious practice, and so devotees must place their hope in the power of Amitābha Buddha's vows to take them to his Pure Land in the West after death.

Beginning with Taixu, the contemporary debates place both of these positions on the "traditionalist" side, which has exerted efforts to harmonize them over the past several centuries and has also opposed them with the modernist view that the present order is not simply given and that the world can indeed become the Pure Land, though not for those individuals who have achieved enlightenment alone. It becomes the Pure Land when society as a whole orchestrates mass movements to alleviate the sources of suffering within itself: poverty, pollution, and injustice. The spirit of the Mahāyāna Buddhist's bodhisattva vow should lead the masses neither to escape from the sources of suffering to the west nor to simply see the sources through the rose-colored glasses of enlightenment, but to organize others for direct action to ameliorate suffering. Only then will the Pure Land in the Human Realm become a reality.

NOTES

1. Bruce B. Lawrence, *Defenders of God: The Fundamentalist Revolt against the Modern Age* (New York: Harper and Row, 1989), p. 27.

2. Ibid., p. 57.

3. See Michel Foucault, *The Order of Things: An Archaeology of the Human Sciences* (New York: Random House, 1971; rpt. New York: Vintage, 1994), pp. 255, 259, and 275, and Lawrence, *Defenders of God*, p. 57.

4. See Joseph M. Kitigawa, "Primitive, Classical, and Modern Religions: A Perspective on Understanding the History of Religions," *The History of Religion: Essays on the Problem of Understanding*, ed. J. M. Kitigawa (Chicago: University of Chicago Press, 1967), pp. 61–62. Quoted in Don A. Pittman, *Toward a Modern Chinese Buddhism: Taixu's Reforms* (Honolulu: University of Hawaii Press, 2001), pp. 292–294.

5. Pittman, *Toward a Modern Chinese Buddhism*, pp. 292–294.

6. Holmes Welch, *The Buddhist Revival in China*, Harvard East Asian Studies 33 (Cambridge: Harvard University Press, 1968).

7. See ibid., chap. 3, and Pittman, *Toward a Modern Chinese Buddhism*.

8. Yang Huinan, "Cong 'rensheng fojiao' dao 'renjian fojiao" (From "Buddhism for Human Life" to "Buddhism in the Human Realm"), in *Dangdai fojiao sixiang zhanwang* (A survey of contemporary Buddhism) (Taipei: Dongda, 1991), pp. 76–86. Pittman, *Toward a Modern Chinese Buddhism*, pp. 170–171.

9. Burton Watson, trans., *The Vimalakirti Sutra* (New York: Columbia University Press, 1997.

10. Shengyan, *Renjian jingtu* (The Pure Land in the Human Realm) (Taibei: Fagu, 1997), pp. 29–31. Pittman, *Toward a Modern Chinese Buddhism*, pp. 226–229.

11. Pittman, *Toward a Modern Chinese Buddhism*, p. 294.

12. Charles B. Jones, "Buddhism and Marxism in Taiwan: Lin Qiuwu's Religious Socialism and Its Legacy in Modem Times," *Journal of Global Buddhism* 1 (2000): 94. (http://jgb.la.psu.edu).

13. Ibid., p. 95.

14. See, for example, the eminent modem Chinese Buddhist scholar-monk Shengyan, who refers to Yinshun's book *Cheng fo zhi dao* (The way to buddhahood) as "the new standard manual for Chinese Buddhism" (p. 6).

15. Yinshun, *Youxin fahai liushi nian* (Sixty years of swimming in the sea of Dharma) (Taibei: Zhengwen, 1985), pp. 4–5.

16. Ibid.

17. Yinshun, "Bing xue da di sazhong de chihan: 'Taiwan dangdai jingtu sixiang de xin dongxiang' du hou" (A fool scattering seeds on a big Weld of ice: After reading "New Directions in Contemporary Taiwan Pure Land Thought"), in Jiang Canteng, *Renjian jingtu de zhuixun-zhongguo jinshi fojiao sixiang yanjiu* (In search of a Pure Land in the Human Realm: A study in contemporary Chinese Buddhist thought) (Taibei: Daoxiang, 1989), p. 221.

18. Yinshun, *Fo zai ren jian* (Buddha is in the Human Realm), rev. ed., Miaoyun ji, xiabian, 1 (Taibei: Zhengwen, 1992), p. 14.

19. Ibid., p. 88–94.

20. Ibid., p. 12

21. Ibid., pp. 17–18.

22. Ibid., pp. 99.

23. Yinshun, "Jingtu xin lun" (A new treatise on the Pure Land), in *Jingtu yu chan* (Pure Land and Chan), Miaoyunji, 17 (Taipei: Zhengwen, 1970), pp. 1–75.

24. Charles B. Jones, *Buddhism in Taiwan: Religion and the State, 1660–1990* (Honolulu: University of Hawaii Press, 1999), pp. 126–131.

25. Yinshun, "Jingtu xin lun," pp. 9–11.

26. Ibid., pp. 20–31 and passim.

27. Ibid., pp. 20ff.

28. Ibid., pp. 9–10.

29. Ibid., p. 12.

30. Ibid., p. 70.

31. Li Zhenglong, "Gongjian renjian jingtu de shehui fuli gongzuo" (The social welfare work of building a Pure Land in the Human Realm together), in the *Fojiao Wenhua* pilot issue (December 1989), p. 2, and "Shenme shi renjian jingtu?" (What is Pure Land in the Human Realm?), *Fojiao Wenhua* 1 (January 1990): 2.

32. Li Zhenglong, "Shenme shi renjian jingtu?"

33. Li Zhenglong and others, "Jianshe renjian jingtu: zuotanhui" (Building a Pure Land in the Human Realm: A symposium), *Fojiao Wenhua* 1 (January 1990): 10–16, and "Shamen tan-jianshe renjian jingtu: zuotanhui" (Clergy discussion— building a Pure Land in the Human Realm: A symposium), *Fojiao Wenhua* 2 (February 1990): 9–16.

34. Li Zhenglong and others, "Jianshe renjian jingtu: zuotanhui," p. 15.

35. Li Zhenglong and others, "Shamen tan-jianshe renjian jingtu: zuotanhui," p. 11.

36. Ibid., p. 12.

37. Mci Naiwen, "Cong nüxing zhuyi jiaodu kan renjian jingtu" (The Pure Land in the Human Realm from a feminist perspective), unpublished paper presented at the Third Chung-hwa International Conference on Buddhism, 19–21 July 1997.

38. Ibid., p. 1.

39. Ibid., p. 5.

40. Jiang Canteng. "Shilun Yinguang dashi de jingtu sixiang" (An experimental discussion of the Pure Land thought of the great master Yinguang), in *Renjian jingtu de zhuixun—zhongguo jinshi fojiao sixiang yanjiu* (In search of a Pure Land in the Human Realm—a study in contemporary Chinese Buddhist thought) (Taibei: Daoxiang, 1989), pp. 168–169.

41. Tong Shijun, *The Dialectics of Modernization: Habermas and the Chinese Discourse of Modernization*, University of Sydney East Asian Series 13 (Sydney: Wild Peony Pty Ltd., 2000).

42. Ibid., pp. 109–110.

43. Ibid., pp. 59–70.

6

Won Buddhism

*The Historical Context of Sot'aesan's
Reformation of Buddhism for the
Modern World*

Bongkil Chung

Opening of the Modern World and Material Civilization

It seems entirely appropriate to analyze the historical context of the
foundation of Won Buddhism in a volume that addresses itself to the
relevance of Buddhism for modernity in that Won Buddhism has
grown out of the movement to reform and renovate Buddhism for
the modern world. This implies that Buddhism in Korea at the
beginning of the twentieth century needed reformation and renovation to be relevant to the modern world. In 1916 the founder of Won
Buddhism, Pak Chung-bin (1891–1943), better known by his cognomen Sot'aesan,[1] attained enlightenment. At that time he made a
prediction no one in Korea could understand that the world was
entering a new era of material civilization. His warning that humans
would be enslaved by the formidable power of material civilization
largely went unheeded. Like a sharp knife that can be either a useful
tool or a lethal weapon depending on its user's spiritual condition,
the by-products and side effects of material civilization have polluted
the air, water, and earth to an alarming extent. For example, the
production and unsafe disposal of nuclear arsenals that can destroy
all the sentient beings many times over demonstrates the way
modern civilization can become a lethal force.

However, Sot'aesan did not hold a totally negative view of
material civilization as the salient feature of the modern world, nor
did he suggest that the world must return to a primitive lifestyle
devoid of modern conveniences. He compared the state of the world

that is materially advanced but spiritually backward to a physically healthy though mentally sick person; and the world that is spiritually advanced but materially backward, to a mentally healthy though physically crippled person.[2] Furthermore, he recognized that it would be impossible to undo the achievements and developments of material civilization; hence, it was necessary for modernity to strengthen spiritual power in order to cope with the unruly and destructive effects of materiality. In Sot'aesan's view, the only way to accomplish this was to have faith in truthful religion and training in sound morality. Moreover, he believed that the best religion for this spiritual strengthening was Buddhism, which had been somnolent for five centuries during the Chosŏn dynasty (1392–1910).

When Buddhism in Korea was still hibernating in deep mountain valleys as a result of the Chosŏn dynasty's pro-Confucian persecution of Buddhism that lasted five hundred years, Sot'aesan made a prediction that Buddhism would become the main religion of the world. He advocated that what should be learned, taught, and practiced from then on was the Buddha Dharma.[3] This implies that he chose the Buddha Dharma from among several religions in Korea at that time as the best means to deliver not just Korea but the whole world. It was clear to him, however, that Buddhism in the future should be reformed and renovated if it were to expand and strengthen the spiritual power of humankind. The Buddha Dharma that he believed was necessary for the world should be simple enough for all sentient beings to practice and yet potent enough to edify them effectively. As I will illustrate, the religious doctrine of Won Buddhism is a syncretism of the religious tenets of Buddhism, Confucianism, and Taoism, with the Buddha Dharma as the central tenet.[4] Thus, Sot'aesan began a religious movement under the slogan: "*Since material power is opening, let us open the spiritual power accordingly.*"[5]

In "The Founding Motive of the Society for the Study of Buddha Dharma," Sot'aesan has briefly elaborated the meaning of the slogan after stating that humankind was about to be enslaved by the power of material things: "Thus, the founding motive of this religious order lies in the intention to lead all sentient beings who are suffering in the bitter seas of misery to a vast, immeasurable paradise by expanding spiritual power and thereby subjugating material power through faith in truthful religion and training in sound morality."[6]

Sot'aesan's idea of "opening" expressed in the founding motto is a continuation of the same idea by two previous prophets, Ch'oe Che-u (1824–1864) and Kang Il-sun (1871–1909), the founders of *Tonghak* (the Eastern Learning) and *Chŭngsan'gyo* (the teaching of Chŭngsan), respectively.[7] In addition to this pivotal idea, Sot'aesan's religious thought includes such tenets as "symbiosis through resolution of grudges and resentment," and the "treatment of all beings as heaven." These were the salient tenets of the two earlier indigenous Korean folk religions.

Furthermore, the opening of a new era was the prediction made by the two prophets, influencing Sot'aesan's idea of the new world as a highly advanced scientific, material civilization. The Chinese ideograph for "opening" as used by these prophets carries the connotations of genesis, splitting of the universe into a new heaven and earth, or creation of a new universe. Thus, these prophets had the vision of the world splitting open like a new day breaking, or the beginning of an early spring after a long, cold winter. The visions of the new world and of the ways of building a new spiritual order were different, although there are some common tenets. This point is clearly indicated in a dialogue between Sot'aesan and his disciples, who declared that "if we compare [the establishment of Sot'aesan's order] to a year's farming, we can say that Ch'oe Che-u told people to prepare the land for farming as it thawed, Kang Il-sun showed people the calendar of farming, and you, our Master, directed us to farm, can't we?" To this Sot'aesan said, "What you have just said is plausible."[8]

Moreover, Sot'aesan recognized the two founders (see appendix for a comparison) as rare prophets, saying that they would be highly respected when his new religion became widely and firmly established.[9] There is no clear evidence in the literature of Won Buddhism as to how much help Sot'aesan received from the two prophets, especially because he took the Buddha Dharma as the central tenet of his new religious order. But, we can properly understand the nature of Sot'aesan's reformation of Buddhism for the modern world only if we take a brief look at the history and some of the central tenets of Tonghak (the Eastern Learning) and Chŭngsan'gyo (the Teaching of Chŭngsan). It should be noted here that Tonghak was renamed Ch'ŏndogyo (the Teaching of the Heavenly Way) by its third patriarch; hence, Ch'oe Che-u never heard of the name Ch'ŏndogyo. Sot'aesan's order was Pulbŏp yŏn'guhoe (the Society for the Study of Buddha Dharma), which was renamed Wŏnbulgyo (Won Buddhism) by the second patriarch. Thus, Sot'aesan also never heard of the name of the current order. We will return to Sot'aesan's renovations of Buddhism after a brief examination of the two prophets.

The Degenerate Age and Ch'oe Che-u's Tonghak (Eastern Learning)

The waning period of the Chosŏn dynasty of Korea in which Ch'oe Che-u lived belongs to the putative degenerate age. Korea during this period was plagued with internal corruption and the plundering of common people by the ruling class of the Confucian elites in the capital and rural areas, and the persistent inroads made by foreign powers against the impotent Chosŏn court. The corrupted government lost its proper direction as the consequence of the bloody wrangling among the factions of the Confucian ruling class. The common people, especially peasants, suffered from the oppression, plundering, exploitation, and extortion carried out by the aristocratic class and the wealthy local families. In addition, there were recurrent epidemics, floods, severe cold in the winter, and famine, so that common people endured great misery.

It was during this degenerate age of injustice, poverty, and disease that Ch'oe Che-u appeared as a spiritual leader to deliver Korean people from misery and protect the identity of his nation. One day in April 1860, Ch'oe received a divine revelation from what people call the Supreme Lord, which advised him to teach people the Eastern Way against the Western Way (Catholicism) that was spreading rapidly amid the upper class.[10] The religious doctrine of *Tonghak* is a syncretism of the Eastern religions of Buddhism, Confucianism, and Taoism, which Ch'oe Che-u thought should not be replaced with the Western Learning. He claimed, however, that the three Eastern ways were individually insufficient.[11]

The appeal of the *Tonghak* movement was both religious and sociological. As a reaction to Western Learning, *Tonghak* was supported by people from farming villages. The ruling class had suppressed the grievances of peasants against aristocratic society until the mid-nineteenth century; therefore, the peasants were able to find expression in the religious movement of *Tonghak*. As the number of people following him increased, Ch'oe Che-u began to propagate his way in June 1861. *Tonghak* asserted that the era had come when the nation should be strengthened and the livelihood of the people assured, and this called for a reform of the corruption-ridden government. This millenarian aspect led the Chosŏn court to view with alarm the spreading popularity of the *Tonghak* faith. The Chosŏn court and its Confucian ruling class started to oppress followers, just as they persecuted the Korean Christians. Eventually, in 1863, Ch'oe Che-u was arrested on charges of misleading the people and sowing discord in society, and he was executed the following year.[12]

Upon his trial and execution, many of his followers hid in the mountains, and for a time, the popularity of *Tonghak* waned. But its second patriarch, Ch'oe Si-hyŏng (1829–1898), systematized the doctrine of *Tonghak* as a new religion and had it published in the *Canon of Tonghak Doctrine* (*Tongkyŏng taejŏn*).[13] The peasants' deep hostility toward the aristocratic class and its resistance to the inroads of foreign powers helped the *Tonghak* movement gradually gain momentum. In 1894, a peasant uprising broke out against the local government in North Chŏlla province, and Chŏn Pong-jun (1853–1895) organized the *Tonghak* army that defeated the government army overwhelmingly. Threatened, the Chosŏn court asked Japan for military reinforcement to defend itself from the rebellion. The Chinese (*Qing*) government, feeling its interests in Korea being threatened, sent its army there and eventually faced defeat in the Sino-Japanese war (1894–1895), thereby giving Japanese imperialists the rationale to put an end to the Chosŏn dynasty. Now threatened by the Japanese presence in Korea, the Chosŏn dynasty turned to Russia for help and the Russian presence led to the Russo-Japanese War (1904–1905), which resulted in Japanese victory. In 1910, Korea (*Taehan* dynasty) was annexed to Japan, losing its national identity, and the Korean people had to endure oppression for thirty-six years under the Japanese Colonial Government until the end of World War II.

On July 20, 1898, Ch'oe Si-hyŏng was executed on charges of instigating the *Tonghak* rebellion. Upon the execution of the second patriarch, Son Pyŏng-hŭi (1861–1922), the third patriarch, tried to straighten out the adverse condition only to face the government's persistent and intensive pursuit. Son Pyŏng-hŭi fled to Japan but continued to recruit and organize members of the *Tonghak* in Korea. In 1905, he renamed the *Tonghak* order "Ch'ŏndogyo" (the Teaching of the Heavenly Way). It should be noted here that Son Pyŏng-hŭi was one of the thirty-three representatives who signed the *Korean Declaration of Independence* for the March First Independence Movement in 1919.

The central religious tenet of *Ch'ŏndogyo* lies in man's ability to realize a heaven on the earth by having faith in and following the heavenly way. Heaven originates in the human mind, and the ultimate unifying principle lies in the spirit of man. The Lord on high, or God, is enshrined in one's body, so that the human mind is none other than God's mind. The most salient feature of *Ch'ŏndogyo* theology is that the mind is heaven; hence, man should be treated as heaven. This tenet aims at restoring the dignity, liberty, and equality of humanity from the deplorable conditions of the oppressed class in the Chosŏn dynasty.

The idea of "opening" that was adopted by the subsequent two indigenous religions of Korea, *Chŭngsan'gyo* and Won Buddhism, was expressed first in *Ch'ŏndogyo*. In the latter, "opening" means the advancement of a new culture, civilization, and humanity based on a momentous unfolding of the universal energy. *Ch'ŏndogyo* divides history into "prior heaven" and "posterior heaven." The "opening of the posterior heaven" means that the past culture and civilization has closed and the new culture for the future has opened. The opening of the posterior heaven means for *Tonghak* a spiritual opening, the opening of the Korean race, and a social opening, through which a universal humanitarian culture will unfold. While *Ch'ŏndogyo*'s soteriology claim is to deliver sentient beings in general through its teachings, Ch'oe Che-u made the steady maintenance of the destiny of Korea the first and foremost priority. Specifically, a warning can be found in the scripture of *Ch'ŏndogyo* against the invasion of Korea by Japan and the West and a strong denunciation of the Chinese (*Qing*) domination of Korea.

The Degenerate Age and Kang Il-sun's *Chŭngsan'gyo*

The *Tonghak* peasant revolution that arose in the North Cholla province in 1894 was a social movement launched by the alienated and oppressed peasants during the waning period of the Chosŏn dynasty. The revolution failed to achieve its goal. Some of the extremists of the low class that participated in the rebellion could not return to their normal life and searched for a new way of social reform. Kang Il-sun (1871–1909), better known by his cognomen "Chŭngsan,"[14] followed the *Tonghak* army and observed the course of rebellion without participating in any battles.[15] Observing the failure of the *Tonghak* revolution and the ensuing social chaos, Kang Il-sun believed that the situation could not be straightened out by the existing religious or human power. He believed that only a divine, magical art could open a new world. In order to attain such power, he studied all sorts of things: the doctrines of Confucianism, Buddhism, and Taoism; *yin-yang* philosophy; geomancy, divination, and medicine; and such occult disciplines as calling rain and hail, and the magic art of transforming his own body into something else. He then wandered about Korea for three years, to find a clear understanding of national and social conditions.[16]

Upon returning to his home village in 1901, Kang Il-sun started ascetic practice at Taewŏn-sa, a Buddhist temple, in Mt. Moak in North Chŏlla province, wishing to attain omniscience with which to deliver the world.[17] He attained spiritual awakening to "the great way of heaven and earth." The news of his enlightenment attracted followers from 1902 on. He practiced Chinese medicine; those who were cured of illness believed him to be a divine man. He gave sermons that he had the great authority to rule heaven, earth, and humankind, and that he had come to the world in order to open a new heaven and earth, a paradise into which he would deliver all men and women suffering in the bitter seas. Accordingly, Kang Il-sun was believed in as the messiah, the incarnation of God. His claim to be the supreme lord of heaven is related to three factors: the chaos after the failure of *Tonghak* revolution; the Buddhist beliefs in Maitreya Buddha's coming; and the rumor on Ch'oe Che-u's resurrection.[18]

Kang Il-sun's followers were mostly the peasants of North Chŏlla province who participated in the *Tonghak* revolution and other people in the lower social classes. He propagated his religion from 1902 to 1909 without systematizing his order. Still, he called his religious work "the reconstruction of heaven and earth," which was the essence of his religious planning. Some of the followers, however, complained about the delay of the promised opening of the new heaven and earth. They frequently pleaded with him that paradise be realized quickly. In the midst of this, however, Kang Il-sun died in 1909 and those followers who were disillusioned at his death dispersed without even attending the funeral, and only a few followers were said to have remained to hold the funeral.

In 1911, his wife, Head Woman Ko (1880–1935), fainted while she was making an offering to her husband's spirit and revived from the swoon four hours later. Thereafter, Head Woman Ko declared that her husband's divine spirit was transferred into her own. As news of this episode spread, Kang Il-sun's old followers gathered around her and an order was formed in 1914. They set up Kang Il-sun as the founder and Head Woman Ko as the head of the order named *Sŏndogyo*. The order's influence started to grow instantly; however, Ch'a

Kyŏng-sŏk (1880–1936), Head Woman Ko's cousin by a maternal aunt and an old adherent of Kang Il-sun, started to divert the members of *Sŏndogyo* to his new order, *Poch'ŏn'gyo*. In 1919, Head Woman Ko separated her own order with the new name *T'aeŭlgyo*.

While Ch'a Kyŏng-sŏk was feuding with Head Woman Ko, Kang Il-sun's followers either left the order for good or started to establish new orders of their own, each claiming to have received Kang Il-sun's religious insignia. Among the many branches, once numbered over one hundred, Ch'a Kyŏng-sŏk's order was the largest in number and power and aroused a great deal of social interest as well as criticism. Rumor had it that his order grew to be so powerful as to purchase one-tenth of the territory of Korea and that he presumed to be the son of heaven or new emperor and paraded his power and authority, setting Kang Il-sun's teachings and authority at naught. Inevitably, antagonisms began to surface, which resulted in some officials and believers of *Poch'ŏn'gyo* breaking away. The order began to dissolve as Ch'a Kyŏng-sŏk failed to enthrone himself as the emperor and his order was wracked by further schisms. The decisive blow was the Japanese government general's ordinance to crack down on pseudoreligions.[19]

After Korea's liberation in 1945, the various orders of *Chŭngsan'gyo* tried to unite their stagnant sects. However, this attempt faced difficulties because of the differences in their interpretations of the *Chŭngsan'gyo* doctrine. *Chŭngsando* (the way of Chŭngsan) claimed to be the only legitimate *Chŭngsan'gyo* order, with Kang Il-sun as their heavenly supreme lord and Head Woman Ko as the leader of the order. Since that time, the religious identity of *Chŭngsando* has remained quite healthy and their religious mission is currently very active.[20]

The idea of "opening" a new world underwent a dramatic change in Kang Il-sun's thought. He thought that he was standing at the juncture of "the prior heaven" and "the posterior heaven."[21] He thought that the ideological foundation of "the posterior heaven" could only be laid with a new syncretism of the merits of all religions.[22] His doctrine contained elements of traditional shamanism, Taoism, *yin-yang* philosophy, and geomancy. The Confucian cardinal moral virtues were highly regarded as the moral ideals, and *Tonghak's* moral virtues were taken as its moral discipline.[23] The syncretism further included the Buddhist thought of *Maitreya* Buddha descending to the earth, *Tonghak's* practice of chanting spells and hymns, and Christian faith in Christ's second advent.

The idea of a degenerate age in *Chŭngsan'gyo* cosmology was tied to that of "the schedule of the universe" that could be controlled by the authority and power of Kang Il-sun, the supreme heavenly lord.[24] In *Chŭngsan'gyo*, the preestablished world is divided into the prior and posterior heavens, and the age when the prior heaven is replaced by the posterior heaven is regarded as the degenerate age. The main characteristics of the prior heaven are extreme inequality, absurdity, and injustice, as was demonstrated during Kang Il-sun's time, while those of

the posterior heaven are equality, justice, and prosperity. During the degenerate age, all the facts accumulated in the prior heaven are clearly exposed and
all hidden oppositions and conflicts come to the surface with extremely violent social tension, struggles, and chaos. This is due to "the reconstruction of
heaven and earth" performed by Kang Il-sun, so that the schedule of the universe was readjusted toward the opening of the posterior heaven. The promised paradise will be constructed in the posterior heaven with all the conflict
and antagonism dissolved.

When the relationship between gods and man is explained, the *Chŭngsan'gyo*
theology separates the realm of divinity from that of humanity, but regards
such objects of reverence as gods, soul, angel, and ghosts as nothing but meta-
morphoses of human nature that is confined in the human body. *Chŭngsan'gyo*
theology holds that god and man act simultaneously, such that if fighting
breaks out in the human world, fighting breaks out also among the ancestor
spirits in heaven. It is believed that what happens in the realm of humanity is
the reflection of what happens in the realm of divinity, and that the situation
in the divine realm is the reflection of the situation in the human realm. Since
the realm of divinity and that of humanity are inseparably related, the realm
of divinity at the present age is in total chaos, and hence there is no harmony
between gods and men. Kang Il-sun thought, moreover, that the established
religions that are apt to quarrel with each other have lost the ability to open
the true path for men to follow. Through his "reconstruction of heaven and
earth," Kang Il-sun is said to have provided the ways to save the world; and
thus, he is worshiped as the supreme lord with the absolute divine authority
to open a new world.

He is said to have called to a meeting all the divine spirits to form a "government of creative transformation" for the reconstruction of heaven and earth.
This consisted of (1) the plan to readjust the "schedule of heaven and earth";
that is, the plan to open the posterior heaven where men can avoid chaos and
misfortune; (2) purification of the realm of spirits to provide the way of cooperation for the unity of divinity and humanity; and (3) the project to give instructions for the way of personal moral perfection, by which to avoid the misfortune
of the degenerate age through the harmonious cooperation with the divine spirits
and participation in the opening of the posterior heaven. One of the salient features of Kang Il-sun's thought is the "resolution of grudges and enmities"; he
identified the cause of tension, enmity, and fighting of the present age as related to the grudges characteristic of the prior heaven, in which the principle of
mutual opposition was in charge of human affairs. Consequently, the universe
was full of grudges and enmity so that the murderous spirits exploded to cause
all the cruelty and calamity in the human world. So, Kang Il-sun intended to
mend the blueprint of heaven and earth by correcting the way of divinity so that
he could resolve the grudges from all antiquity and erect a government of creative transformation.

Sot'aesan's Society for the Study of Buddha Dharma

When Sot'aesan attained spiritual awakening in 1916, Korea, which had been annexed to Japan in 1910, was still under Japanese colonial rule, and Korean people were suffering the consequence of losing their national identity.[25] As Kang Il-sun died one year before the annexation, he did not experience the reality of what he called the degenerate age in which Sot'aesan found himself as a young man of age twenty-five. In Sot'aesan's precognition, the future of Korea was not hopeless. He predicted that the Japanese occupation of Korea was dated, and he was optimistic that Korea would be liberated, even hinting to his followers that they would see the day of liberation. He died a sudden death in 1943, two years before the liberation of Korea at the end of World War II. Sot'aesan taught his followers under the name of the order *Pulbŏp yŏn'guhoe* (Society for the Study of Buddha Dharma), holding summer and winter Zen retreats, each lasting three months. Before examining the content of his teachings, we must see whether Sot'aesan and Chŏngsan (1900–1962) owed much to the influence of the two prophets of *Tonghak* and *Chŭngsan'gyo*, since they openly praised the two prophets.

Both Sot'aesan and Chŏngsan had some connections with *Chŭngsan'gyo* prior to laying the groundwork for establishing the new religious order. In July 1916, Sot'aesan learned from a follower of *Poch'ŏn'gyo* a method of sacrificial service to the spirits of heaven and earth, offering seven days of sacrificial services with some of his villagers. This event attracted about forty followers in a couple of months.[26] Sot'aesan selected eight serious followers among them, forming a ten-member body including Sot'aesan himself as the leader for the new life movement with the center position vacant, which was filled by Chŏngsan in 1918. Except for this episode, Sot'aesan had no further connection with *Chŭngsan'gyo*, though his thought contains such ideas as "opening of the posterior heaven" and "resolution of grudges," which were the salient features of Kang Il-sun's religious thought. For Sot'aesan, however, the opening of the posterior heaven meant the bursting open of a great material civilization, and resolution of grudges was not something that could be achieved by the magic art of a single messiah, as Kang Il-sun said it could. For Sot'aesan, the main cause of enmity, hatred, and conflicts among individuals, families, societies, and nations was resentment, which must only be transformed into gratitude by individuals, families, and so on. Thus, changing resentment to gratitude became the central tenet of the religious and moral doctrine of his new religious order.

However, the affinity of Won Buddhism with *Chŭngsan'gyo* did not stop with Sot'aesan's episode. Chŏngsan, whom Sot'aesan ushered into his order in 1918, had moved from North Kyŏngsang province to North Chŏlla province in search of the right mentor in 1917. Chŏngsan happened to stay briefly at Kang Il-sun's house after meeting with Ch'a Kyŏng-sŏk, the founder of *Poch'ŏn'gyo*, while Kang Il-sun's wife, Head Woman Ko, was establishing her own order. What Chŏngsan, still a teenager, learned from the two founders of the *Chŭngsan'gyo* sects is not known, though it is clear that he did not find the right mentor within them. He moved to Taewŏn-sa to do ascetic practice in 1917, the same Buddhist temple where Kang Il-sun had attained spiritual awakening.[27] After a brief stay at the temple, Chŏngsan moved to Kim Hae-un's house and stayed there offering prayers in 1918. Sot'aesan from South Chŏlla province located him by using his clairvoyance and received him as the new order's "chief legislator of the doctrine (Dharma)" and his successor. Thus, it is hard to argue that Won Buddhism had no affinity with *Chŭngsan'gyo,* though there is no clear concept of *Chŭngsan'gyo* theology in the *Correct Canon of Buddhism (Pulgyo chŏngjŏn).*

Still, Sot'aesan seems to have done what is comparable to Kang Il-sun's "reconstruction of heaven and earth" in a totally different way; he provided the foundation of a new religious order. With his nine disciples, he took a year from 1918 to 1919 to erect an embankment for the reclamation of a tidal land for farming. At the beginning, he was roundly ridiculed by the villagers for undertaking such a novel project. However, this reclamation of the tidal land became a model for the movement and provided the financial foundation of the new religious order he was establishing. Upon the completion of the embankment project, his disciples asked him what they should do when the March First Independence Movement (1919) was underway throughout Korea against Japanese occupation. It is noteworthy that Son Pyŏng-hui, the third patriarch of *Tonghak,* was the first of the thirty-three national representatives who signed their names on the Declaration of Korean Independence. Sot'aesan, still a young man, told his disciples that the roar of the March First Hurray Movement was an advance notice of the "opening of the new heaven and earth," not merely for Korea, but for the whole world. He said: "We have no time to waste and there are urgent things to be done. All the great individuals and great organizations have their historical missions, which the divine truth endows at the right time. Let us hurry up to complete the embankment project and pray to the numinous spirits of heaven and earth so that the destructive energy of enmity under heaven can be harmoniously resolved."[28]

He ordered his nine disciples to offer sacrificial prayers to the spirit of heaven and earth so that their sincere wish to devote themselves for the realization of a paradise on earth could be authenticated, saying further:

> There is an old saying, "One sacrifices oneself in order to preserve one's integrity." There were some who performed miracles by following this principle. Why would not the numinous spirits of heaven and earth be affected if you would not mind sacrificing your life for the well being of all sentient beings? In the near future, a great way (religion) with correct doctrine will be established in the world and the disturbed mind of men will be corrected thereby, contributing to the blessings of sentient beings. If so, you will be the

savior of the world and the hidden merit of yours will be eternal. Hence, you must show your views on this matter from your true hearts.[29]

The prayers lasted for about five months until their sincerity was recognized by the numinous spirits of heaven and earth with some miraculous event. This event is called "the dharma authentication" for the establishment of a new religious order; it can be interpreted as Sot'aesan's way of doing what Kang Il-sun called "the reconstruction of heaven and earth." What moved the numinous spirit of heaven and earth was their sincere resolution to sacrifice their lives for the public's well-being. Sot'aesan laid the spiritual foundation of the new religious order by fostering in their minds the spirit of "sacrifice with no regret and selfless service for the public."

When the dual foundations for the new religious order were completed, Sot'aesan sent Chŏngsan to a Buddhist temple, Wŏlmyŏng-am, as a novice to Zen Master Paek Hang-myŏng (1867–1929). However, nothing is known of what Chŏngsan studied or learned from the Zen master except that Sot'aesan warned him not to read the Buddhist scriptures such that he did not even look at the scripture lectern. Sot'aesan moved to Mt. Pyŏn where the temple was; he built a cloister, close to Wŏlmyŏng-am, and spent five years drafting the essential tenets of the doctrine of his order. The doctrine drafted there with Chŏngsan's assistance has formed the central doctrine of Won Buddhism.[30] Upon the completion of the doctrine in 1924, Sot'aesan with his assistants moved to Iksan County, where he started the communal life with his followers under the order's name *Pulbŏp yŏn'guhoe* (Society for the Study of Buddha Dharma). As the name of the order implies, Sot'aesan sought to implement Buddha Dharma as the best religious principle and practice to deliver the world from the tormenting seas of misery. We can surmise that in Sot'aesan's view neither of the two earlier Korean indigenous religions could be truthful and sound enough to do the job.

Why Sot'aesan chose Buddha Dharma as the skillful means to deliver sentient beings in the world to come is explained by the fact that not long after his enlightenment in 1916 he was introduced to the *Diamond Sūtra*[31] in a dream, and subsequently one of his followers borrowed it for him from a Buddhist temple.[32] Upon perusing it, he decided to take Buddha Dharma as the central tenet of a new religious order he was about to establish, saying that Śākyamuni Buddha is the sage of all sages and that he would take the Buddha Śākyamuni as his ancestral Buddha. However, he did not express his intention to rely on Buddhism right away upon enlightenment, as no one would have followed him if he had tried to edify him or her with Buddha Dharma, which was still a taboo in Korean society ruled by Confucian norms.

Once the signboard of his order was put up, the Japanese government authority tried to find fault with Sot'aesan until his death in 1943; they were cracking down on any society or company that was not overtly pro-Japanese. However, the Japanese colonial government could not find any pretext for suppressing Sot'aesan's order, declaring that it could ably govern a state. Upon the outbreak of the Pacific War in 1941, the Japanese government general in Korea tried to transform Korean Buddhism into Japanese Imperial Buddhism.[33] As Sot'aesan's order appeared lukewarm to their policy, the Japanese governor general took a firmer stance either to suppress it or make it a pawn for their colonial policy. The Japanese governor general ordered Sot'aesan to go to Japan to pay homage to the Japanese emperor; while preparing for his trip, however, Sot'aesan re-ceived a notice that he did not have to go to Japan. The Japanese government general thought that once Sot'aesan was gone, his order would die with him. Sot'aesan chose his death so that his order could survive. He became ill on May 16 and died on 1 June 1943, at a hospital, suddenly dropping his head while he was sitting in a chair talking to O Ch'ang-gŏn, one of his first nine disciples.[34] As the local Japanese authorities were afraid of Sot'aesan's ability to revive, they urged the order to cremate his body as soon as possible.[35]

Sot'aesan's Reformation of Buddhism for the Modern World

With his spiritual awakening, Sot'aesan felt it was urgent to reveal the way "to deliver sentient beings" and " to cure the world of moral illness." In 1924, he held an inaugural meeting for the foundation of *Pulbŏp yŏn'guhoe* (Society for the Study of Buddha Dharma) in Iri City (now Iksan City) and trained his fol-lowers with the newly canonized system of Buddha Dharma. Being aware of the imminent end of his life, Sot'aesan urged his main disciples to finish the compilation of his teachings in a volume, which was published as the *Correct Canon of Buddhism* (*Pulgyo chŏngjŏn*) just two months after his death in 1943.[36] It was used as the order's main canonical textbook until 1962. In 1947, two years after Korea's liberation, the second patriarch of the order, Chŏngsan, renamed the order *Wŏnbulgyo* (Won Buddhism). By 1962, Chŏngsan had the order's new canonical text *Wŏnbulgyo kyojŏn* (the scriptures of Won Buddhism) compiled; it was published several months after his death.[37] Sot'aesan's thought on the ref-ormation of Korean Buddhism was expressed in the draft of *Chosŏn bulgyo hyŏksillon* (a treatise on the reformation of Korean Buddhism) in 1920 while he was at the cloister in Mt. Pyŏn; this monograph was published in 1935.[38] The treatise contains seven chapters: "The View of Buddhism in Korean Society in the Past"; "The Life of Korean Monks"; "The Wisdom and Ability of the Bud-dha"; "Indigenization of Foreign Buddhism into Korean Buddhism"; "Propa-gation of Buddhism to the Public"; "Unifying the Subjects of Buddhist Practice That Are Divided"; and "Replacing the Buddha Statue with *Irwŏnsang* (unitary circular form) as the Object of Worship." From the contents of the treatise, we can see that Sot'aesan tried to make Buddha Dharma relevant to the modern world when Korean Buddhism was still hibernating as the consequence of the

Buddhist persecution for five centuries by the pro-Confucian Chosŏn dynasty. We must bear in mind, however, that Sot'aesan's intention to reform Korean Buddhism was not for the sake of the viability of Korean Buddhism but for the practical application of Buddha Dharma as a means to the realization of his religious aspiration "to deliver sentient beings" and "to cure the world of moral illness." In his view, one cannot be delivered from the tormenting seas of misery unless one is enlightened to one's Buddha nature; and the main cause of the phenomena of the degenerate age full of grudges and enmities was resentment, which can only be removed when one is aware of indebtedness to the source of one's life. Thus, Sot'aesan's ideal person in the modern world is one who is enlightened to one's own Buddha-nature and lives the life of gratitude to the source of one's own life.

This can be seen in the declaration of the order's four religious platforms: (1) Correct enlightenment and right practice; (2) Awareness and requital of beneficence; (3) Popularization of Buddhism; (4) Selfless service for the public. Since the whole doctrine expounded in the *Pulgyo chŏngjŏn* is expounded as the theoretical basis for the four platforms, we must examine the meaning of each platform.

Of these, the first two platforms are the main objectives of the order: the first for " the deliverance of sentient beings" and the second for "curing the world of moral illness." And the central religious tenets in the *Pulgyo chŏngjŏn* are systematized as the means to realize these dual objectives. For the objective of "correct enlightenment and right practice," Sot'aesan relied on Buddha Dharma; and for "awareness and requital of beneficence," he synthesized the Confucian ethics of filial piety with the Buddhist worship of making offerings to Buddha statues. This is expressed in the principle, "Requital of beneficence as making offering to the Buddha." I will analyze Sot'aesan's central doctrine that expounds the ways of realizing the first two platforms shortly; first, I must examine the ways for the realization of the third platform "popularization or propagation of Buddhism," the meaning of which is expressed in a few mottos for the reformation of Buddhist practice.

1. *Everywhere is the Buddha statue; hence do all things make an offering to Buddha.* By this motto, the traditional Buddhist ritual of making offerings to the Buddha statue for supplication was replaced with a new way of being blessed by treating all beings as incarnations of *Dharmakāya* Buddha, the cosmic truth body of the Buddha, which in the metaphysics of Hua-yen Buddhism is referred to as *Vairocana* Buddha.[39] In Sot'aesan's view, everything in the universe is the manifestation of the cosmic body of Buddha with the power and authority to bless or punish. He demonstrated this reformation of the Buddhist worship with an example. An old couple that suffered from their unfilial daughter-in-law was advised to treat her as if she were a living Buddha instead of making offerings to the Buddha statue enshrined in the temple. Following the advice, they transformed her to be filial, changing a hell to a paradise.[40] However, the central

principle of making an offering to Buddha lies in requiting beneficence; there are four sources of beneficences as the manifestation of *Dharmakāya* Buddha: heaven and earth, parents, brethren, and laws. The theory of obligations in Won Buddhist religious ethics explicates how they are the sources of beneficence and how to requite them, as summarized later. In Sot'aesan's view, the Buddha statues have been worshiped for more then two millennia and proven to be ineffective; the new era needs a new form of Buddhist worship that can be of true service to the realization of a limitless paradise in the mundane world.

2. The second motto that expresses Sot'aesan's idea of the Buddhist reformation suggests that one should keep the Zen mind anytime and anywhere: *Timeless Zen and Placeless Zen*. Of course, this is not new with Sot'aesan, but he thought it necessary for everyone to practice Zen. In a chapter of the *Pulgyo chŏngjŏn*, the principle and method of timeless Zen are expounded.[41] Sot'aesan was well aware of the history of different, controversial approaches to Zen practice among different Zen schools. The fact that he adopted and included in the *Pulgyo chŏngjŏn* Chinul's *Susimgyŏl* (*Secret on Cultivating the Mind*) implies that he approved the approach developed through the Hoze lineage.[42] Sot'aesan's point in the chapter reflects Hoze Shenhui's idea that one should take "true emptiness as the substance" and "marvelous existence as the function" of one's own nature,[43] and "concentration [*samādhi*] as the substance and wisdom [*prajñā*] as the function" of one's own nature.

It is also evident that Sot'aesan chose the Zen approach of sudden enlightenment and gradual cultivation, as he says:

> Whenever one confronts adverse conditions, therefore, one should remind oneself of the opportunity to cultivate one's mind, checking only whether one's mind is being attracted to the conditions. To see if the occasions in which one's mind is under control in any conditions are increasing, it is necessary to test one's mind against conditions that are usually loved and conditions that are usually abhorred. If the mind is still disturbed in such situations, one's moral sense is immature. If the mind is not disturbed in such conditions, this may be regarded as the sign of one's mind becoming mature.[44]

If Zen without enlightenment is like the sun without heat and light, as D. T. Suzuki claims, and if Zen monks spend years in remote mountain valleys to attain enlightenment, some serious question arise concerning Sot'aesan's way of Timeless Zen. One can maintain the Zen mind or true mind in adverse mental spheres only if one is awakened to one's own nature. If not, one will be unable to disperse the thick clouds of greed, anger, and delusions that create bitter seas of misery. Sot'aesan's view on this issue is that henceforward enlightenment to one's own nature will be done at home during one's youth. Furthermore, awakening to one's own nature is the only necessary condition for realizing Buddhahood. Whether one is truly practicing Zen at any time and any place can be determined, in Sot'aesan's view, by testing whether the One Mind is cultivated so that one's six senses are free from distractions, as well as whether one can commit to justice and forsake injustice when the six senses are engaged.[45]

3. Sot'aesan took a critical approach on the traditional Buddhist mind with the reformative motto: *Maintain One Mind in motion and at rest; perfect both soul and flesh.* This set of mottos requires one to maintain True Thusness of One Mind, not only in quiet mountain valleys but also in troublesome urban life. It also requires that Buddhist practitioners improve a sense of balance in both the spiritual and physical spheres. By this, Sot'aesan criticized the century-old Buddhist *sangha* system in Korea, reminding one of Baizhang's rule about communal labor, "A day without work is a day without eating."[46] Sot'aesan encouraged his followers to eliminate poverty, ignorance, and disease by having a sound occupation while putting the doctrine of One Mind into practice in daily life. With this set of mottos, Sot'aesan attempted to correct the views of the past that the practitioner of the way should only improve soul or mind, thereby ignoring or even despising anything material, including his or her own body.

4. In Sot'aesan's view, the traditional view that Buddha Dharma can be practiced only by the Buddhist *sangha* in deep mountain valleys was irrelevant to the secular world where it was needed more than anywhere else. Thus, he set up the motto: *Buddha Dharma is living itself; living is Buddha Dharma itself.* While Confucianism provided the norms for the secular world of human affairs, Buddhism taught the relative lack of importance of secular norms, which the Neo-Confucians in China and Korea judged to be evil teachings. At the point of opening the new era of great material civilization, Sot'aesan was concerned with providing norms for the mundane world just as Confucius had, and he advocated the virtues of benevolence (*ren*) and righteousness (*yi*) as the main principles of morality, while condemning trickery and deception.[47] Thus, Sot'aesan sought to synthesize the otherworldly teaching of Buddha Dharma and the worldly teaching of Confucianism, as is further explained later. His philosophical synthesis of the two heterogeneous religions can best be seen in his answer to an avid Confucian who was just converted to this new style of Buddhism. He said, "However, if you end up with emptiness and ultimate quiescence, you cannot become a superior man of the way. In order to practice the perfect and great way, one should be able to apply the truth to all human affairs, taking the way of emptiness and quiescence (Buddhist *nirvāṇa*) as the substance of the way and benevolence [*ren*], righteousness [*yi*], propriety [*li*], and wisdom [*zhi*] as its function."[48]

This synthesis is based on his view that the fundamental truths of Buddhism and Confucianism are of the identical source.[49] In Sot'aesan's approach, any attempt to propagate Buddha Dharma in Korean society could be successful only if the central tenets of the Confucian moral system were integrated into Buddhism and soteriology.

Dharmakāya Buddha-Irwŏnsang

The most salient feature of Won Buddhism is the tenet of *Irwŏnsang* (unitary circular form), which is used as the symbol of *Dharmakāya* Buddha. The *Dharamakāya* refers to the ineffable ultimate principle of Mahāyāna metaphysics and the *Irwŏnsang* provides a phenomenal expression in terms of a circular form. This symbol is offered by Won Buddhism to the deluded as part of an attempt to bring the profound transcendental Buddha Dharma to the secular world. This is expressed in the first of the four religious platforms of Won Buddhism: "*Correct Enlightenment and Right Practice* means, first, for one to be enlightened to and model oneself on the truth of *Irwŏn*, namely, the mind-seal, which Buddhas and patriarchs correctly transmit from one to the other; and second, for one to act perfectly and without partiality, attachment, excessiveness, or deficiency, when one uses the six sense organs: (eyes, ears, nose, tongue, body, and mind)."[50]

It should be noticed here that Chŏngsan is using the term *Irwŏn* (unitary circle without circumference) as another name for *Dharmakāya* Buddha in contrast to *Irwŏnsang* (unitary circular form), which is the phenomenal symbol of the ultimate reality beyond form. And the essential religious tenets of Won Buddhism are epitomized in the unitary circular form (*Irwŏnsang*). While the phenomenal world is none other than *Dharmakāya* Buddha to the enlightened, the former cannot be identified with the latter to the deluded. Sot'aesan, therefore, used the unitary circular form as a sign pointing at it just as a finger can be used as a pointer to the moon.[51] In the *Pulgyo chŏngjŏn*, the circular form *Irwŏnsang* is also identified with "circular emptiness," which is "(1) the fundamental source of all things in the universe; (2) the mind seal that has correctly been transmitted through all Buddhas and patriarchs; and (3) *Vairocana* Buddha of pure *Dharmakāya*."[52]

What is asserted in this description of *Irwŏnsang* falls completely within the metaphysics of such Mahāyāna Buddhist schools as Huayan, Tiantai, and Chan/Zen; for the circular form is nothing but a symbol of *Dharmakāya* Buddha, which is their metaphysical ultimate. Chŏngsan has expressed "the truth of *Irwŏnsang* [*Dharmakāya* Buddha]," as follows:

> *Irwŏn* is the noumenal nature of all beings in the universe, the original nature of all Buddhas and patriarchs, and the Buddha-nature of all sentient beings.
>
> It is the realm where there is no differentiation of noumenon from phenomenon or being from nonbeing, the realm where there is no change of arising and ceasing or going and coming, the realm where the karmic retribution of good and evil has ceased, and the realm where the verbal, audible, and visible characteristics are utterly void.

Owing to the light of [the mind-essence of] empty and calm, numinous awareness, the differentiation of noumenon from phenomenon and being from nonbeing appears. And, thereby, the distinction between good and evil karmic retribution comes into being, and the verbal, audible, and visible characteristics become clear and distinct so that the three worlds in the ten directions appear like a jewel on one's own palm.

And the creative wonder of true emptiness cum marvelous existence freely conceals and reveals through all beings in the universe throughout incalculable aeons without beginning. This is the truth of *Irwŏnsang*.[53]

Notice that this discourse starts with *Irwŏn* (unitary circle) as the name of *Dharmakāya* and ends by stating that the truth of *Irwŏnsang* is the theory of "causation by true-thusness or suchness of existents [*bhūtatathatā*]," a Buddhist theory of causation that explains the relationship between reality and appearance.[54] In Chŏngsan's view, the immutable reality appears as the phenomenal world owing to the light of "[the mind-essence] of void and calm, numinous awareness." And the nature of two realms is the dual aspects of "true emptiness cum marvelous existence."[55] Thus, it can readily be shown that in the "truth of *Irwŏnsang*" can be discerned the essentials of the Mahāyāna Buddhist metaphysics: Nāgārjuna's *śūnyatā-vāda*, Asanga's and Vasubandhu's *vijñāna-vāda*, the concept of One Mind in the *Awakening of Faith*, and the concept of the mind-essence with its dual aspects of true emptiness cum numinous awareness expounded in the Chan/Zen tradition of Shenhui (670–762), Zongmi (780–841), and Chinul (1158–1210).[56]

Now, in Sot'aesan's reformed Buddhist order, the unitary circular form *Irwŏnsang* is enshrined as the symbol of perfection of practice and as the object of religious worship; it is identified for Sot'aesan's soteriology as "the Buddha-nature of the *Tathāgata*"[57] and "the fundamental source of the four beneficences." These two are approached through two gates: the gate of practice and the gate of worship, respectively.

The gist of the first platform is expressed in the section "Practice of *Irwŏnsang*" as follows:

One is to establish the model of practice by having faith in the truth of *Irwŏnsang*. The method of practice is: first, being enlightened to the truth of *Irwŏnsang*, to know one's own mind, which is as perfect, complete, utterly fair and unselfish as *Irwŏn*, namely, *prajñā*-wisdom; second, fostering one's own mind, which is as perfect, complete, utterly fair and unselfish as *Irwŏn*, namely *prajñā*-wisdom; and using one's own mind, which is as perfect, complete, utterly fair and unselfish as *Irwŏn*, namely, *prajñā*-wisdom. Herein lies the practice of *Irwŏn*.[58]

Since *Dharmakāya* Buddha cannot be seen in one's mind until one is enlightened to it, one must start the practice of *Irwŏn* with a firm faith that there is the original enlightenment of *Irwŏn* in one's mind. But there is no genuine practice without awakening to *Irwŏn*, namely, *prajñā*-wisdom. Once awakened, one can know, foster, and use one's own mind that is as perfect, complete, utterly fair, and unselfish as *Irwŏn*, namely, *prajñā*-wisdom. This is the way of realizing the goal of the first platform: correct enlightenment and right practice. So far, there is no point of reformation on the Buddhist practice; for it can readily be shown that knowing, fostering, and using one's own mind are none other than the Buddhist threefold practice: wisdom (*prajñā*), concentration (*samādhi*), and morality/precepts (*śīla*), which are, according to Huineng, the three attributes of one's own nature (*Dharmakāya*). The elements of Sot'aesan's reformation lie in the threefold practice—(1) cultivation of spirit, (2) inquiry into facts and principles, (3) heedful choice in karmic action—the elements of which are as follows:

1. Spirit means the mental state, that being clear and calm is devoid of mental differentiation or dwelling on anything. Cultivation means the nourishment of a clear and calm spirit by the removal of internal differentiation or dwelling on anything, and, by keeping the mind from external distraction.

2. Facts means rightness, wrongness, gain and loss in human affairs; principles means the absolute and the phenomenal, and being and nonbeing of all things in the universe. The absolute means the noumenon of all beings in the universe, and the phenomenal means the phenomenal world diversely differentiated in the universe. Being and nonbeing means: (a) the cycle of four seasons of heaven and earth, namely, spring, summer, autumn, and winter; (b) the atmospheric phenomena of winds, clouds, rain, dew, frost, and snow; (c) the birth, aging, illness, and death of all things; and (d) the transformation of rising and falling, and of prosperity and decline. Inquiry means study and investigations of facts and principles.

3. Karmic action means the operation of the six sense organs: eyes, ears, nose, tongue, body, and volition. Heedful choice means choosing what is just and forsaking what is unjust.[59]

Thus, the Buddhist Triple Discipline is given an extensive reorientation as the Threefold Practice in such a way that it can be relevant for the modern world. Here Chŏngsan explains the difference between them:

You find the Triple Discipline in traditional Buddhism; but our Threefold Practice is different from it in scope. While *śīla* is focused on one's keeping the monastic precepts, Heedful Choice in Karmic Action is an essential discipline necessary for individual moral cultivation, regulating the family, ruling a nation, and putting the world at peace. While *prajñā* emphasized the wisdom emanating from one's self-nature, Inquiry into Facts and Principles is the way of attaining well-rounded knowledge and wisdom on all facts and principles. While *samādhi* emphasized calmness in meditation, Spiritual Cultivation is the discipline of keeping One Mind without going astray from the self-nature in motion and at rest. Success in anything that one does lies in following this Threefold Practice, thus no other way can be more perfect than this.[60]

Thus, the tenet of the Buddhist threefold discipline is revived in Won Buddhism through the expansion of its scope of the practical application in handling world affairs, providing the meaning of the slogan, "daily living is Buddha Dharma itself and Buddha Dharma is daily living itself." It provides also the method of the first platform: correct enlightenment and right practice. Finally, it provides the concrete agenda for the practice of Timeless Zen and Placeless Zen, the gist of which is that when the six sense organs are free from distraction there should be the development of the One Mind by eliminating worldly thought; and when they are engaged in worldly activity, it is necessary to maintain justice by forsaking injustice.[61]

Sot'aesan's idea of "curing the world of moral ills" borrows its force from the religious aspect of *Dharmakāya* Buddha, which is enshrined in the symbolism of *Irwŏnsang* (unitary circular form). In his view, the content of *Dharmakāya* Buddha is all things in the universe, which he categorized as the four sources of beneficences: heaven and earth, parents, brethren, and laws. These are the sources of beneficence because one owes one's life to them; he challenges us to think whether we can exist and maintain our lives without them, and then asks what could be a greater beneficence if our life is utterly dependent on them.[62] In Sot'aesan's view, human existence depends on "the universal beneficence of nature," just as fish in the sea depend on the beneficence of water; this universal beneficence of nature is none other than the four beneficences, which in turn are none other than the content of *Dharmakāya* Buddha. In his view, this is the principle of justice that one ought to pay what one owes. From this, Sot'aesan formulates the theory of religious and moral duties, providing the ground of the ethics of Won Buddhism.[63]

While there are twenty-two articles of moral duties to requite the four beneficences, the essential ways of requital are fourfold: (1) the way of no mind while rendering beneficence to others like heaven and earth; (2) the way of protecting the helpless like parents; (3) the way of benefiting oneself by benefiting others like fellow beings; and (4) the way of doing justice and forsaking injustice like the spirit of laws. One can truly follow the first two ways only if one practices the Confucian moral virtue of benevolence (*ren*) and the remaining two ways only if one practices the Confucian moral virtue of righteousness (*yi*).

While the four beneficences are the content of *Dharmakāya* Buddha, the requital of them can be done only if one cultivates the two cardinal moral virtues of Confucianism. Sot'aesan's reformative synthesis of Buddhism and Confucianism is expressed in the motto: *Requite the beneficence as making an offering to the Buddha.*

Thus, the Won Buddhist way of making an offering to Buddha is not to take emoluments to the Buddha statues enshrined in the Buddhist temples for supplication; it lies in following the essential ways of requiting the four beneficences. Thus, one can put into practice the motto, "Everywhere is the Buddha image, do all things as making an offering to the Buddha," only if one follows the essential ways of the requital of beneficence. In Sot'aesan's view, this is the only realistic way of curing the world of moral ills. In this way, Sot'aesan seems to have provided philosophical justifications for the *Tonghak*'s dictum that man should be treated as heaven and the *Chŭngsan'gyo*'s soteriology of resolving grudges and enmities in the posterior heaven.

APPENDIX: A COMPARATIVE CHART OF THE THREE RELIGIONS

Items of Comparison	Ch'ŏndogyo *(religion of heavenly way)*	Chŭngsan'gyo (religion of Chŭngsan)	Wŏnbulgyo (consummate Buddhism)
The name of the founder	Ch'oe Che-u	Kang Il-sun	Pak Chung-bin
Cognomen	Suun (Water-clouds)	Chŭngsan (Cake-steamer)	Sot'aesan (Young-great-mountain)
Dates	1824–1864	1871–1909	1891–1943
Initial name of the order	Tonghak (Eastern Learning)	No name of the order during Kang's life	*Pulpŏp yŏn'guhoe* (The Society for the Study of Buddha-dharma)
Object of religious worship	*Hanulnim* (Heavenly Lord); man as heaven	*Chŭngsan*, the Heavenly Lord	*Dharmakāya* Buddha (as symbolized by unitary circular form)

NOTES

1. Since Pak Chung-bin has been known by "Sot'aesan" in the West, the latter name will be used in this chapter.

2. See *the Scripture of Sot'aesan* 2: 31 in Bongkil Chung, *The Scriptures of Won Buddhism with an Introduction* (Honolulu: University of Hawaii Press, 2002). The latter contains two books: *The Canon* and *The Scripture of Sot'aesan*. The two books will be referred to as *The Canon* and *The Scripture of Sot'aesan* hereafter in this chapter. When a reference is made to the whole volume, *The Scriptures of Won Buddhism* will be used.

3. *The Scripture of Sot'aesan* 1: 15.

4. See *The Scripture of Sot'aesan* 2: 1.

5. This is the founding motto stated in a page after the frontispiece of *The Canon*. The Korean for "open" in the motto is *kaebyŏk* (C. *kaipi*), which means "open" or "split open."

6. *The Canon*, part 1, chap. 1.

7. For the descriptions of the histories and doctrines of the two Korean indigenous religions, see Chung, *The Scriptures of Won Buddhism*, "*Study*," part 1: 1, c, d.

8. *The Sot'aesan Scripture* 6: 32

9. See *The Scripture of Sot'aesan* 6: 31 and 32, "Since our precursors [Choe Che-u and Kang Il-sun] helped the later sages to come, the latter will venerate their precursors."

10. See *Tonggyŏng taejŏn* (Great Canon of the Eastern Learning) (Seoul: Ŭryu Munhwasa, 1973), p. 33.

11. *Tonggyŏng taejŏn*, p. 8; Yang Ŭn-yong, "Han'guk chonggyo sasang esŏ bon shin chonggyo" (New Religions Viewed in the Context of the History of Korean Religions), *Han'guk Chonggyo* (Korean Religions) 23 (1998): 164.

12. See Ki-baik Lee, *A New History of Korea*, trans. Edward W. Wagner with Edward Shulz (Cambridge: Harvard University Press, 1984), pp. 258–259.

13. *Tonggyŏng taejŏn*, see n. 10.

14. See *The Teachings of Chŭngsando*, at <http//www.jsd.or.kr> chap.1, part 4, "He [Kang Il-sun] was born into this world around midnight on the nineteenth day of the ninth lunar month (November 1), 1871"; Ibid. ch. 2: 19: "Finally I stopped in this Eastern land of Korea, where the Buddhist monk Chin-p'yo devoted his whole life at Kŭmsan-sa in Mt. Moak mountain to my incarnation as a human child. I stayed in the Maitreya statue of Kŭmsan-sa for thirty years. There I gave Ch'oe Che-u the great heavenly mandate and spiritual teaching for him to rectify humanity's violation and open up great enlightenment. Yet, he was unable to move beyond the boundaries of Confucianism to bring forth the true law and direct the ways of spiritual faith and human knowledge to open up the great, unified truth. Thus, in the year of *Kapcha* (the year of the rat, 1864) I withdrew my heavenly command and spiritual knowledge from him. And, finally, I came down to earth on my own accord, as a human child, in the year of *shinmi* (the year of the ram, 1871). 'Sangje' (the Supreme Lord in person), who emerges from the book of *Tonggyong-taejŏn* and the songs of *Suun kasa*, speaks of me" (style modified for this chapter). This work is referred to as *JeungSanDo* hereafter.

15. See *Taesun chŏn'gyŏng haesŏl* (explanations of the scripture of great itinerary) (Kimje, Korea: Chŭngsan'gyo Ponbu, 1984) 1: 14 (p. 14). This work is referred as *Taesun chŏn'gyŏng haesŏl* hereafter.

16. *Taesun chŏn'gyŏng haesŏl* 1: 27 (p. 15).

17. *Taesun chŏn'gyŏng haesŏl* 2: 1 (p. 18).

18. *Taesun chŏn'gyŏng haesŏl* 3: 44 (p. 170) for his claim: "Those who believe in Jesus Christ wish for the coming of Jesus, those who believe in Buddha wait for the coming of Maitreya Buddha, those who believe in *Tonghak* (Eastern Learning) wait for the rebirth of Ch'oe Che-u. No matter who comes, as long as the one person comes, all will proclaim that their teacher has come and follow him."

19. See Yun E-heum, "Han'guk Minjok Chonggyo ŭi yŏksajŏk Silt'ae" (Historical Reality of Korean Folk Religions), *Han'guk Chonggyo* (Korean Religions) 23

(1998): 87–120. According to the *Ordinance No. 83*, officially recognized religions were Shinto, Buddhism, and Christianity.

20. The current (1999) order of *Chŭngsando* has discredited the *Taesun chŏn'gyŏng* (the Scripture of Great Itinerancy) after they published the JeungSanDo Tojun (*Chŭngsando dojŏn* [sic]) (the Scripture of *Chŭngsan's* Way), which is 1,200 pages long, an expansion of the former.

21. See *Taesun chŏn'gyŏng haesŏl* 4: 142 (p. 370).

22. *Taesun chŏn'gyŏng haesŏl* 5: 3 (p. 393).

23. The Confucian cardinal moral virtues are benevolence (*ren*), righteousness (*yi*), propriety (*li*), wisdom (*zhi*), and faith (*xin*), and *Tonghak's* moral virtues are sincerity (*sŏng*), respect (*kyŏng*), and faith (*shin*).

24. See *Taesun chŏn'gyŏng haesŏl* 5: 4 (pp. 395–396).

25. For a biographical information of Sot'aesan, see Bongkil Chung, *The Scriptures of Won Buddhism with an Introduction*: "Study," part I.

26. See *Wŏnbulgyo kyosa* (A History of Won Buddhism) (Iri, Korea: Wŏnbulgyo Chŏnghwasa, 1975), 3, 3. This work is referred to as *Wŏnbulgyo kyosa*.

27. See *Wŏnbulgyo sasang* (Won Buddhist thought) (Iri: Won Kwang University Press) 15: *Chongsan Chongsa Yŏnbo* (Chronology of Master Chŏngsan).

28. See Bongkil Chung, *The Dharma Words of Master Chŏngsan* (Iksan, Korea: Wŏn'gwang Publishing, 2000), *Dharma Words* 3: 3. This seems to have reflected Kang Il-sun's thought of "resolving grudges and bitterness."

29. See *Wŏnbulgyo kyosa*, p. 47; for a description of the circumstances, see Chung, *The Scriptures of Won Buddhism*, "Study," part 1, 4: B.

30. The central religious tenets of Won Buddhism drafted at the cloister were Fourfold Beneficence (heaven and earth, parents, brethren, laws); Four Essentials (equal rights of man and woman, the wise one as the standard, education of the children of others by those with no child, treatment of those devoted for the public as one's own father); Threefold Practice (cultivation of spirit, enquiry into facts and principles, mindful choice of karmic action); and Eight Articles (to proceed: faith, zeal, doubt, devotion; to forsake: disbelief, greed, laziness, delusion). The tenet of *Irwŏnsang* (unitary circular form) as the symbol of *Dharmakāya* Buddha was added in 1935.

31. Sanskrit, *Vajraccedikha Prajñāpāramitā Sūtra*; Chinese, *Jinkang qing*; Japanese, *Konggōkyō*; Korean, *Kŭmganggyŏng*.

32. The scriptures he perused include *The Four Classics* and the *Xiaoqing* (Filial Piety) of Confucianism; the *Jinkang qing* (*Diamond Sūtra*), the *Sŏnyo* (Essentials of Zen), the *Pulgyo taejŏn* (A Compendium of Buddhism), and the *P'alsangjŏn* (Eight Aspects of the Buddha's Life) of Buddhism; *Yinfuqing* (Secret Planning), and *Yushuqing* (Jade Hinge) of Taoism; the *Tonggyng taejŏn* (Canon of Eastern Learning) and the *Yongdam Yusa* (Hymns from Dragon Pool) of *Tonghak*; and *The Old and New Testaments* of Christianity. See the *Wŏnbulgyo kyosa*, part 1, chap. 3, sec. 1.

33. In 1915, the Japanese government general promulgated its statute no. 83, "Rules for Propagation," which aimed at putting all religious activities under Japanese control. See Yun E-heum, "Han'guk minjok chonggyo ŭi yŏksajŏk silt'ae."

34. See *Taejonggyŏng sŏnoerok* (collected writings not included in *The Scripture of*

Sot'aesan) (Sot'aesan chronicles not included in the *Scripture of Sot'aesan*) (Iri, Korea: Wŏn'gwang Press, 1982), chap., 21, pp. 137–149, "Kyodan sunan chang" (The Order's Suffering).

35. *Ibid.*, pp. 147–148.

36. Sot'aesan could not get permission to publish the book from the Japanese authorities; it was published under the name of a pro-Japanese Buddhist monk who was the publisher of a Buddhist newspaper. This edition has three books: book 1 is the only new writings on the central doctrine of the new order, books 2 and 3 are collections of the Buddhist *sūtras* and *śastras*.

37. This edition contains two books: book 1 is a redaction of the book 1 of the *Pulgyo chŏngjŏn*, and book 2 is Sot'aesan analects, *The Scripture of Sot'aesan*. With the publication of this new canonical text, Won Buddhist ecclesia claims that it is not a sect of Korean Buddhism but a new form of Buddhism with Śākyamuni as the ancestral Buddha and Sot'aesan as the founder of the new order.

38. This treatise was inserted in the *Pulgyo chŏngjŏn* of the 1943 edition as its part 1, but it was removed from the *Canon* of the 1962 edition, which is the redaction of book 1 of the former. The treatise in question is redacted as part of chapter 1 of the *Scripture of Sot'aesan*.

39. See "Cessation and Contemplation in the Five Teachings of the Hua-yen" (*Huayen wu jiao zikuan*), in *Taishō shinshū daizōkyō* (Tokyo: 1924–1935), 45:513 [this work referred to as *T* hereafter]; Thomas Cleary, tr., *Entry into the Inconceivable: An Introduction to Hua-yen Buddhism* (Honolulu: University of Hawaii Press, 1995), p. 68, "The reality body of the Buddha is inconceivable; Formless, signless, without comparison, It manifests material forms for the sake of beings. In the ten directions they receive its teachings, Nowhere not manifested." See also *Mo hezhikuan* in *T* 46:75b, "Vairocana Buddha is ubiquitous; how can you say that objects of vision and thought are not true dharmas? This is the truth of neither being nor nonbeing."

40. For the anecdote, see the *Scripture of Sot'aesan* 2: 15.

41. See the *Canon*, part 3, chap. 7.

42. For an incisive treatment of the different Zen schools in China and Korea, see Robert E. Buswell Jr., *The Korean Approach to Zen* (Honolulu: University of Hawaii Press, 1993), pp. 39–71; for his translation of *Susimgyŏl*, pp. 140–157.

43. Shenhui (670–762) in *Xian zongji* 30, *T* 51.458c, explains, "True void is the substance and marvelous existence is the function." Here true void and marvelous existence should be understood as synonymous with the "meditative calmness and concentration" (*śamatha*) and the "insight contemplation (*vipaśyanā*)," respectively. See Neal Donner and Daniel B. Stevenson, *The Great Calming and Contemplation* (Honolulu: University of Hawaii Press, 1993), p. 82.

44. For testing the mind's maturity, see Chi-nul, *Chin-sim chiksŏl* in *T* 2019.48: 1003a-b; Buswell, *Korean Approach to Zen*, p. 179: "If there comes a time when you want to test true mind, you should take all the hateful and lustful situations you have encountered throughout your whole life and imagine that they are right before you. If a hateful or lustful state of mind arises as before, your mind of the path is immature. If hateful or lustful thoughts do not arise, your mind of the path is mature."

45. See *Canon*, part 3, chap. 7, "Timeless Meditation."

46. See Heinrich Dumoulin, *Zen Buddhism: A History—India and China* (New York: Macmillan, 1988), p. 171.

47. See the *Scripture of Sot'aesan* 1: 5.

48. *Ibid.*, 6: 20.

49. *Ibid.* "However, *Wuji* (the ultimate of nonbeing) or *taiji* (the great ultimate) in the *Chou-i* [the Book of Changes] is the true essence of emptiness and ultimate quiescence [*nirvāṇa*] with no selfish desires. The moral virtue of *ren* (benevolence) Confucius taught in the *Lun-yu* [*The Confucian Analects*] is emptiness and ultimate quiescence [*nirvāṇa*] with no selfish desire. The mental state of equilibrium Zisi taught in the *Chongyong* cannot be the silent and unstirred state of equilibrium unless it is emptiness and ultimate quiescence. And the illustrious virtue in the *Taxué* cannot be manifested without emptiness and ultimate quiescence. Thus, various religions use different words and names, but the fundamental source of all truths is identical."

50. See Chung, *The Scriptures of Won Buddhism*, the *Canon*, part 1, chap. 3. See *Fohsing lun* 1, *T* 1610.31: 787a, "All sentient beings are endowed with Buddha nature." See also *Tashĕng zhiquān famen, Taishō* 1924.46: 642b: "The Buddhas of all the three ages together with sentient beings, all equally have this one mind as their substance. All things, both ordinary and sagely, each have their own differences and diverse appearances, whereas this genuine mind is devoid of either diversity or appearance.

51. See Chung, *The Scripture of Sotaesan* 2: 6 "Kwang-jŏn asked further, 'Are you saying then that the circular figure drawn on the wooden board contains in itself such truth, potency, and the way of practice?' The Master answered, 'That circular figure is a model which is adopted to make the true *Irwŏn* (unitary circle) known. This is analogous to the fact that the finger used to point at the moon is not itself the moon. Therefore, the cultivator of the Way should discover the true *Irwŏn* through its symbol, *Irwŏnsang*, keep the true nature of *Irwŏn*, and apply the perfect mind of *Irwŏn* to daily affairs so that the truth of *Irwŏnsang* can be realized in our daily life.'"

52. See the "Doctrinal Chart" in the *Pulgyo chŏngjŏn*. In the *Wŏnbulgyo kyojŏn* (The Scriptures of Won Buddhism), this has been modified as: *Irwŏn* (unitary circle) is Dharmakāya Buddha; it is the fundamental source of all things in the universe, the mind seal of all Buddhas and all sages, and the original nature of all sentient beings. See the "Doctrinal Chart" in the 1962 edition.

53. See the *Canon*, part 2, chap. 1, sec. 1.

54. *Bhūtatathatā* is the reality as opposed to the appearance of the phenomenal world; it is immutable and eternal, whereas forms and appearances arise, change, and pass away. The other Buddhist metaphysical theories of causation are: the theories of causation by "action influence," "*Ālayavijñāna*," and "*dharma-dhātu*."

55. The true void is the mysteriously existing; truly void, or immaterial, yet transcendentally existing. Shenhui (670–762) in *Xian zongji* 30, *T* 2076.51:458c, explains, "True void is the substance and marvelous existence is the function." Tongshan Liangjiè (807–869), in "Five Ranks" uses true void as the absolute and marvelous existence as the relative-phenomenal. See Dumoulin, *The Development of Chinese Zen* (New York: Oriental Book Store, 1990), p. 26.

56. Chinul says, "This is your pure mind-essence of void and calm, numinous awareness." *Koryŏguk pojosŏnsa susim kyŏl, T* 2020.48.1007a–b; Buswell, *The Korean Approach to Zen*, p. 147.

57. *Tathāgata* is one of the ten titles of the Buddha, meaning literally "the thus-come one" or "the thus-perfected one" referring to one who on the way to truth has attained supreme enlightenment. In the Mahāyāna, the *tathāgata* is the Buddha in his *nirmaṇākaya* aspect. He is both the perfected man who can take on any form and disposes of the ten powers of a buddha and the cosmic principle, the essence of the universe, the unconditioned. In the absolute sense, *tathāgata* is often equated with *prajñā* and *śūnyatā*.

58. See *The Canon*, part 2, chap. 1, sec. 3. This translation is from the section in the *Pulgyo chŏngjŏn*; this section in the *Wŏnbulgyo kyojŏn*, which is the redaction of the former, is significantly different from the former. I have shown there that in the latter, the light of the Buddha's wisdom has been dimmed.

59. *The Canon*, part 2, chap. 4.

60. Chung, *The Dharma Words of Master Chŏngsan: Dharma Words* 6: 13.

61. See *The Canon*, "The Doctrinal Chart."

62. *The Canon*, part 2, chap. 2.; for a philosophical analysis of the tenet of "beneficence," see Bongkil Chung, "Beneficence as the Moral Foundation in Won Buddhism," in *Journal of Chinese Philosophy* 23 (1996): 193–211.

63. See Bongkil Chung, "The Ethics of Won Buddhism: A Conceptual Analysis of the Moral System of Won Buddhism." Ph.D. dissertation, Michigan State University, 1979.

7

Abbreviation or Aberration

The Role of the Shushōgi *in Modern Sōtō Zen Buddhism*

Steven Heine

Although karmic retribution for evil actions invariably infiltrates all three stages of time, the act of repentance [*zange*] transforms and lessens the effects considerably, and results in the eradication of wrongdoing or sin [*metsuzai*] and the attainment of purity. Therefore, let us repent before the Buddha in all sincerity, and realize that when we do this the merit-power of repentance not only saves and purifies us, it also stimulates the growth within us of pure, doubt-free faith and earnest effort. When pure faith appears it changes others just as it changes us, and its benefits encompass all beings, both animate and inanimate.

Shushōgi

Sōtō Zen (or the Sōtō-shū) is the largest of the three Zen sects in Japan by far and, with 10 million adherents, stands as one of the larger of the traditional forms of Buddhism.[1] Its 14,000 affiliated temples rank as the greatest number for any Buddhist institutional network, and it enjoys a growing clerical community of monks, nuns, temple priests, and ordained lay leaders. Like the other Japanese sects, Sōtō has survived challenges stemming from a variety of internal and external forces and pressures in the modern period, beginning with the Meiji Restoration in 1868 that caused a general decline of Buddhist influence. These forces included the termination of the *danka seidō* (family affiliation or "parish" system) accompanied by government suppression and the persecution of Buddhist institutions and symbols in an era of increasing nationalism and militarism, as well as the rise of syncretic New Religion movements and competition from foreign ideologies such as Christianity in addition to modern Western scientific and philosophical thinking.

As with the other sects, part of the staying power for Sōtō has been the role of "funerary Buddhism" (*sōshiki Bukkyō*), in that many of the main religious functions include performing mortuary, ancestor veneration, and ghost festival rites for which there is a regular, ongoing demand in Japanese society. Another crucial factor in the continuing popularity of Sōtō Zen is the short, compact text, the *Sōtō Kyōkai Shushōgi* (The Meaning of Practice-Realization in the Sōtō Zen Fellowship), better known simply as the *Shushōgi*, created in the late nineteenth century when the compilers selected passages from Dōgen's *Shōbōgenzō*. According to Heinrich Dumoulin, "One of the achievements of the Sōtō school during the Meiji period that had broad, positive effects was the publication of the *Shushōgi*."[2]

The *Shushōgi* is used in funeral liturgies, but its function and significance go well beyond this role. The aim of the *Shushōgi* is to foster *shūi anjin* (peace of mind attained through the founder's ideas), which helps link theory and practice, ideals and rituals, and monks and laity, and the text thus serves as a centerpiece in the modern development of the sect.[3] As the epigraph indicates, the *Shushōgi* as a Meiji-era compilation puts a strong emphasis on repentance as a means of eradicating evil karma. This seems to be odds with the mainstream of Dōgen's thought, although the injunctive is expressed in terms of the notion of the universality of ultimate reality, which is in accord with Dōgen. Furthermore, the *Shushōgi* does not mention zazen or the need for meditation a single time, which seems unusual, although its emphasis on the role of the precepts reflects some elements in Dōgen's approach to Zen. What was the nature of the construction of this text as a response to various challenges and the need for religious reform in Meiji Japan?

The conventional view is that the history of the Sōtō sect's doctrine has been based consistently on (1) the teachings of founding patriarch Dōgen (1200–1253) that were (2) delivered at Eiheiji temple in Echizen (currently Fukui) province about (3) the priority of the practice of just-sitting or zazen-only (*shikan taza*), as (4) expressed in his major work, the *Shōbōgenzō*. However, a careful study indicates that all four components of the mainstream view of the sect's history must be problematized by giving weight to other factors that were important in framing Sōtō religiosity. Although Dōgen is considered the first patriarch, for long periods he was regarded as no more important than several other ancestors, particularly fourth patriarch Keizan and Giun, the fifth patriarch of Dōgen's temple Eiheiji, which often competed with the main temple founded by Keizan, Sōjiji, originally situated in the Noto peninsula but relocated to Yokohama in 1898. Sōtō Zen has long had two head temples or *honzan*, yet over 90 percent of the temples in the sect's vast network are affiliated with Sōjiji rather than Eiheiji. Also, while many of the writings of Dōgen and Keizan often stress the priority of zazen training, some of the important works emphasize the signifi-

cance of other types of practice based on the study of kōans, the role of the precepts, the doctrine of causality, or syncretism with indigenous beliefs. Finally,
the *Shōbōgenzō* is not a single text but has been collected in a variety of editions.
Its role has often been superseded by other texts of Dōgen or other sources,
including the abbreviated version of the *Shōbōgenzō* that is both studied for content and recited as a key component of the sect's liturgical repertoire.

The *Shushōgi* is a 5-section, 31-paragraph text that consists of selections of
brief passages extracted from the 95-fascicle edition of the *Shōbōgenzō*.[4] This
text was created over a few years in the late 1880s by several contributors or
editors, especially lay leader Ōuchi Seiran (1845–1918), one of the giants of Meiji-
era Buddhism, and it was published in 1890 by the Sōtō sect headquarters. The
Shushōgi outlines the Zen religious life, which is based on the following principles (paraphrasing the titles of the five sections): understanding the problem
of life-and-death (*shōji*) and the universality of karmic retribution; penitence
leading to the eradication of evil karma (*zange metsuzai*); receiving the sixteen
precepts (*jukai nyūi*); benefiting others through a vow of benevolence (*hotsugan
rishō*); and expressing gratitude by means of constant practice (*gyōji hōon*). The
Shushōgi was declared the sect's manual for lay devotion, as well as for monastic ritual, by a joint edict issued in 1892 by the abbots of Eiheiji (Takitani or Takiya
Takashū) and Sōjiji (Azegami Baisen). The joint edict was a major component
of the truce, or hiatus in bickering, between the representatives of Eiheiji and
Sōjiji temples, which were vying for the role of the head Sōtō temple but were
also willing for a time to declare the compromise doctrine of "two head temples,
one essence." In 1876 the first formal Sōtō fellowship, or *kyōkai*, was created,
and in 1888 the first handbook of ritual and liturgy was distributed. Then Takitani
Takashū was selected the sixty-third chief abbot of Eiheiji, although he was then
serving as abbot of one of Sōjiji's main branch temples in the Kantō region,
Saijōji in Kanagawa prefecture (this was before Sōjiji was moved toYokohama).
Takitani was also a strong proponent of the thesis that Keizan was equal in stat-
ure to Dōgen. At the time Sōjiji was a proving ground for ascension at Eiheiji,
and Takitani played a unique role in bridging the gap between the two temples.
However, shortly after the edict dealing with *Shushōgi* was announced, the head
temples severed relations for about two years. This action was reversed at the
insistence of Eiheiji, which had the most to lose in the controversy because it
supported only a fraction of the number of branch temples found in Sōjiji's
nationwide network.[5]

Because of the prominence attributed to the abbreviated text by both head
temples, Dōgen has generally been known in modern times, not primarily for
the *Shōbōgenzō*, which throughout history was largely lost, misunderstood, or
limited in distribution to a highly specialized faction, but for the *Shushōgi*, which
is short and readily accessible.[6] Through the twentieth century the brief, user-
friendly *Shushōgi*, expressing a view of repentance based in part on a response
to the challenge of Christianity during the Westernization process of the Meiji

era, was memorized or chanted by Sōtō followers. The demanding *Shōbōgenzō* still remains largely unread, even in various modern Japanese renderings (*gendaigoyaku*) that try to make the opaque original comprehensible to the average reader. The effective use of the *Shushōgi* is often given credit for much of the success and popularity of the Sōtō sect in modern Japan.[7]

This situation raises a key question pertaining to the authenticity and value of the abbreviated text. To what extent is it a distillation or a condensed yet essential expression of Dōgen's thought, capturing the ideas of the sect's founder? Or, to the contrary, is it an arbitrary and rather misleading summative digest that bears only a surface resemblance to the sources? Should the relative popularity of the text that compresses the source material into a nutshell version be attributed to the "replica culture" (*migawari no bunka*) of Japan, for which surrogates, doubles, and replacements regularly substitute for the original or genuine source?[8] In the Japanese Buddhist style of imitative expression (*nazoraeru*), for example, chanting a sūtra substitutes for reading it, reciting the title replaces the entire text, and gazing at the sūtra replicates chanting it.

Despite the warning of Ōuchi Seiran, who cautioned against trying to understand the *Shōbōgenzō* through a reading of the *Shushōgi*,[9] many commentators concur with Yokoi Yūhō, who considers the abbreviated text an ideal synopsis and introduction to the *Shōbōgenzō*: "With its emphasis on the importance of a thorough understanding of life and death, the need for repentance, and acceptance of the sixteen Bodhisattva precepts, it serves as possibly the best introduction to the *Shōbōgenzō* presently available. Furthermore, its presentation of the meaning and expression of compassion, as well as of gratitude, is undoubtedly one of the finest in all Buddhist literature."[10]

Yokoi implies that in some ways, particularly in its compactness and its emphasis on the themes of repentance and compassion, the *Shushōgi* may even surpass the original in the effect it has on the audience. This view is supported by a recent commentator, Matsubara Taidō, who refers to the *Shushōgi* as the "essence of the *Shōbōgenzō*" in a book titled *Shushōgi ni Kiku: Dōgen Zen no Shinzui* (*Listening to the Shushōgi: The Core of Dōgen Zen*).[11]

Yet the primary function of the *Shushōgi* is for ritual activities, such as recitations during funeral ceremonies, ancestral veneration, and communal meals, a function that is far removed from intensive studies of the complexities and subtleties of the entire *Shōbōgenzō*. Also, the *Shushōgi* does not make any mention of zazen (or *shikan-taza*), perhaps the central teaching of Dōgen, and its focus on repentance seems at odds with much of the *Shōbōgenzō*, in which this theme is treated only sporadically.[12] On the other hand, the *Shushōgi* seems to reflect the teaching of the 12-fascicle *Shōbōgenzō*, a product of Dōgen's later years, although it is distanced from the 75-fascicle *Shōbōgenzō*, which was the main work of the early part of Dōgen's career. The 75-fascicle *Shōbōgenzō* Dōgen is generally considered Dōgen's primary text. Most people who hear that the *Shushōgi* is based on the *Shōbōgenzō* would simply jump to the conclusion that this implies a profound connection with the 75-fascicle *Shōbōgenzō*; many would not be aware or well informed of the distinction between the 12-fascicle and 75-fascicle editions or realize that this holds the key to understanding the role of the *Shushōgi*.

Furthermore, the *Shushōgi* has been criticized in recent years for its apparent endorsement of the doctrine of "repentance equals the eradication of evil karma," or *zange metsuzai*, as a panacea for the consequences of improper or sinful behavior. But does this doctrine reflect Dōgen's thinking, and should he be the target of criticism? Or, should the criticism be directed to the *Shushōgi* itself as a misappropriation of Dōgen? In that case, what accounts for the gap between the founder of the sect and the role played by "Dōgen Zen," or the history of sectarian appropriations and applications of Dōgen's thought, which parasitically selects from and yet becomes a surrogate for Dōgen? At the same time, we must recognize that reading the *Shushōgi* often inspires further studies of the *Shōbōgenzō*, and can help clarify our understanding of the relation between the 75-fascicle and 12-fascicle editions of Dōgen's magnum opus. Thus, the *Shōbōgenzō* and *Shushōgi* are inextricably linked.[13]

Like another abbreviated text that is important in the history of Dōgen Zen, the *Eihei Goroku*, which is a condensed version of the *Eihei Kōroku* collection of Dōgen's sermons and verses that must be understood in terms of the historical context whereby the post-Dōgen Sōtō sect was seeking to establish continuity with the Ts'ao-tung school in China, the *Shushōgi* needs to be seen as the product of its age.[14] A critical analysis of the role of abbreviation in the *Shushōgi*, therefore, must consider several interrelated issues: (1) the editors' intentions reflected in the *Shushōgi*'s textual structure as seen in light of the historical context of anti-Buddhist policies and reactions to Christianity, as well as the ritual functions of the text in modern practice; (2) the patterns of inclusion and exclusion of passages from the *Shōbōgenzō*, especially in terms of how this reflects the respective concerns of the 75-fascicle *Shōbōgenzō* and 12-fascicle *Shōbōgenzō* editions; and (3) recent philosophical criticism of the *Shushōgi* for promoting the notion of *zange metsuzai*, which can be understood as an automatic, mechanical confession devoid of genuine spirituality or moral transformation.

Historical Background

The religious and intellectual life of Meiji Buddhism was largely shaped by challenges stemming from both inside and outside of Japanese society. This was a precarious yet stimulating period in Buddhist history when dangers and obstacles also presented some opportunities for renewal and expansiveness. The termination of the Tokugawa-era *danka* system was a mixed blessing because, although the system required universal affiliation with Buddhist temples, this had been been carried out by the shogunate primarily for bureaucratic rather than genuinely spiritual reasons. Yet, with the elimination of this system, the Meiji era was the time of direct attacks on Buddhism through the policy of *haibutsu kishaku* (desecration of icons of Buddhas and Śākyamuni), or quasi-official campaigns causing the suppression and destruction of Buddhist images that resulted in real acts of violence.[15] In addition, the separation of Buddhist deities and Shinto kami (*shinbutsu bunri*) further limited the power and growth of the Buddhist sects.

Also, the end of the hegemony of Confucianism as the ideology of the *bakufu* was accompanied by the restoration of imperial order and the revival of a nationalist breed of Shinto, which also brought on both legal and unofficial measures designed to discredit and diminish Buddhism through the policy of *ippa ichidera* (amalgamation of sects into a single main temple) and the nationalization of temple lands. These policies were intended to strengthen Shinto shrines and cause the deterioration or elimination of Buddhist temples. One effect was that "[I]n short order the Zen clergy, like all Buddhist clerics, lost all of the centuries-old status perquisites that they had enjoyed, [and] became subject to state mandates regarding universal conscription and compulsory education."[16] In addition, clergy felt the impact of the decriminalization of clerical meat-eating and marriage taboos. After centuries of the valorizing of celibate, vegetarian monastic practice, they were now encouraged or even required to marry and eat meat.

Buddhism was also challenged from within Japanese society by the popularity of the syncretic, charismatic, and millenial elements of New Religions that first began to emerge during the *bakumatsu* (or the end of the *bakufu*) period. But in many ways the most serious challenge to Meiji Buddhism came from competition with Christianity, a worldwide religious institution claiming universal efficacy for its distinctive styles of worship, which offered an alternative vision of religious fulfillment based on allowing the lay community greater access to salvific truth. This was achieved either through the Protestant use of quotations from the Bible as a basis for sermons and ritual life or the Roman Catholic emphasis on the redemptive power of confession. Both types of practice—one stressing the study of selected passages from scripture, and the other the rite of penitence—are reflected in the creation and function of the *Shushōgi*. (See fig. 7.1 for an outline of the evolution of Japanese Buddhism.)

The production of the *Shushōgi* was part of a series of reforms in the Sōtō sect taking place nearly seven hundred years after Dōgen's birth (the centennial anniversary of the *Shushōgi* was celebrated in 1990). During the same decade, Sōtō established its first modern university. In 1882 the Sendan Rin, an Edo academy founded in 1592 in the precincts of Kichioji Temple in Surugadai, was moved and reorganized as Komazawa University.[17] In 1898 one of the sect's two head temples, Sōjiji, was moved from remote Noto peninsula to a more central location outside Yokohama (although the original temple still functions).

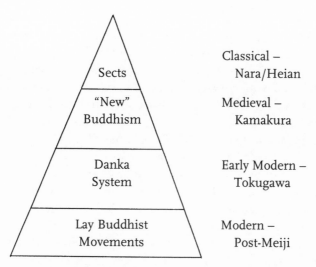

Sects	Classical – Nara/Heian
"New" Buddhism	Medieval – Kamakura
Danka System	Early Modern – Tokugawa
Lay Buddhist Movements	Modern – Post-Meiji

FIGURE 7.1. The evolution, and increasing democratization of Japanese Buddhism: in the classical period, the sects were restricted and approved by official government edicts; in the medieval period, the "New" sects arose, including Zen, Pure Land, and Nichiren; in the early modern period, the sects performed the function of supervising the *danka* or parish system; and in the modern period, there has been a new emphasis on developing Buddhism for laypersons. I thank Yoshizu Yoshihide of Komazawa University for suggesting this schema.

In addition, Sōtō Zen had among the traditional Buddhist sects created the largest number of lay teaching assemblies and fraternal societies—numbering over a thousand—although this also created a need for a greater emphasis on developing an effective method for instructing lay disciples (*zaike kyōkehō*). One of the sect's manuals of the late 1880s stressed the notion of peace of mind attained through the founder's ideas (*shūi anjin*), as the key for lay instruction, and this was considered complementary with Dōgen's doctrine of *honshō myōshu*, or the unity of original realization and marvelous practice.[18]

The Sōtō reforms were part of a widespread effort to restructure and create new institutions as the Buddhist response to the Meiji Restoration. Sōtō Zen, like other medieval Buddhist sects, sought to modernize by extricating itself from the rut of performing the primary function of funerary Buddhism and expressing a sense of self-identity in terms of a global awareness, or a clarification of the role of Buddhism on the international stage, with an emphasis on local implications for the lay community. One of the ways of accomplishing this was through the revival of traditional textual studies and, at the same time, the attempt to simplify voluminous collections into a single, handy "Buddhist bible," as well as to glorify the role of their traditional founders. The Meiji government also required the sects to submit formal summaries of doctrine and rules to the central authorities. The doctrinal summaries that sometimes became Buddhist bibles were often lengthy, comprehensive compilations, but the *Shushōgi* is a condensed scripture preaching the doctrine of confession as a vehicle to salvation.[19] It reflected a new emphasis on propagation of the faith among lay practitioners, who were at once encouraged and hindered by the mainstream sectarian leadership in starting up lay organizations and teaching assemblies.

Another important element of Meiji intellectual life was the attempt of Japanese writers and intellectuals traveling to Europe, such as Mori Ōgai and Natsume Sōseki, who were in turn stimulated by Western travelers and cultural critics like Lafcadio Hearn, to interpret their cultural identity for a global audience.[20] Japanese participated for the first time in national and international conferences on religion and religious education, such as the World Parliament on Religions in 1893. Some Meiji intellectuals who influenced Sōtō thinkers identified five types of worldwide religious experience in a comparative context: piety, such as Pure Land Buddhism, *bhakti* Yoga, or fundamental Christian faith; esoteric or mystical ritualism, such as Tendai-Shingon *mikkyō* Buddhism, popular Taoism, or Kabbalah; nationalistic spirituality, such as state Shinto, caste-centered Hinduism, or ritual Judaism; ethical discipline, such as *Vinaya* Buddhism, Confucianism, or Mosaic/Halachic law; and reason, as in basic Buddhist doctrines of causality and dependent origination and the Western theological rational arguments of Maimonides and Aquinas, among other philosophers of religion.[21] Sōtō Zen thinkers considered their school to be exemplary of the path of reason based on Buddhist conceptions of causality understood, not as an abstract or strictly logical approach, but an eminently concrete experience grounded on rigorous and mindful yet intuitive religious training.

Structure of the Text

The *Shushōgi* is considered a highly condensed form of the *Shōbōgenzō*. Table 7.1 sums up the five sections of the text, along with brief characterizations of the themes of the thirty-one paragraphs. There are two readings offered for these themes: mine, and (my translation of) commentator Matsubara Taidō's modern Japanese version. In some cases, Matsubara sums up the paragraphs by alluding to their moral lessons or by citing key phrases.

First, let us consider how the text was created as part of the Meiji-era process of compiling state-approved uniform sectarian regulations and doctrinal summaries. The publication of the *Shushōgi* was the result of a complex process of editing that actually evolved over a period of seventy years based on consulting forty to fifty medieval and early modern commentaries on the *Shōbōgenzō*. In the 1880s, the *Shushōgi* was commissioned as a collaborative

TABLE 7.1. The Topics of the Thirty-one Paragraphs of the *Shushōgi*

Sections of Shushōgi	
Heine	Matsubara
I. General Introduction	Life and Death
1. Thorough clarification of birth-and-death	Living in the present
2. Do not waste precious time	Making the most of this fleeting existence
3. Universality of impermanence	The ruddy face of youth has disappeared[a]
4. Law of causality (*inga*)	Law of dependent origination (*engi*)
5. Karmic retribution	Feeling the effects of cause-and-effect
6. Consequences of evil acts	Each person stands on his own
II. Eradication of Evil Karma Through Repentance	Great Confession
7. Repentance lessens effects of karmic retribution	Gateless gate
8. Merit-power of repentance	Offering repentance
9. Compassion of Buddhas and patriarchs	Past Buddhas the same as ordinary people[a]
10. Invisible help of Buddhas and patriarchs	Receiving the effects of repentance
III. Ordination and Enlightenment	Children of the Buddha[a]
11. Venerate three treasures [first three precepts]	Three Treasures
12. Do not worship local deities	True faith
13. Taking refuge in Buddha, Dharma, *Sangha*	Taking refuge
14. Spiritual communion—Buddha and disciple	Transmission from mind to mind
15. Other precepts [three "pure" and ten "grave"]	For the sake of the children of the Buddha
16. Realizing supreme bodhi-wisdom	Attaining the mind of the Buddha
17. All-pervasive manifestations of enlightenment	Mountains and trees preach the Dharma[a]
IV. Vow of Altruism	Vow to Save All Beings
18. Bodhisattva vow	Helping others before oneself
19. All are potentially teachers	All are teachers
20. Merits of the vow	Good fortune
21. Giving offerings	Making offerings
22. Power of loving words	Power of loving words
23. Benevolence	For the sake of others
24. Nonduality of self and others	Self-interest and altruism
25. Saving all beings	Vowing to practice the bodhi-mind
V. Gratitude Through Ceaseless Practice	Gratitude by Living the Buddha Way
26. Gratitude for being born as human	Living in the world
27. Gratitude for being born under Dharma	Gving thanks for being born human
28. Gratitude for Śākyamuni	Understanding the meaning of gratitude
29. Selfless practice	Each and every day of life[a]
30. Value of ceaseless effort	Living a full life
31. Mind itself is Buddha	Mind itself is Buddha

The Heine list translates the titles and encapsulates the themes ([a] indicates direct quote from the text). The two lists give Heine's and Japanese commentator Matsubara Taido's readings of the *Shushōgi*.

effort by the Sōtō Fushūkai, a lay organization consisting of over a thousand confraternities or fellowships, which was interested not only in developing a private *jukai* (precepts) ceremony but in dealing with a variety of issues affecting the practices of both monks, or home-leavers (*shukke*), and laypersons, or householders (*zaike*). The latter group of believers was able to demonstrate its importance for the overall growth of the sectarian institution for the first time in the Meiji era.

The project to distill the *Shōbōgenzō* began formally in 1887, two years after the Ministry of Home Affairs' notification that all sects were required to submit doctrinal summaries. The most influential precursor works that were similarly based on passages extracted from Dōgen's *Shōbōgenzō* considered particularly relevant for householders included Menzan Zuihō's eighteenth-century "Eihei Kakun," which in turned influenced two works by Honshū Yūran in the early nineteenth century, "Tōjō Shōshūketsu" and "Eihei Shōshū kun." Prominent lay leader Ōuchi Seiran, an author/editor who had converted to Sōtō from a Nishi Honganji affiliation and helped create the Sōtō Fushūkai, became the leader of the project.[22] Based on reading and intensively studying each and every passage of the *Shōbōgenzō* seven times, according to traditional accounts, Ōuchi created the "Tōjō Zaike Shushōgi," the immediate predecessor to the *Sōtō Kyōkai Shushōgi* or *Shushōgi*.[23]

Ōuchi's text consisting of four sections in thirty-two paragraphs with over 4,000 words remains very similar to the final product. It covers four cardinal points, *zange metsuzai, jukai nyūi* (ordination and enlightenment), *hotsugan rishō* (vow of altruism), and *gyōji hōon* (gratitude through ceaseless practice), which are all related to the basic doctrine of *honshō myōshu* (original realization and wondrous practice). One basic difference is that Ōuchi's "Tōjō Zaike Shushōgi," which is primarily directed to laypersons as the title suggests, lacks an introductory section, or rather integrates the prefatory material into the first substantive section.[24] The text was apparently revised by editors in the Sōtō Central Office so as to integrate some of the concerns of monastics, especially by adding a title for the preface that highlighted the issue of the meaning of birth and death. The *Sōtō Kyōkai Shushōgi*, which was prescribed by the central office as a standard of faith for both laymen and monks, consists of five sections but is a bit shorter than Ōuchi's work, as indicated in table 7.2.[25]

The term "Shushōgi" (Principle of Practice-Realization) derives from the doctrine of *shushō ittō* (oneness of practice-realization, or *shushō funi*) initially expressed in the "Bendōwa" fascicle, the earliest writing included in the *Shōbōgenzō* that is also often listed as the opening fascicle of the 95-fascicle *Shōbōgenzō* edition, although it is not contained in either the 75-fascicle *Shōbōgenzō* or 12-fascicle *Shōbōgenzō* editions. As recorded in "Bendōwa," in response to a question about whether one should practice zazen in order to attain a realization of the Buddha Dharma, Dōgen argues:

To suppose that practice-realization [*shushō*] are not one is the view of a non-Buddhist. In the Buddha Dharma, practice-realization are one [*shushō ittō*]. Because practice right now is practice-realization, the practice of the mind first [aroused to seek realization] is the whole body of original realization. . . . Because this is the realization of practice, realization is limitless. Because this is the practice of realization, practice is beginningless.[26]

The doctrine of *shushō ittō* is often explained by many commentators as being more or less identical to the notion of the unity of original realization and marvelous practice (*honshō myōshū*).[27] Based on the importance of this doctrine, most commentators suggest a threefold division of the *Shushōgi* as indicated in table 7.2: (1) "Preface," or an introductory section added to Ōuchi's original work; (2) "Honshō" (Original Realization), which includes the second and third sections on the spiritual rewards of repentance and precepts based on the primordial Buddha-nature; and (3) "Myōshu" (Wondrous Practice), which includes the last two sections on the priority of altruism and the need for constant effort to perpetuate original realization.

Relation to the *Shōbōgenzō*

The message about the identity and ideology of Zen that the framers of the *Shushōgi* apparently sought to convey highlighted a dimension of religious experience based on reason (*dōri*), which may be consistent with the thought of Dōgen.[28] But does the *Shushōgi* represent the essence of the much longer and more substantial *Shōbōgenzō*? Or is it a streamlined version of the source material that shifts the priorities of Dōgen's philosophy, which stresses zazen training under a true master, to a focus on the rituals of precepts and repentance primarily intended for laypersons in accord with the concerns of the Meiji era?

TABLE 7.2. The Length in Paragraphs and Word Count of the *Shushōgi*, along with the Three Thematic Divisions

Section	Paragraphs/ sentences	Word count	Division
1	6/16	667	Preface
2	4/7	388	Honshō
3	7/18	897	"Shushō ittō or Shushō funi"
4	8/20	994	Myōshū
5	6/21	758	
Total 5	31/82	3,704	

Understanding the philosophy of the *Shushōgi* requires that one clarify how it is linked to the multiple versions of the *Shōbōgenzō*. What is the *Shōbōgenzō* in the first place, and which version does the *Shushōgi* reflect? Although many commentators continue to echo a fallacious idea that the *Shushōgi* contains passages from each and every one of the ninety-five *Shōbōgenzō* fascicles, this has been shown to be completely off base.[29] In fact, the *Shushōgi* cites just twenty-four fascicles, and the great majority of these are from the 12-fascicle *Shōbōgenzō*.[30]

The first step in the analysis is to recognize the existence of multiple editions: The *Shōbōgenzō* is a text published in numerous versions with differing numbers of fascicles that are grouped together based on apparently diverging aims and ideological foci. Which editions, or which portion of them, does the *Shushōgi* best reflect? At the time of the composition of the *Shushōgi*, the main, if not only, version consulted was the 95-fascicle *Shōbōgenzō*, a compilation of all of the available fascicles first published in 1691. The 75-fascicle *Shōbōgenzō* of the early, pre-1246 period (before the change of the name of Daibutsuji temple to Eiheiji) that was first compiled and commented on by Senne and Kyōgō shortly after Dōgen's death was well-known. But by the Meiji it was generally studied out of the context of the longer edition. The 12-fascicle *Shōbōgenzō* of the later, post-1248 period (after Dōgen returned to Eiheiji from a trip to Kamakura) was long rumored to exist. But it was not verified as an independent text until the discovery of an obscure manuscript in 1930 certified its status. The fascicles contained in both the 75-fascicle and 12-fascicle *Shōbōgenzō* editions, along with eight other fascicles, had been incorporated into the 95-fascicle *Shōbōgenzō* (a 92-fascicle edition eliminates three supplementary fascicles).

The *Shushōgi* seems to have a special affinity with the controversial 12-fascicle *Shōbōgenzō*, which has in recent years received considerable criticism, as well as praise, in some quarters for its emphasis on the inexorability of karmic causality and the value of repentance. The *Shushōgi* appears to have a far less important connection with the 75-fascicle *Shōbōgenzō*, known for its emphasis on metaphysical issues such as time, language, and Buddha-nature, although these topics are addressed. Perhaps the framers of the *Shushōgi* were either not clear or somewhat disingenuous about their aims in relation to the various versions of the *Shōbōgenzō*. In any case, their emphasis on the 12-fascicle *Shōbōgenzō* highlights the period of the late Dōgen, especially the final section of this period, which can be referred to as the late late Dōgen.

The impression given by the *Shushōgi* and the role it plays in contemporary Sōtō practice seems to diverge from Dōgen's works in several respects. The *Shushōgi*'s emphasis on repentance and the precepts, rather than on zazen, does not seem to convey the doctrine of *shushō ittō*—a term not even mentioned in the body of the text. *Shushō ittō* emphasizes meditation as the continuing practice (*shu*) of monks that leads to realization (*shō*) in a manner consistent with the 75-fascicle *Shōbōgenzō*. Rather, it expresses the notion of *zen-kai itchi* (oneness of Zen and the precepts), which highlights the role of the moral discipline of laypersons consistent with some aspects of the 12-fascicle *Shōbōgenzō* (which in other ways is a text designed for entry-level monastics). However, the *Shushōgi* focuses on a couple of aspects of the 12-fascicle *Shōbōgenzō* teaching, and gives a primacy to a particular line of interpretation by emphasizing *zange metsuzai* that does not appear in the source text.

An analysis of the contents of the *Shushōgi* indicates that there are a number of references to the 75-fascicle *Shōbōgenzō* concerning a variety of doctrines evoking the nonduality of self and others, including the "one mind" or "mind itself is Buddha" (*sokushin zebutsu*) (paragraph 31); the equality of Buddha-nature encompassing men and women as well as all social classes in "Raihaito-kuzui" (no. 19); and an imperative for constant practice (*gyōji*), although this is not expressed in terms of zazen but a more vague evocation of "daily Buddhist training" (no. 30). Another reference in paragraphs 8 and 9 is to the 75-fascicle *Shōbōgenzō* "Keisei sanshoku," yet this is the passage from the anomalous, concluding section of the fascicle that emphasizes repentance in a way that recalls the 12-fascicle *Shōbōgenzō*.

Other *Shushōgi* passages cite fascicles from the 95-fascicle *Shōbōgenzō* (that is, fascicles not contained in either the 75-fascicle or 12-fascicle *Shōbōgenzō* editions). These include the unity of practice-realization and the all-pervasive, dynamic universality of enlightenment as in "Bendōwa" (no. 17); and the inseparability of life and death in "Shōji" (no. 1). However, most of the 95-fascicle *Shōbōgenzō* citations deal with devotional themes of veneration, offerings, benevolence, and loving words in "Bodaisatta shishōbō" (nos. 21–24), which recalls the 12-fascicle *Shōbōgenzō*.

A more detailed examination, illustrated in tables 7.3 and 7.4 showing the probable sources for the *Shushōgi* (although in some instances the specific *Shōbōgenzō* fascicle is unclear), more vividly demonstrates the text's reliance on the 12-fascicle edition.[31] Table 7.3 lists the sources of each paragraph.

The numbers demonstrate that the *Shushōgi* is, if anything, a distillation of the 12-fascicle *Shōbōgenzō* in its doctrines of causality and repentance. The great majority of *Shushōgi* passages are extracted from the 12-fascicle *Shōbōgenzō* dealing with the topics of causality (*inga*) and the impact of karma and the effect of retribution extending through three (current, next, and future) lives (*sanjigo*) (especially nos. 1 and 4).[32] These themes are treated in a way that resembles the Āgama (J. *Agonkyō*) literature of primal Buddhism (*genshi Bukkyō*). Other *Shushōgi* passages taken from the 12-fascicle *Shōbōgenzō* include "thou shalt not" prohibitions and admonitions to adhere to the sixteen precepts or *jukai*, including the three treasures, three pure precepts, and ten grave prohibitions, as enunciated in the "Kiesanbō" and "Jukai" fascicle (nos. 11 and 15), the doctrine of the veneration of buddhas (*kuyō shobutsu*) (no. 11) accompanied by a repudiation of local divinities (no. 12), and the notions of arousing the bodhi-mind (*hotsubodaishin*) (no. 16) and reciprocal spiritual

TABLE 7.3. *Shushōgi* sources by Paragraph

Paragraph	Source	Fascicle
1.1	95-SH	Shōji
1.2	12-SH	Kiesanbō
1.3	12-SH	Shukke kudoku
1.4	12-SH	Jinshin inga
1.5	12-SH	Sanjigo
1.6	12-SH	Sanjigo
2.7	12-SH	Sanjigo
2.8	75-SH	Keisei sanshoku
2.9	75-SH	Keisei sanshoku
2.10	other	[Kegon Kyō]
3.11	12-SH	Kiesanbō
3.12	12-SH	Kiesanbō
3.13	12-SH	Kiesanbō
3.14	12-SH	Kiesanbō
3.15	12-SH	Jukai
3.16	12-SH	Shukke kudoku
3.17	95-SH	Bendōwa
4.18	12-SH	Hotsubodaishin
4.19	75-SH	Raihaitokuzui
4.20	12-SH	Hotsubodaishin
4.21	95-SH	Bodaisatta shishōbō
4.22	95-SH	Bodaisatta shishōbō
4.23	95-SH	Bodaisatta shishōbō
4.24	95-SH	Bodaisatta shishōbō
4.25	75-SH	Raihaitokuzui
5.26	12-SH	Hotsubodaishin
5.27	75-SH	Raihaitokuzui
5.28	75-SH	Gyōji , part 2
5.29	75-SH	Gyōji, part 2
5.30	75-SH	Gyōji, part 1
5.31	75-SH	Sokushin zebutsu

SH indicates *Shōbōgenzō*.

communion (*kannō dōkō*) (no. 14), along with the basic virtues of compassion, loving words, and benevolence.

The basic orientation and scriptural reliance of the *Shushōgi* is surprising because, although they had studied the fascicles contained in the 12-fascicle *Shōbōgenzō* since these were all part of the 95-fascicle *Shōbōgenzō*, the *Shushōgi* framers were unaware, or at least uncertain, of its status as a separate, independent edition. The 12-fascicle *Shōbōgenzō* originally stemmed from the latest period in Dōgen's life, following his return from what was probably a disappointing eight-month visit to the temporary capital in Kamakura of the new shogun, Hōjō Tokiyori in 1247–1248. It expresses a unique ideology based on causality and repentance that is at once somewhat consistent—as in the notion of the nonduality of self-others (*seishin seii*)—and yet to a great extent at odds with the 75-fascicle *Shōbōgenzō*.

Another way of clarifying the relation of the *Shushōgi* to the editions of the *Shōbōgenzō* is by comparing the *Shushōgi* with a successor text, the *Shōbōgi*, created by Nakabata Gidō in 1952 (Sendai: Shōdenan) to mark the 700th anniversary of Dōgen's death. The *Shōbōgi* was an attempt to rewrite and reorient the *Shushōgi* in terms of the needs of monks and the importance of zazen meditation. It consists of five sections: Preface (5 paragraphs, 851 words); True Faith in the True Dharma (5, 848); Learning the Way Through Body-Mind (7, 1136); Original Realization and Marvelous Practice (6, 964); and Just-Sitting (Shikantaza, 7, 992) (Total = 30, 4,791).[33] It is clear that the *Shōbōgi* was designed as a remedy for the *Shushōgi* by culminating in an emphasis on zazen meditation rather than ignoring it.

According to Fukase Shunji, Ōuchi's text, the *Zaike Shushōgi*, focuses on precepts for laypersons while assuming the role of zazen for monks; the *Shushōgi* focuses on precepts for laypersons and for monks; and the *Shōbōgi* focuses on zazen for laypersons and monks. The *Shōbōgi*, which was influenced by the *Dōgen Zenji Shōkun* (1924), mainly cites "Bendōwa" (fourteen times), with "Gyōji" (four times) in second place; the predecessor text cites "Bendōwa" twelve times and "Busshō" eight times. Fukase's analysis is shown in Table 7.5.

The Eradication of Evil Through Repentance

The key issue in understanding the *Shushōgi*'s relation to the *Shōbōgenzō* is not just that it focuses on repentance, because there is some consistency in that this topic appears in both the 75-fascicle *Shōbōgenzō* "Keisei sanshoku" as well as

TABLE 7.4. The Total Figures for *Shushōgi* Sources by Paragraph

Shushōgi sources	Number of paragraphs/number of sentences	
12-*Shōbōgenzō*	15	(Kiesanbō-5, Sanjigo-3, Hotsubodaishin-3, Shukke kudoku-2, Jinshin inga-1, Jukai-1)/34 (Kiesanbō-12, Hotsubodaishin-7, Shukke kudoku-6, Sanjigo-4, Jukai-3, Kesa kudoku-1, Jinshin inga-1)
75-*Shōbōgenzō*	9	(Raihaitokuzui-3, Keisei sanshoku-2, Gyōji 2–2, Gyōji 1–1, Sokushin zebutsu-1)/32 (Keisei sanshoku-8, Gyōji 1–6, Gyōji 2–5, Raihaitokuzui-5, Kenbutsu-2, Shoaku makusa-1, Immo-1, Makahannyaparamitsu-1, Bukkyō-1, Osakusendaba-1, Sokushin zebutsu-1)
95-*Shōbōgenzō*	6	(Bodaisatta shishōbō-4, Shōji-1, Bendōwa-1)/13 (Bodaisatta shishōbō-6, Bendōwa-2, Shōji-2, Jūundōshiki-1, Dōshin-1, Bussoshōden bosatsu-1
non-*Shōbōgenzō*	1	(Kegon Kyō)/3 (Kegon Kyō-1, grammatical constructions-2)

TABLE 7.5. Comparison of the Themes in Three Texts

Text	Audience	Practice	Source
Zaike Shushōgi	[Monks	Zazen]	12-Shōbōgenzō
	Lay	Precepts	
Shushōgi	Monks	Precepts	12-Shōbōgenzō
	Lay	Precepts	
Shōbōgi	Monks	Zazen	75-Shōbōgenzō
	Lay	Zazen	

Brackets indicate unexpressed tendency of the text.

the 12-fascicle *Shōbōgenzō* "Sanjigo." Rather, the point is that the *Shushōgi* emphasizes a specific and perhaps rather extreme approach to repentance, that is, the notion of the eradication or elimination of sins, transgressions, or defilements according to the notion of *zange metsuzai*. This phrase, which is used as the title of the second section, was never mentioned in Dōgen's writings. It does not even appear in the 12-fascicle *Shōbōgenzō*, although it seems to highlight a tendency of thought in that text. The *Shushōgi*'s use of the term has become the target of criticism in the recent debate over Critical Buddhism, a new methodological movement that emphasizes social reform. Critical Buddhism has charged that Buddhism fosters problems of social injustice, ethnic discrimination, and nationalism/militarism, in that the basic notion of original enlightenment proclaims a false sense of equality on the absolute level while allowing conflicts based on inequities and hierarchical distinctions to be perpetuated on the everyday level.[34] According to the Critical Buddhist approach, *Shushōgi* and other Zen texts are problematic because they endorse a viewpoint of original purity and presume that all transgressions, including those committed by Buddhists, as in discrimination against untouchables or *burakumin* in funerals and other ceremonies, can be wiped clean through the attainment of a state of formlessness.[35]

Dōgen is known for stressing that the realization of authentic spiritual attainment requires going beyond the ritualization of repentance, as when he cites his mentor Ju-ching's utterance in "Bendōwa": "To study Zen is to cast off body-mind. It is not burning incense, worship, recitation of Amida's name, repentant practice (*shū-zan*), or reading sūtras, but the singleminded practice of zazen-only."[36] But what is Dōgen's view on confessing, forgiving, and overcoming misdeeds? Some aspects of Dōgen's approach suggest a stern, puritanical, and unforgiving attitude consistent with the earliest Zen Buddhist monastic rules text attributed to Pai-chang, the *Ch'an-men Kuei-shih* (J. *Zenmon Kishiki*), which threatens banishment and excommunication even for minor offenses.[37] For example, Dōgen's biography, the *Kenzeiki*, records the case of the Gemmyō incident when Dōgen dismissed and expelled a monk he suspected of corrupt behavior by having his seat in the meditation hall dug up and removed.[38] This seems at odds with the message of "Shushōgi," which supports repentance in a conventional, ritualistic sense.

The *Shushōgi* view, in turn, seems to stand in contrast, or even opposition, to the emphasis on "formless" repentance in the *Platform Sūtra* attributed to sixth patriarch Hui-neng.[39] According to the *Platform Sūtra*, there is no need for confession of specific sins (*ji-zange*) when one realizes the primordial state of the formless purity that is untainted and free of defilement. On the other hand, the messages of the *Shushōgi* and the *Platform Sūtra* can also be seen as converging in that both seem to provide a rationale that vitiates the need for a systematic approach to *ji-zange* confession. According to the *Shushōgi*: "If you repent in the manner described, you will invariably receive the invisible assistance of the buddhas and patriarchs. Keeping this in your mind and following the rules for your bodily behavior, you must repent before the buddhas whose power will lead to the elimination of the causes of wrongdoing at their roots." This passage emphasizes the virtue of repentance in transforming evil deeds based on the power of forgiveness and the compassion of buddhas, which "you will invariably receive." It appears close to a mythological, supernatural perspective but still requires some degree of self-discipline and meditative training. Yet, like the *Platform Sūtra*, the *Shushōgi* suggests that wrongdoing can be fully eliminated and a state of sinlessness attained. In other words, both the *Platform Sūtra*'s notion of the nonproduction of karma and the *Shushōgi*'s notion of the destruction of evil karma (*metsuzai*) imply that ultimate human nature (or Buddhanature or original enlightenment, *hongaku*) remains untainted and unaffected by the effects of evil actions. The underlying ethical problem is that by giving priority to transcendence these approaches may overlook some of the unintended consequences that arise from a decreased emphasis on recognizing and feeling remorse and repentance for actual wrongdoings in the phenomenal realm of karmic causality. For Critical Buddhism, this sense of facile confession gives rise to immoral tendencies that derive from the doctrine of original enlightenment that claims the inherent moral purity of all beings. This tendency is a consequence of Dōgen Zen rather than the thought of Dōgen himself.[40]

Furthermore, the *Shushōgi*'s view of *zange metsuzai*, which implies the purification of evil karma through the power of forgiveness of compassionate buddhas, bodhisattvas, and patriarchs, can be distinguished from the notion of *zangedō*, generally translated as "repentance" or "metanoesis," to borrow the term that forms the center of Tanabe Hajime's postwar philosophy, which implies a personal, existential struggle with one's sense of wrongdoing.[41] *Zangedō* can also

be referred to as self-reflection and self-criticism (*jigo hihan*). Ironically, the
Shushōgi text created by culling and editing Dōgen's Zen sayings seems to suggest a mechanical and devotional model of repentance, whereas Tanabe's Pure
Land approach appears more individualistic and intuitive (keeping in mind that
his message was directed to the nation and particularly his fellow philosophers,
whose prewar writings contributed to a militarist ideology that suffered defeat
and humiliation in the war). The distinction between *zange metsuzai* and *zangedō*
can also be used to encompass a distinction between repentance *toward* Buddhism due to preceptual transgressions and repentance *for* Buddhism because
of its wrongdoings vis-à-vis society at large. For Critical Buddhism, this distinction also epitomizes the discrepancy between the concerns of Dōgen's philosophy, which is characterized by authentic self-criticism (*zangedō*), and those of
Dōgen Zen, which in seeking to popularize and evangelize a dimension of Dōgen
(*zange metsuzai*) ends in distorting his essential teaching.

Concluding Comments on the Distillation of Dōgen

There are two issues involved in analyzing this question of whether the *Shushōgi*
is a distillation of Dōgen? The hermeneutic issue is, is Dōgen distillable? And
the historical question is, if so, is it in the manner that would or could result in
the production of this text? The first issue raises the question of whether the
notion of distillation is in keeping with or in violation of the spirit of Dōgen's
teaching. Although Dōgen seems to be a proponent of speech over silence, or
of expressing the Dharma through discourse rather than abandoning the scriptures, his writings suggest a flexible standpoint that does not prohibit abbreviation. In principle, the sense of abbreviation represented by the *Shushōgi* does
not stand in opposition to Dōgen. However, the issue of whether or not this
particular abbreviated text represents either a distillation/essence of Dōgen or a
kind of condensation that skews the message cannot be dealt with in abstract
theoretical terms. That is, the first issue immediately transmutes into the second issue because the text was the creation of his followers, who were not fully
aware of or perhaps somewhat oblivious (in their preoccupation with other,
modern agendas) to the priorities of Dōgen's thought. Thus, interpreting the
abbreviated text is a matter of historical contextualization—to see how, when,
and why the abbreviation was created as well as the function it serves. It seems
clear that Ōuchi Seiran and other Meiji lay leaders created a view of repentance
in *Shushōgi* based in large part on the challenge of Christianity during the Westernization process.

    At the same time, the popularity of the *Shushōgi* is largely due, not to its
conceptual content, but to the fact that it is easy to understand and memorize.
It works well as a text that can be chanted by both monks and laypersons, especially as a liturgical vehicle used during the sect's main rituals of funeral cer-

emonies, thereby contributing to a kind of esoteric religiosity or piety. The *Shushōgi* functions as a nutshell version that appeals to those who participate in the replica culture. When seen in the context of Japanese religions that are generally characterized by the pursuit of worldly benefits (*genze riyaku*), the appeal on this level may be seen as complementary and not necessarily in contradiction to the attainment of genuine spiritual aspirations.[42]

The historical level of significance reflects the fact that the *Shushōgi* demonstrates the importance of, and sharpens our focus on, the later period of Dōgen, an area of inquiry that has generally been much overlooked but highlighted recently by Critical Buddhism. The period of the late Dōgen refers to the time that begins around 1246, when he was fully settled into Eiheiji and had completed the 75-fascicle *Shōbōgenzō*. He then turned to the production of the *Eihei Kōroku* record of sermons and, eventually, the 12-fascicle collection of *Shōbōgenzō* sermons. But a study of the abbreviated text shows that the late Dōgen is complex—it is not a single period, but a multifaceted sequence of subperiods. A key turning point in the late Dōgen is the period beginning around 9/1, 1249, when Dōgen dedicated himself to the 12-fascicle *Shōbōgenzō*. This was also the time when Gien took over the editing of the *Eihei Kōroku*, and the general tenor of Dōgen's sermons changed from emphasizing the model of Chinese Zen patriarchs to an emphasis on causality that is quite compatible with the 12-fascicle *Shōbōgenzō*. The emphasis of the *Shushōgi* seems to be on this subperiod—the late late Dōgen. While most Dōgen scholarship has been preoccupied with the 75-fascicle *Shōbōgenzō*, the abbreviated text may be pointing to the most significant stage in Dōgen's career, in part through a broken lens.

Thus, the hermeneutic issue refers to the way the abbreviated text cannot help but lead back to an appropriation of Dōgen. Although not a pure distillation that provides an ideal introduction to the *Shōbōgenzō*, as some commentators claim, it is also not altogether arbitrary but an extension that preserves yet distorts the source. Despite Ōuchi's warning about not interpreting the *Shōbōgenzō* through the lens of the *Shushōgi*, Hee-Jin Kim writes of the *Shushōgi*, "This book was originally designed to be a manual for Zen believers' daily devotional life. However, the task of making the work required some unexpectedly painstaking efforts relative to linguistic, textual, and literary studies of *Shōbōgenzō*. These efforts gave an impetus in subsequent years to genuinely scholarly and systematic endeavors for basic research."[43]

No historical figure, or text that he or she creates, is an island. Dōgen stands in a dynamic, reciprocal relationship with Dōgen Zen, or his appropriators and critics, as truth to errancy and untruth to truth. Dōgen and Dōgen Zen are entangled in an ongoing process of creative misunderstanding and creative hermeneutics. This shows that "Dōgen" is not a static entity that can exist apart from how he is perceived and received (heard, understood, interpreted, translated, commented on, transmitted—and distilled, even in a culture of convenience and simulation).

NOTES

The Japanese text of the *Shushōgi* is in Mizuno Kogen, *Shushōgi no Bukkyō* (Tokyo: Shunjusha, 1968), pp. 3–12 (the passage in the epigraph is on p. 5). The *Shushōgi* is based primarily on the *Shōbōgenzō*, in *Dōgen Zenji Zenshū*, vols. 1 and 2. See also Yoshizu Yoshihide, *Shushōgi ni yoru Bukkyō nyūmon* (Tokyo: Daizō shuppan, 1999). A full translation of the *Shushōgi* appears in Yūhō Yokoi, *Zen Master Dōgen*, with Daizen Victoria (New York: Weatherhill, 1975), pp. 58–63.

1. The other Zen sects are Rinzai and Obaku, and the largest sects in Japan are the Pure Land sects, Jōdo-shū and Jōdo-shin-shū, which has several subdivisions. The other traditional sects include among others Kegon, Hosso, Tendai, Shingon, and Nichiren.

2. Heinrich Dumoulin, *Zen Buddhism: A History*, vol. 2, *Japan* (New York: Macmillan, 1990), p. 414.

3. The *Shushōgi* is not popular in American Zen, which is dominated by non-Japanese, but it is used extensively in Sōtō Zen in Brazil, which is largely an immigrant religious group.

4. An important area to be discussed later is the difference between various versions of the *Shōbōgenzō*, including the comprehensive 95-fascicle edition and the more specialized 75-fascicle and 12-fascicle editions.

5. See William M. Bodiford, *Sōtō Zen in Medieval Japan* (Honolulu: University of Hawaii Press, 1993), pp. 82–84.

6. This may seem somewhat surprising to those who have witnessed a boom in translations and studies of the *Shōbōgenzō* in recent years, both in Japanese and in English, but it is an accurate portrayal of Dōgen Zen. On the other hand, the neglect of the *Shōbōgenzō* (as well as the *Eihei Kōroku*) during the medieval period does not necessarily indicate an absence of intellectual life or the persistence of a sectarian "dark ages," as is often interpreted, because the vigorous activity of commentaries on the *Eihei Kōroku* and other texts belies that argument.

7. This remark is based on comments consistently made by a number of leading scholars at Komazawa University and the affiliated Sōtō Shūgaku Kenkyūjō interviewed in May 1999.

8. See Marilyn Ivy, *Discourses of the Vanishing: Modernity Phantasm Japan* (Chicago: University of Chicago Press, 1985).

9. Ōuchi's comments are cited in Ozaki Masayoshi, "*Shōbōgenzō to Shushōgi no aida*," *Shūgaku Kenkyū* 33 (1991): 23–30; this is in a special issue of the journal marking the 100th anniversary of the *Shushōgi*.

10. Yokoi, *Zen Master Dōgen*, p. 58. Dumoulin also remarks, "Meditation and enlightenment were not extolled and details of monastic living were omitted in order to focus more clearly on the main elements of Zen Buddhist teaching." Yet, he declares, "Relying as it did on Dōgen's writings, [the *Shushōgi*] offered an effective introduction to the thought of this great master, who has been presented to the West as a central figure in Zen," in *Zen Buddhism*, p. 414.

11. Matsubara Taidō, *Shushōgi ni Kiku: Dōgen Zen no Shinzui* (Tokyo: Chōbunsha, 1996). The remark on "essence" (*essensu*) appears on the "obi" around the jacket cover.

12. As discussed later, exceptions are the final section of "Keisei-sanshoku" in the 75-fascicle *Shōbōgenzō* and "Sanjigo" in the 12-fascicle *Shōbōgenzō*.

13. There are similar concerns about the *Eihei Goroku*, which a translator refers to as "a distillation of *Eihei Kōroku*" that is based on what was "considered the creme." Thomas Cleary, trans., *Eihei Goroku*, unpublished (held at San Francisco Zen Center Library, n.d.), p. 1. The passages selected for the *Eihei Goroku* present a view of Dōgen as a Zen master who behaved very much in the mold of his Chinese predecessors, particularly Hung-chih and Dōgen's mentor Ju-ching, as a preceptor of monastic rituals and transmitter of the Ts'ao-tung lineage. But are these passages an adequate reflection or distillation of the entire *Eihei Kōroku* that was composed primarily during Dōgen's later period? The picture that emerges from a variety of writings stemming from this period, especially the 12-fascicle edition of the *Shōbōgenzō*, is that the late Dōgen emphasized the doctrine of "true belief in causality" (*jinshin inga*) in a way that seems to diverge from the Chinese models. This historical point reinforces the emphasis on the 12-fascicle edition in the *Shushōgi*. Also, Dōgen's criticisms found in the *Eihei Kōroku* of syncretism and indigenous religiosity, as well as the exclusivism that characterized the Ch'an/Zen school, are missing from the *Eihei Goroku* selections. Nevertheless, a reciprocal relation exists in that studies of the *Eihei Goroku* may lead to a reexamination of the source text.

14. I am publishing another essay, "An Analysis of the *Eihei Goroku*: Abbreviation or Aberration?" to be included in a volume edited by Carl Bielefeldt based on an October 1999 conference on Sōtō Zen held at Stanford University.

15. James Edward Ketelaar, *Of Heretics and Martyrs in Meiji Japan: Buddhism and Its Persecution* (Princeton: Princeton University Press, 1993).

16. Richard Jaffe and Michel Mohr, "Editors' Introduction: Meiji Zen," *Japanese Journal of Religious Studies* (special issue on Meiji Zen) 25 nos.1–2 (1998):3. The authors also point out, "Through a combination of state mandates and sectarian initiatives, all Buddhist denominations were profoundly changed by the creation of the chief abbot [*kanchō*] system; the rise of sectarian universities; the compilation of state-approved uniform regulations and doctrinal summaries; the appropriation and redistribution of large portions of temple lands by the state [particularly relevant for understanding the formation of the *Shushōgi*]; the open establishment of temple families; and the general spread of the familial inheritance to the majority of local, non-training temples," pp. 3–4.

17. The school was renamed Sōtō-shū Daigaku in 1904 and Komazawa Daigaku in 1925, but 1882 is considered the founding date of Komazawa University.

18. The notion of *shūi anjin* was depicted in the *Sōtōshū Shūsei* (in a preamble to the fourth section known as the *Sōtōshū Shūkyō Taii*), which advocated a radical distinction between monastics and laity. See Ikeda Eishun, "Teaching Assemblies and Lay Societies in the Formation of Modern Sectarian Buddhism," *Japanese Journal of Religious Studies* 25 nos. 1–2 (1998): 36-39. Ikeda points out that within a few years there was a reversal of emphasis, with a new focus on lay practice developing, which in turn greatly influenced monastic practice. He also shows that the Sōtō Fushūkai organization died out in the 1890s—and a similar process occurred in other Buddhist sects—largely because the main ideas of the ground-level organiza-

tion were co-opted and reabsorbed into the administration of the central denomina-
tional institution. Unfortunately, the uniformity of the sect's approval of the *Shushōgi*
was part of a very short-lived truce between the rival Eiheiji and Sōjiji branches,
based largely on the role of Takitani Takashū, who had moved up the ranks as abbot
of Saijōji in Kanagawa Prefecture affiliated with Sōjiji and yet became abbot of
Eiheiji. The truce ended with the secession of the Sōjiji and its branch temples in
1892.

19. The Bukkyō Dendō Kyōkai organization continues the process of providing
and disseminating Buddhist bibles and related materials. Also, it should also be
noted that, based on an analysis of other kinds of documents, it appears that Ōuchi
and other members of the lay group were under the sway of the increasing tendency
of Meiji Buddhism to accomodate and capitulate to the chauvinism and militarism of
the Imperial Way. Buddhists sought to show that their cooperation with imperialism
was an element of religion that was not shared by and was thus superior to Christianity. See Brian Victoria, *Zen at War* (New York: Weatherhill, 1997), pp. 18, 52.

20. For example, the first decade of the twentieth century saw the publication
of two short but extremely influential books in English by Japanese scholars dealing
with the spiritual values of Japan, Okakura Kakuzo or Tenshin's *Book of Tea* and
Nitobe Inazo's *Bushido, the Warrior's Code*.

21. Mizuno, *Shushōgi no Bukkyō*, p. 13.

22. Ōuchi's father was a Sōtō member and his mother followed the Jodō-shin-shū.

23. See Hoshi Shundō, "*Shushōgi* ni kansuru ikkōsatsu," *Shūgaku Kenkyū* 33
(1991): 69–75. For a detailed textual comparison of the Ōuchi text and the *Shushōgi*,
see Kaneko Kazuo, "Shushōgi seiritsu no ikkōsatsu (part 2)," *Sōtōshū Kenkyūin
Kenkyū Kiyō* 22 (1991): 93–118. In addition, for a translation of other, more recent
Sōtō lay texts see Ian Reader, "Contemporary Zen Buddhist Tracts for the Laity:
Grassroots Buddhism in Japan," *Religions of Japan in Practice*, ed. George J. Tanabe,
Jr. (Princeton: Princeton University Press, 1999), pp. 487–498.

24. On the other hand, Ōuchi's text opens with some general comments to the
reader that have been left out of the *Shushōgi*.

25. According to Tagami Taishū, over 1,700 hundred words were deleted from
the 4,003–word Ōuchi text and over 1,450 new words were added to the *Shushōgi*; in
"*Shushōgi* no seiritsu ni tsuite," *Budda kara Dōgen e*, ed. Nara Yasuaki (Tokyo: Tokyo
Shoseki, 1992), pp. 325–330.

26. Kagamishima, *Dōgen Zenji Zenshū*, vol. 2, p. 470. In "Genjōkōan" Dōgen
also writes, "To undertake practice-realization (*shushō*) of the ten thousand things in
terms of the self is delusion; to undertake practice-realization of the self through the
ten thousand things is *satori*."

27. Although the term *shushō ittō* is found in Dōgen's writings ("Bendōwa"),
the term *honshō myōshu* appears to be a Meiji-era invention probably attributable to
Ōuchi's concern with finding a handy slogan.

28. Hirakawa Sukehiro suggests that Dōgen's ideal of self-cultivation was put
forth as part of a Meiji intellectual conservatism, which valorized traditional Japanese and East Asia values in the face of the pragmatism of Westernization. For
example, in the *Shōbōgenzō Zuimonki*, Dōgen writes, "The jewel becomes a jewel
through polishing. Man becomes benevolent through training." This echoes the

Book of Rites, which states, "Unless the jewel is polished, it does not become a jewel; unless men study, they do not learn the Way." In "Japan's Turn to the West," *Modern Japanese Thought,* ed. Bob Tadashi Wakabayashi (Cambridge: Cambridge University Press, 1998), p. 84. Also Katō Shūkō notes that Dōgen used the term *dōri* at least 272 times (and the related term *kotowari* twelve times), in *Shōbōgenzō yōgo sakuin,* 2 vols. (Tokyo: Risōsha, 1962–1963.

29. Mizuno states that the *Shushōgi* cites "each of the 95 fascicles," and Yokoi suggests that it uses "all ninety-two sections" of the *Shōbōgenzō.*

30. Azuma Ryūshin, *Sōtō-shū: Waga Ie no Shūkyō* (Tokyo: Daihōrinkan, 1983), p. 136.

31. For a comprehensive analysis of the source passages of each of the sentences in the *Shushōgi,* see Sōtō shūmuchō, eds., "*Shushōgi to Shōbōgenzō to no taihi,*" *Genshaku Kenshū* 12 (1991) and 13 (1992).

32. Mark Unno suggests that Dōgen's view of *shikan-taza* is an exception to the Kamakura-era "demand for a simple and direct soteriology that deals with the problem of karmic evil," as found in Hōnen, Nichiren, and Myōe; in "Recommending Faith in the Sand of the Mantra of Light: Myōe Kōben's *Kōmyō Shingon Dosha Kanjinki,*" in *Re-Visioning Kamakura Buddhism,* ed. Richard K. Payne (Honolulu: University of Hawaii Press, 1998), p. 171. However, it seems that the 12-fascicle *Shōbōgenzō* is precisely Dōgen's effort to deal with karma.

33. See Fukase Shunji, "*Shushōgi to Shōbōgi o megutte,*" *Shūgaku Kenkyū* 33 (1991): 62–68.

34. See Jamie Hubbard and Paul L. Swanson, ed., *Pruning the Bodhi Tree: The Storm Over Critical Buddhism* (Honolulu: University of Hawaii Press, 1997).

35. See, for example, Okabe Kazuo, "*Shushōgi* seiritsu no jidai o kangaeru," *Budda kara Dōgen e,* pp. 331–341.

36. Kagamishima, *Dōgen Zenji Zenshū,* vol. 2, p. 462. The same passage is cited in "Gyōji" of the 75-fascicle *Shōbōgenzō, Eihei Kōroku,* and *Hōkyōki.*

37. The *Ch'an-men Kuei-shih* is in the *Ching-te Ch'uan-teng Lu, chuan* 6, *Taishō,* vol. 51.

38. Kōdō Kawamura, ed., *Shohon Taikō Eihei Kaisan Dōgen Zenji Gyōjō— Kenzeiki* (Tokyo: Taishūkan, 1975), pp. 63–64; and Ōkubo Dōshū, *Dōgen Zenji Den no Kenkyū* (Tokyo: Chikuma shobō, 1966), pp. 276–278. In an interesting discursive juxtaposition, probably the two main features of Dōgen's hagiography in the late period are the Gemmyō incident and an emphasis on the role of *rakan*-veneration in his approach to lay religiosity.

39. The *Platform Sūtra,* nos. 22 and 33. According to David Chappell, five kinds of repentance are communal repentance to the sangha to ensure monastic conformity; personal repentance of karmic history; mythological repentance to a supermundane Buddha; meditation repentance of incorrect perceptions and attachments; and philosophical repentance of wrong concepts and discrimination; in "Formless Repentance in Comparative Perspective," *Report of International Conference on Ch'an Buddhism* (Taiwan: Fo Kuang Shan, 1990), p. 253.

40. Hakamaya Noriaki, *Hongaku Shisō Hihan* (Tokyo: Daizō Shuppan, 1989), and "Nihonjin to Animizumu," *Komazawa Daigaku Bukkyōgakubu Ronshū* 23 (1992): 351–378.

41. Tanabe Hajime, *Zangedō toshite no Tetsugaku*, in *Tanabe Hajime Zenshū* (Tokyo: Chikuma Shobo, 1963, vol. 9; trans., *Philosophy as Metanoetics*, Takeuchi Yoshinori with Valdo Viglielmo and James W. Heisig (Berkeley: University of California Press, 1986).

42. Ian Reader and George J. Tanabe, Jr., *Practically Religious: Wordly Benefits and the Common Religion of Japan* (Honolulu: University of Hawaii Press, 1998).

43. Hee-Jin Kim, *Dōgen Kigen—Mystical Realist* (Tucson: University of Arizona Press, 1975), p. 321. Kim cites Kagamishima Hiroyuki, "Dōgen Zenji Kenkyū no Dōkō Kaiko," *Dōgen Zenji Kenkyū* 1, no. 1 (1941): 341–368.

8

"By Imperial Edict and Shogunal Decree"

*Politics and the Issue of the Ordination
Platform in Modern Lay Nichiren Buddhism*

Jacqueline I. Stone

Observers are often struck by the "engaged" or even "political"
character of modern Japanese Nichiren Buddhist movements. In the
first decades of the twentieth century, the movement known as
Nichirenshugi ("Nichirenism"), led by Tanaka Chigaku (1861–1939)
and Honda Nisshō (1867–1931),[1] deployed Nichiren Buddhist
doctrine in a way that bolstered modern nationalistic agendas and
justified militant imperialism; in the postwar period, the small
monastic order Nipponzan Myōhōji espoused a stance of absolute
pacifism, taking active part in the anti-nuclear campaign, while the
rapidly expanding lay organization Sōka Gakkai ran candidates for
the National Diet and even started a political party. More recently the
Sōka Gakkai—like Risshō Kōseikai movement, another large lay
Buddhist organization with roots in the Nichiren tradition—has
become a nongovernmental organizational member of the United
Nations and now engages in global networking for peace, protection
of the environment, aid to refugees, and a host of other issues. This
"activist" orientation, on one hand, exemplifies the emphasis on
social engagement found in Buddhist modernism worldwide. On the
other hand, such efforts can be seen as attempts to reappropriate, in
modern or contemporary contexts, the vision of the founder
Nichiren (1222–1282), who taught that exclusive devotion to the
Lotus Sūtra could transform the present world into a Buddha land.

One aspect of the medieval Nichiren Buddhist vision, however,
has proved difficult for modern practitioners. This is the tradition

that, someday, a great ordination platform (*kaidan*) would be erected "by imperial edict and shogunal decree," symbolizing the fusion of Buddhism and worldly
rule and the conversion of the sovereign and his people to Nichiren's teaching.
One might expect that this ideal, framed in such obviously medieval terms, might
be allowed to lapse into obscurity, or be interpreted in purely symbolic fashion.
Such has, indeed, been the mainstream tendency within the various Nichiren
Buddhist temple denominations. Nonetheless, there have also been two significant attempts within the last century to reframe the goal of establishing the
kaidan in a literal sense, in the context of political milieus that Nichiren's medieval followers never imagined: the militant imperialism of the first part of the
twentieth century and the parliamentary democracy instituted after the Pacific
War. This chapter will consider, first, Tanaka Chigaku's religious nationalism,
forged during Japan's modern imperial period, and second, the postwar Sōka
Gakkai's entry into politics, focusing in both cases on their refigurations of the
future ordination platform that was to represent the fusion of government with
the *Lotus Sūtra*. First, however, it will be helpful to touch briefly on those elements in the earlier Nichiren Buddhist tradition that both movements would
reappropriate and reconfigure in defining their aims.

Nichiren's *Lotus* Exclusivism and the *Honmon No Kaidan*

Nichiren taught a doctrine of exclusive devotion to the *Lotus Sūtra* and stressed
as a primary practice the chanting of its *daimoku* or title in the formula, "Namu-
myōhō-renge-kyō." In medieval Japan, the *Lotus Sūtra*, with its promise that
"all shall achieve the Buddha Way," was widely revered as the highest of the
Buddha's teachings, reconciling all others within itself. For Nichiren, however, the *Lotus Sūtra* was not simply one teaching supreme among many but
the sole Dharma that could lead to Buddhahood now in the Final Dharma age
(*mappō*), preached by the Buddha expressly for the people of this degenerate
time. In his estimation, the other Buddhist forms current in his day—Pure
Land, Zen, and the esoteric teachings—being provisional and incomplete, no
longer led to liberation in the *mappō* era; to embrace them and reject the *Lotus
Sūtra* was a pernicious inversion of high and low, a form of "disparaging the
Dharma" (*hōbō*) that could only invite suffering. Drawing on traditional
Mahāyāna ideas of the nonduality of individuals and their container world,
the "realm of the land" (*kokudo seken*), Nichiren insisted that it was precisely
this evil, a neglect of the *Lotus Sūtra's* perfect teaching, that had brought down
on the populace the calamities of his day: drought, famine, earthquakes, and
the threat of invasion by the Mongols. Conversely, Nichiren held that the spread
of exclusive faith in the *Lotus Sūtra* would banish such disasters and manifest
this world as an ideal realm:

When all people throughout the land enter the one Buddha vehicle, and the Wonderful Dharma [of the *Lotus*] alone flourishes, because the people all chant Namu-myōhō-renge-kyō, the wind will not thrash the branches nor the rain fall hard enough to break clods. The age will become like the reigns of [the Chinese sage kings] Yao and Shun. In the present life, inauspicious calamities will be banished, and the people will obtain the art of longevity. . . . There can be no doubt of the sūtra's promise of "peace and security in the present world.[2]

Since, in his view, the devotion paid to outdated and ineffectual teachings was inviting disastrous social consequences, Nichiren saw the dissemination of his message as a matter of urgency. Accordingly, he stressed the practice of *shakubuku*, an assertive approach to proselytizing in which one actively rebukes attachment to views deemed inferior or false. Nichiren practiced *shakubuku* by preaching and writing, engaging in doctrinal debate with fellow clerics, and admonishing officials of the Bakufu, the recently established shogunate or military government that shared power with the imperial court. The place of "the ruler" in Nichiren's thought is a complex one. Nichiren himself often directed his efforts in *shakubuku* toward those in positions of power because of their influence over the people at large. But at the same time, he strictly subordinated the authority of worldly rule to that of the true Dharma of the *Lotus*. A ruler's obligation, in his view, was to protect the *Lotus Sūtra* and the monks who upheld it while denying support to those who "disparage the Dharma"; this would ensure general peace and prosperity. If, on the contrary, the ruler gave support to misleading teachings, disaster would plague his realm. This claim was articulated in Nichiren's famous admonitory treatise *Risshō ankoku ron* (Treatise on establishing the true [Dharma] and bringing peace to the land), submitted to the Bakufu in 1260.

The rhetoric of leading Buddhist institutions of Nichiren's day held that the "Buddha-Dharma" (*buppō*) and the ruler's dharma (*ōbō*) exist in mutual dependence. In practice, this generally meant providing rites of thaumaturgical protection for the emperor or sovereign (*tennō*), the shogun, or other officials in exchange for a guarantee of privileges and economic support. For Nichiren, however, such reciprocal arrangements were untenable where the ruler opposed or was indifferent to the *Lotus Sūtra*, or revered it only as one teaching among many. Until those in power embraced the True Dharma, he held, devotees of the *Lotus* must maintain an oppositional stance, admonishing the ruler, even at the risk of their lives, to take faith in it for the sake of the country and the people's welfare. In this way, Nichiren's *Lotus* exclusivism contained an element critical of authority and established a moral basis for defiance of worldly rule in the Dharma's name.[3]

However, certain Nichiren writings indicate that, when at some future point the ruler should embrace the *Lotus Sūtra*, a more cooperative relationship of *ōbō* and *buppō* could then be instituted. Envisioning that time, he wrote: "Of my disciples, the monks will be teachers to the sovereign and retired sovereigns, while the laymen will be ranged among the ministers of the left and right."[4] But the clearest statement attributed to him of a future unity of Buddhism and worldly rule appears in an essay known as the *Sandai hihō shō* (On the three great secret Dharmas):

> When the ruler's dharma [*ōbō*] becomes one with Buddha-Dharma
> [*buppō*] and the Buddha-Dharma is united with the ruler's dharma, so
> that the ruler and his ministers all uphold the three great secret
> Dharmas of the origin teaching . . . then surely an imperial edict and a
> shogunal decree will be handed down, to seek out the most superlative
> site, resembling the Pure Land of Sacred Vulture Peak [where the
> *Lotus Sūtra* was expounded], and there to erect the ordination plat-
> form. You have only to await the time. . . . Not only will this be [the
> site of] the dharma of the precepts [*kaihō*] by which all people of the
> three countries [India, China, and Japan] and the entire world (Skt.
> Jambudvīpa; Jpn. Ichienbudai) will perform repentance and eradicate
> their offenses, but [the great protector deities] Brahmā and Indra will
> also descend and mount this ordination platform.[5]

Nichiren had taught that Buddhism for the time of *mappō* consisted in essence of "three great secret Dharmas" (*sandai hihō*) implicit in the depths of the
origin teaching (*honmon*) of the *Lotus Sūtra*—the "origin teaching" being the
latter half of the *sūtra*, which presents itself as the teaching of an eternal Buddha who constantly abides in this world. These three secret Dharmas are (1) the
daimoku, or invocation of the *Lotus Sūtra's* title, "Namu-myōhō-renge-kyō," the
central practice of Nichiren's Buddhism and said by him to encompass all
the eternal Buddha's merits and virtues; (2) the object of worship (*honzon*), the
calligraphic maṇḍala that Nichiren had devised, depicting the assembly of the
Lotus Sūtra as the eternal Buddha's enlightened realm; and (3) the "ordination
platform." The first two Nichiren had himself discussed in detail. But, while
some of his later writings make reference to the "ordination platform of the origin
teaching" (*honmon no kaidan*), no authenticated work of his explains precisely
what he meant by this. Only this one writing, the *Sandai hihō shō*, clearly presents it as an officially sponsored ordination platform, to be erected in the future when "the ruler and his ministers" have embraced the *Lotus Sūtra*.

However, the *Sandai hihō shō* does not survive in Nichiren's handwriting, and
in the modern period his authorship has been heatedly disputed. In particular, in
the years following Japan's defeat in the Pacific War, in the mood of revulsion
against institutional Buddhism's support for the nation's ill-judged imperialist
venture, some scholars of the Nichiren tradition denounced the work as a forgery

and denied that Nichiren would ever have embraced a state-sponsored *kaidan* as a religious ideal.[6] Nonetheless, from the time of Buddhism's introduction to Japan in the sixth century, the ordination of monks had at least in principle been regulated by the imperial court, and the four ordination platforms existing in Nichiren's day were all court sponsored. He and his rather marginal religious community existed outside this official system of ordination, and it seems quite possible—whether he personally wrote the *Sandai hihō shō* or not—that he envisioned the establishment of an "ordination platform of the origin teaching" mandated by the court and the Bakufu, the two ruling structures of his day, as symbolic of the official acceptance of his Buddhism. Whatever Nichiren's own views, throughout premodern times, the future establishment of an imperially mandated *kaidan* was widely accepted within the Nichiren tradition as a task whose achievement Nichiren had entrusted to his later followers. Rival lineages sometimes debated over whose head temple would house the eventual *kaidan* structure. Yet at the same time, perhaps in part because the likelihood of realizing this goal seemed so remote, a corollary interpretation emerged in which the *honmon no kaidan* referred simply to that place, wherever it might be, where the follower of Nichiren embraces faith in the *Lotus Sūtra* and chants Namu-myōhō-renge-kyō—a reading closely linked to Nichiren's own claim that wherever one chants the *daimoku* of the *Lotus Sūtra* is the Buddha land. Under the rule of the Tokugawa shogunate in the early modern period (1603–1868), when religious proselytizing was severely restricted, this abstract interpretation of the *kaidan* became the predominant one. Not until the Meiji period (1868–1912), with a radical restructuring of Japan's government, would the ideal of an imperially sponsored *kaidan* be reimagined as something achievable in concrete terms.[7]

Tanaka Chigaku's Religious Nationalism

The first person to reenvision the establishment of the *kaidan* in a modern context was Tanaka Chigaku (1861–1931). As a young man, Tanaka had abandoned his training for the priesthood of Nichirenshū, the chief denomination of Nichiren Buddhism, to embark on a career of lecturing and proselytizing as a lay teacher. What he advocated was not the traditional Nichiren Buddhism of temples and priests but "*Nichirenshugi* [Nichirenism]," a popularized, lay-oriented Nichiren doctrine applicable to contemporary social realities. In particular, he saw Nichirenshugi as providing a spiritual basis for Japan as a modern state, and "the fusion of Dharma and nation" (*hōkoku myōgō*) would be his lifelong concern. In 1881 Tanaka founded the Rengekai (Lotus Blossom Society) in Yokohama to propagate Nichirenshugi ideals. It was reorganized in 1885 as the Risshō Ankokukai (after Nichiren's *Risshō ankoku ron*) and again in 1914 as the Kokuchūkai, or "Pillar of the Nation Society"(after Nichiren's words, "I will be the pillar of Japan"). Over the course of his career, Tanaka would shift his base of activities from

Yokohama to Tokyo, Kyoto and Osaka, Kamakura, Miho in Shizuoka, and then
back to Tokyo, all the while continually traveling to preach and lecture. His was
not a large organization; Kokuchūkai membership has been estimated at only
somewhat more than 7,000 at its height in 1924.[8] But Tanaka's influence extended
well beyond his immediate circle. He was outspoken in defense of clerical marriage and a passionate advocate of lay Buddhism.[9] His style of lay organization
appears to have influenced modern Nichiren Buddhist new religions.[10] He made
innovative use of print media to disseminate his message; Kokuchūkai published
a number of magazines and journals that made Nichiren Buddhist teachings
available in the vernacular language, interpreting them in light of contemporary
events. Tanaka also sponsored the compilation of the first dictionary of Nichiren's
teachings.[11] The literary figure Takayama Chōgyū (1871–1902) and the poet
Miyazawa Kenji (1896–1933) were drawn to Tanaka for a time, though they would
ultimately reject his nationalistic views. Perhaps his most famous disciple was
General Ishiwara Kanji (1889–1949), operations officer of the Kwantung Army,
whose actions during the so-called Manchurian Incident (1931) seem to have been
inspired by his apocalyptic reading of Tanaka's nationalistic Nichirenism.[12] Here,
however, our concern is not to present a detailed overview of Tanaka's career but
to consider how he reappropriated medieval Nichiren Buddhist visions of the
ruler's future conversion and the establishment of the *honmon no kaidan* in the
context of modern Japanese nationalism.[13]

Tanaka's Millenarian Vision and the State-Sponsored *Kaidan*

Tanaka first addressed these themes in detail in his 1901 essay *Shūmon no ishin*
(Restoration of the [Nichiren] sect), a manifesto for radical sectarian reform.
Tanaka excoriated the traditional Nichiren temple institutions of his day as
outmoded, parochial, and indifferent to the needs of modern Japan. "Nichiren
Buddhism should not exist for its own sake," he admonished, "but for the sake
of the nation. It is the doctrine that can protect the Japanese state, and to which,
in the future, all humanity must inevitably convert."[14] Toward Buddhist practice, he urged a spirit of restoration and in particular, a return to Nichiren's
foundational emphasis on *shakubuku*, directly challenging the teachings of other
sects. Under the Tokugawa regime (1603–1868), when Buddhism had been
incorporated into the shogunate's administrative apparatus and religious debates
were prohibited by law, the practice of assertive proselytizing by *shakubuku* had
been largely abandoned. Doctrinal interpretation had assumed an accomo-
dationist stance, one inherited by Nichiren sectarian leaders of the Meiji period. In addition, in the wake of the brief but violent anti-Buddhist persecution
(*haibutsu kishaku*) that had erupted in the early 1870s, Buddhist leaders saw their
best chance of institutional survival in transsectarian cooperation. Tanaka de-
spised this ecumenical move; Nichiren had taught that only the *Lotus Sūtra* could

protect the country, and, now that Japan was struggling to assume a place among the world's powers, refutation of inferior teachings by *shakubuku* was what the times demanded.[15] In the areas of education, proselytizing, and sectarian organization, however, Tanaka stressed reforms. He urged, for example, that the various Nichiren denominations transcend their divisions and unite as one tradition, not by abandoning their separate lineages and institutional identities but by establishing a common head temple.[16] He also recommended modern methods of proselytizing, including preaching at roadsides, in halls and auditoriums, at military installations, at hot-spring resorts, and aboard ships; the publishing of a daily newspaper and other propaganda materials in colloquial Japanese; and the organizing of lay women into a nursing corps and the establishment of charitable hospitals run by the sect.

In its wealth of concrete detail, *Shūmon no ishin* gives the impression of a blueprint for action, but it is more accurately understood as a highly embellished millennial vision, decked out with modern trappings. This becomes clear especially in the appendices to Tanaka's essay, which outline a fifty-year plan for world conversion to Nichiren Buddhism, beginning from the year that his envisioned sectarian reform should have been achieved. Here Tanaka plotted with charts and maps the growth he estimated in the numbers of students, doctrinal instructors, and adherents of the sect, as well as its capital, income, and expenditures over ten five-year periods. Adherents, he imagined, for example, would increase over this period from three million to well over 113 million. The Nichiren sect would steadily dominate the nation's economy and infrastructure by building and maintaining railways, shipping lines, and a national bank. He also envisioned the progress of conversion efforts in foreign countries on a "Map of World Unification through Propagation [of Faith in the *Lotus Sūtra*] throughout Jambudvīpa," giving the locations of projected Nichirenist colonies and missionary bases throughout the world.

Central to Tanaka's millenarian vision was the *honmon no kaidan*, the ordination platform of the origin teaching, to be established, according to the *Sandai hihō shō*, by "imperial edict and shogunal decree." Substituting the relevant political structure of his own day, Tanaka argued that the mandate for the *kaidan's* establishment would now have to come from the Imperial Diet; it would be, in his terms, a *kokuritsu kaidan*, a "national *kaidan*" or, literally, a "*kaidan* established by the state." To win a majority of sympathizers in both Diet houses, it would be necessary to convert a majority of the Japanese populace by *shakubuku*. Tanaka depicted a scenario in which, one by one, other religions, acknowledging the superior righteousness of the *Lotus Sūtra*, would declare their own dissolution and convert. Within Buddhism, Hossō and Kegon would capitulate first; their temples, passing to the Nichiren sect, would be respectfully preserved and offered to the state as national treasures. Tendai and Shingon would follow suit, and so, after some initial resistance, would Jōdo and Zen. Jōdo Shinshū and Christianity would resist mightily, and a great Dharma battle

would ensue, but before the fifty years were out, the whole nation would embrace the one vehicle, and establishment of the *kaidan* would be proclaimed.

Tanaka also considered the location and funding of this structure. Its site
would be that of the future "single head temple" of a restored Nichiren sect,
which Tanaka said should be built in Shizuoka at the foot of Mt. Fuji, "the sacred place at the center of Japan, which is the sacred country at the center of the
world." He calculated that, if even a quarter of all believers were to take out
hundred-yen life insurance policies with the head temple as beneficiary, careful management of such funds could, over a fifty-year period, result in a sum of
1,190,151,541 yen, sufficient to build the *kaidan*.[17] Tanaka's 1909 decision to
relocate his headquarters to Miho in Shizuoka was evidently informed by his
vision of this future *kaidan*. As noted above, the *Sandai hihō shō* stipulates that
the ordination platform should be erected at "the most superlative (*saishō*) site,
resembling the Pure Land of Sacred Vulture Peak." For Tanaka, Mt. Fuji corresponded to "Vulture Peak," and Miho, to the "most superlative site" where the
kaidan would be built. The name of his new headquarters, the Saishōkaku ("pavilion of the most superlative [site]"), is derived from this passage. The top floor
of this new structure even contained a room prepared to house the imperial edict
that would mandate the *kaidan's* establishment.[18]

Tanaka's vision underwent elaboration in his lectures and writings over the
next few years. He divided the *mappō* era, the Final Dharma age for which the
Lotus Sūtra was intended, into three periods: the founding period, when Nichiren
had lived and declared his teaching; the era of dissemination, when faith in the
Lotus Sūtra was destined to spread; and the era of unification, when all people
would embrace it.[19] For Tanaka, this era of unification would be the "golden
age" of *ōbutsu myōgō*—the merging of the ruler's dharma with the Buddha-
Dharma—another phrase he derived from the *Sandai hihō shō*. At this time, a
majority of the nation having been converted, the Diet would pass an amendment revising the constitutional article allowing for freedom of religion and make
Nichiren Buddhism the state creed, and an imperial edict would be issued to
build the *kaidan*, thus formalizing the merger of Buddhism and government.
Politics, society, ethics, thought—all would all be unified on the basis of the *Lotus
Sūtra*, a goal that Tanaka referred to as the "realization of Buddhahood by the
land" (*kokudo jōbutsu*). This goal was "not like heaven or the Pure Land, which
are never actually expected to appear before our eyes. We predict, envision, and
aim for it as a reality that we will definitely witness."[20]

Tanaka's Theory of the "National Essence"

Tanaka may well have been the first person in modern Nichiren Buddhist history to have imagined the universal spread of Nichiren's teachings and the establishment of the *kaidan*, not as a remote future ideal but as a target within

actual reach. The appeal of his vision to followers and sympathizers, however, lay not merely in its immediacy but in the central role it assigned to Japan and its resonance with both official ideology and the popular patriotic sentiments of the day, which had been fanned by Japanese victories in the wars with China (1894–1895) and Russia (1904–1905), the annexation of Korea (1910) and later imperial expansion on the Asian continent. The "Buddhahood of the land," in the sense of peace, just rule, and the manifestation of the *Lotus Sūtra's* blessings in all spheres of human activity, was something Nichiren himself had envisioned. But neither Nichiren nor his medieval followers had understood this goal as necessarily allied to any specific regime or form of government; whether court or Bakufu, any government that upheld the *Lotus Sūtra* would serve to help realize this ideal. For Tanaka, however, "the Buddhahood of the land" was to be exemplified, mediated, and extended to all humanity by the imperial Japanese state. Already in *Shūmon no ishin*, he had written:

> At that time [when the *kaidan* is established]—being exhaustively interpreted in connection with our holy founder Nichiren, who in his own person manifested the original Buddha Śākyamuni and the original Dharma of the *Lotus Sūtra*—the sacred plan of the divine ancestors of great Japan, her wondrous and unsurpassed national essence [*kokutai*], and her imperial house, divinely descended in a direct line, will manifest their true worth. Thus the authority of our teaching and the light of our country will fill the universe and instruct the people of all nations. This will accomplish the spiritual unification of the world, without need of a single soldier or sword.[21]

Nichiren Buddhism and Japan, in Tanaka's view, shared a divine mission to unite the world.

This theme would become increasingly prominent in Tanaka's writings from the time of the Russo-Japanese War (1904–1905). At this point, Tanaka consciously shifted his efforts from internal reform of the Nichiren sect to "study of the national essence" (*kokutaigaku*), by which name he termed his attempt to interpret the Japanese *kokutai* from the standpoint of Nichirenshugi. The notion of Japan's unique national essence formed the ideological pillar of the modern state; its key elements included the myth of an unbroken imperial line, descended directly from the Sun Goddess and her grandson, Emperor Jinmu, and the concept of the emperor as benevolent father to the "family" of his subjects. The myth of the *kokutai* was disseminated through the media, school ceremonies, educational curricula, and observances on national holidays, and was iconized in ubiquitous pictures of the Meiji emperor. Especially as the nation prepared for war, notions of Japan's divine destiny were promoted to rally public support for the sacrifices this venture would demand. Buddhist sects and other religious institutions for the most part offered wholehearted support, sending chaplains to the front, conducting prayers for victory, and, as the fighting continued, providing aid to bereaved families.[22] At this juncture, Tanaka felt increasingly compelled to communicate his conviction that only Nichirenshugi could provide the spiritual basis for the realization of Japan's unique destiny. Ritualized expressions of reverence for the emperor, with a Nichirenshugi slant, were incorporated into Risshō Ankokukai observances; at the organization's headquarters in Osaka, for example, during the New Year's ceremony, portraits of the imperial couple were hung at either side of the Nichiren mandala, and prayers were conducted for the eventual realization of ōbutsu myōgō.[23] Toward society at large, Tanaka now began to offer his emerging Nichirenist version of kokutai theory.[24]

Tanaka first seriously addressed this issue in a lecture delivered in Nara in 1904, shortly before the war's outbreak, to some two hundred participants in a study training session whom he had taken on a visit to Emperor Jinmu's tomb. It was published as a pamphlet titled Seikai tōitsu no tengyō (The divine task of world unification), and several thousand copies distributed to soldiers departing for the front. Its central argument, in Buddhist terms, was that the kokutai is the truth to be interpreted (shoshaku), and Nichirenshugi, that which interprets it (nōshaku).[25] Tanaka's hermeneutical strategy, here and in later writings, was to homologize the Lotus Sūtra, or, more specifically, Nichirenshugi, with the Japanese national essence through a logic of analogy and numerical correspondence. From the legendary account of Emperor Jinmu's founding of the Yamato kingdom, as related in the eighth-century chronicle Nihon shoki, Tanaka drew three phrases describing Jinmu's achievements—"fostering righteousness, accumulating happiness, and increasing glory"—which he identified as the three original acts that had established the Japanese kokutai. These he in turn equated with the three imperial regalia—the sword, mirror and jewel—and with Nichiren's three great secret Dharmas: the daimoku, the object of worship, and the ordination platform.[26] The mission of Japan was the divine task of world unification inherited from Emperor Jinmu, to extend the blessings of the kokutai to all people. It would be spearheaded by the emperor, who was at once both Jinmu's lineal heir and also the "wheel-turning monarch" of Buddhist tradition, who supports and protects the Dharma. At the same time, its fulfillment required the spiritual basis provided by Nichirenshugi; incomplete religions, such as Christianity or other forms of Buddhism, could never supply it. "Nichirenism is precisely Japanism," Tanaka wrote. "Nichiren Shōnin appeared in order to interpret Japan's spiritual essence as Buddhist doctrine, providing all humanity throughout the ten thousands years of the Final Dharma age with the ultimate refuge. The great teaching of Nichiren is the religion for Japan, and the religion for Japan is the religion for the world."[27]

From this point, Tanaka's writings increasingly suggest that the underlying purpose of the Lotus Sūtra and Nichiren's teaching was to explicate the Japanese national essence. "Śākyamuni, being in India, preached the Japanese kokutai as Buddhism," he asserted. Japan was "the country that gave form to the *Lotus Sūtra*" while the *Lotus Sūtra* "spiritualized Japan."[28] By thus identifying the *Lotus Sūtra* with the Japanese *kokutai*, Tanaka elevated a particular "national essence" to the status of universal truth. This rhetorical move abolished the critical distance that the early Nichiren tradition had advocated toward rulers who do not embrace the *Lotus Sūtra* and legitimated unreserved support for the imperial system. It also conflated the spread of the *Lotus Sūtra* by *shakubuku* with the expansion of Japanese hegemony. At this point, Tanaka's "spiritual unification of the world, without need of a single soldier or sword" gave way to frank endorsements of militant imperialism.

Tanaka's conviction that only Nichirenshugi could manifest the Japanese national essence led him, in 1923, to take the unprecedented step of founding a political party. "Now is the time for adherents of Nichirenshugi to assume their places to the emperor's right and left and take up the reins of a government based on the *Lotus Sūtra*. The time for realizing rule based on the true Dharma has come," he said.[29] The party was called the Rikken Yōseikai, or Constitutional Party for Fostering Righteousness; Kokuchūkai leaders were appointed as party officials. As the name suggests, its platform was to be grounded in the three essential principles of the *kokutai*—"fostering righteousness, accumulating happiness, and increasing glory"—that Tanaka had formulated nearly two decades earlier based on his reading of the *Nihon shoki*. Tanaka and two other Kokuchūkai members stood for the May 1924 election to the House of Representatives, running in Nihonbashi in the fifth Tokyo electoral ward. None of the three was elected. Yet, as the first Japanese religious organization to found a political party, Tanaka's Kokuchūkai set a historically significant precedent—one that would be followed, with far greater success, by the postwar Sōka Gakkai.

Tanaka, on the one hand, inherited the totalizing vision of his medieval Nichiren Buddhist forebears, in which temporal government, and indeed, all worldly activities, would someday be based on the *Lotus Sūtra*. On the other hand, Tanaka's reinterpretation was innovative, in being indissolubly linked to the modern imperial state. In the latter part of his career, he increasingly identified "the *Lotus Sūtra*" with the Japanese national essence, an interpretive move that raised the Japanese *kokutai* to the status of universal truth and served to legitimate the armed extension of Japanese empire. It was a distinctly "Nichirenist" mode of *kokutai* exegesis, different in that regard from more prevalent discourses on the *kokutai* expressed in the language of state Shinto. But it stood in unequal competition with the structurally very similar, totalizing vision of official ideology, in which government, public affairs, and eventually the world itself would be united under sacred imperial rule. By asssimilating to Nichirenshugi elements of imperial ideology, such as the myth of Japan's divine origins and the uniqueness of its national essence, Tanaka drew his message ever closer into alignment with the official program. As Edwin Lee notes, he stood among "that group of men who helped in an important, if indirect, way to provide the context within which the leaders of government were able to achieve many of their goals."[30]

Within the context of the Nichiren tradition, however, he was the first individual to redefine the goal of the unity of government and the *Lotus Sūtra* and the establishment of the *honmon no kaidan* in a modern context. These efforts set an important precedent for another such modern revisioning in the postwar period.

Sōka Gakkai's Postwar Vision

The next individual to envision a modern unity of politics and the *Lotus Sūtra* was Toda Jōsei (1900–1958), second president of the Sōka Gakkai, which is now Japan's largest lay Buddhist movement.[31] Like Tanaka's Kokuchūkai, the Sōka Gakkai under Toda's leadership would run candidates for political office with the aim of eventually winning a majority in the National Diet, in order to establish a state-sponsored ordination platform. There was no direct connection between the two; they had emerged from very different streams within the Nichiren tradition, and, where Tanaka had framed his goals in terms of the rhetoric and ideology of modern imperialism, Toda drew on those of postwar participatory democracy. To my knowledge, Tanaka is nowhere mentioned in Toda's writings. Nonetheless, Toda's vision undoubtedly owed something, however indirectly, to Tanaka's precedent.

The Sōka Gakkai (originally Sōka Kyōiku Gakkai) was founded in 1930 by Makiguchi Tsunesaburō (1871–1944), an educator who had converted to Nichiren Shōshū, a small independent sect of Nichiren Buddhism. The society's original aim was to implement Makiguchi's system of value creative pedagogy (*sōka kyōiku*) on the basis of Buddhist principles. In the 1940s—faithful to Nichiren Shōshū doctrine, which condemns all objects of worship other than Nichiren's mandala as heretical—Makiguchi defied the wartime government policy of religious control, which sought to enforce the observances of state Shinto by demanding that all citizens enshrine the talismans of the imperial Ise Shrine. He was arrested on charges of *lèse majesté* on July 6, 1943, along with other leaders of the society, and died in prison the following year.

Makiguchi's disciple Toda, who had been among those imprisoned, was released in 1945, shortly before the end of the Pacific War, and began the task of rebuilding. He renamed the society "Sōka Gakkai" to reflect an expanded orientation that would seek to implement Buddhist principles, not only in education but in all human activities. Toda devoted the first few years of his postwar efforts to establishing an economic foundation for the organization's activities and training leaders through doctrinal study. He also emphasized *shakubuku*, which for Sōka Gakkai members meant converting individuals specifically to the Buddhism of Nichiren Shōshū. Such activities centered on local discussion meetings (*zadankai*), the chief venue for the society's proselytizing since Makiguchi's day. In a manner reminiscent of Nichiren's explanation for the calamities of his own day, Toda stressed that Japan's sufferings during the war and its aftermath were fundamentally attributable to "disparaging the Dharma"; that is, a willful neglect of the *Lotus Sūtra*. Only by embracing the practice of Nichiren Shōshū could the country, indeed the world, achieve happiness and peace. The term *"kōsen-rufu,"* the universal spread of faith in the *Lotus Sūtra*, was used to designate this ideal.[32] Where Tanaka had linked *shakubuku* to the spread of divine imperial rule, Toda, who was active in the years immediately following the collapse of the empire, saw it as the means to create a world in which the sufferings epitomized by the recent war could not happen again. His message also appealed on an individual level, emphasizing the power of chanting the *daimoku* and converting others to bring about good health, improved material conditions, harmony in personal relations, and similar benefits. Sōka Gakkai practice thus promised to generate merit for individuals and, at the same time, bring about a harmonious world.

Toda's Vision of The *Kaidan*

Toda's particular vision of the *honmon no kaidan* began to emerge from the time of his formal inauguration as the Sōka Gakkai's second president on 3 May, 1951. This *kaidan* would be located in Shizuoka near Mt. Fuji—not in Miho, at the future head temple of a someday-to-be-unified Nichiren sect, as Tanaka had envisioned, but in Fujinomiya at Taisekiji, the specific head temple of Nichiren Shōshū. Nichiren Shōshū had a deeply rooted sense of its unique sectarian identity and had long claimed, among the various Nichiren Buddhist lineages, to alone uphold Nichiren's true teachings. According to its tradition, someday its precincts would house the *honmon no kaidan*, to be built by imperial decree.[33] Thus, in Toda's vision, the building of the *kaidan* would not only signify the official acceptance of Nichiren's teaching but also legitimate Nichiren Shōshū over other forms of Nichiren Buddhism. In speaking of this goal, Toda used the terms that Tanaka had popularized—*ōbutsu myōgō* and *kokuritsu kaidan*—but in a manner shorn of their earlier nationalistic connections. Toda himself had experienced firsthand the repressive policies of the wartime government, which he held responsible for his teacher Makiguchi's death, as well as the economic hardships, dislocation, and general misery that followed in the wake of defeat. In his inaugural address, he made certain to divorce the goal of building the *kaidan* from imperial ideology:

> There are those who think that *kōsen-rufu* can be achieved by having
> the emperor accept a *gohonzon* [personal object of worship, i.e.,
> Nichiren's mandala] and issue an imperial edict [for the building of
> the *kaidan*] as soon as possible, but this is a foolish way of thinking.
> Today, *kōsen-rufu* means that each of you must grapple with false

teachings and convert the people in this country through *shakubuku* one by one, having everyone receive the *gohonzon*. Only then will the *honmon no kaidan* be established.[34]

Similarly, Toda's rhetoric of *ōbutsu myōgō*, the fusion of Buddhism and government, had little to do with the nation-state. Ordinarily, Toda observed, government was willing to sacrifice the interests of individuals, small businesses, and so forth to implement its policies; in having sacrificed the lives of so many of its own citizens, Japan's wartime government had been "the worst government in the world." The aim of Buddhism, however, was to enable each individual to flourish. When that spirit would be implemented in public policy, a fusion of the two could take place and bad government would vanish. The spirit of *ōbutsu myōgō* was that prosperity and happiness should obtain on both an individual and societal level.[35]

At the time of Toda's inauguration, the Sōka Gakkai numbered only about three thousand households. Yet Toda fervently believed that he was living at a key historical juncture, when an extraordinary effort could make the goal of *kōsen-rufu* a reality in the space of a mere twenty-some years. In his inaugural address, he announced a seven-year proselytizing campaign—the "great march of *shakubuku*"—vowing to achieve a membership of 750,000 households before his death. This massive undertaking was supported by a thorough organizational restructuring and the systematic promotion of doctrinal study, geared toward one-on-one conversion efforts. The campaign was spearheaded by the youth division, which was organized in a military-style corps under Toda's direct leadership. They planned strategy and often confronted leaders of other religious groups, forcing them to engage in debate.[36] The "great march of *shakubuku*" drew much criticism, even some official scrutiny, for high-pressure conversion tactics.[37] At the same time, however, the Sōka Gakkai's promise of personal benefits and a chance to participate in creating an ideal world clearly appealed to many. Toda's goal of 750,000 member families would be achieved well before his death in 1958.

In addition to gaining converts through *shakubuku*, a second prong of Toda's campaign focused on "cultural activities" aimed at winning broad-based support for Sōka Gakkai's aims within the larger society. In particular, Toda decided that Sōka Gakkai should enter the political arena. The society ran fifty-two candidates for the 30 April, 1955 local elections, chiefly ward assemblies in the Tokyo metropolitan area. Of these, fifty-one were elected, including the Sōka Gakkai general director, Koizumi Takashi. Subsequent efforts would also prove remarkably successful, and by 1967, there would be nearly 2,000 Sōka Gakkai members serving in local assemblies. In 1956, three Sōka Gakkai members were elected to the House of Councilors, the Upper House of the National Diet.[38]

Several reasons have been adduced for Sōka Gakkai's entry into politics. Electing Sōka Gakkai members to political office helped promote internal solidarity and demonstrate the organization's presence to the larger society; it may also have been seen as a defense against the possibility of repressive measures.[39] Fundamentally, however, the venture into politics was driven by Toda's religious vision of an ideal world in which politics, economics, government, and all human activity would be informed by the *Lotus Sūtra*—a unity symbolized by the establishment of the *honmon no kaidan*. His mid-1950s editorials in the society's newpaper are quite frank about this: The culmination of *kōsen-rufu* will be the establishment of the *kokuritsu kaidan*, and for that purpose, a resolution by the Diet will be necessary. Thus, it is needless to say that representatives of those people with firm convictions as to the truth or falsity of religion, people who desire the establishment of the *kokuritsu kaidan*, must occupy a majority in the Diet.[40] Or, more explicitly yet, "We must establish the *kokuritsu kaidan* at Mt. Fuji, and make Nichiren Shōshū the state religion. For that purpose, we must occupy a majority of the Diet within the next twenty years."[41]

Tanaka Chigaku's vision, as we have seen, while in competition with the official ideology of his day, was nonetheless structurally similar to it; both, although from different perspectives, aimed at the unification of all humanity within the sacred Japanese *kokutai*. It was this structural similarity that made the two visions mutually comprehensible and won Tanaka support from prominent figures, even outside Nichiren Buddhist circles. However, Toda Jōsei's vision of the unity of government and Dharma was profoundly at odds with the dominant political ideology of the postwar period, which mandated a clear "separation of church and state" and relegated religion to the private sphere. On one hand, Toda seems to have strongly supported postwar democratic principles; he hailed the establishment of religious freedom, which made his "great march of *shakubuku*" possible.[42] On the other hand, he appears genuinely not to have recognized that the very goal of a state-sponsored *kaidan*, to be established by a resolution of the Diet, was fundamentally inconsistent with postwar religious policy. Writing in 1956, he dismissed the concerns of others who clearly did discern an incompatibility:

> The campaign for the last House of Councilors election drew
> considerable attention from society. That we, as a religious organiza-
> tion, should put forward some of our members as politicians has
> provoked debate on various points both internally and externally. At
> present, all sorts of deluded opinions are being bruited about, for
> example, that we intend to make Nichiren Shōshū the state religion,
> or that in several decades our members will dominate both houses of
> the Diet, or that Sōka Gakkai will seize control of the Japanese
> government. But our interest in politics lies solely in *kōsen-rufu*, the
> spread of Namu-myōhō-renge-kyō of the Three Great Secret
> Dharmas. Establishing the *kokuritsu kaidan* is our only purpose.[43]

Toda maintained throughout that the Sōka Gakkai had no interest in founding its own political party, nor would it run candidates for the House of Representatives (the Lower House, which elects the prime minister and thus exerts a correspondingly greater influence than the Upper House in national politics). But the fundamental tension between the Sōka Gakkai's goal of a state-sponsored ordination platform and the postwar ideal of the separation of government and religion persisted, and Toda's successor would be forced to address it.

Ikeda Daisaku and the Privatizing of the *Kaidan*

Ikeda Daisaku (1928–), Toda's youth division chief of staff, assumed leadership of the Sōka Gakkai as general director after Toda's death and was inaugurated as the third president on 3 May 1960. Initially, he reiterated Toda's earlier assurances that the Sōka Gakkai would neither form a political party nor run candidates for the Lower House. But the society was soon expanding sufficiently to consider bolder plans. At the twenty-seventh general meeting, held on 3 May 1964, with the membership nearing four million households, Ikeda made a startling announcement. Sōka Gakkai would formally establish a party, Kōmei Seiji Renmei (Clean Government League) or Kōseiren, to conduct its political activities. Though institutionally distinct, the society and the party would be "one and indivisible" in spirit. Moreover, the Kōseiren would run candidates for the Lower House.

Kōseiren—renamed Kōmeitō (Clean Government Party) in November of the same year—adopted the goals of "*ōbutsu myōgō* and Buddhist democracy" in its party platform.[44] With the Sōka Gakkai's formidable organizational resources mobilized for campaigning, it enjoyed considerable success. In 1965, eleven Kōmeitō candidates were elected to the Lower House; In 1967, twenty-five were elected. In 1969, when the number of its representatives in the Lower House rose to forty-seven, Kōmeitō emerged as the third largest party in the country. But, as its influence grew, public criticism mounted. Where earlier criticism had focused on the Sōka Gakkai's aggressive proselytizing, from around the mid-1960s books and articles by scholars and journalists now raised questions about the legality of Sōka Gakkai's political activities under Article 20 of the Constitution, which prohibits religious bodies from exercising political authority. Increasingly, fears were expressed that the Sōka Gakkai's political aims, including the establishment of a state-sponsored ordination platform, were inimical to democracy and the freedom of religion. Poor media management on the Sōka Gakkai's part compounded the problem, and matters would reach a head when Kōmeitō leaders tried to block publication of a book highly critical of the Sōka Gakkai by the political scholar Fujiwara Hirotatsu.[45] Fujiwara went public with the incident, precipitating a public relations crisis.

When such criticism first emerged, around the time of the Kōmeitō's establishment in 1964, Ikeda began attempting to redefine the term "state-sponsored ordination platform" (*kokuritsu kaidan*) in a neutral manner, or even to replace

it with the original and more doctrinally precise expression *honmon no kaidan*.
To a gathering of the Sōka Gakkai student division, he explained:

> Mr. Toda occasionally used the expression [*kokuritsu kaidan*], and
> because he did so, I, too, have used it from time to time. But in the
> *gosho* [Nichiren's writings], the writings of Nikkō Shōnin [1246–1333,
> founder of Taisekiji], and in the works of Nichikan Shōnin [1665–
> 1726, systematizer of Taisekiji doctrine], the expression *kokuritsu*
> *kaidan* does not occur. "*Kaidan*" refers to the *honmon no kaidan*, the
> ordination platform of the origin teaching of the *Lotus Sūtra*.[46]

Alternatively, he suggested that *kokuritsu* or "national" should be understood
simply as "belonging to the public" in the sense of a national art museum or a
national stadium, and that the establishment of the *kaidan* was "nothing to be
feared, nothing special at all" but, rather, comparable to erecting a commemo-
rative marker symbolizing the goal of the people's happiness.[47] For the Sōka
Gakkai study journal, Ikeda wrote: "In a democracy, the collective will of the
people is at the same time the will of the nation, so if one speaks of a nationally
established *kaidan* in that sense, there is nothing strange about it."[48]

Such apologetics, however, would ultimately prove inadequate. Under the
mounting pressure of external criticism, the Sōka Gakkai officially revised its
stance on several points concerning both the *honmon no kaidan* and its own
political activities. In his address to the thirty-third general meeting of the Sōka
Gakkai in 1970, Ikeda announced that, in consultation with the society's directors and with the Reverend Hosoi Nittatsu, chief abbot of Nichiren Shōshū, the
term "*kokuritsu kaidan*" would henceforth be abandoned. He offered assurances
that the Sōka Gakkai was not aiming to make Nichiren Shōshū the state religion; as a religion for all humanity it did not require that sort of political support. Moroever, the *honmon no kaidan* would be built, not by resolution of the
National Diet but "by the power of the people who maintain pure faith." Ikeda
elaborated: "The former president, Mr. Toda, and I thought seriously about a
Diet resolution [to establish the *kaidan*], as an expression of the people's demand.
However, in terms of the spirit of the Constitution, that would not be appropriate, and we abandoned that idea long ago." He further assured his listeners that
abandoning the notion of a state sponsored *kaidan* was in no way a betrayal of
doctrine; rather, to establish the *kaidan* "by the collective will of pure believers"
would be far more significant. Lastly, reversing Toda's declaration of some years
before, Ikeda declared that "[our] venture into politics is in no way a means to
establish the *kaidan*. Its purpose is simply to promote the welfare of the people,
and I would like to confirm, once again, that it is unrelated to the various [reli-
gious] activities of Nichiren Shōshū and the Sōka Gakkai."[49] In the same address, Ikeda further announced that, while Sōka Gakkai and Kōmeitō were united
in a common desire for the people's peace and happiness, use of the expression
"one and inseparable" to describe their relationship had invited misunderstand-

ings. Henceforth, the activities of the two organizations would be separate, and Kōmeitō officials would no longer hold leadership positions within the Sōka Gakkai.[50] The next month, at the eighth general meeting of the Kōmeitō, the expression ōbutsu myōgō was dropped from the party platform, and Kōmeitō assumed a more secular self-definition.[51]

This sweeping redefinition was in a sense liberating for both bodies. Freed from its explicitly religious ties, Kōmeitō was now able to join forces with other opposition parties, while the Sōka Gakkai from this point began to assume a more moderate, mainstream orientation, modulating its criticism of other religions. But Ikeda's announcement also marked a major readjustment of the society's religious vision. The Sōka Gakkai had entered politics as a means to achieve the goal of a state-sponsored kaidan, by winning a majority in the Diet. Ironically, its very success in advancing this means, as measured by the Kōmeitō's growing influence, aroused the criticism that would ultimately force the original goal of a state-sponsored ordination platform to be abandoned.[52] This did not mean abandoning the goal of establishing the honmon no kaidan in and of itself. It was simply now to be "established by the people" (minshūritsu) rather than "by the state" (kokuritsu). Passages in the major Sōka Gakkai handbooks were revised to reflect the change.[53]

What, exactly, did that mean? Some years earlier, at the twenty-seventh general meeting in 1964—the same occasion when he had declared the founding of Kōseiren—Ikeda had also announced that the society's members would raise money to donate to Taisekiji, a large, imposing hall of worship to accommodate increases in the number of pilgrims resulting from the Sōka Gakkai's shakubuku campaign. It would be called the Shō Hondō, or grand main sanctuary. At the time, it was designated simply as the latest in a series of buildings donated to the head temple by Sōka Gakkai members. By the following year, however, Ikeda had begun to speak of this project as the "de facto" (jijitsujō) establishment of the honmon no kaidan.[54] This suggests that he may already have foreseen the need to distance the Sōka Gakkai from the goal of a state-sponsored ordination platform, well before that goal was publicly renounced in 1970.

It would be hard to overstate the excitement and level of commitment that the Shō Hondō project generated within the society. When the plans were first announced in 1964, members were encouraged to save money to contribute during a fundraising drive that would be held for only four days, 9–12 October of the following year. The money, collected through the Mitsubishi Bank at more than 16,000 locations nationwide, amounted to more than thirty-five and a half billion yen, mostly from Sōka Gakkai members. The noted Yokoyama Kimio was retained as chief architect, and six construction firms were contracted for the project on a joint-venture basis.[55] The honmon no kaidan, the goal of Nichiren Shōshū for seven hundred years, would now be realized, and it was Sōka Gakkai members, under Ikeda's leadership, who were going to make it happen.

Tanaka Chigaku's plan for establishing the *honmon no kaidan* by decision of the Imperial Diet had marked the first reinterpretation of this goal in a modern political context and reflected the ideology of an emerging nation-state. In the postwar period, Toda Jōsei also aimed at establishing the *kaidan* by a resolution of the National Diet, a vision similar to Tanaka's but stripped of its imperialistic connotations and assimilated specifically to Nichiren Shōshū. Ikeda Daisaku's "*kaidan* established by the people," however, marked a major hermeneutical innovation in that it was to be built, not by government authority at all but as a privatized venture of the Sōka Gakkai. It offered, somewhat belatedly, a vision of the *kaidan* consistent with the postwar separation of church and state in a way that notions of a *kokuritsu kaidan* were not. At the same time, however, it was more difficult to legitimate in light of traditional doctrine and presented new definitional problems.

The Rise and Fall of the "De Facto" *Kaidan*

According to Nichiren Shōshū teachings, the *honmon no kaidan* was to be built when *kōsen-rufu,* or the spread of faith in the *Lotus Sūtra*, had been achieved. Though the Sōka Gakkai by the mid-1960s numbered an impressive five million households, still, no one could claim that a majority of the Japanese people— let alone of the world—embraced Nichiren Shōshū. Thus, the goal of *kōsen-rufu* itself had to be redefined in a more immediate manner. Ikeda accordingly introduced the concept of *Shaie no san'oku,* or the "three hundred thousand of Śrāvastī," a phrase from the *Dazhidulun* (Treatise on liberation through great wisdom) referring to the great difficulty of encountering the Dharma. According to this classic Chinese Buddhist work, although the Buddha taught in the city of Śrāvastī for twenty-five years, only one-third of Śrāvastī's nine hundred thousand households had seen him; another third had heard of but not seen him; and the remaining third had never seen or heard of him. In Ikeda's reading, however, the "three hundred thousand of Śrāvastī" became a formula for *kōsen-rufu.* If one-third of Japan's population were to embrace Nichiren Shōshū and another third become Kōmeitō supporters, he said, then, even if the remaining third were opposed, *kōsen-rufu* would virtually have been achieved.[56] Considering the Sōka Gakkai's rate of expansion at the time, converting one third of the population probably did not seem altogether inconceivable. Redefining *kōsen-rufu* in "de facto" (*jijitsujō*) terms not only made it seem more accessible but also served to legitimate the "de facto" *kaidan* that was to symbolize it.

Not everyone, however, found Ikeda's redefinitions persuasive. Even as the majestic framework for the Shō Hondō began to rise, new difficulties were brewing, this time within Nichiren Shōshū. Although Sōka Gakkai was by now the wealthiest and most powerful of Nichiren Shōshū's *kō* or lay affiliates, some of the older *kō* resented its growing influence within the sect. Particularly strident criticisms were voiced by the Myōshinkō, formed in 1942. This lay association took a more literalist reading of the *Sandaihihō shō*: The ordination platform was *supposed* to be nationally sponsored, and the attainment of *kōsen-rufu*, which should precede its establishment, had not yet been achieved. Supported by some sympathetic members of the Nichiren Shōshū priesthood, Myōshinkō members accused the Sōka Gakkai of distorting doctrine, and the head temple, of endorsing their error. Myōshinkō protests culminated in 1974 with a large anti–Sōka Gakkai demonstration staged in Meiji Park in Tokyo. Angered at the group's intransigence, Nichiren Shōshū's chief abbot, Hosoi Nittatsu, eventually ordered the Myōshinkō to dissolve.[57] But he also required the Sōka Gakkai to cease equating the Shō Hondō with the *honmon no kaidan*—although he left open the possibility that it might later be so designated when *kōsen-rufu* had actually been achieved. Just days before the newly completed structure was to be formally dedicated, an article appeared in the Sōka Gakkai's newspaper under the byline of General Director Izumi Satoru, which read:

> In light of [Nichiren] Daishōnin's great resolve to save all humanity, at present, only the first step toward *kōsen-rufu* has been achieved. Accordingly, the Shō Hondō does not yet represent the establishment of the *kaidan* referred to in the *Sandai hihō shō*. . . . Thus it would be a mistake to think that, in building the Shō Hondō, we have finished something, or fulfilled [Nichiren's] will, or accomplished *kōsen-rufu*.[58]

The Shō Hondō, with its glistening marble surfaces and soaring suspension roof, the largest in the world, was accounted an architectural marvel. Upon its completion, Taisekiji did indeed become a major pilgrimage site, visited annually by millions who came to worship, including Sōka Gakkai members from throughout Japan and from the member nations of the rapidly expanding Sōka Gakkai International. A network of facilities, lodging, shops, and transportation services, including a new bullet train station (Shin Fuji), sprang up to serve their needs. But the Nichiren Shōshū leadership had made clear that the structure in which they worshiped, imposing though it might be, was not the *honmon no kaidan*. Nor, today, does the possibility even remain that the Shō Hondō might someday be so redefined. Long-standing tensions between Nichiren Shōshū and the Sōka Gakkai, already evident at the time of the Shō Hondō's construction, escalated over time into mutual mistrust and hostility, eventually leading to a bitter schism in 1991. In a burst of anti-Gakkai sentiment, and over the protests of architects worldwide, the current chief abbot of Nichiren Shōshū, Abe Nikken, had the Shō Hondō demolished in 1998–1999.[59] Briefly catapulted to the status of a world religion by Sōka Gakai's international proselytizing efforts, Nichiren Shōshū has reverted to its historically more familiar role as a small, marginal sect within the larger Nichiren Buddhist tradition. Sōka Gakkai, for its part, now undergoing a period of self-redefinition, has reoriented its goal of an ideal society based on faith in the *Lotus Sūtra* in a manner consistent with Buddhist modernism more generally, joining the global network of socially engaged religionists. Its fierce exclusivistic truth claims of the postwar period—difficult for any religious institution with mainstream aspirations to sustain—have given way to a rhetoric of interfaith dialogue and cooperation. While the goal of *kōsen-rufu* remains, there is no longer talk of timetables or of concrete plans to build the *honmon no kaidan*. The millennial expectations that the *kaidan* represents have been returned to the indefinite future.

Afterword

Practitioners of any historical period who envision for their religion an active social role must continually negotiate two requirements: fidelity to their received tradition, which confers legitimacy, and responsiveness to the needs of the present, by which vitality is maintained. Not infrequently, these two demands—for orthodoxy and for contemporary relevance—are in tension. When that happens, the received tradition undergoes redefinition: hitherto prominent elements may be marginalized or overlooked; others, half forgotten, may be resurrected; and still others, reinterpreted. The hermeneutical strategies by which such choices are made are the vehicles by which traditions continually define and sometimes reinvent themselves. This is by no means a new process, though the attempts of Buddhist traditions to adjust to the social and intellectual transformations of the last two centuries place it in stark relief.

In this light, it is important to note that, from the standpoint of the broader Nichiren tradition, the attempts of Tanaka Chigaku and the Sōka Gakkai—to envision or even build Nichiren's *honmon no kaidan* as an actual institution supported by contemporary political structures—represent a minority move, one seldom encountered in the traditional Nichiren denominations consisting of priests, temples, and lay parishioners. From the early modern period, when Buddhist temples were subsumed within the state administrative apparatus and widespread *shakubuku* became impracticable, Nichiren Buddhist ideologues tended to interpret the *honmon no kaidan* in an abstract sense. The *kaidan* was wherever a practitioner might embrace the *Lotus Sūtra* with faith and chant Namu-myōhō-renge-kyō. Or, the entire realm of the eternal Buddha—the cosmos seen through the awakened eyes of faith—could be understood as the *honmon no kaidan*. The mandate found in the *Sandai hihō shō* for the building of an actual physical structure, symbolizing the conversion of the ruler and the people, was indefinitely postponed. What impact Tanaka's ideal of an actual *kaidan* as the spiritual center of Japan's envisioned world leadership may have made on traditional Nichiren temple Buddhism during Japan's modern imperial period remains a question for further investigation. In the postwar period, however, the mainstream Nichiren temple institutions have, on the whole, been content to let the establishment of the *kaidan* recede into the indefinite future.[60] More radical postwar scholars of Nichiren, as we have seen, have vigorously challenged the authenticity of the *Sandai hihō shō*, and with it, the entire notion of the *kaidan* as an actual institution; if Nichiren did not write this text, then abandoning the very idea of the union of Buddhism and government that it suggests could be construed as a return to orthodoxy.[61] This move has been driven less by textual evidence calling into question the *Sandai hihō shō's* authenticity than by a desire to define Nichiren Buddhism in a manner dissociated, both from the Buddhist nationalism of the modern imperial period, such as Tanaka's, and from the controversial political activities of the postwar Sōka Gakkai. Not coincidentally, it is also consistent with the postwar liberal ideal of the separation of religion and state.

It is significant that both Tanaka's Risshō Ankokukai (later Kokuchūkai) and the Sōka Gakkai were newly organized lay societies, quite different from the Nichiren Buddhist temples or lay associations of the past. In their initial emphasis on a "return to *shakubuku*," both societies drew, whether consciously or not, on a legitimating strategy used by reformers and schismatic lineages throughout the history of the Nichiren tradition: those who actively confront and repudiate the doctrines of other religions are the ones who can be said to be truly faithful to Nichiren's teachings.[62] Inspired by dramatic changes in modern forms of government—the emergence of the Japanese empire and the establishment of postwar democracy—their respective plans to realize the *honmon no kaidan* as an actual institution supported by the contemporary political structure served a similar legitimating purpose; in each case, it was the new movement, rather than the traditional institutions, that could claim to be striving to achieve what Nichiren had mandated. The political activities of these modern Nichirenist movements must be seen, not only in the context of Buddhist modernism, with its demand for this-worldly social engagement, but also within the history of the Nichiren tradition and the competing strategies of legitimation by which rival groups and institutions within that tradition have sought to define their orthodoxy.

NOTES

1. Japanese names are given in the traditional order, with the surname first. In notes, I have followed whichever order is used in the sources being cited.

2. *Nyosetsu shugyō shō, Shōwa teihon Nichiren Shōnin ibun* (hereafter *Teihon*), ed. Risshō Daigaku Nichiren Kyōgaku Kenkyūjo (Minobu-chō, Yamanashi Prefecture: Minobusan Kuonji, 1952–1959; revised 1988), 1: 733.

3. On this element in Nichiren's thought and in his subsequent tradition, see Satō Hiroo, "Nichiren's View of Nation and Religion," *Japanese Journal of Religious Studies* 26, nos. 3–4 (1999): 307–23, and my "Rebuking the Enemies of the *Lotus*:

Nichirenist Exclusivism in Historical Perspective," *Japanese Journal of Religious Studies* 21 (1994): 231–259.

4. "Shonin gohenji," *Teihon* 2: 1479.

5. *Teihon* 2: 1864–1865. The formal title of this essay is *Sandai hihō honjōji.*

6. On Nichiren's *homon no kaidan* and the politics of the dispute over the *Sandai hihō shō's* authenticity, see Pier P. Del Campana, "*Sandaihihō-shō*: An Essay on the Three Great Mysteries by Nichiren," *Monumenta Nipponica* 26, nos. 1–2 (1971): 205–224; Sueki Fumihiko, "Nichiren's Problematic Works," *Japanese Journal of Religious Studies* 26, nos. 3–4 (1999), especially pp. 264–273; and Jacqueline I. Stone, *Original Enlightenment and the Transformation of Medieval Japanese Buddhism* (Honolulu: University of Hawaii Press, 1999), pp. 288–290.

7. For an overview of the history of interpretation of the *honmon no kaidan*, see Watanabe Hōyō, "Kaidan," in *Nichirenshū jiten*, ed. Nichirenshū Jiten Kankō Iinkai (Tokyo: Nichirenshū Shūmuin, 1981), pp. 43–47. Nichiren himself understood the merit of receiving and keeping the precepts to be encompassed in the act of upholding the *Lotus Sūtra*, an interpretation which facilitated modern refigurings of the *kaidan* as relevant to lay Buddhists.

8. Ōtani Eiichi, *Kindai Nihon no Nichirenshugi undō* (Kyoto: Hōzōkan, 2001), p. 404.

9. See Richard M. Jaffe, *Neither Monk nor Layman: Clerical Marriage in Japanese Buddhism* (Princeton: Princeton University Press, 2001), pp. 165–188.

10. For Tanaka's influence on the Reiyūkai's founder, Kubo Kakutarō, see Helen Hardacre, *Lay Buddhism in Contemporary Japan* (Princeton: Princeton University Press, 1984), pp. 11–13. When Niwano Nikkyō established the Risshō Kōseikai in 1938, he sought the organizational assistance of two Kokuchūkai members, who initially served as Kōseikai's general and vice general director. See Niwano's *Lifetime Beginner: An Autobiography*, trans. Richard L. Gage (Tokyo: Kosei Publishing Co., 1978), p. 88.

11. The three-volume *Honge seiten daijirin* (Great dictionary of the sacred writings of Nichiren), published in 1920. One of the project's chief editors, Tanaka's disciple Yamakawa Chiō (1879–1956), helped to pioneer the modern academic study of Nichiren.

12. Iokibe Makoto, "Ishiwara Kanji ni okeru Nichiren shūkyō," *Seikei ronsō* 19, nos. 5–6 (February 1970): 121–147 and 20, no. 1 (April 1970): 69–100.

13. The most detailed study of Tanaka's career to date appears in Ōtani Eiichi, *Kindai Nihon no Nichirenshugi undō*. Other useful overviews include Edwin Lee, "Nichiren and Nationalism: The Religious Patriotism of Tanaka Chigaku," *Monumenta Nipponica* 30, no. 1 (Spring 1975): 19–35, and Nakano Kyōtoku, "Tanaka Chigaku: Hōkoku myōgōron kara Nihon kokutairon e no tenkai," *Kindai Nichiren kyōdan no shisōka*, ed. Nakano Kyōtoku (Tokyo: Kokusho Kankōkai, 1977), pp. 147–98.

14. *Shōmon no ishin* (1901; 9th printing, Tokyo: Shishiō Bunko, 1919). A more recent edition of the text, minus Tanaka's appendices, appears in *Gendai Nihon shisō taikei*, vol. 7, ed. Yoshida Kyūichi, (Tokyo: Chikuma Shobō), pp. 165–196. For further discussion of this work, see Lee, "Nichiren and Nationalism," pp. 26–27, and Ōtani *Kindai Nihon no Nichirenshugi undō*, pp. 69–75.

15. On Meiji-period transsectarian constructions of Buddhism, see James E. Ketelaar, *Of Heretics and Martyrs in Meiji Japan: Buddhism and Its Persecution* (Princeton: Princeton University Press, 1990). On the significance of *shakubuku* for Tanaka, see George J. Tanabe, Jr., "Tanaka Chigaku: The *Lotus Sutra* and the Body Politic," in *The Lotus Sutra in Japanese Culture*, ed. George J. Tanabe, Jr., and Willa Jane Tanabe (Honolulu: University of Hawaii Press, 1989), pp. 191–208.

16. In referring collectively to Nichiren Buddhism, Tanaka used the term Honge Myōshū, meaning the lineage (*shū*) of the Wonderful Dharma (*myō[hō]*), i.e., the *Lotus Sūtra* (Jpn. *Myōhō-renge-kyō*), borne by those bodhisattvas who are the eternal Buddha's disciples (*honge*), taught by him, not in his provisional manifestation as the historical Buddha, but at the time of his original enlightenment in the remotest past, as described in the origin teaching of the *Lotus Sūtra*. The Nichiren tradition identifies Nichiren as the leader of these "original disciples," the bodhisattva Jōgyō (Skt. Viśiṣṭacārita). Honge Myōshū was not the name of any existing Nichiren Buddhist institution but rather suggested an idealized, unified tradition.

17. *Shūmon no ishin, furoku*, pp. 32, 7.

18. Ōtani, *Kindai Nihon no Nichirenshugi undō* pp. 152–53.

19. *Honge myōshū shikimoku kōgiroku* (1904), vol. 1. For discussion, see Ōtani, *Kindai Nihon no Nichirenshugi undō*, pp. 95–103.

20. Ibid., quoted in Ōtani, *Kindai Nihon no Nichirenshugi undō*, p. 98.

21. *Shūmon no ishin, furoku*, p. 25.

22. See for example Yoshida Kyūichi, *Kaitei zōho Nihon kindai Bukkyō shakaishi kenkyū 2, Yoshida Kyūichi chosakushū 6* (Tokyo: Kawashima Shoten, 1991), pp. 120–35.

23. See Ōtani, *Kindai Nihon no Nichirenshugi undō*, pp. 119–20.

24. On the shift in Tanaka's orientation at the time of the Russo-Japanese War, and the development of his *kokutai* thought more generally, see Lee, "Nichiren and Nationalism," pp. 28–33; Nishiyama Shigeki, "Nichirenshugi no tenkai to Nihon kokutairon," *Ronshū Nihon Bukkyōshi*, vol. 9, ed. Kōmoto Mitsugu (Tokyo: Yūzankaku, 1988), pp. 136–140; and Ōtani, *Kindai Nihon no Nichirenshugi undō*, pp. 114–28.

25. Ōtani, *Kindai Nihon no Nichirenshugi undō*, p. 123.

26. The hermeneutical strategy of establishing identifications by correspondence and analogy constitutes a key feature of medieval Japanese Buddhist secret transmission texts. Interestingly enough, it was widely deployed in the modern period by Buddhist ideologues of every sect to argue that Buddhist teachings were consistent with the imperial project (see, for example, Christopher Ives, "The Mobilization of Doctrine: Buddhist Contributors to Imperial Ideology in Modern Japan," *Japanese Journal of Religious Studies* 26, nos. 1–2 [Spring 1999], especially pp. 89–94). To what extent Tanaka may have set the precedent for this interpretive approach will bear further investigation.

27. "Kōshū no kenkoku to honge no daikyō," *Myōshū* 7, no. 2 (February 1904), quoted in Ōtani, *Kindai Nihon no Nichirenshugi undō*, p. 123.

28. *Nihon kokutai no kenkyū*, quoted in Nishiyama, p. 140.

29. Quoted in Ōtani, *Kindai Nihon no Nichirenshugi undō*, pp. 297–298. See also pp. 322–329.

30. Lee, "Nichiren and Nationalism," p. 35.

31. The Sōka Gakkai today claims more than eight million member families (<www.sokagakkai.or.jp/sokanet/Syoukai/data>, accessed 12/30/01). Useful sources on the postwar Sōka Gakkai include Murakami Shigeyoshi, *Sōka Gakkai, Kōmeitō* (Tokyo: Aoki Shoten, 1967), and Kiyoaki Murata, *Japan's New Buddhism: An Objective Account of Soka Gakkai* (New York: Weatherhill, 1969). For this chapter, I am particularly indebted to Nishiyama Shigeki's "Nichiren Shōshū Sōka Gakkai ni 'honmon kaidan' ron no hensen," in *Nichirenshū no shomondai*, ed. Nakao Takashi (Tokyo: Yūzankaku, 1974), pp. 241–265.

32. In the text of the *Lotus Sūtra*, the expression *kōsen-rufu*, literally "to widely declare and spread," refers specifically to the Bodhisattva Medicine King chapter, which may have circulated independently (*Myōhō-renge-kyō, Taishō* no. 262, 9: 54c). Nichiren used *"kōsen-rufu"* to refer to the spread of his teaching.

33. See Murakami, *Sōka Gakkai*, pp. 74–82, for an overview of the *kaidan* in Nichiren Shōshū doctrine. On similarities and differences between Tanaka's view of the *kaidan* and that of the Taiseiki lineage, see Nakano, "Tanaka Chigaku: Hōkoku myōgōron kara Nihon kokutairon e no tenkai," pp. 180–184.

34. *Toda Jōsei zenshū*, ed. Toda Jōsei Zenshū Shuppan Iinkai (Tokyo: Seikyō Shinbunsha, 1981–), 3: 430. An exception to Toda's refusal to invoke the authority of the imperial house is a series of references, made in lectures delivered in the fall of 1954, to the *shishinden gohonzon*, a maṇḍala held by Taisekiji, which Nichiren is said to have inscribed for bestowal upon the emperor at such time as he should embrace the *Lotus Sūtra* (ibid., 4: 195, 198, 201, 211). Toda's references to this mandala, however, serve to stress, not so much the authority of the emperor as the sole legitimacy of Nichiren Shōshū among all Nichiren Buddhist lineages, by virtue of its possession of this maṇḍala.

35. Toda's views on *ōbutsu myōgō* were first adumbrated in an editorial in the Sōka Gakkai journal *Daibyakurenge* ("Ōbō to buppō," 10 March 1950, reproduced in *Toda Jōsei zenshū* 1: 26–29), and elaborated in his essay "Ōbutsu myōgōron," serialized from August 1956 through April 1957 (ibid., 1: 200–253).

36. The young men and women who had joined Sōka Gakkai just after the war came primarily from the urban working class; with little access to formal higher education or career-track jobs, they were drawn by Toda's personal charisma, his vision of an ideal society, and the opportunity he offered them to exercise their abilities in leadership roles. For the importance of the youth division in the Sōka Gakkai's postwar growth, see Murakami, *Sōka Gakkai*, pp. 119–120, 129, 139, 140–141, 143–147; Murata, *Japan's New Buddhism*, pp. 98–101. It is worth noting that, in the 1920s, the youth of the Kokuchūkai had also been organized into military-style corps and charged with direct responsibility for proselytizing (Ōtani, *Kindai Nihon no Nichirenshugi undō*, pp. 299–301); the question of whether or not their activities inspired Toda's manner of organizing of his youth division will require further research.

37. In 1952, Toda was required by the special investigations bureau of the Department of Justice (Hōmufu Tokushinkyoku) to deliver in writing a statement to the effect that Sōka Gakkai members would refrain from the illegal use of violence or threats in conducting *shakubuku* (*Kyōke kenkyū* 2, ed. Sōtōshū Kyōke Kenkyūjo [December 1957], p. 122, cited in Murakami, *Sōka Gakkai*, p. 136).

38. Hiroshi Aruga, "Soka Gakkai and Japanese Politics," in *Global Citizens: The Soka Gakkai Buddhist Movement in the World*, ed. David Machacek and Bryan Wilson (New York: Oxford University Press, 2000), pp. 107–108.

39. Nishiyama, "Nichiren Shōshū Sōka Gakkai ni okeru 'honmon kaidan' ron no hensen," p. 247.

40. *Seikyō shinbun* (7 April 1955), cited in ibid., p. 249.

41. *Seikyō shinbun* (17 April 1955), cited in ibid., p. 249.

42. According to Ikeda Daisaku's fictionalized treatment of the Sōka Gakkai's postwar history, Toda saw Douglas MacArthur, head of the American Occupation forces, as carrying out the work of "Brahmā," the Buddhist tutelary deity who punishes those disparaging of the Dharma and protects Buddhism, in this case, by dismantling the wartime religious controls and instituting freedom of religion (*Ningen kakumei*, vol. 1 [Tokyo: Seikyō Shinbunsha, 1965], pp. 132, 149, 152).

43. "Ōbutsu myōgō" (1 August 1956), *Toda Jōsei zenshū* 1: 200. Not much more than a year earlier, Toda himself had spoken of winning a majority in the Diet and making Nichiren Shōshu the state religion (see notes 40 and 41); it is not clear here whether he was being disingenuous or simply inconsistent, or had perhaps begun to shift his thinking.

44. On Kōmeitō's history and policies, see for example Daniel A. Métraux, *The Soka Gakkai Revolution* (Lanham, Md.: University Press of America, 1994), pp. 39–69, and Hiroshi Aruga, "Soka Gakkai and Japanese Politics," pp. 97–127.

45. Hirotatsu Fujiwara, *I Denounce Soka Gakkai* (*Sōka Gakkai o kiru*), trans. Worth C. Grant (Tokyo: Nisshin Hodo, 1970).

46. Address to the seventh student division general meeting (30 June 1964), quoted in Nishiyama, "Nichiren Shōshū Sōko Gakkai ni okeru 'hommon kaidan' ron no hensen," p. 251.

47. Ibid.

48. *Daibyakurenge*, November 1964, quoted in ibid., p. 252.

49. "Ningen shōri no daibunka mezashite," *Shinpan Ikeda Kaichō zenshū* (Tokyo: Seikyō Shinbunsha, 1977–1980), 1: 13–16.

50. Ibid, pp. 18–22.

51. Nishiyama, "Nichiren Shōshū Sōko Gakkai ni okeru 'hommon kaidan' ron no hensen," p. 257.

52. This problem has been analyzed in detail by Nishiyama Shigeki. Acording to Nishiyama, the process by which a religious movement's original goal is modified or abandoned while the means of organizational preservation and expansion become ends in themselves characterizes the transformation of a "sect" into a mainstream "denomination."

53. Nishiyama has compared the 1961 and 1968 editions of the *Shakubuku kyōten* (Manual for *shakubuku*), as well as the 1962 and 1967 editions of *Nichiren Shōshū Sōka Gakkai*, noting that in both texts, references to the state-sponsored ordination platform in the earlier edition have been revised in the later one to reflect the notion of a *kaidan* erected "by the people" (Nishiyama, "Nichiren Shōshū Sōka Gakkai ni okeru 'hommon kaidan' ron no hensen," pp. 254–256). Similarly, one notes that references to a state-sponsored ordination platform in Toda's posthumously published complete works are qualified by endnotes that repudiate the term

as one no longer in use and explain it as a *kaidan* sponsored by the people (see for example *Toda Jōsei zenshū* 1: 201–202).

54. See Murata, Japan's New Buddhism, pp. 129–132; Nishiyama, "Nichiren Shōshū Sōko Gakkai ni okeru 'hommon kaidan' ron no hensen," pp. 252–53.

55. For architectural details, see *Pictorial Report of the Sho Hondo* (Tokyo: Seikyo Press, 1972).

56. The *Dazhidulun* reference appears at *Taishō Shinshū Daizokyō* no. 1509, 25: 125c. For Ikeda's reading, see Murata, *Japan's New Buddhism*, pp. 129–132, and Nishiyama, "Nichiren Shōshū Sōko Gakkai ni okeru 'hommon kaidan' ron no hensen," p. 254.

57. Nishiyama, "Nichiren Shōshū Sōko Gakkai ni okeru 'hommon kaidan' ron no hensen," pp. 256, 259–259. Myōshinkō reorganized in 1982, however, as the Nichiren Shōshū Kenshōkai, and is now growing rapidly.

58. *Seikyō shinbun*, 3 October 1972, quoted in Nishiyama, "Nichiren Shōshū Sōko Gakkai ni okeru 'hommon kaidan' ron no hensen," p. 257.

59. Jane Hurst, "A Buddhist Reformation in the Twentieth Century: Causes and Implications of the Conflict between Sōka Gakkai and the Nichiren Shoshu Priesthood," in *Global Citizens*, pp. 69–70. The relevant websites cited by Hurst are no longer active; see however <www.nichiren.com/e03/htm>, accessed 30 December 01. On the schism more generally, see Trevor Astley, "A Matter of Principles: A Note on the Recent Conflict between Nichiren Shōshū and Sōka Gakkai," *Japanese Religions* 17, no. 22 (July 1992): 167–175; Jan Van Bragt, "An Uneven Battle: Sōka Gakkai vs. Nichiren Shōshū," *Bulletin of the Nanzan Institute for Religion and Culture* 17 (Spring 1993): 15–31; and Daniel A. Métraux, *The Soka Gakkai Revolution*, pp. 71–97.

60. For example, a Nichirenshū handbook explains the *kaidan* as a formal place of practice symbolizing universal conversion to the Wonderful Dharma but says nothing about when or where it might be erected, or about state sponsorship (*Nichirenshū dokuhon*, ed. Asai Endō and the Risshō Daigaku Nichiren Kyōgaku Kenkyūjo [Kyoto: Heirakuji Shoten, 1989], pp. 166–169). An exception to this general trend is Itō Zuiei. See his *Naze ima Sandai hihō shō ka* (Kyoto: Ryūmonkan, 1997).

61. See, for example, the chapter titled "Nichiren o kegasu *Sandai hihō shō*" ("The *Sandai hihō shō* that defiles Nichiren") in Tokoro Shigemoto's *Nichiren no shisō to Kamakura Bukkyō* (Tokyo: Fuzankaku, 1965), pp. 152–67.

62. On this point, see my "Rebuking the Enemies of the Lotus: Nichirenist Exclusivism in Historical Perspective," *Japanese Journal of Religious Studies* 21/2–3 (1994): 231–59.

9

The Making of the Western Lama

Daniel Cozort

Tibetan Buddhism was virtually unknown outside of its Himalayan
stronghold before the Chinese occupation of Tibet, which precipitated an exodus eventually numbering more than 100,000, including most of its prominent lamas.[1] Almost immediately, Westerners
began to find their ways to India and Nepal, to establish relationships with these teachers, and to invite them to travel and live in the
West. In little more than forty years, this little known branch of the
world's quietest major religion has reached around the globe to
establish a presence in nearly every major city and area of the West.
Hundreds of thousands of Westerners are now involved in some way
with Tibetan Buddhism, and while it may or may not eventually
become a major religion in the West, it has become clear that there
is only one major barrier to its further expansion: the emergence of a
cadre of Western-born teachers.

Even if there were enough qualified Tibetan teachers who were
willing to live in the West (and there are not, given the rapid
expansion of Tibetan Buddhism), there are many reasons that
reliance on Tibetan teachers alone would impede the development
of Tibetan Buddhism there. Tibetan lamas need financial support
that is beyond the means of many smaller Buddhist centers. They
have their own problems dealing with life in a foreign place where
they are often isolated from other Tibetans and by the language
barrier. They may not be up to the demands of teaching laypeople,
who have complex lives, who may have significant personal problems, more than half of whom usually are women, who may not

be interested in philosophy, and who may be hesitant to enter into a student-mentor relationship.[2]

But the most important reason may be the cultural divide. Because Buddhism is a religion in which individuals must work for their own salvation, it has always placed great emphasis on the teacher-student relationship. When the teacher is a Tibetan and the student is not, that relationship can be fraught with difficulties. There is in most cases a considerable language barrier; the student almost never understands any Tibetan and the teacher either cannot communicate in the student's language at all or at least cannot communicate subtle aspects of the Buddhist *Dharma*. And there is an inevitable cultural barrier. Although at times it is trivial—the teacher tells a story that falls flat, or the student asks a question that refers to technology that is unknown to the teacher— at times it is more serious, stemming from the neuroses peculiar to the Western mind. Once when His Holiness the Dalai Lama was teaching at Harvard, he was asked to advise students dealing with self-hatred and had to confer at length with several advisors to address a concept theretofore absent from his understanding of human nature. And the Dalai Lama probably knows as much about the Western mind as any Tibetan teacher anywhere.[3]

In short, as brilliant, compassionate, and generous as the Tibetan lamas are, many Western students simply need or want to hear the *Dharma* from the lips of their cultural cohorts. Several of the most prominent Tibetan teachers have long recognized themselves the need to train Westerners as *Dharma* teachers. They are the founders of a few energetic organizations, which like church associations, promote the establishment of new centers for study and meditation and provide links to unify those that already exist. The two largest and perhaps fastest growing of these organizations are the Foundation for the Preservation of the Mahayana Tradition (FPMT), founded by Lama Thubten Yeshe, and the New Kadampa Tradition (NKT), founded by Geshe Kelsang Gyatso. Together they have between 500 and 600 centers and branches around the world.[4] This chapter will examine the formal training programs each has begun in the 1990s and reflect on the ways in which these programs differ from the Tibetan curriculum that is their model.

The Traditional Course of Study at Sera Je Monastery

Both Geshe Kelsang Gyatso and Lama Thubten Yeshe were monks of the Gelukpa (*dge lugs pa*) order at Sera Je (*se ra byes*) monastery, near Lhasa, which has been reestablished near Bylakuppe in Karnataka state in south India. The teacher training programs at FPMT and NKT are based upon the curriculum of study for the Geshe degree at Sera Je, which is similar in most respects to the curricula at other Gelukpa monasteries. Because it is so lengthy and arduous, adapting the Tibetan model for Westerners involved many difficult choices.

THE MAKING OF THE WESTERN LAMA 223

Grueling does not seem too strong a word to apply to the path to the Geshe degree, requiring twenty to twenty-five years of study and debate. The title "geshe" has been applied historically to many teachers within all the Tibetan orders, including some laypeople.[5] Dge ba'i bshes gnyen is the Tibetan translation of kalyāṇamitra, "spiritual friend," a common way of explaining what it means to be a guru (Tibetan: lama, bla ma). However, in the twentieth century it was established as the name of the academic degree of the three major Lhasa-area Gelukpa monasteries of Ganden, Drepung, and Sera.

Although texts by renowned Indian scholars are formally the basis of study, special monastic debate manuals (yig cha) are used extensively. Each monastic college (grwa tshang) has its own. Sera Je's were written long ago by Jetsun Chogyi Gyeltsen (rje btsun chos kyi rgyal mtshan, 1469–1568). The debate manuals systematize the sometimes terse and ambiguous Indian texts and provide a rich blend of commentary drawn from Indian and Tibetan sources, along with helpful summaries and hypothetical debates on controversial points. Teachers teach the root texts and the debate manuals, following which students engage each other in long, formal sessions of dialectical debates on the material. The works of Gelukpa founder Tsongkhapa Losang Drakpa (tsong kha pa blo bzang grags pa, 1357–1419) are also important, and the better students become familiar with them as well. Some of the debate manuals are commentaries on Tsongkhapa's major works, which are themselves commentaries on Indian texts.

The curriculum for the Geshe degree is very ambitious. It has five phases:

1. Collected Topics on Valid Cognition (bsdus grwa). The aspiring scholar is grounded in topics in logic, epistemology, and psychology for at least three years.[6] He relies on his debate manual, the basis for which is the Pramāṇavārttika by Dharmakīrti (seventh cent.). Much emphasis is placed on learning how to debate as the student considers topics such as sameness and difference, subjects and objects, karma, and part and wholes. Also studied at this time are the topics of Types of Mind (literally, "awareness and knowledge," blo rig) and Signs and Reasoning (rtags rigs).

2. Perfection of Wisdom. For five years, he studies seventy topics related to the spiritual path of Buddhist practitioners at all levels, based on Maitreya's (fourth cent.) Abhisamayālaṅkāra, various commentaries, and the Sera Je debate manual.

3. Middle Way. For four years, in two separate classes, he studies the Mādhyamika philosophy based on the debate manual, which is essentially a commentary on Tsongkhapa's commentary on Candrakīrti's (seventh cent.) Madhyamakāvatāra. The ten Bodhisattva perfections and grounds are covered, although the main topic is emptiness (śūnyatā).

4. Monastic discipline. For four years, he studies Buddhist ethics as delineated in the rules of monastic life through the debate manual based on Guṇaprabha's (fourth cent.) *Vinayasūtra*.

5. Abhidharma. For four years, he studies topics such as cosmology, meditative states, and psychology through commentaries on Vasubandhu's (fourth cent.) *Abhidharmakośa*.

There were many small additions to this curriculum, such as the annual winter debating sessions on the *Pramāṇavārttika* and time spent memorizing rituals and prayers. Students were organized into classes with teachers who met with them in the mornings and imparted a commentary on the text. Then, many hours were spent in memorization and debate. Monks were expected to learn by heart many texts, such as the Indian root texts for their classes, as well as the definitions, divisions, and illustrations of the debate manuals. They were not allowed to bring books to the debating courtyard, but rather had to cite passages from memory. In Tibet, as many as eight hours per day were spent debating.[7] In India, Sera Je's schedule includes two hours in the morning and two hours in the evening.

Viewed from the perspective of Western pedagogical standards, it may seem that the Sera monk has a course of study that is at once broad and narrow, deep and shallow. On the one hand, he learns only Buddhist philosophy; what is learned about other systems is limited and polemical. What he learns about Buddhist philosophy is also limited; there is nothing, for instance, from the East Asian or Theravāda traditions. He deals with only certain kinds of texts on a regular basis; he reads little of the *sūtra* or even commentarial literature except what is filtered through the debate manuals. On the other hand, the range of topics he covers is remarkable; the debate manuals he uses, which are anthologies of pertinent texts from across the Indian and Tibetan traditions, present him with multiple points of view; and he explores the topics in fine detail through testing them in the debating courtyard.

The Sera Je curriculum is considered to be an exhaustive study of everything of great importance on the sutra side of Buddhism. The formal study of esoteric Buddhism, tantra (also known as secret mantra or the Vajrayāna), comes after the Geshe degree. Of course, many monks learn a great deal about tantra through acquiring initiations and performing their practices, and there are those who attend the tantric colleges without having completed the Geshe course; but the placement of tantric college after the attainment of the Geshe degree is meant to imply that the latter is preparatory for and is in fact the ideological basis of these higher practices.

Gelukpas are sometimes felt to equate spiritual development with education, but no one is elevated to the post of abbot—and thereby be in a position to become himself a Rinpoche who might begin a line of incarnations or tulku (*sprul sku*)—without thorough training in the tantras and time set aside for meditation retreats. Still, there is no denying that this tradition places more emphasis on philosophical study than any other. Whereas Westerners, and some Tibetans, tend to consider "practice" more important than "study," Gelukpas make no such division. As Geshe Jampa Gyatso, teacher of FPMT's main teacher-training program, says, "If one is ignorant, one cannot meditate. The Kadampa geshes have a saying that 'mediating without having listened to teachings is like someone without hands trying to climb a snow mountain.'"[8] Study and debate are supposed to remove misconceptions and sharpen the mind so that meditation can be more effective.

Teacher Training in the FPMT

The FPMT is a large Western movement of more than 130 *Dharma* centers in twenty-nine countries throughout the world operating under the spiritual guidance of Lama Zopa Rinpoche, a Gelukpa monk. The founder of FPMT, and its main teacher until his death in 1984, was Lama Thubten Yeshe.[9] In addition to *Dharma* centers, the FPMT sponsors health clinics and hospices, a prison program, monasteries and nunneries, and a revitalization of Buddhism in Mongolia, and is planning the world's tallest statue (of Maitreya, the future Buddha) in Bodh Gayā, India. Its Education Department designs and facilitates various formal programs including several to train teachers, which will be described later.[10]

Lama Yeshe was born in 1935 near Lhasa and was identified as a tulku as a small child. He entered Sera Je monastery at age six and remained there until 1959, when he escaped to India, living first in Buxaduar and later in Darjeeling. Among his teachers was the Dalai Lama's junior tutor, Trijang Rinpoche (who later was to suggest that Geshe Kelsang Gyatso come to England to teach in Lama Yeshe's Manjushri Institute). The young Zopa Rinpoche became his disciple at the request of Geshe Rabten, who himself later became an influential teacher of Westerners in Switzerland.

Lama Yeshe and Zopa Rinpoche became teachers of Westerners in the mid-1960s through the friendship of an American woman who became their student, took ordination, and helped them to establish a course for Westerners near Boudhanath and its famous *stūpa* in the Kathmandu Valley of Nepal. They acquired land and built the Kopan Monastery, then called the Nepal Mahayana Gompa Center, in 1971–1972. Their first meditation course was attended by about twenty students, but within three years attendance had to be limited to 200. In 1972 they also purchased land in Dharamsala, the headquarters of the Dalai Lama in Himaschal Pradesh, and in a house previously owned by Trijang Rinpoche they established Tushita Retreat Center for Westerners. They founded the first organization of Western monks and nuns, the International Mahayana Institute, at Kopan in December 1973.

The Western monastic community at Kopan became the first participants in a deliberate *Dharma* teacher-training program.[11] Basic topics in the Stages of the Path (*lam rim*) were taught systematically, followed by discussions and examinations that consisted of a prepared talk on the subject to the Western visitors, with questions from Lama Yeshe and Zopa Rinpoche as well as the audience. The Western monks also served as teaching assistants and discussion group leaders for the meditation courses.

Soon, Lama Yeshe began to move toward the establishment of a Geshe Studies program that would include most of the features of the Sera Je education. In 1975, Lama Yeshe encouraged the students who attended the year-end meditation course to return to their countries and start meditation centers, promising that he would travel from place to place. He envisioned the centers as staffed by a geshe, an interpreter, and a Western monastic. In 1978, the Geshe Studies program was begun at the Manjushri Institute in England. It was a very serious program that demanded twelve years of study and was taught initially by Geshe Jampa Tegchok, with coordination by a Western monk, Ven. Thubten Pende, who became one of Lama Yeshe's monks in 1974 and who has played a variety of key roles in every subsequent effort to educate Westerners.

The difficulties of the course, and differences of opinion about its direction (especially from Geshe Kelsang Gyatso, the first resident geshe of the Manjushri Institute), led to its demise.[12] In 1982, Lama Yeshe established Nalanda Monastery in France for his Western monks and Geshe Jampa Tegchok and Thubten Pende tried again to institute a Geshe Studies program there. However, it did not go very well; even with nuns from nearby Dorje Palmo Nunnery, there were not enough students attracted to the philosophical study of the geshe curriculum.[13]

The latest formal programs for teacher training, the Basic Program (BP) and the Masters Program (MP), were developed in the mid-1990s and launched in 1998. The BP is designed for those who want to go more deeply into Buddhist philosophy but either do not wish to or cannot commit to the longer and more difficult MP. It is a five-year course comprised of nine subjects with another three recommended. It qualifies its graduates to teach the topics they have studied, and the range of subjects is broad enough to serve the needs of all but the larger and more active *Dharma* centers. The MP was created by Geshe Jampa Gyatso and Thubten Pende, drawing on firsthand experience with the previous programs that had to be abandoned. It is a seven-year program of study followed by a year of retreat on the topics of the Stages of the Path, and some of its graduates will become the senior teachers of the FPMT.

The BP is currently offered at eight centers of the FPMT,[14] the Masters only at the Instituto Lama Tsong Khapa at Pomaia, Italy. About forty students from various European countries, the United States, Canada, Japan, Singapore, and Taiwan started the MP in 1998.[15] The two programs are quite distinct, and potential students must choose between them. The BP is not a prerequisite for the Masters, nor would its completion shorten the length of the MP if a Basic graduate decided to enroll in it.[16]

The FPMT Basic Program

The BP is a wide-ranging program that covers all the topics of great interest to Western laypeople but also some of the more advanced philosophical studies that are taught in Gelukpa monasteries. Texts are in English, and in most cases are translations of Tibetan works, although there are some seminal Indian Buddhist texts. In some cases a particular commentary is also a text for the class. The core curriculum of the BP is as follows:

1. The Stages of the Path. A study of Tsongkhpa's *Medium Exposition of the Stages of the Path* (*lam rim 'bring*). This survey of the entire Buddhist path is called "medium" because of its length (he wrote longer and shorter *lam rim* texts).
2. Heart Sūtra. This very short Mahāyāna sutra on emptiness is "unpacked" with a commentary by Tendar Lharampa.
3. Mahāyāna Mind Training (*blo sbyong*). This genre is similar to the Stages of the Path literature but is succinct, practice oriented, and concentrated on the generation of altruistic compassion. The text is Dharmarakṣita's *Wheel of Sharp Weapons*.
4. Bodhisattva Deeds. A study of Śāntideva's *Engaging in the Bodhisattva Deeds* (*Bodhisattvācāryāvatāra*), the seminal ninth-century text on the perfections of giving, ethics, patience, effort, meditation, and wisdom.
5. Types of Mind. Epistemology and psychology, based on a typology of consciousness, using two Tibetan texts on "awareness and knowledge" (*blo rig*).
6. Tenets. A Tibetan doxography of Indian Buddhist philosophical schools.
7. Ornament for Clear Realization. The fourth chapter of Maitreya's *Abhisamayālaṅkāra*, which is the principal source for delineation of gradations in the spiritual path and is considered the root of the Stages of the Path teachings.
8. Sublime Continuum of the Mahāyāna. The first chapter of Maitreya's *Mahāyāna-uttaratantra*, on "the Tathagatha Essence," or qualities of Buddhahood.
9. Tantric Grounds and Paths. A survey of the four classes of tantra, discussion of pledges and vows, and general outline of the Highest Yoga Tantra methods and gradations of experience, based on Tibetan texts that are themselves based on Tsongkhapa's *Great Exposition of Secret Mantra* (*sngags rim chem mo*).

Centers will teach certain other supplemental texts: the FPMT recommends Jetsun Chokyi Gyeltsen's *Seventy Topics* (a summation of the *Abhisamayālaṅkāra*); a text on death, intermediate state, and rebirth by Yangjen Gaway Lodro (*dbyangs can dga ba'i blo gros*), and a Highest Yoga Tantra commentary. These may or may not be made the basis of an examination.

Certain themes are repeated in slightly different ways as students progress through these texts. The Stages of the Path, Mind Training, and Bodhisattva Deeds texts and the commentaries on them cover much of the same ground, and the *Ornament for Clear Realization* and *Sublime Continuum* teachings expand upon the teachings on grounds and paths and Buddhahood given in them.

The BP requires examinations at the end of each of its nine subjects and has an optional comprehensive examination at the end of the curriculum. Students must participate in the support program as provided by the center where they attend the BP. This consists of discussions, meditations, and homework assignments (again including meditation), as well as, ideally, short retreats as an integrated part of each subject. To qualify for the final exam, they attend at least one one-month retreat on the Stages of the Path at the end of the program.

In addition, BP students have certain behavioral criteria. BP students, as future teachers, should be especially concerned about trying to generate an altruistic motivation and reducing the degree to which their minds are dominated by desire and anger. Patience is a particularly important quality for a Western teacher, who may be required to deal with students of many different backgrounds, dispositions, and personal problems. Ideally, all five precepts for laypeople (not to harm, steal, lie, take intoxicants, or misuse sex) should be kept, but in the West some exemption from the fourth precept on intoxicants has become customary.

The FPMT Masters Program

The MP is FPMT's top-level training program.[17] It requires seven years of intense study in Italy and therefore attracts only those very serious about the study of Buddhism and establishing competence to teach about more advanced subjects and who can overcome financial and other difficulties to devote themselves to a long course of study.[18] Reflecting the FPMT's intent to integrate even the MP study with the life of practice, its only prerequisite is a year of study on the Stages of the Path (such as one might receive at an FPMT center by attending weekly talks); a three-month retreat is highly recommended. (If it has not been undertaken, the retreats done during the program will add up to one.) Some students are ordained, but most are not.[19]

Two Tibetan geshes teach students of the MP with assistance from two highly qualified assistants for the English- and Italian-speaking students, respectively. The principal teacher is Acharya Geshe Jampa Gyatso, who was a friend of Lama Yeshe, a fellow Sera Je lharampa geshe who also graduated from the Gyume tantric college and received the Acharya degree for Sanskrit study in

Varanasi. Geshe Tenzin Tenphel is also a lharampa geshe; he teaches nonobligatory supplemental topics such as the "Collected Topics" that are the subjects in early monastic education, and the texts and subjects of the BP (since MP graduates may well become teachers of the BP).

The teaching assistant for English-speaking students is Jampa Gendun, a Canadian who was a monk for eighteen years and studied at the Buddhist School of Dialectics in Dharamsala for nine years. He leads review classes, teaches debating, and so on. Lorenzo Rosello (Ven. Losang Tarchin) works with Italian-speaking students. He is a monk who studied with Geshe Jampa Gyatso in the previous incarnation of the Master's program and therefore is familiar with much of the course work.

In many ways, the program resembles the forms of Western secular education: classes break for the Christmas holiday and from mid-July to mid-September; they meet Monday to Friday; there are review and discussion sessions with teaching assistants; written quizzes are given weekly and exams are taken every three months. On the other hand, students participate in weekly Stages of the Path meditation sessions, attend a monthly Stages weekend teaching, do a yearly group retreat, and contribute five hours of community service per week. In addition, they keep a daily journal of "self-evaluation" as part of an ongoing to effort to modify behaviors such as anger and envy. Graduates of the MP must be judged by the MP staff to be exemplary individuals in addition to being learned if they are to be posted as teachers in the FPMT *Dharma* centers.

The curriculum for the MP is actually simpler than that of the BP, but each subject is approached with much greater depth, and there is more emphasis on the classic Indian Buddhist texts (although as always much use is made of Tibetan commentaries and some Western texts).[20] The topics are as follows:

1. Ornament for Clear Realization. Maitreya's *Abhisamayālaṅkāra*.
2. Entrance to the Middle Way. Candrakīrti's *Madhyamakāvatāra*.
3. Treasury of Knowledge. Vasubandhu's *Abhidharmakośa*.
4. Tantric Grounds and Paths. An overview of tantra using Tibetan sources.
5. Guhyasamāja Tantra. A deeper study of tantric grounds and paths focusing on a single tantra whose system is a model. This requires that the students have received an initiation into its practice.

The first three topics correspond to three of the five areas of the Sera Je geshe curriculum. The time spent on each subject ranges from one to two years.[21] In addition, Geshe Tenphel teaches many subjects that are not required (and therefore not the subject of examinations), but which future teachers of the BP should know: the Collected Topics, Tenets, Types of Mind (*blo rig*), Cittamātra (*sems tsam*), Maiteya's *Uttaratantra*, and so on.

Only those who can undertake the full residential program in Italy will be granted the final teaching certification, but the program is open to others who want to study a single topic as it comes up in the rotation, and there is a thriving correspondence program. Each day the staff and students produce transcriptions of the lectures of Geshe Jampa Gyatso and supplementary material such as outlines and charts that are made available to subscribers through the Insituto Tsongkhapa website (and eventually collected on compact disks). Twenty-some prisoners in the United States and Canada are among those who receive the material gratis.

Teacher Training in the NKT

The NKT is a large and rapidly growing Western organization with its headquarters in northern England and many local *Dharma* centers, particularly in the United Kingdom and United States. It is the result of a quarter century of teaching in the West by Geshe Kelsang Gyatso, although it was not formally established until 1991. Geshe Gyatso was born in Tibet in 1931 and became a monk at the age of eight at Ngamring Jampaling Monastery in Western Tibet.[22] In 1950 he enrolled at Je college of Sera Monastery, one of the three main Gelukpa monasteries near Lhasa. He left Tibet in 1959 and resided in northern India, first at Buxa and then Mussoorie, for much of the next eighteen years, teaching and undertaking retreats.[23] He came to England in 1977 and has stayed there ever since, eventually becoming a British citizen.

The NKT is the final product of Geshe Gyatso's Western mission. He originally entered England to be the resident teacher of the Manjushri Institute near Ulverston, which was established by his former classmate Lama Thubten Yeshe as part of the network of centers that later came to be known as the FPMT. However, by 1979 he had begun to establish centers under his own direction and by 1990 there were fifteen in the United Kingdom and Spain. After visits to North America in 1990, centers were established in the United States, Canada, and Mexico. The NKT was formally established on 31 May 1991, and subsequently became a charitable (nonprofit) company registered in the United Kingdom, administered by four directors who are elected annually by the administrative directors and education program coordinators of the NKT centers. By 1992 the NKT had forty-five centers and branches; by 1997, over 170 in the United Kingdom and 100 in eighteen other countries; by the end of 2001, there were at least 400.[24]

The name of the organization recalls the name Tsongkhapa used in the fifteenth century for his monastic order, the New Kadam (*dka 'gdams gsar ma*), which has become better known as the Gelukpa. However, while firmly rooted in the teachings of Tsongkhapa—virtually all of Geshe Gyatso's books are commentaries on Tsongkhapa's works—the NKT does not consider itself part of the Gelukpa order. Geshe Gyatso, in a 1997 interview, said, "We are pure Gelukpas. The name Gelukpa doesn't matter, but we believe we are following the pure tradition of Je

Tsongkhapa."[25] However, when asked whether the NKT is synonymous with the Gelukpa, he replied, "Because the New Kadampa Tradition is in Western countries, most of the followers of this tradition are Westerners, so their way of studying and practicing is different." In other words, the NKT is a Western order that draws primarily upon the teachings of the Gelukpa tradition but is not subordinate to Tibetan authorities other than Geshe Gyatso himself.

The NKT stops short of proclaiming itself to be an emerging "fifth order" of Tibetan Buddhism. The Vajralama Buddhist Center in Seattle, for instance, states:[26]

By using this title to describe the association of Centres following his spiritual direction, Geshe Kelsang Gyatso is making it clear that practitioners of this tradition are principally following the teachings and example of Atisha and Je Tsongkhapa. The word "new" is used not to imply that the tradition is newly created, but to show that it is a fresh presentation of Buddhadharma in a form and manner appropriate to the needs and conditions of the modern world. New programs such as the General Program, Foundation Program, and Teacher Training Program have been specially designed to meet the needs of Western practitioners. By using the title "Kadampa," Geshe Kelsang Gyatso encourages his disciples to follow the perfect example of simplicity and purity of practice shown by the ancient Kadampas.

The fortunes of the NKT suffered a dip in 1996, when it was broadly criticized in the British press and elsewhere for picketing the Dalai Lama during a visit to Britain. The issue was one that was and is difficult for Westerners to comprehend: the Dalai Lama had opposed the worship of Dorje Shugden, a *Dharma* protector (*dharmapāla*), on the grounds that Shugden was not a Buddha but rather was an evil spirit who caused dissension in the Tibetan exile community, and Geshe Gyatso, a Shugden worshiper, considered this to be unwarranted meddling in a legitimate spiritual practice. In particular, he objected to the Dalai Lama's refusal to give tantric initiations to anyone who continued the propitiation of Shugden. Although to many Western observers the controversy seemed to be a strange remnant of Tibet's shamanistic past, the propitiation of Shugden is widespread and was promoted by some of the leading lamas of the twentieth century.[27] It continues to be an important part of NKT practices.

In any case, the NKT has clearly recovered from the negative publicity and has continued on a path of rapid growth. One key to this growth has been the establishment of a multilayered educational program that can largely be taught by Geshe Gyatso's Western disciples and that is designed to produce a continual supply of lay and ordained teachers for the new centers. The development of new teachers from within the organization is crucial, since the NKT has a policy that all of those who teach at NKT centers must be graduates of or at least participants in its own teacher training program. Even Gelukpa geshes would not be invited to teach.[28]

The names of the levels are the General Program, the Foundation Program, and the Teacher Training Program. The General Program is simply the ongoing general instruction for all comers at NKT centers or wherever NKT teachers find a venue for teaching. The Foundation and Teacher Training programs, on the other hand, are curriculums designed to turn Western students into *Dharma* teachers, the latter being the "finishing school" that all resident teachers ideally should complete.

The NKT Foundation Program

The Foundation Program is meant for serious students who want a guided study at a deeper level than they can get through the series of lamrim talks, usually all pitched to a beginner's capacity, that normally constitute the fare of Western *Dharma* centers. Some of the Foundation Program participants may be aspiring *Dharma* teachers, but they are not yet prepared to commit themselves to the Teacher Training Program. The program has been designed to resemble the format of study at a British or American university, with textbooks, lectures, small and large group discussion, and examinations. The five subjects cover the main topics of interest to Westerners involved with Tibetan Buddhism, exclusive of tantra:

1. The Stages of the Path.
2. Mahāyāna Mind Training.
3. The Heart Sūtra.
4. Types of Mind.
5. Bodhisattva Deeds. A study of Śāntideva's *Engaging in the Bodhisattva Deeds*.

In all cases, the textbooks are published books of Geshe Gyatso's teachings, which in turn are commentaries on Gelukpa works, especially those of its founder Tsongkhapa: *Joyful Path of Good Fortune*, *Universal Compassion*, *Heart of Wisdom*, *Understanding the Mind*, and *Meaningful to Behold*.

Students of the Foundation Program are expected to attend all classes and special study days prior to examinations, which are set for whole texts or parts of larger ones; to memorize essential points of each text; to take examinations; and to attend at least one special *pūjā* per week at their centers. The structure of each class meeting is as follows:

1. Preliminary practices consisting of a special *pūjā* (e.g., to Tara, Mañjuśrī, etc.) and recitation of a portion of the root text under consideration (e.g., for a class on Geshe Gyatso's *Meaningful to Behold*, it would be part of Śāntideva's *Engaging in the Bodhisattva Deeds*).

2. A guided meditation related to the topic of the previous class.
3. A "transmission": the reading aloud of a portion of the class textbook by the teacher, followed by a brief commentary.
4. Discussion, first in pairs and then as a group.
5. Dedication of merit.

Many pursue the Foundation Program by correspondence, which is offered at the larger NKT centers, which make audiotapes of classes and have copying equipment. In lieu of attending classes, correspondence students are asked to submit monthly "study summaries"—notes on the texts and to make special efforts to attend the special "study days" at their center. The study summaries can include questions directed to the teachers who read the correspondence. They are asked to listen to an audiotape of the real class, chanting along with the *pūjā*, participating in the guided meditation, and listening to the transmission and commentary. They are given the transmission again in person on the specified study days. In lieu of coming to a center for a special *pūjā* each week they are asked to practice privately at home, perhaps guided by an audiotape. They take the same written examinations as the other students, assessed by Geshe Gyatso and the program teacher.

James Belither, the international program coordinator of the NKT, estimates that at least half of the NKT centers and branches are holding Foundation Program classes. The numbers in the classes vary as widely, as does the intensity. At smaller centers, the program classes may occur only on weekends for a couple of hours, whereas larger centers can run daily classes. Correspondence students are generally involved with the larger centers and must be highly motivated to stay with a faster moving program, but many do.[29]

The teachers for the Foundation program are described as having "the transmission, lineage, and blessings of Geshe Gyasto's teachings and books."[30] In practice, this means that they are themselves involved in the Teacher Training Program. This Program has two levels, the first of which is roughly equivalent to the Foundation Program; the first three of its four subjects are exactly the same as the first three subjects of the Foundation Program. Indeed, one may transfer from one to the other at any time. However, few centers offer both programs simultaneously.[31]

The NKT Teacher Training Program

The Teacher Training Program is NKT's most ambitious undertaking. With twelve subjects (again based on Geshe Gyatso's commentaries) for a Study Program, as well as a Meditation Program of scheduled retreats and a Teaching Skills Program of monthly discussions, it aims not only to produce graduates who can teach the basics to newcomers at *Dharma* centers, but who are able to give tantric initiations and serve as tantric gurus. Geshe Gyatso himself has said:[32] "If you engage in the three programmes sincerely, maintain a pure motivation, view, and discipline, there is no doubt that sooner or later you will become a qualified Dharma Teacher. Eventually you will become a qualified Vajra Master like Buddha Vajradhara and lead thousands of disciples into the Vajrayana paths." The two levels of the Study Program are projected to take about eight years to complete. Those who reside at the Manjushri Mahayana Buddhist Center, the current name of the nineteenth-century Conishead Priory complex which is Geshe Gyatso's home and NKT's flagship center, are able to undertake classes four times per week and to participate in special retreats and spring and summer festivals.[33] Their approach to the subjects is far more intensive than is possible for Foundation students at the various centers offering those programs. Their classes are similar, except that group discussion is a special session at the end of each week rather than a feature of each class, and every fourth week there is a special "teaching skills" class.

Those who reside away from the Manjushri Center can complete the first level by pursuing the Foundation Program at their own centers or by correspondence and when ready can move on to the subjects of the second level by correspondence and occasional residence at Manjushri Center. Virtually all of the resident teachers at NKT centers around the world are in the position of already being teachers yet simultaneously being students in the Teacher Training Program, rather like graduate students who teach undergraduate courses while pursuing their own Ph.D.'s. The term used for all ordained resident teachers outside the United Kingdom is "Gen" (*dge rgan*, "spiritual elder"); lay resident teachers are called "Kadam" (*bka 'gdams*), a neutral term that neither implies an academic degree nor the special relationship that one may have with a "lama."

The principal difference between the first level of the Teacher Training Program and the Foundation Program is that there are four subjects rather than five, with the study of types of mind and Śāntideva's *Engaging in the Bodhisattva Deeds* being moved to the second level of the program and the study of the Bodhisattva vow put in its place. The four subjects of the first level are projected to take about three years to complete:

1. The Stages of the Path.
2. Mahāyāna Mind Training.
3. The Heart Sūtra.
4. Bodhisattva Vow.

The subjects of the second level, projected to take about five years to complete, are as follows:

1. Bodhisattva Deeds. A study of Śāntideva's *Engaging in the Bodhisattva Deeds*.
2. Middle Way. A study of Candrakīrti's *Entrance to the Middle Way*.
3. Vajrayāna Mahāmudrā.

4. Types of Mind (*blo rig*).
5. Offering to the Spiritual Guide.
6. Vajrayoginī Tantra.
7. Grounds and Paths of Tantra.
8. Heruka Body Maṇḍala.

The subjects are, like the Foundation subjects, based on Geshe Gyatso's commentaries to important texts in the Gelukpa order.[34] The first, second, and fourth are part of the Sera Je geshe curriculum. The latter does not include tantric topics, which comprise much of the subject matter here. Vajrayāna Mahāmudrā and Tantric Grounds and Paths are both surveys of principles and stages common to all *sādhanas* (the specific practices, or "means of achievement," of particular Buddhist deities) of the highest class, Highest Yoga Tantra (*annutarayogatantra*). They correspond, on the level of esoteric tantric practice, to the Stages of the Path literature of the exoteric level, and draw on Tsongkhapa's two longest works, the *Great Exposition of the Stages of the Path* (*lam rim chen mo*) and *Great Exposition of Secret Mantra* (*sngags rim chen mo*). The Vajrayoginī and Cakrasaṃvara material is the most detailed and revealing commentary on specific tantric practices yet to be published in a Western language.

Many graduates of the Foundation Program will want to move on to the subjects of the Teacher Training Program even if they do not aspire to become teachers, because it is only on that level that tantra is studied in detail. By the time they have finished the Foundation Program, most students will have received empowerments in Highest Yoga Tantra practices and will want to understand them better. But the time commitment is considerable, even though recently Geshe Gyatso has allowed centers to offer a schedule of two classes per week, half of what was required previously, with a reduced retreat commitment in exceptional circumstances.

Participants in the Teacher Training Program are asked, like the Foundation students, to attend all classes, to attend at least one *pūjā* per week, to memorize certain root texts and essential points, and to pass examinations. They are expected to review continually what they have learned before, so that before beginning a new subject they will be examined on their ability to remember root texts and "condensed meanings" such as definitions and divisions.

The subjects can be studied in any order, for new students may join at the beginning of any subject, or even at the commencement of a new section within a larger subject. However, once one has joined the program one is asked to complete all twelve subjects without interruption. The NKT wants to discourage people from coming and going as they please before they have finished the curriculum, and someone who fails to keep up with the pace may not be allowed to continue.[35]

Teachers in training are also expected to be students of Vajrayāna, and therefore to undertake a week of retreat each year on each of the preliminary practices (sngon 'gro): going for refuge, maṇḍala offering, guru yoga, and Varjasattva purification practice. There is a retreat in the summer to work on these. Normally, the preliminary practices are series of 100,000–plus repetitions that are done one practice at a time, but it is not unusual, especially in the West, for most of the practice to occur in structured retreats that mix them.

Trainees also participate in month-long retreats during the winter on either tantric grounds and paths, a particular tantric deity, or the Vajrayāna Mahāmudrā. Before completing the program they must have spent a total of two month's retreat each on Stages of the Path and Vajrayāna Mahāmudrā and a close retreat on a deity of Highest Yoga Tantra. Geshe Gyatso has taught only the practices of Vajrayoginī and Cakrasaṃvara, and so the January retreats organized by centers that have teacher training programs are devoted either to one of these deities or to the Stages of the Path.

Conclusions

What Was Omitted?

I have used as a baseline for comparison the Sera Je monastic education. Both the FPMT and the NKT curricula skip subjects that Tibetan monks spend years learning and debating. One major area is that of the "Collected Topics," the fare of early Sera Je education. This is treated only in some centers of the FPMT BP, briefly and optionally in its MP, and only in part (in Types of Mind, blo rig) in the NKT programs. How essential is this material?

Young monks learn to debate through topics such as colors, sameness and difference, subjects and objects, karma, and parts and wholes, and go on to a study of the classifications of types of reasoning, and a study of types of consciousness. All of this study provides a sort of grounding in the Buddhist way of dividing up the world and in the specialized philosophical vocabulary that is useful later when one studies higher topics, but that can probably be introduced well enough to students as they need it, if they do. This may be what occurs in the FPMT MP classes, which are being conducted by a fully qualified Tibetan geshe, and hence the future Western teachers may be getting all they really need from that material. But they will presumably teach other things as well, and it remains an open question as to whether Western teachers, whose exposure to these topics might be minimal, will see when it might be advantageous to introduce some of these topics, or realize that subtle points in the texts they teach might be connected to them.

Monks also spend two years studying the rules of monastic discipline (Vinaya). Although both the FPMT and NKT train ordained monks and nuns, the communication of the essentials of monastic discipline is apparently left up to ad hoc teaching from the Geshe Gyatso in the case of NKT or the resident geshes in the case of FPMT. Much of this material would not be relevant to lay teachers in these programs and it would have extended considerably the length of the programs to include it, although there is a good deal of discussion of Buddhist ethics within it.

Other areas within the Sera Je curriculum are covered in some programs but not others. The FPMT MP includes all the monastic subjects with the exception of those just mentioned; its BP has far fewer, although it includes a chapter of Maitreya's *Ornament for Clear Realization*, a Sera Je "types of mind" text, and refers to some other texts by Jetsun Chogyi Gyeltsen. The NKT Foundation Program does not use any Sera Je sources. While some of the same topics such as the stage of the path, emptiness, compassion, the bodhisattva perfections, and so forth, are covered in the alternate texts, they would not be treated in similar detail or terminology, and many other topics, for example, the cosmologies and other subjects in the Abhidharma literature, would be missed. The NKT Teacher Training Program studies Candrakīrti's *Entrance to the Middle Way* but otherwise uses different texts than Sera Je. What it adds to the Foundation Program is much more material on tantra than from the monastic curriculum.

The Content of the Western Programs

Both the NKT and FPMT have two tracks, one for very serious students who may become resident teachers, the other for students whose aspirations, abilities, or circumstances are more constrained. In both tracks in both organizations there is a heavy emphasis on the Stages of the Path literature, and meditation, something formally absent from the Sera Je monastic curriculum. And in all but the NKT Foundation Program level there is instruction in the theory of tantra and required meditation retreats, neither of which is included in the formal Sera Je curriculum.

The Stages of the Path approach is clearly regarded as "foundational" and "practical" for the West, and there is no hesitation to teach about esoteric tantric practices just because they are considered more advanced. Moreover, all of the programs incorporate meditation retreats that would be rare for a Sera monk in the midst of a geshe program. All in all, the NKT and FPMT programs respond to the desires of Western *Dharma* students, who feel that Buddhism is mainly about meditation, who want their philosophy mixed with practice, and who want to progress as quickly as possible toward the higher tantric teachings.

The lower level tracks, the Foundation Program of the NKT and the BP of the FPMT, are particularly alike. The latter includes all of the subjects of the former, adding four more that extend the BP another year or two beyond the Foundation Program and adding material on tantra, which an NKT student would receive only by progressing to the next program. In essence, the BP is more self-contained and can lead to a teaching position whereas the Foundation Program is more of a warm-up to the higher plane of the Teacher Training Program.

The MP of the FPMT and Teacher Training Program of the NKT differ most in their fidelity to the Sera Je model. The Masters requires seven years of study in Italy; the Teacher Training, eight years, some of which would have to be spent in northern England. But the MP copies the Sera Je curriculum with its lengthy courses on *Ornament for Clear Realization*, *Entrance to the Midddle Way*, and the *Abhidharmakośa*, differing mainly in its omission of Collected Topics and monastic discipline and its addition of tantric theory. The NKT Teacher Training Program more resembles the FPMT Basic Program than it does the Masters Program, except in length. It has twelve subjects (the FPMT Basic Program has nine) and many are the same. The Basic Program differs in including a study of tenets, *Ornament for Clear Realizations*, and *Sublime Continuum of the Mahāyāna*. They differ somewhat in the way they approach tantra; the NKT program includes Vajrayāna Mahāmudrā, Guru Offering, and the Vajrayoginī and Heruka Body Maṇḍala, whereas the FPMT program uses a Highest Yoga Tantra commentary and a text on death, intermediate state, and rebirth.

In the end, the similarities of the programs are more striking than their differences, and to truly assess their variation in coverage and intensity would require lengthy firsthand observation. Neither organization has yet produced its graduates and so it remains to be seen whether the choices of texts, the length of program, the examination standards, and the pedagogical methods were appropriate.

The Western programs differ from the Sera Je model most significantly in their emphasis on tantra and in their requirement for meditation retreats. The latter is clearly an attempt to "correct" for the Gelukpa tendency to sacrifice meditation to study; meditation is always said to be important, but there is little time for it in the monastery. That tantra is studied early and often, however, is an interesting decision given the long history of secrecy surrounding its practice and the oft-expressed reservations about its difficulties and danger. A Gelukpa monk who studies for the geshe degree defers the study of tantra until he has finished, entering a special tantric college or going into retreat.

Westerners clearly want to try what they have heard is the "highest" teaching, and at least at this point, Tibetan lamas do not seem concerned about the problems that might ensue. Of course, there are gradations of tantras and levels of initiation within the Highest Yoga Tantra practices that are given commonly. One must prove adept at the lower practices before progressing to the higher ones, and the degree of difficulty is such that not many Westerners will do so. But eventually Westerners will be authorized to give initiations and work with students and the standards of secrecy, of working with a guru, and so forth, will be tested.

Is Language Study Necessary?

Western languages, usually English, are used exclusively in all of these training programs. There is no required training in Tibetan or Sanskrit, although the

FPMT MP intends to have weekly classes in reading Tibetan. Students rely on written translations and, in the case of FPMT, oral translation for the discourses of some of the Tibetan teachers. (This slows to at least half-speed the pace of teaching, no matter how efficient and accurate the translation.)

This means that students can rely only on those sources that have been translated into English, and that they cannot reply upon their own resources to read translations critically. It also means that they are not equipped to receive teachings directly from a Tibetan teacher, unless that teacher speaks very good English, and that they would not be able to apply their knowledge to the many texts that have not yet been translated.

However, we have now reached the point where a great deal of essential material, especially that which is from the Gelukpa tradition, has been translated into Western languages and much more will follow in the coming years. Given their charge as teachers, to relate the essential *Dharma* to fellow Westerners, it probably makes little difference that these teachers have not studied the original languages.

Is Debating Necessary?

The FPMT's Geshe Jampa Gyatso has commented, "In the monastery, teaching tends to be easier. There, we teach in such a way that the students can then debate with each other and ask each other questions. In a monastery, it is said that 25% of one's understanding of the subject comes from the teacher's lecture, 25% from self-study, and 50% from debating."[36] Does a Western student need to use debating in the process of learning *Dharma* topics in order to become a qualified teacher?

The Sera Je monk studies his material very carefully and subjects it to thorough scrutiny in the debating courtyard. The debate process ensures a fairly high level of intellectual probing. One monk serves as the defender, the other, the challenger. The challenger often begins by asking the defender to recite a passage or definition and explain it. His task is then to explore the consequences of the view he has been given; ultimately, he attempts to find a consequence that the defender cannot accept and that will cause him to contradict his original assertion. A skilled debater can hold virtually any position and can find approaches to attack even those points with which he is in agreement. As can be imagined, the practice of dialectics cultivates impressive habits of mind over the years, training the monk to respond spontaneously to all manner of statements with critical reflection. It is done with considerable enthusiasm, being one of the main physical outlets available to monks and the only real sport allowed at the monastery.

But is debate necessary, or even possible, in a Western setting? The FPMT tried to incorporate it in its earlier training programs, with mixed results.[37] It decided not to include the classic "debating" texts in its required curriculum, and it decided that it was too difficult to require debate as a study method for the others. The Chenrezig Institute in Australia runs a BP that uses debate, but most other centers lack the materials and trained staff to make it successful, even if the students were the sort who would be willing to undertake the special requirements of debating. Among the other objections raised in FPMT's discussions were that: debate works only with a great deal of memorization, at which Westerners are not very adept; what is memorized for debating purposes is often relatively trivial; a majority of students are too "practice"-oriented to want to devote themselves to something so "academic"; the dialectical format discourages free discussion; the debate material does not deal with the sorts of questions that a Western program ought to cover; most of the debate texts that have been translated exist only in English; and debating only works well if there are a sufficient number of students at a particular place who are on the same level.

Westerners who study the *Dharma* without debate can still inculcate analytical habits of mind, of course, especially if they are taught by those trained in the method. This would be far more likely in the present FPMT programs that are taught by Tibetans, but it will occur less as time goes by. Memorization and analysis are not wholly absent from the Western programs: the students of the NKT programs and the FPMT Masters Program are asked to memorize some root texts and commit main points to memory, and they undoubtedly use their review classes and discussion sessions to test their views. However, the NKT discussion in pairs and in the group that follows is meant to reinforce Geshe Kelsang Gyatso's teachings rather than engage in hard-eyed analysis. On the positive side, the discussion method is used to provoke students into realizing how the points they are learning can be integrated with their own daily practice, which is something that the older Western laypersons who are the core of the classes want and need.

Is the NKT Training Too One-Sided?

Whereas FPMT students draw upon a variety of published sources and receive teachings from a number of teachers, NKT students rely entirely upon the published works of Geshe Kelsang Gyatso. Kelsang Gyatso is a highly trained geshe, and his teaching through these books is very much in the mainstream of his tradition, but it is still only one voice and one point of view. This is unusual in the Tibetan tradition. Although it is true enough that for Gelukpas, Tsongkhapa is considered virtually infallible, in general no source is considered immune from criticism.

Although nothing prevents NKT students from reading the books of other teachers, many might not see the point or have little time to do so. Somewhat of a counterweight to this is that the NKT, as it describes itself, is an "association of independent centers" with a weak center.[38] The teachers of the NKT are largely on their own, teaching in far-flung centers around the world with only occasional, perhaps not even yearly, contact with Geshe Gyatso and other NKT teachers. Also, as Westerners they have come to Buddhism from many directions, including other teachers and traditions. Their teaching is enriched by their own experience and by the challenge of teaching those who come to their centers, who themselves come to Buddhism with many different backgrounds.

What Kind of Teachers Will They Be?

The most essential question is whether or not these Westerners will be "lamas" in the best sense of the word, teachers with the inner qualities to inspire others and lead them along the spiritual path. Will there prove to be any correlation between the type and quality of training they have received and their ability to perform this vital function?

It is not yet possible to answer these questions. But it has always been considered essential to have a deep relationship with a spiritual teacher oneself in order to achieve the inner transformation that would make one a great teacher and potential spiritual mentor oneself. NKT students have only one lama, Geshe Kelsang Gyatso, and it is not clear that graduates of the TTP will ever have established a very close relationship with him except through the medium of his books. Will that suffice? Current FPMT students have relationships with the Tibetan geshes who teach the BP at certain centers or with Geshe Jampa Gyatso if they are in the Masters Program in Italy. But in the future, will students establish similar relationships with Western teachers?

However it turns out that the Western teachers will be as spiritual mentors, they will undoubtedly teach in a style at times highly different from the Tibetan model. Tibetan teachers become skilled commentators on texts, but they never self-consciously study public speaking skills such as gesture, modulation of voice, use of visual aids, provoking audience participation, and so forth. And, of course, they are not trained to address audiences of laypeople, especially Western laypeople, some of whom may be very new to Buddhism, some of whom are in deep psychological distress, and nearly all of whom bring into the lecture hall the basic outlook of Western culture with its scientific materialism, consumer mentality, and skepticism about religious authority. Many in the audience at *Dharma* talks lack the Asian ability to sit quietly and attentively for extended discourses. They prefer an interactive style, with plenty of opportunities for their own contributions in the form of questions or even opinions and revelations of personal experience. That Tibetan teachers have generally been successful anyway is a testament to the power of the ideas of Buddhism and the West's readiness to receive them, but few have been able to communicate effectively in English or another Western language and to address the peculiar concerns of typical *Dharma* students.

The Western *Dharma* teachers are bound to adopt Western styles in their teaching anyway, but the programs of the NKT and FPMT are devoting some attention to teaching styles. NKT Teacher Training students work on "teaching skills," which means that they take turns preparing talks that are given to their fellow students and critiqued by the group afterward. The program teacher also gives individual guidance on teaching methods. A yearly special three-week International Teacher Training Program gives those who are already teaching the opportunity to share ideas and problems and is becoming, says Belither, "a kind of 'Master Class' for teachers."[39] The FPMT is also beginning to make these matters a regular part of its curriculum. The BP as taught at the Chenrezig Institute in Australia includes teaching skills training for prospective *Dharma* teachers, and this may soon become a model for other centers. MP students are promised occasional workshops on teaching and counseling skills.

Those Who Are Already Teachers

All of the well-established Western Buddhist organizations already have prominent Westerners who function as teachers but who have not, of course, been through the training programs that have just begun. Most have studied with their Tibetan teachers for many years and may even have studied at a monastery in India. But with the exception of Georges Dreyfus and Michael Roach, no Westerners have earned the Geshe degree or its equivalent and a relative handful have undertaken formal study of the great texts with memorization, examinations, and so forth.

Hence, these organizations are creating designations for senior Western teachers to allow them an exemption from some of the criteria that otherwise apply to teachers. Shambhala International, the Kagyu organization founded by Chögyam Trungpa Rinpoche, may have been the first to give a special title to its longtime Western teachers when nine of them were named Acharyas (a Sanskrit title for a "learned one"; there are now eighteen) in 1996 by their current leader, Trungpa's son. These individuals are empowered to teach broadly, to give refuge vows and reading transmissions (*lung*) and to teach the tantric preliminary practices (*sngon 'gro*).

The FPMT is planning to designate as Lopon (*slob dpon*) a group of senior teachers who will carry the most authority.[40] As with the Shambhala International Acharyas, the FPMT Lopon designation is in part a way to recognize the status quo wherein there are a number of high-profile teachers who have not had the formal education of the FPMT Basic or Masters Program. Lopons are approved by the spiritual director of FMPT, Lama Thupten Zopa Rinpoche. The principal criteria for Lopons is that they have at least ten years of service to the FPMT, that they be respected and accepted as a teacher by the general public, which usually means that they travel frequently to teach at centers away from home, and of course that their conduct be regarded as virtuous.

Lopons can teach broadly, although some of them will not have had any formal study of some of the topics covered in the Masters Program classes. They can also confer certain types of vows.[41] "Refuge Vows" involve following the examples of the Buddha, *Dharma*, and *Sangha*. The "Five Precepts" are the ethical undertakings common to all Buddhists (not to harm, steal, lie, take intoxicants, or misuse sex). The "Bodhisattva Vows" revolve around the special aspiration to seek enlightenment from a base of compassion. The "Eight Mahāyāna Precepts" are one-day vows that may be taken anytime but that are normally undertaken at the time of the new, full, or quarter moon; they are an expanded version of the Five Precepts involving some small austerities such as sexual abstinence and limiting food intake. In addition, Lopons can give transmissions (*lung*) of mantras for students who have been advised to do a practice but have not formally been coached in the mantra recitation it requires. In other words, Lopons can function as lamas, although they will not give tantric initiations.

Titles for Teachers

In this chapter I have explored the way in which two Western organizations of the Tibetan Buddhist tradition are attempting to certify teachers for its students. It is a question that arises for every other Western teacher in the Tibetan Buddhist tradition, of course.

I have already referred to Shambhala International and its use of the Acharya designation for senior teachers. Other Western Buddhist organizations in the Nyingma and Kagyu traditions have begun to use the term "lama" for senior Western teachers who meet certain qualifications. They include the Dzogchen Foundation of Lama Surya Das (a Westerner); the Rigpa Fellowship founded by Sogyal Rinpoche; and the Chagdud Foundation of Chagdud Tulku Rinpoche. There are, in addition, many Western *Dharma* teachers who trained with Kalu Rinpoche in traditional three-year, three-month retreats and received the title "lama" from him upon their completion. They are not necessarily part of any formal organization nor do they necessarily use the title.

I have been concerned here with the Tibetan tradition, but there are many other examples. The conferences of Western Buddhist Teachers in Dharamsala have become forums for the discussion of the problems of certification and other adjustments to Western culture.[42] To cite two examples, at the third conference, Rōshi Bernie Glassman of the Zen Peacemakers Order headquartered in New York talked about the hesitation of Japanese Zen masters to confer the title "Rōshi" on Americans. Ven. Sumedo of the Amaravati Monastery in England, which follows a Thai Theravāda tradition, spoke about how Thai elders encouraged them to institute new norms for nuns in England (which they would not dream of introducing in Thailand).

What makes a person qualified to be a teacher of the *Dharma*? And who is to say? In Asia, these questions were relatively simple to answer. A qualified teacher of the *Dharma* was a senior monastic who had proved himself (or herself, far less often) worthy by excelling at monastic training under the tutelage of a recognized master. But in the West, where the tradition of monasticism is weak at best, and where even the ordained are not undertaking the classic training, the answers are less far clear. The FPMT and NKT will graduate its first teachers soon and we shall see what happens.[43]

NOTES

1. I am using the term "lama" (Sanskrit: *guru*) in the broadest sense as "teacher." The ideal lama is someone who actually has the personal qualities to lead others to enlightenment, which in the context of Tibetan Buddhism also means someone who can confer tantric initiation and fulfill the intense student-teacher relationship that may result. There are no universal objective standards for use of the term "lama," although it tends to be used automatically for tulkus (*sprul sku*; recognized reincarnations of prominent teachers), for graduates of the tantric colleges of the Geluk (*dge lugs*) monastic order, and for the best of graduates of three-year retreats in the Kagyu (*bka 'brgyud*) and Nyingma (*rnying ma*) order; in Ladakh it is used for all monks and in Mongolia for the caretakers of temples. See Alexander Berzin, *Relating to a Spritual Teacher* (Ithaca, N.Y.: Snow Lion, 2000), p. 37. Otherwise, it seems that someone is a lama if he or she has a student who regards him or her as one! For a full discussion, see Berzin's second chapter.

2. These and many other problems are discussed in various places in Berzin, *Relating to a Spiritual Teacher*. The context of a modern Western *Dharma* center, where a teacher is essentially hired, at salary, with benefits, to teach classes to students, is a very alien environment to traditional Tibetans and that so many have been able to adjust anyway is a testament to their kindness and flexibility.

3. Although there ought to be a clear demarcation between a spiritual teacher and a psychotherapist, in fact many students with problems tend to blur the distinction. Berzin makes some excellent points (pp. 61–63) about the difference. But the trend seems to be to combine roles; many Western Buddhist teachers actually make a living as therapists, combining a Buddhist perspective with other kinds of training. A case for combining classical psychotherapy with Buddhist training is made by several practicing therapists, such as Mark Epstein in his book, *Thoughts without a Thinker* (New York: Basic Books, 1995).

4. I should make it clear at the outset that I am not now nor have I ever been a member of either organization. I gained familiarity with the Gelukpa educational system through my graduate studies at the University of Virginia, where the Buddhist studies program directed by Jeffrey Hopkins was modeled on the Gelukpa monastic curriculum. Estimates of the numbers of centers and "branches" (associations or fellowships of students, usually in towns or cities where their numbers are insufficient to establish a permanent center) as of the beginning of 2002 were provided by the education staff of the organizations.

5. Sherpa Tulku, Khamlung Tulku, Alexander Berzin, and Jonathan Landaw, "The Structure of the Ge-lug Monastic Order, *Tibet Journal* 2, no. 3 (Autumn 1977): 67.

6. Geshe Lhundup Sopa, *Lectures on Tibetan Religious Culture*, unpublished manuscript, 1972, pp. 41–42. Circumstances could easily extend the time required; brilliance and hard work could shorten it. Geshe Rabten (38) who also attended Sera

Je, differs from this account only in noting that after the Abhidharma class there is a Karam (*bka 'ram*) class that reviews discipline and Abhidharma in detail.

7. Geshe Rabten, *Life and Teaching of Geshe Rabten*, ed. B. Alan Wallace (London: George Allen and Unwin, 1980), pp. 50–51.

8. Geshe Jampa Gyatso, "Climbing a Mountain with Both Hands" *Mandala* magazine (the FPMT publication), July 1997, p. 28.

9. Biographical information comes from the FPMT website (http://www.fmpt.org). Although Lama Yeshe has passed away, he is returning: his reincarnation was identified as a Spanish boy, born in 1985, who is studying at Sera Monastery in India as Lama Tenzin Osel and is expected in a few years to become director of FPMT.

10. There are now four formal programs: Discovering Buddhism, Foundation of Buddhist Thought, Basic Program, and Masters Program. The latter two are teacher training programs. The new "Discovering Buddhism" program is meant to be a way to "give participants a solid footing in the practice of Mahayana Buddhism" (FPMT website) in the period of approximately two years. The subject areas range from "Mind and Its Potential" to "Introduction to Tantra"; after a residential retreat of at least two weeks on the topics of the Stages of the Path, a student receives a certificate of completion. The course is being offered already by eight centers and another eighteen are gearing up for it, according to the FPMT International Office. Another foundational course covering approximately the same areas is the correspondence course in "Foundation in Buddhist Thought" offered by Geshe Tashi Tsering, a Tibetan who is the resident teacher of the Jamyang Buddhist Center in London. According to an article by Julia Hengst in the June 2001 *Mandala*, "Dharma Teachers: Seven Years in the Making", pp. 48–51, eighty students in London have completed the course over the four years prior to the article. It was to be made available to students elsewhere around the world starting in January 2002. The two-year course is divided into six modules ("The Four Noble Truths," "The Two Truths," "Buddhist Psychology," "The Mind of Enlightenment," "Emptiness According to the Prasangika-Madhyamika School," and "An Overview of Tantric Grounds and Paths"). Students listen to teachings on CD or cassette, read texts, do daily practice, participate in e-mail discussion groups, take exams, and write essays.

11. Information about the chronology of FPMT education programs is from a personal communication from Thubten Pende.

12. This and other disagreements led to a rift between Lama Yeshe and his students and Geshe Kelsang Gyatso and his, and eventually the Manjushri board of directors (comprising of Geshe Gyatso students) severed the connection of the between institute and FPMT. Few current students of either organization are aware of their past connection, but it is an unpleasant memory for some senior members.

13. This was true in Tibet as well; as few as a quarter of the monks in major monasteries engaged in serious study toward the monastic degree.

14. The BP is currently offered in centers located in Malaysia, the Netherlands, Australia, New Zealand, and the U.S.

15. In an article in *Mandala* in January 1999, "The Birth of the Master's Program", p. 58, Geshe Jampa Gyatso said that there were thirty-one students in residence and over 100 who were doing the correspondence course. At the start of

each new subject it is possible for new students to join. An interview with one student, Don Hanrick of the U.S., in the June 2001 *Mandala* reports that the ages of the students range from early twenties to early sixties, with most between twenty-five and thirty-seven, over half of whom are women (Hengst, "Dharma Teachers," p. 50).

16. Although there is a certain overlap in the subjects of the Basic and Masters courses, the subjects are treated in much greater depth in the Masters Program and the standards for behavior and practice are stricter. Hence, a graduate of the Basic Program who developed a desire to do the Masters Program would not be allowed to skip any of the stages but would need to start from the beginning.

17. Information about the Masters Program is drawn from the FPMT website.

18. There is a scholarship program that pays one-half of the room and board costs, and there are work-study possibilities; still, many students must spend all of their holidays and summer vacation months earning money to stay in the program (Hengst, *Mandala*, "Dharma Teachers," p. 50).

19. About one-quarter are ordained. Some became ordained at the beginning of the program and some during, but the majority are still lay persons (*Mandala* June 2001).

20. *Meditation on Emptiness*, by Jeffrey Hopkins (London: Wisdom, 1983), a lengthy and detailed analysis of many of the topics treated in the MA curriculum, is held in such esteem that an effort is underway, funded by an anonymous donor, to translate it into French, Spanish, Italian, German, Chinese, and Japanese.

21. Classes on the Ornament for Clear Realization ran from January 1998 to December 1999 and were followed by classes on the Entrance to the Middle Way; the Masters Class is scheduled to complete the Treasury of Knowledge classes in December, 2002.

22. Information about Geshe Kelsang Gyatso is from James Belither, the international programme coordinator of the NKT, in *Modern Day Kadampas* (NKT, 1997), the http://www.kadampa.org site, and from a November 2001 private communication.

23. Belither relates an account in which Geshe Kelsang Gyatso attended an examination at Tashilungpo Monastery prior to leaving Tibet, after which he was referred to as a Geshe; however, he also had a Geshe offering ceremony at Sera Je before coming to England. Since the normal procedure for a Geshe candidate was to pass examinations in his own monastery, with a final examination for candidates in the higher lharampa class at the time of the festival of New Year in Lhasa, and since only the three big Lhasa area monasteries offered the Geshe degree, it seems likely that Geshe Gyatso's examination at Tashilungpo was not for his own Geshe degree.

24. Estimates by Belither. The exact number of "branches" is difficult to determine because some smaller local groups, meeting at members' homes or public or rented places, come into existence or disband without communicating with the central office.

25. Donald Lopez, "An Interview with Geshe Kelsang Gyatso," *Tricycle: The Buddhist Review*, vol. 7, no. 3 (Spring 1998): 74.

26. http://www.vajralama.org, October 2001. This is clearly adapted from Belither, *Modern Day Kadampas* (NKT, 1997), p. 12.

27. For a summation of the controversy, and interviews with Geshe Kelsang

Gyatso and Thubten Jigme Norbu, a *tulku* (reincarnate lama) and elder brother of the Dalai Lama, see articles by Stephen Batchelor and Donald S. Lopez in the Spring 1998 issue of *Tricycle: The Buddhist Review*. One of the most famous Shugden worshipers was Trijang Rinpoche, one of the Dalai Lama's own tutors. Geshe Gyatso was one of Trijang Rinpoche's disciples, a fact often stressed in material about him. According to Belither, Trijang Rinpoche suggested to Lama Yeshe that Geshe Gyatso be asked to come to England and teach. Trijang Rinpoche wrote an effusive foreword for Geshe Gyatso's first book, *Meaningful to Behold*. Many other prominent lamas, including Lama Yeshe, were Shugden worshipers before the Dalai Lama's decision.

28. As Belither pointed out, one reason for this stipulation is that there be consistency throughout the organization in the presentation of topics. Every monastic college has its own set of unique positions on certain usually rather minor topics in Buddhist philosophy and may also differ with regard to the performance of rituals, etc., inasmuch as they will rely upon different texts. Of course, the ongoing disagreement with the Dalai Lama over Dorje Shugden practice would make it difficult for many Tibetan teachers to teach at NKT centers anyway.

29. Belither estimated that at least forty of the sixty students actively enrolled in the Foundation Program correspondence course at the Manjushri Center have been consistently completing the requirements.

30. From the NKT pamphlet, "A Meaningful Life: The Foundation Programme in Kadampa Mahayana Buddhism," p. 4, n.d.

31. Belither states that some centers wait until the completion of the five foundation courses before continuing on with the additional seven teacher training courses, and offer the latter only if there is sufficient interest; otherwise, they begin a new round of foundation courses.

32. Geshe Kelsang Gyatso, February 1994, in "A Guide to Becoming a Qualified Teacher" (NKT 2001), p. 4.

33. Belither says that a group of students connected to the Madhyamaka Centre in the U.K. was close to finishing the cycle of twelve subjects at the end of 2001 and another group is on its last subject at the Manjushri Center.

34. For the Stages of the Path, *Joyful Path of Good Fortune*; for Mahāyāna Mind Training, *Universal Compassion*; for the Heart Sūtra, *Heart of Wisdom*; for the Bodhisattva Vow, *The Bodhisattva Vow*; for the Bodhisattva Deeds, *Meaningful to Behold*; for the Middle Way, *Ocean of Nectar*; for Vajrayāna Mahāmudrā, *Clear Light of Bliss*; for Types of Mind, *Understanding the Mind*; for Offering to the Spiritual Guide, *Great Treasury of Merit*; for Vajrayoginī Tantra, *Guide to Ḍākinī Land*; for Grounds and Paths of Tantra, *Tantric Grounds and Paths*; for Heruka Body Maṇḍala, *Essence of Vajrayāna*.

35. Belither commented that although the program is flexible to allow for circumstances that might dictate the failure of a student to complete a topic, "people have been asked to leave when it was felt that they weren't really interested and their participation was having a detrimental effect on the class. People do not have to pass the exams and perform memorizations, just participate sincerely and try." Private communication.

36. Unpublished interview with Ven. Joan Nicell.

37. This summary was provided by Olga Planken of the FPMT Education

248 BUDDHISM IN THE MODERN WORLD

Department, who has been involved with the formation of FPMT educational programs since the 1970s. She was herself part of the original Geshe studies course that tried to use the Tibetan language and use debate as a method for learning.

38. There are only three unpaid part-time workers in the NKT Office at Manjushri Institute according to Belither, *Modern Day Kadampas* (NKT, 1997), p. 14.

39. Private communication, November 2001.

40. The Lopon designation had not yet been instituted as of this writing. Information supplied by Merry Colony, director of the FPMT Education Department at the FPMT International Office in Taos, New Mexico, U.S.A.

41. Unlike monastic vows or tantric vows, the vows on this list are not initiatory in the sense that they authorize specific practices. It is not necessary to participate in a formal ceremony to practice the five precepts or generate bodhicitta, etc.

42. Thubten Pende, private communication.

43. My speculation is that like so much else that is true of these training programs, they will continue to imitate secular academic training. In that world, the standards have gradually increased until it is now virtually impossible to obtain a college teaching post without the Ph.D. degree already in hand. I anticipate that the growth of centers of Tibetan Buddhism will eventually mean that to become the teacher of a major center one will need to have completed a course of study even more rigorous than those that we have examined in this essay. However, I would also imagine that the program of study will be more mixed, with even less time spent on the texts of a particular tradition of Buddhism and more spent on the skills of counseling and on a more "academic" approach to Buddhism including studies of its history, interreligious dialogue, and so forth.

IO

"Liberate the Mahabodhi Temple!"

Socially Engaged Buddhism, Dalit-Style

Tara N. Doyle

Setting the Stage

In the early morning hours of Buddha Purnima 1992, some eight hundred Buddhists from Maharasthra entered the Mahabodhi Temple compound and congregated in front of the locked doors leading into the main sanctuary.[1] There at the site, and on the day,[2] of the Buddha's enlightenment these Dalits[3] lit twenty-two candles commemorating the vows made by their deceased leader, Dr. Bhimrao Ambedkar, when he and a half-million of his untouchable followers formally renounced Hinduism and embraced Buddhism on 14 October 1956.[4] But on this morning, a twenty-third candle was lit and a new promise ardently added to the others: "Let it be known that today, here in Bodh Gayā, we vow to liberate this temple from Hindu hands! *Jai Buddha ki jai! Jai Jai Bhīm!* (Hail Buddha! Hail Bhim [Ambedkar]!)"

Just before sunrise, another group—comprising monks from the various Bodh Gayā monasteries, Buddhist pilgrims, Indian politicians, and visiting dignitaries—wound its way through town and ended under the Bodhi Tree. The annual *pūjā* began, as usual, with the monks chanting: first the Southeast Asians, then the Tibetans, and finally the Japanese. Next, speeches were given by a handful of notables, including the high commissioner of Sri Lanka, Neville Kanakaratne. In his speech, which was being broadcast live over Sinhalese radio, Kanakaratne announced his government's plan to install a gold-plated railing around the Bodhi Tree and asserted that Bodh Gayā should be seen in the same light as Mecca, Jerusalem, or the Vatican.[5]

The Maharashtrians did not join these Buddhists, however. They stationed themselves in front of the temple, opposite a building called the Pancapandav Mandir. This small complex, named after the five brothers of the Mahabharata, is under the jurisdiction of a local Shaiva *mahant* (abbot), and contains a collection of ancient Buddhist statues identified, by the brahmin priests who oversee their worship, as Hindu heros and gods. To the ex-untouchable Buddhist converts, this identification is not only inaccurate but deeply offensive. Furthermore, they deem the presence of a Hindu shrine within the Mahabodhi complex unacceptable. But most obnoxious in their eyes is that the Mahabodhi Temple *itself* is managed by a committee of five Hindus and four Buddhists, with the top two positions held by Hindu members. Thus their campaign to "liberate the Mahabodhi Temple" began quite self-consciously in front of this Hindu shrine, on Buddha Purnima—the day commemorating Buddhism's most central event.

After the Maharashtrians had congregated in front of the Pancapandav Mandir, they started shouting: "*Paṇḍāgiri bandh karo! Vihār baudhom ko do!* [End Hindu priestcraft! Return the (Mahabodhi) Temple to the Buddhists!]" Then a leader of the group accused the brahmin on duty of falsely identifying the Buddha images there as Hindu deities, ripped off the clothes covering these statues, and displayed them to the cheering crowd. Several Dalits entered another part of the Pancapandav complex and smashed the clay pots of water that had been ritually established over *liṅga*s marking the *samādhi*s (graves) of the Bodh Gaya Math's first mahants. At some point during this ruckus, the brahmin priest was shoved to the ground.[6] Around this time, news reached the people assembled under the Bodhi Tree that all hell had broken loose in front of the temple. The Gaya District Magistrate (D.M.), Rajbala Verma, quickly diffused the situation. No one was arrested, but the Maharashtrians were ordered to leave town by the next day. Before going, the Dalits circulated a memorandum outlining their grievances to a number of bystanders, including members of BBC and SLBC (Sri Lanka Broadcasting) radio crews. Chief among their complaints was the 1949 Act (known among this community as *kālā kānūn*, or the "black law"), which stipulates that the temple be managed by a committee comprising four Buddhists and five Hindus. The Dalits contended that the Mahabodhi should instead be administered by those who considered it most sacred (i.e., Buddhists), in line with the management of sacred sites worldwide. This said, they vowed to return in much greater numbers later that year.[7]

Within a few days, sensational headlines such as "Another Ayodhya-type Issue in the Offing," "Bihar Temple Dispute Hots Up," and "Yet Another Disputed Shrine Sparks Off Communal Trouble"[8] began appearing in newspapers, and became daily fare for the next few weeks. And while the situation in Bodh Gayā returned to normal, certain signs of discord began to manifest, both locally and farther afield. For instance, gun-toting police were stationed in front of the Pancapandav temple and a notice signed by the D.M. was posted forbidding the immersion of (what could only be understood as Hindu) images in the

Mahabodhi pond. Furthermore, the chief minister of Bihar, Laloo Yadav Prasad, a powerful Rashtriya Janata Dal (RJD) party chief noted for his anti-brahmin, pro-backward-caste politics,[9] began circulating a draft bill that would give sole management of the Mahabodhi Temple to Indian Buddhists. And in Nagpur, Maharashtra, a group headed by Japanese monk and naturalized Indian citizen Surai Sasai, held a meeting to discuss the Mahabodhi situation. Calling themselves the *Akhil Bhāratiya Mahābodhi Mahāviār Mukti Andolan Samitī* (All-India Mahabodhi Temple Liberation Action Committee),[10] they announced plans for a Dhamma Mukti Yatra (Buddhist Liberation Procession), which would begin in Bombay, travel through Delhi, and end with a demonstration in Bodh Gayā on 22 October 1992 (fig.10.1).[11]

In response to all this, graffiti began appearing on the outer wall surrounding the Mahabodhi compound. Scrawled in large red letters, the messages claimed the Mahabodhi a Hindu temple, decried Laloo Yadav Prasad, accused the Dalit Buddhists of being Pakistani agents, and asserted that the immersion of images would continue and that the Pancapandav Mandir would remain in the hands of the mahant. Most were signed "BJP" (Bharatiya Janata Party) and accompanied by the lotus symbol of this Hindu-nationalist party, which was at that time making the razing of the Babri Masjid in Ayodhya, and the building of a Ram temple on that site, a central plank in their campaign. Pamphlets were also distributed by local members of Vishva Hindu Parishad (VHP), a powerful

FIGURE 10.1. Poster for rally held in Delhi during the Mahabodhi Action Committee's Dhamma Mukti Yatra in 1992.

cultural organization closely aligned with the BJP, alleging that agitation for Buddhist control of the Mahabodhi was part of a "grand foreign design."[12] Finally, statements by prominent members of these groups began appearing in newspapers. For instance, the vice president of the VHP, Ashok Singhal, issued a press release saying that "the temple belongs not just to the Buddhists, but to the entire Hindu society,"[13] while a local member of the RSS (Rashtriya Swayamsevak Sangh), a paramilitary organization connected with the BJP, warned: "If the need arises, we are ready to shed blood to maintain Hindu dominance over the temple."[14]

By and large, however, the residents of Bodh Gayā wanted nothing to do with either the Dalit or BJP/VHP/RSS factions. Most feared that "another Ayodhya-type" situation would engender communal strife, keep pilgrims away, and thus disrupt business. Furthermore, international Buddhist response, at least at the official level, was not particularly supportive of the Dalits' actions. For instance, the Sri Lankan high commissioner wrote his foreign ministry: "In this sensitive and complicated area, it is my view that the Sri Lankan government, should, at least for the present, refrain from involving itself in what, to the outside world, will be purely an internal domestic problem of the Indian state."[15] He also wrote that the demonstration in Bodh Gayā, with its "unfortunate result" of damage to the Hindu shrine, had led to the issue becoming "seriously politicized" and could well lead to a hardening of attitudes along "Hindu and non-Hindu lines."[16] All other foreign governments with large Buddhist populations were similarly cautious and refrained from making official statements in support of the Dalits' campaign.

The 1992 Buddha Purnima demonstration was the first in a series of processions (yātrā), agitations (andolan), rallies (sammelan), and strikes (dharna) held in Bodh Gayā by the Mahābodhi Mahāvihār Mukti Andolan Samiti (henceforth, Mahabodhi Liberation Committee). All these protests have continued to revolve around amending the 1949 Act and, thereby, "liberating" the Mahabodhi Temple from Hindu and, to a lesser extent, what they see as "elite" foreign and Indian Buddhist influence. But unlike the first agitation, these subsequent gatherings have remained nonviolent, although most have been marked by angry, militant rhetoric, with threats of violence occasionally made.

Unlike practices described in the other chapters in this volume, the Buddhism practiced by members of the Mahabodhi Liberation Committee is quite new, stemming as it does from the 1956 conversion of Dr. Bhimrao Ambedkar. However, like many individuals and movements discussed here, it reflects "reformist" (as opposed to "neotraditional") tendencies and traits. In order to locate the Mahabodhi Liberation movement within the larger contemporary Buddhist arena, I have chosen to view it as an expression of what has recently come to be called Socially Engaged Buddhism. Therefore, I begin by discussing this phenomenon, arguing that the Mahabodhi Liberation Committee can best be understood within this rubric as a *militant* Buddhist Liberation Movement.

With respect to its militancy, the historical factors and modern forces that have influenced this group are many, but I would say two sets are particularly significant. This first is Buddhist, and comprises the Nichiren background of its leader Surai Sasai; the late nineteenth- and early twentieth-century attempts by the Sinhalese nationalist and Buddhist reformer, Anagarika Dharmapala to wrest control of the Mahabodhi Temple from the Bodh Gayā mahants; and the group's inheritance from Bhimrao Ambedkar of a socially engaged, militant style of Buddhism that includes anti-Hindu dimensions.

It is important to note, however, that this movement is driven to a large extent by contemporary Indian politics, which during the last few decades have been articulated and organized along caste and religious lines, with the reclaiming or retaining of sacred centers central to the discourse, actions, and goals of major political parties and chauvinist groups. This communalization of Indian politics, and in particular the Sangh Pariwar's recent campaign to "liberate" Ayodhya, I consider the second set of influences on the militant strategies and goals characterizing the Mahabodhi Liberation Committee. But, as we shall see, they draw heavily on the nonviolent tactics perfected and popularized by Gandhi, as well.

Finally, the fact that the Mahabodhi Temple is now frequented by a rapidly escalating number of international Buddhist pilgrims, and has become quite wealthy in the process, has prompted the Dalits to reach out for support from foreign Buddhists, and thereby place their movement on the contemporary international Buddhist stage. This attempt to globalize their campaign, however, has proven rather unsuccessful, as their militant tactics, anti-elite Buddhist rhetoric, and Ambedkarite style of Buddhism have stimulated many foreign Buddhists to either distance themselves from or actively disparage the Dalits' liberation campaign.

Socially Engaged Buddhism—Expanding the Definition

Given its members' strong emphasis on both the reformation of Buddhism and sociopolitical activism, the Liberate the Mahabodhi Temple Movement might well be included in what has come to be called Socially Engaged Buddhism or, more simply, Engaged Buddhism. Yet the militant nature of this group (with its angry, anti-Hindu rhetoric, aggressive tactics, and occasional threats of violence) makes the inclusion of this movement somewhat problematic, given how Socially Engaged Buddhism has tended to be defined.

The term "Engaged Buddhism" is attributed to the Vietnamese meditation teacher and social activist Thich Nhat Hanh, who wrote a book with this title in 1963. Since that time, Nhat Hanh has in many ways come to stand as the exemplar of this socially conscious, politically active, meditation-in-action style of Dharma. But during the 1980s and 1990s, other illustrious teachers, both Asian and Western, have been associated with this movement. These include most prominently the Dalai Lama, A. T. Ariyaratne, Sulak Sivaraksha, Mahaghosananda, Aung San Suu Kyi, Buddhadasa, Aitken Rōshi, Joanna Macy, Gary Snyder, Bernie Glassman, Christopher Titmus, and Joan Halifax.

While earlier works on Engaged Buddhism[17] focused almost exclusively on those Buddhist teachers who combine meditation, social activism, and a firm commitment to pacifism and reconciliation, Christopher Queen and Sally King broke new ground with their 1996 volume *Engaged Buddhism: Buddhist Liberation Movements of Asia* by including more strident figures and groups, several of whom mention meditation or "inner peace" not at all. Indeed, Queen and King's subtitle immediately, and quite self-consciously, brings to mind Third World liberation movements and Christian liberation Theologies. But they are quick to note that whereas many liberation movements in developing countries have been "typified not by peaceful or symbolic protests, but rather by open ethnic and class warfare, terrorism, and protracted armed struggle," the "Buddhist movements are *always nonviolent* and, indeed, often contribute innovative ideas and actions to the global discourse on the theory and practice of nonviolence."[18] I shall return to this caveat on nonviolence below.

The new, more militant groups and individuals found in Queen and King's volume—either in their introduction and conclusion or in full-length articles—comprise the fiery and iconoclastic Nichiren, the Buddhist nationalist Anagarika Dharmapala, the "political monks" of Sri Lanka (including Walpola Rahula), the strident untouchable Buddhist convert B. R. Ambedkar, and the wealthy, aggressively missionizing lay organization Sōka Gakkai. While both Queen and King seem at times hard-pressed to justify the volume's inclusion of these figures, they assert that, in the end, all qualify as *liberation movements* by virtue of "their focus upon the relief of concrete economic, social, political, and environmental ills," and as *Buddhist* due to "their commitment to pursue this end on the basis of Buddhist spirituality and heritage."[19] In her conclusion, King further clarifies the difference between figures such as Nobel Peace Prize winner the Dalai Lama (who counsels forgiveness and reconciliation with respect to Chinese aggression), and the leader of India's ex-untouchable Buddhist converts, Dr. Ambedkar (noted for his fiery invectives against upper-caste Hindus). Here she contends that the former (and others like him) utilize the modality of "love" when attempting to change oppressive social and political situations, while the latter (and strident figures such as those mentioned earlier) use the "prophetic voice." She explains these modalities as follows:

> The prophetic voice maintains a separation between self and other and does not hesitate to denounce what it sees as error and those whose actions are in error. Those who use this approach take up an oppositional stance with respect to an opponent or entity . . . and

take it as a goal to remove that opponent or entity from its position. In contrast, there are others who fundamentally and on principle recognize no enemy, who are averse to taking up an oppositional stance and who prefer to effect change in a manner that affects no enemies.[20]

Certainly the Mahabodhi Liberation Committee qualifies as a Buddhist Liberation Movement, as many of its members are involved in, and see their temple campaign as integrally linked to, a larger struggle aimed at eradicating the centuries-old social, political, economic, and psychological ills of untouchability. Furthermore, in both arenas, they draw heavily on Buddhist figures, ideas, symbols, and practices to justify and explain their actions, all the while reworking these Buddhist elements to fit their modern concerns. Finally, there can be no doubt that Surai Sasai and his Dalit followers fit King's description of Engaged Buddhists who utilize the "prophetic voice." For they maintain a strong separation between themselves and caste Hindus, forcefully denounce orthodox Hinduism and what they perceive of as elite Buddhism, are stridently oppositional in their rhetoric and tactics, and are determined to remove Hindus and elite Buddhists from the Mahabodhi Temple Management Committee, thereby eliminating (or at least curtailing) their influences at this site.

I thus find the ideas laid out in this volume extremely useful, and in particular the category of "prophetic voice." And yet, I have two problems with the way in which this category has been framed. First, would not a less culturally specific (i.e., less historically western) term be more useful when referring to a non-Abrahamic tradition such as Buddhism? Why not use the Sankrit terms *ugra* (wrathful) and *śānta* (peaceful), or the more neutral categories "oppositional" and "non-oppositional," as King does in her description, or the more standard designations "militant" and "pacifist" instead? While this may seem a minor complaint, it reflects a larger concern I have with a premise that frames this volume: that is, that what makes Engaged Buddhism a historically new tradition (as opposed to one with substantive precedents in Buddhist history) is the late nineteenth-century influence of European and American religious (particularly Protestant) and political thought.[21]

I have no trouble accepting Engaged Buddhism as a historically new tradition, one engendered by distinctly modern forces and conditions; yet it seems to me that this premise overly credits Anglo-American influence. As John Holt, Charles Hallisey, and others have noted when critiquing similar theories, Catholicism was also prevalent in colonies where Buddhist reform movements were occurring during much the same period; while in places such as Thailand and Japan, indigenous influences and historical precedents have been as significant as those new ideas and systems imported from the West. But more important, such theories often have the unintended consequence of overlooking or underplaying not only non-Anglo-American influences but the substantial agency of Buddhist actors in reforming their own traditions during the last two centuries, thereby perpetuating a basic strut of Orientalist constructions of knowledge vis à vis "the East."[22] In order to avoid this pitfall, at the level of semantics, I would thus prefer to use the term "militant"—as opposed to "prophetic voice"—to describe the Mahabodhi Liberation Movement and its Dalit participants.

This said, I would place this particular group on the far end of the militant spectrum. For in addition to utilizing angry, aggressive rhetoric, they have taken their movement—through processions, strikes, demonstrations, and agitations—into the streets. While these are standard items in the nonviolent activist's toolbox, there has been the implied threat of violence in several of the Mahabodhi Liberation campaigns. All of this leads me to wonder what exactly is the difference between militant words and actions or, for that matter, between militancy and violence? Where do the lines get drawn, and why? Furthermore, and perhaps more important, what is it about our understanding—our *construction*— of Buddhism that makes the inclusion of militancy so discomforting, and that of violence such an anathema? While I too am uncomfortable with these modes of expression and action—especially in the context of recent escalations of religiously justified violence, both worldwide and in South Asia—it seems crucial that such modalities be more fully explored. Thus, by introducing a militant group that *threatens* but does not engage in violence, all the while drawing on Buddhist ideas and figures to explain and justify their actions, it is my hope that this study will begin to answer some of these questions, and in the process contribute to ongoing discussions regarding Engaged Buddhist strategies for eradicating contemporary social ills.

Buddhist Roots of Militancy: Nichiren, Dharmapala, and Ambedkar

The militancy of the Mahabodhi Liberation Committee should come as no surprise, given the personalities and contemporary movements that have influenced the goals, rhetoric, and modus operandi of this group. While Ambedkar is primary with respect to the construction of their liberationist ideology and base of support, three other influences are important, especially regarding their goals and strategies. These are Surai Sasai's Nichiren background coupled with his emergence as a Dalit religious leader, Anagarika Dharmapala's nineteenth- and early twentieth-century campaign to wrest control of the Mahabodhi Temple from Bodh Gayā's *mahants*, and the Sangh Pariwar's movement to build a Ram temple in Ayodhya on the site of an already existing mosque. In this section I will deal with the Buddhist members of this group (Sasai, Dharmapala, and Ambedkar), while in the next I will take up the influences of the Sangh Pariwar.

Surai Sasai—Fulfilling Nichiren's Prophecy?

Surai Sasai was born Minoru Sasai in Okayama, Japan, in 1934.[23] At the age of fourteen he was ordained under his Tendai teacher, Shujuma Yamamoto, who named him Tenjit Surai, or "Light of the Sun, Beautiful Mountain Peak." Since then he has been known as Surai Sasai. Following his ordination, Sasai studied for five years at Taisho University in Tokyo. In 1955, his teacher sent him to Thailand, where he studied Vipassan meditation. Eleven years later he went to India, where he met Nichidatsu Fuji (the founder of Nipponzan Myōhōji, a Nichiren organization devoted to world peace).[24]

Fuji Guru-ji, as he was known in India, recruited Sasai to help in the construction of Shanti Stūpa in Rajgir (Bihar), India's first "peace pagoda."[25] By all accounts, including Sasai's own, Fuji's emphasis on a fusion of religion and social activism, interest in reviving and building Buddhist sacred places in India, and strong belief in Nichiren's prophesy that a monk from Japan would bring Buddhism back to the land of its birth, all strongly influenced the Japanese newcomer. But in 1969, within weeks of the *stūpa's* completion, the two men had a falling out, and Sasai decided to return home. However, while in Calcutta awaiting his flight, an event occurred that would send him in the opposite direction: west, to Maharashtra, where his thirty-year affiliation with Buddhists there would begin. That event, in his own words, is as follows:

> On the night of the full moon, I stayed awake all night, in deep *samādhi* (concentration), and had a vision. A giant of a man, with a huge head and long beard appeared to me. This man looked like Nagarjuna, as he is depicted in Japan. In his hand was a sharp weapon, with which he pierced me, and then he said, in Japanese: "Don't go to Japan, go to Nagpur. That is my *karmabhūmi* (place of action), now it will be your *karmabhūmi*." This divine being then removed the weapon from my body and disappeared. So I thought: "What can I do? I must go. *Then* I'll return to Japan."
>
> When I arrived at Nagpur station, I started beating my drum, chanting "*Namu myoho renge kyo,*"[26] and a crowd gathered. I asked where there might be a Buddhist temple, and was taken to meet a colleague of Dr. Ambedkar's, V. R. Godbole.[27] Inside his house was a Buddha statue and a picture. I was shocked to see that the man in this picture was the one in my vision, except that this one had no beard. When I asked who the man was, Godbole said "Babasaheb Ambedkar." I realized then that I was in the right place.

Despite this last claim, a professor at Nagpur University relates that the Nichiren monk was initially considered "strange, an outsider. People abused him, and threw away his drum. But then he started to say 'Jai Bhim' and build

Buddhist *vihāras* (temples). People were impressed and thought: He is our man. After this, his popularity started to grow."[28] In July 1987, however, a court case was filed that attempted to deport Sasai, as his visa had long since expired. Some Nagpur Buddhists objected and held a large procession. The matter was also taken up in the Maharashtra assembly, after which a delegation of his students went to see Rajiv Gandhi. As a result, Surai Sasai was granted citizenship.

Since becoming a naturalized citizen, Sasai's involvement in local and regional activities has escalated, thus moving him into a leadership position, particularly in Maharashtra, where the vast number of Dalit Buddhists live. He has organized an annual procession in Nagpur on Ambedkar's birthday, built a number of schools, hospitals, and *vihāras* in Maharashtra (using, many say, Japanese money), and helped establish a huge Buddha statue in the middle of the Hyderabad reservoir. It is clearly the Mahabodhi Temple issue, however, which has propelled him into the Maharashtrian, Indian national, and international limelight. Given his central role in this movement, I shall return to him many times later.

Dharmapala's Unfinished Campaign

When hearing about Surai Sasai's campaign, one is immediately reminded of Anagarika Dharmapala, the Sinhalese nationalist and Buddhist reformer who visited Bodh Gayā for the first time in 1891. Finding the site of the Buddha's enlightenment in the hands of the local Shaiva mahant, he launched a full-fledged crusade for Buddhist control of the temple. This battle he would wage, unsuccessfully, until the end of his life.[29] In order to precipitate his campaign, Dharmapala founded the Mahabodhi Society, the aims of which were to "make known to all nations the sublime teachings of . . . Buddha Shakya Muni, and to rescue, restore and reestablish as the religious centre of this movement, the holy place Buddha Gaya."[30] But he was quite clear that this organization should remain nonsectarian, writing: "The society representing Buddhism in general, . . . shall preserve absolute neutrality with respect to doctrines and dogmas taught by sections and sects among Buddhists."[31] In short, Dharmapala wanted to forge an international, ecumenical movement, using Buddhist jurisdiction over the Mahabodhi Temple as its central, unifying cause.

In order to accomplish this, Dharmapala went on worldwide speaking tours (including the 1893 Parliament of Religions), met and corresponded with numerous Buddhist leaders and rulers, wrote countless articles, attempted to purchase the Mahabodhi Temple outright, appealed to Indian independence leaders, and spent eight years contesting the mahant's jurisdiction over the temple in court. But to no avail: the temple remained firmly in the hands of the Bodh Gayā mahant. Two years after independence, however, the 1949 Bodh Gaya Temple Act was passed stipulating that the Mahabodhi Temple should be handed over by the mahant and managed by a committee comprising four Buddhists and five Hindus. It also stipulated that the committee would have no jurisdiction over the Pancapandav complex, which the Math was allowed to retain. Although the Bodh Gayā mahant fought this act, both in the courts and through *goonda* (thug) activity, the Mahabodhi Temple was finally handed over to a joint Hindu-Buddhist management committee on Buddha Purnima, 1953.

Dharmapala is featured prominently in Dalit historical narratives regarding the Temple,[32] while the present movement to liberate the Mahabodhi Temple is represented by its members as being a "continuation of Dharmapala's unfinished campaign."[33] Sasai certainly sees it this way. In fact, he claims to be an incarnation of the Sinhalese Buddhist revivalist, who died one year before Surai Sasai's birth in 1934.[34] Through this narrative, Sasai takes up Dharmapala's mantle, and makes his own movement "chapter two" of the latter's internationally famous, albeit unsuccessful, crusade. It should be noted, however, that the Japanese monk's constituency is quite different. Dharmapala's base of support comprised well-known Western sympathizers (e.g., Col. Henry Olcott, Edwin Arnold, and Thomas Edison), influential foreign Buddhists (the prince of Thailand, Gendun Choepal, and monastic leaders in Sri Lanka, Burma, and Japan), and upper-class, liberal Hindus (many of whom were members of the Mahabodhi Society). By contrast, the vast majority of Sasai's followers are poor Indian converts (particularly from Maharashtra, Delhi, and Uttar Pradesh), who have alienated many caste Hindus and failed to attract much foreign Buddhist sympathy or financial support. Indeed, most Western and Asian Buddhists are either unaware of or have actively distanced themselves from this new campaign.

Ambedkar's Socially Engaged Dhamma

Certainly the most significant influence on Sasai's rhetoric, goals, and constituency is Bhimrao Ambedkar, the undisputed founder and champion of the Dalit Buddhist community. Like Ambedkar, Sasai is a charismatic, driven, hot-tempered individual working for the uplift of the Dalit community and the spread of Buddhism in India. Unlike Ambedkar, however, Sasai is a foreigner, and has thus needed to establish connections between himself and his Dalit followers. And yet he does this by drawing on Ambedkar's charisma, theories, and agendas. This is not surprising, as anyone who wishes to forge a following among Dalits (especially those in Maharashtra) must affiliate him- or herself with Babasaheb ("Respected Father") Ambedkar.

Ambedkar was born into an untouchable family in 1891, but due to his brilliance, and the financial support of the liberal maharaja of Baroda, he obtained Ph.D.'s at both Columbia University and the University of London, as well as a British law degree. Returning to Maharashtra in 1923, he had his untouchable status, nonetheless, cruelly driven home: office clerks would not touch his papers, he was forcibly evicted from housing, and he received beatings and death threats from caste Hindus. According to Christopher Queen, "These ex-

periences convinced him that neither the patronage of liberal Hindus and British colonialists nor the heroic efforts of isolated individuals could make a lasting difference; only a social revolution . . . would end [caste-related] prejudice
and violence."[35]

Thus, during the 1920s and early 1930s Ambedkar led numerous nonviolent campaigns for access to water tanks and temples, and publicly burned the
Hindu Law Book, or *Manusmṛti*. All this brought him tremendous popularity
among untouchables but garnered little actual change. He consequently became
convinced that his people's uplift would never occur as long as they remained
Hindu, and turned his attention away from agitation toward conversion, urging his people, in 1935: "If you want to gain self-respect, change your religion;
if you want a just society, change your religion; if you want power, change your
religion."[36] After much consideration, he became a Buddhist in 1956.[37] He died
within forty-four days of this great event, however, leaving his fledgling movement leaderless. But through his speeches, articles, and magnum opus, *The
Buddha and His Dhamma*, he indicated what he wanted for his people, both
socially and religiously.

The Buddhism that Ambedkar bequeathed his community was a liberation
ideology par excellence. To begin with, he considered the Four Noble Truths
misguided interpolations of monastic editors, and defined suffering instead as
material poverty and social exploitation, the source of suffering as caste prejudice
legitimated by Hindu ideology, the cessation of suffering as the eradication of social
and economic injustice, and the path as the way to remove injustice and inhu-
manity.[38] He also denied that karma affected rebirth, as this implied that the
untouchables' plight was the result of their own ignorant past actions rather than
caste prejudice. Finally, Ambedkar was deeply critical of the modern *Sangha* for
their preoccupation with either worldly concerns or meditation and ritual, and
held that the spread of Buddhism in India could happen only if monks engaged
in social activism. Thus, gone is the emphasis on psychological bondage, meditative techniques, monasticism, and enlightenment. For, like most Third World
liberation theologies, and the beliefs of many militant Socially Engaged Buddhists,
Ambedkar's Buddhism addresses the economic, political, and social vicissitudes
of his community, with scant reference to spiritual practices and release.

One of the most important dimensions of Ambedkar's Buddhism was the
explicit, angry rejection of Hinduism. His "Twenty-two Oaths" include much
to this effect. These oaths, which he took at his own conversion ceremony and
which his followers continue to take to this day, include not only the basic Buddhist percepts, but such statements as: "I will not regard Brahma, Vishnu, and
Mahesh as Gods nor will I worship them,"; 'I do not believe that Lord Buddha
was the Incarnation of Vishnu"; "I will never perform any [Hindu rituals]"; and,
finally, "I embrace today the Buddha Dhamma discarding the Hindu Religion. . . . I believe that today I am taking New Birth."[39] With this final vow,

Ambedkar launched one of the greatest Buddhist movements in contemporary times, stimulating as he did the subsequent conversion of some eight to ten million Dalits, and thus the revival of Buddhism in its native land.

As can be seen from this overview, Ambedkar left his community with a radically reworked, socially conscious Buddhism. But he also bequeathed them a sense of defiance and angry, militant rhetoric that some, such as Surai Sasai and his followers, have taken into the streets.

Applying Ambedkar's Dhamma

Like Ambedkar before him, Sasai utilizes anti-Hindu rhetoric and emphasizes that to be a Buddhist in this community is very much wrapped up with *not* being a Hindu. As we have seen, Ambedkar's "Twenty-two Oaths" explicitly reject Hindu gods, rituals, and priests. The fact that Buddha statues are being dressed and worshiped as Hindu gods at the site of the Buddha's enlightenment, Hindu ancestral rites regularly performed there, and the temple itself managed by a committee comprising a Hindu majority would obviously be anathema to Buddhists who have taken such vows. It is not surprising, therefore, that Mahabodhi Liberation members see their movement as contributing to and participating in their community's attempt to regain its rightful religious heritage. Nor is it surprising that they have added a twenty-third vow to these others: "The Mahabodhi Temple shall be liberated from Hindu hands!"

Among the more interesting ways in which Sasai has aligned himself with this great Dalit leader are his oft-recounted vision conflating a Japanese-looking Nāgārjuna with Ambedkar and the addition of "Ārya Nāgārjuna" to his name. This vision, Sasai claims, is evidence that Babasaheb authorized his presence and activities among the Dalits, as the deceased leader commanded him: "Don't go to Japan, go to Nagpur. That is my *karmabhūmi* (place of action), now it will be your *karmabhūmi*." Sasai has further emphasized this connection by means of a widely distributed color poster that depicts him flanked by two enormous serpents, with Ambedkar just over his head. He claims that both Ambedkar and these *nāgas* are always with him and function as his protectors, but can only be seen by the magical *siddha*-eye.

While the ancient Mahāyāna philosopher is not himself important to Dalits, the name Nāgārjuna, that is, "Chief of the Nāgas," has significance for them, particularly those based in Nagpur. The reason is that, according to Ambedkar, Nagpur and the surrounding area was the ancient land of the indigenous, non-āryan Nāgas—tribals who were converted to Buddhism by the great "nāga-tamer," the Buddha, and who only later became untouchables at the hands of brahmin priests.[40] Taking Ambedkar's lead, many present-day Dalits believe themselves to be descendants of these Nāgas, who have once again become Buddhists. Thus, by calling himself the "Noble Nāga-tamer," Surai Sasai has established a connection not only with the Buddha and the Indian philosopher Nāgārjuna (who, it should be noted, is very important in Japan) but with Ambedkar and his Dalit followers as well.

Finally, Surai Sasai has skillfully drawn on Ambedkar's belief that Buddhist monks should be social activists and engage in conversion so that Buddhism might once again take root in India.[41] Although Ambedkar did not live to organize such a socially engaged *Sangha*, there is one section in *The Buddha and His Dhamma* that reflects the militant attitude he felt such a *Sangha* should have. This section, entitled "A Bhikkhu Must Fight to Spread Dhamma," begins with the following query: "Warriors, warriors, Lord, we call ourselves. In what way then are we warriors?" The Buddha answers: "We wage war, O disciples, therefore we are called warriors." The *bhikkhus* then ask: "Wherefore, Lord, do we wage war?" To this the Buddha replies: "For lofty virtues . . . for sublime wisdom-for these things do we wage war." This exchange concludes with Ambedkar's commentary: "Where Dhamma is in danger do not avoid fighting, do not be mealy-mouthed."[42]

Sasai, who is far from "mealy-mouthed," has responded to Ambedkar's battle cry in a number of ways. To begin with, he organizes *dikṣhās* (conversion ceremonies) at many of his agitations. Second, he constantly harangues his people to "Go into the villages. Convert!" Finally is the formation of what he calls his Dhammasena: a "Buddhist Army" comprising monks who ordain for the period of his agitations, as well as lay "lieutenants" dedicated to the Mahabodhi cause (fig. 10.2). As we shall see in the following section, comparisons with such militant Hindu organizations as the RSS, Vajrang Dal, and Shiv Sena are obvious. But the Nichiren Buddhist influence is equally clear, given Nichiren's advocation of an aggressive form of proselytism, coached in militaristic language and perpetrated by monks, all of which have characterized this sect until recent times. Indeed, Sasai proudly told me: "My Dhammasena men are true samurais, complete with martial arts training. Unlike other Buddhists, they're not afraid to fight!" Whether Ambedkar would have felt the Mahabodhi issue one worth fighting for, or in this manner, is impossible to determine. But it is likely that much of Surai Sasai's angry, anti-Hindu rhetoric and many of his goals (especially conversion and social uplift) would have met with Ambedkar's approval, as they are certainly in line with his own.

Militant Processions, Nonviolent Strikes

While many of the Mahabodhi Liberation Committee's rhetorical statements, strategies, and goals derive from Buddhist sources, contemporary Indian leaders and movements have had their influence as well. Prime among them has been the BJP's campaign to build a Ram temple in Ayodhya, as this militant, communally based crusade provided the Dalits, in the early stages of their

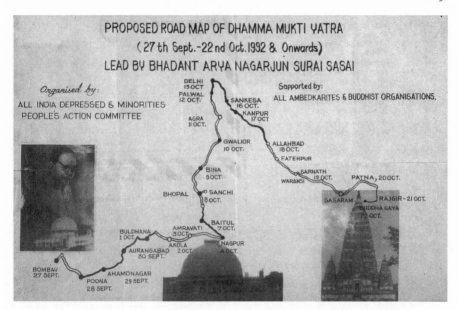

FIGURE 10.2. This map was printed on an inland letter and sent to Buddhists, politicians, social workers and other interested parties to advertise Surai Sasai's 1992 "Liberate the Mahabodhi Temple" procession, which began in Bombay and ended in Bodh Gayā.

Mahabodhi movement, with a model for how they, too, might thrust their social and political grievances onto the national stage. Another influence has strangely enough been Gandhi, who through his perfection and popularization of nonviolent tactics, supplied members of the Mahabodhi Liberation Movement with the strikes and demonstrations they have employed in more recent years.

In the Shadow of Ayodhya—1992 Yatra

Within weeks of the 1992 Buddha Purnima described at the beginning of this chapter, Surai Sasai and his followers announced plans for a month-long Dhamma Mukti Yatra, or "Buddhist Liberation Procession," that would begin in Bombay and end with a demonstration in Bodh Gayā on October 22. In this, they were clearly taking their cues from the highly politicized Rath Yatra (Chariot Procession) from Somnath to Ayodhya, which was led in 1990 by the BJP primo, L. K. Advani, comprised tens of thousands of BJP, VHP, and RSS members, had as its goal the "liberation of the birthplace of Lord Ram," and entailed the removal or, if need be, the destruction of, the Babri Masjid (mosque).[43] While there are clear analogies between the BJP/VHP/RSS Sangh Pariwar's militant rhetoric, actions, and goals and those of the Mahabodhi Liberation Committee, there are important differences as well.

The first similarity revolves around the reclaiming of a specific religious center as both the symbolic and literal focus of a larger, sociopolitical cause. Simply put, for the Sangh Pariwar, building the Ram Temple has come to symbolize the reestablishment of Hindu religious, cultural, and political dominance vis à vis other communities, who they claim have received unfair preferential treatment in the social and political arenas. They focus particularly on Muslims, who they assert should also be held responsible for the historical destruction of countless Hindu temples, including that of Ram's birthplace. For many Dalit Buddhists, on the other hand, the removal of Hindu influence at the Mahabodhi Temple and the establishment of an all-Buddhist committee has come to stand for the eradication of caste prejudice and the regaining of their religious patrimony (i.e., Buddhism)[44] and sociopolitical rights-all of which they assert have been stolen from them by upper-caste Hindus, such as those in the Sangh Pariwar. But whereas the Sangh Pariwar's campaign advocated (and eventually succeeded in) the razing of a Muslim mosque in order to build a Ram temple, the Mahabodhi Liberation group has merely demanded the removal of Hindu members from the Mahabodhi Temple Management Committee—a far less radical, potentially violent goal. In both cases, however, not only the regaining of a religious center but the construction of a religious identity has been key.

Related to this was the self-conscious use of religious iconography throughout both *yātrās*. For like Advani's motorized procession, the Dalits's trucks were decorated with religious symbols and carried religious items important to their group. But whereas the hundreds of vehicles headed toward Ayodhya were emblazoned with paintings of Hindu deities, the proposed Ram temple, and L. K. Advani, the Dalits' dozen-or-so trucks were decorated with pictures of the Buddha, the Mahabodhi Temple, the Dikshabhumi Stupa (site of the first Dalit conversions), and Ambedkar. Furthermore, while Advani's own enormous, glassed-in, air-conditioned vehicle was festooned with saffron flags, designed to look like Ram's royal chariot (*rāth*), and carried both a miniature Ram temple and yellow-clad *sādhus*,[45] Surai Sasai's funky flatbed truck was draped with Buddhist flags and contained a large Thai Buddha image, *stūpas* holding relics of the Buddha and Ambedkar, a few Buddhist monks, and a torch referred to as the *Dhamma Jyoti*, or "Light of the [Buddhist] Dharma," kept burning for the duration of the trip.

While the items mentioned here are benign, certain members of the Sangh—in particular members of the VHP's militant youth wing, the Vajrang Dal (or "Hanuman's Army")—did draw on and carry quite militant religious icons. These included Shiva tridents, Ram bows, and ritually offered pots of blood. There was nothing like this in the Dalit procession. Yet, while the symbols were different, the goal was the same: to publicly proclaim and internally solidify the religious identity of each group for political purposes—a tactic that Gayatri Chakravorty Spivak refers to as "strategic essentialism."[46]

There is another important similarity: the rhetoric used throughout both processions was militantly oppositional, positing a religious enemy that must in some way be removed. For instance, the Dalits spoke continually of wresting control from the "wicked Hindu mahantas" (fig. 10.1) and threatened *"Agar Mahābodhi Mandīr ko paṇḍon se mukta nahin kiya, to Bodh Gayā dusra Ayodhyā ban jayega!* (If the Mahabodhi Temple is not liberated from the priests, then Bodh Gayā will become another Ayodhya!)"[47] However, many Sangh members, particularly the Vajrang Dal, were much more rhetorically violent, singing songs, for instance, about the streets running with Muslim blood.[48]

Yet religious identity is not all these two groups were and remain concerned with. Caste identity, and its correlate caste politics, are equally key, as both movements have attempted to make the regaining of a sacred center the focus of a larger political struggle. With respect to this, the Sangh Pariwar's political agenda revolves around not only reasserting the dominance of a "threatened" Hindu majority over a "pampered" Muslim minority but also fighting against scheduled and backward-caste reservations in government and educational institutions. (The latter was an extremely contentious issue at the time of the 1990 Rath Yatra, given the Janata Dal prime minister V. P. Singh's intention to implement the Mandal Commission's suggestions and substantially increase these "affirmative action" slots.) The RSS/VHP/BJP combine used this communal rhetoric in order to appeal to middle- and upper-caste Hindus, that is, those most likely to suffer from the Mandal Commission's advice and vote for the BJP.

The Mahabodhi Liberation Committee's campaign, in contrast, focuses on the uplift of Dalit minorities,[49] fights against upper-caste oppression and exploitation, and thereby attempts to attract the support of pro-scheduled and backward-caste politicians, as well as those who would likely vote along these lines. In short, gaining political advantage by both perpetuating and appealing to caste identity has played an equally important role in the two campaigns.

There is an important difference here, however. The Mahabodhi movement does not have nearly the same potential to influence or upset Indian politics, as its popular and political base of support is too small.[50] For instance, the 1992 Dhamma Mukti Yatra was led by a nationally unknown figure, comprised only a few hundred people throughout most of its journey, attracted at most 200,000 to its largest rally (on the esplanade in New Delhi), won no support from international Buddhists, and has had little political impact on state or national governments. In contrast, the 1990 Rath Yatra was led by a nationally prominent politician, and was key to electoral campaigns being waged by the BJP throughout northern India. Moreover, it attracted crores of rupees from nonresident Indians, comprised hundreds of thousands of participants, and was greeted by millions of people as it snaked its way through eight states where BJP support was strong. As a result of the Rath Yatra, and the violence that followed it, prime minister V. P. Singh's government was overturned, while in the 1991 elections 119 seats were gained in the Lok Sabha and four state governments were won by the BJP. With a few twists and turns, this once-marginal party continued to rise to power throughout the 1990s, with a moderate BJP prime minister, A. J. Vajpayee, now ruling the country. In short, the "liberate Ayodhya" campaign has been remarkably successful, politically and financially, at the regional, national, and international levels. The same cannot be said of the Mahabodhi Liberation Movement.

Finally, there is another important difference. While both groups utilized militant rhetoric and actions throughout their *yātrās*, the more hard-core wing of the Sangh advocated and actually engaged in violence. The Mahabodhi Liberation Committee, by contrast, did not. The 1990 Rath Yatra resulted in communal rioting, mass arrests, and numerous deaths all along its path. And while Advani was arrested before reaching Ayodhya, 100,000 Sangh Pariwar militants successfully entered the city and damaged the Babri Masjid. Then, in 1992, they razed the mosque to the ground, killed or injured scores of Muslims, and provoked widespread riots (the worst since 1947), not only in India but in Bangladesh, Pakistan, and England. By contrast, only a few thousand Dalits demonstrated in Bodh Gayā that same year, during which they gave angry speeches, led several processions, and planned to form a human chain around the temple until the Bihar government amended the 1949 Act (the latter they were unable to accomplish, due to tight security and the institution of curfew).[51] In short, they neither advocated, stimulated, nor engaged in violence, although the implicit and, occasionally, explicit warning that Bodh Gayā could become another Ayodhya, and talk of "wresting control" of the temple were definitely there.

I have rehearsed these similarities and differences for several reasons. First, it is important to note that the early stages of Surai Sasai's "liberate the Mahabodhi Temple" campaign occurred within the context of, and attempted to influence, a north Indian political scene increasingly articulated, organized, and contested along communal lines. Furthermore, and related to this, its first major agitation was modeled, to a large extent, on Advani's militant crusade to liberate the birthplace of Lord Ram. I also want to underscore that this was not, despite many newspaper headlines to the contrary, "Another 'Ayodhya type' dispute in the offing."[52] The potential for massive political and communal upheaval was and is simply not there. Finally, the issue of violence is important, as it leads me to categorize the Sangh Pariwar as "extremist," due to their advocation and actual destruction of the mosque, as well as the looting, bodily harm, and murder they stimulated, encouraged, or actively perpetrated on members of both the Muslim and untouchable communities before and after this tragic event. On the other hand, as I mentioned at the beginning of this chapter, I would categorize the Mahabodhi temple as "militant," due to their angry, anti-Hindu rhetoric and strident agitations. However, that they have neither advocated physical destruction, nor spoken of Hindu blood running in the streets, nor engaged in violence, qualifies them for inclusion in the category Buddhist Liberation

Movements, albeit at the extreme militant end of this group. As we shall see, however, their militancy has diminished somewhat in recent years.

Sit-Down Strikes and Fasts Until Death

After their 1992 Dhamma Mukti Yatra, the Mahabodhi Liberation Committee staged two Buddha Purnima agitations, one in 1993 and another in 1994.[53] Both attracted some ten to fifteen thousand Dalits, including a number of Sasai's Dhammasena monks who had been ordained specifically for these events. Most of the activists came from Maharashtra, but people from Uttar Pradesh, Gujarat, Andhra Pradesh, Tamil Nadu, and Bihar participated as well. Given the communal tensions that were still rife throughout northern India, security was extremely tight, with hundreds of police stationed in town, metal detectors placed at the front gate of the Mahabodhi Temple, the Pancapandav Mandir and the Mahabodhi's inner shrine room barricaded, and the annual Buddha Purnima celebrations canceled for the first time in forty years (fig. 10.3). Small counter-demonstrations by local members of the VHP were also staged, and in 1994 two truckloads of Shiv Sena militants (a Maharashtrian paramilitary group that has joined ranks with the Sangh Pariwar) were stopped by police before reaching town. Finally, both years the chief minister of Bihar, Laloo Yadav Prasad,

FIGURE 10.3. Surai Sasai (center) and thousands of Dalit monks, most of whom were ordained for this event, leaving the Mahabodhi Temple under armed guard during the 1993 agitation in Bodh Gayā. Photograph by Suresh Bhattia.

promised he would take up the Mahabodhi Liberation Committee's demands in the Bihar Assembly, thus prompting the Dalits to stop their agitations. But when these promises proved empty, Surai Sasai called another gathering on 6 December, 1994—a particularly provocative date, given that this was when the Babri Masjid had been razed.

More moderate leaders had by then joined the movement, however, and this event was thus publicized as a meeting (*sammelan*), not an agitation (*andolan*), with promises made to the local administration that no processions or demonstrations would take place.[54] In response, the D.M. allowed the 25,000 Dalits full access to the Mahabodhi Temple and even provided certain facilities to the crowd. There were conspicuously more children and women at this event, and many more non-Maharashtrians.[55] And while the tone of the speeches was often strident, the usual anti-Hindu rhetoric was toned down. Another change was the presence of a dozen foreign Buddhists on the stage set up for this meeting, including Tibetan and Korean monastics living in Bodh Gayā, and Japanese monks and lay persons who had flown in especially for this event. Also, two conversion ceremonies were staged, at which approximately 150 Indians became Buddhists (fig. 10.4). And in town, business boomed. In short, the feeling was more that of a *melā* (festival) than a siege.

But on the day following the gathering, despite promises made by the movement's more moderate leaders, Surai Sasai and two hundred of his Dhammasena monks staged a sit-down strike in front of the Mahabodhi Temple (fig. 10.5). This moved Laloo to promise that he would reconfigure the Mahabodhi management committee within the next few months. Once again, however, the chief minister did not keep his promise, fearing, I suppose, that this would alienate his backward-caste, Hindu constituency.[56] In response, more radical, nonviolent tactics were adopted by the Mahabodhi Liberation Committee.

These included most centrally fasts until death, both in Bodh Gayā and in Delhi. The hunger strikes, coupled with an upcoming fundraising trip to Thailand (where there was talk of the need for more Buddhist representation on the Temple Management Committee), moved the chief minister, in 1995, to reconstitute the committee so that three out of the four Buddhist positions went to leaders of the Mahabodhi Liberation Committee: Surai Sasai, Bhante Anand (a monk from Agra, with a large following), and Bhante Anand Ambedkar (a monk from Kanpur).[57] While this represented a major victory for the Dalits, Sasai was not satisfied, declaring to a reporter: "The reconstitution of the committee is hardly of any consequence. Our demand is amendment of the (1949) Act. We will continue our agitation till we have achieved it. . . . The utmost we can accept is the continuation of Bodh Gaya Mahanth and the Gaya district magistrate. But the rest of the members have to be Buddhists, which will correct the anomaly inherent in the Act."[58] Yet he ended this interview by saying: "Now we are comfortably placed and can fight it out from both inside and outside the committee."[59]

FIGURE 10.4. Surai Sasai with newly ordained boy from Maharashtra, during 1994 *sammelan* (rally) in Bodh Gayā. Photograph by Tara Doyle.

And "fight it out" they have. From 1995 to 1998, Surai Sasai and his followers accused Hindu members of the Management Committee and several Bodh Gayā Buddhists of immoral behavior and misappropriation of temple funds. Not surprisingly, countercharges ensued, creating a contentious atmosphere in town and attracting much media coverage.[60] The Dalits also staged more indefinite hunger strikes, including an eighteen-month-long fast at Jantar

FIGURE 10.5. Surai Sasai and his Dalit followers engage in a sit-down strike in front of the Mahabodhi Temple after the 1994 *sammelan*. Photograph by Tara Doyle.

Mantar Park, in the heart of New Delhi, where different groups participated for at least a week at a time. Several monks also threatened to immolate themselves unless the 1949 Act was amended.

In 1998, these threats, coupled with Surai Sasai's seriously weakening condition during the Jantar Mantar fast, prompted Laloo to remove the longtime, Hindu general secretary Dwarko Sundrani and appoint Bhante Prajnasheel, a Dalit monk and Surai Sasai's close associate, in his place. The first Buddhist ever to hold this office, Prajnasheel's appointment was heralded as a major success. Furthermore, monks from within the Mahabodhi Liberation Committee were placed in charge of performing *pūja*, collecting donations, and assisting visitors inside the temple—duties that Theravādin monks, particularly those associated with the Mahabodhi Society, had previously performed.[61] Thus firmly and "comfortably" placed on the inside—with three out of four Buddhist Committee slots, the most important position (general secretary), and the day-to-day running of the temple in their hands—their agitations ceased.

But this is not the end of the story. Ugly divisions continue between the Dalit monks and several foreign Buddhists who live in Bodh Gayā. And in the summer of 2001, in a major about-face, Laloo's wife, Rabri Devi (now Bihar's chief minister) removed Bhante Anand from the committee, and replaced the general secretary, Bhante Prajnasheel, with a local RJD politician and Yadav clansman, Kalicharan Singh Yadav.[62] With two Mahabodhi Liberation leaders now ousted from the Management Committee, this left only Surai Sasai in place.[63] Not surprisingly, he and his followers are calling for renewed agitations unless the new committee is dissolved and the 1949 Act amended.[64] However, if the events of the last decade are any indication, and given that the BJP now rules the Central government, I doubt seriously that either the national or Bihar state governments will do this anytime soon.

Gandhian Tactics With a Militant Twist

As a footnote to all this, it is important to note that many of the tactics used throughout the course of the Mahabodhi Liberation campaign have been influenced by Gandhi—a controversial claim among Dalits, given their deep animosity toward this man. Seen by them as a champion of caste Hinduism, and the major opponent of Ambedkar's attempts both to legislate affirmative action and convert to Buddhism, Gandhi nonetheless, through his perfection of these politically successful tactics, provided members of the Mahabodhi Liberation Movement with the nonviolent strikes, processions, and demonstrations they have employed in their attempts to overturn the 1949 Act. These, of course, are now standard items in the toolbox of nonviolent activists worldwide, and in fact figure centrally in Socially Engaged Buddhist movements. But such strategies have particular clout in the Indian political arena. Indeed, the Pariwar Sangh uses them as well. But Gandhi, like pacifist leaders of Buddhist liberation movements, was decidedly nonoppositional, and fought hard against the construction and perpetuation of communal identity in the service of politics. In this, he and Ambedkar were at odds. But following Ambedkar, Surai Sasai and his followers have neither advocated nor engaged in violence; thus, I would term their tactics "Gandhian," with a militant twist.

Conclusion

Here I return once again to the Buddhist dimensions of Sasai's struggle, which have to some extent been lost in the course of my descriptions of the Mahabodhi Liberation Committee's political maneuvering, processions, strikes, and fasts. But I do not apologize for this diversion: the Mahabodhi campaign is a distinctly modern *Indian* movement, one that makes no sense without an appreciation of its national social and political frame. Indeed, given that the Dalits have been unable to garner much foreign Buddhist sympathy or assistance, the regional and national scenes become even more important—both for them, practically, and for our understanding of their tactics, rhetoric, obstacles, and goals. Yet, there can be no doubt that this is a Buddhist movement as well. Given this, one might wonder: what is it, exactly, that makes this movement both Buddhist and modern? And, perhaps more important, why has this struggle not attained more Buddhist recognition and support?

Buddhifying the Issue

Toward the beginning of this chapter, I discussed the various Buddhist leaders and movements that have influenced the Mahabodhi Liberation Committee: Dharmapala's earlier campaign, Ambedkar's socially engaged *Dhamma*, and the influence of Nichiren Buddhism, as manifested by Nichadatsu Fuji, on Surai Sasai himself. All these have certainly contributed to the Buddhist dimensions of this modern movement; but there is more. To begin with, this group draws heavily on Buddhist symbols, particularly those deriving from Theravādin countries, in the course of their demonstrations. These include the Thai Buddha statue and relics of the Buddha found on the lead truck of their Dhamma Mukti Yatra, a small Burmese Buddha statue used during conversion ceremonies in the 1994 Sammelan, and the five-colored Buddhist flag found everywhere at their agitations—a flag that originated during the Sri Lankan Buddhist revival movement but that is now commonly found throughout the contemporary (especially Theravāda) Buddhist world.

The new symbols they have added to this mix include their Dhamma Jyoti, or "Light of Buddhism," which is ritually central at many of their demonstrations, the five-colored epaulets worn by a group of women from Uttar Pradesh, purple flags emblazoned with a white dharma-chakra that are carried by Surai Sasai's "lay lieutenants" and other activists, and the relics of Ambedkar, which were found side by side with those of the Buddha during the Dhamma Mukti Yatra campaign. In short, symbolically, they are creating a Buddhist identity that not only sets them apart from Hindus, but mixes Theravāda and Ambedkarite elements. In this, they are following Ambedkar; yet they have added symbols distinctly their own.

The rituals they perform during their agitations also combine Theravāda and Ambedkarite elements, including as they do *dikṣhās* (conversions), the taking of the three refuges in Pāli, followed by Ambedkar's twenty-two vows in Marathi or Hindi. But now there is a new "*dikṣhā*," that is, the novice ordination taken by Sasai's Dhammasena monks, as well as a twenty-third vow added to the others: "The Mahabodhi Temple shall be liberated from Hindu hands." Also, as we have seen, this group has organized numerous agitations on Buddha Purnima, a day particularly important to Theravāda Buddhists. But other dates have been significant in the timing of their demonstrations, including Ambedkar's conversion day and the day of the razing of the Babri Masjid.

Finally, in the area of nomenclature, they utilize distinctly Buddhist vocabulary. Examples are that they now call Bodh Gayā "Buddhagaya" and the Mahabodhi Temple a "*vihār*" (instead of using the Hindu term *mandir*). But with

FIGURE 10.6. A Dhammasena monk holding a Buddhist flag during the 1994 rally. Photograph by Tara Doyle.

respect to innovation, what I find most interesting is the way in which they have played with the word "*mukti*," a pan-Indian term normally referring to spiritual liberation. However, when placed next to the term *andolan* (agitation, struggle)— as in the name of their committee, the Mahabodhi Mukti Andolan Samiti—they have transformed the meaning to include social and political emancipation (a semantic tactic that reminds one not only of Christian liberation theologies, but

Socially Engaged Buddhist movements as well). Thus, like those of other Buddhist traditions, both historical and contemporary, their symbols, rituals, significant dates, and institutional names reflect classical and modern, as well as traditional and indigenous elements. This complex intermingling provides both continuity with "received" Buddhism and dimensions that are distinctly new *and* local. And this, of course, is how contemporary Buddhist movements get forged.

Globalizing the Struggle

So, why has not the Mahabodhi Liberation Movement received more foreign Buddhist support? The reasons are many, but here I will focus on only four.[65] First, while most foreign Buddhist officials and monastic heads I have spoken to *do* feel that the Mahabodhi Temple should be in the hands of a Buddhist management committee, they have nonetheless been loathe to interfere with what they perceive, in the words of Sri Lanka's high commissioner, as "purely an internal domestic problem of the Indian state."[66] In short, the issue is both too sensitive and, I contend, not important enough to risk putting pressure on the Indian government to amend the 1949 Act. Second, the majority of foreign Buddhists feel that the present arrangement is quite acceptable, especially when compared to the situation before the temple was relinquished by the Bodh Gayā mahant in 1953. The temple is now decidedly Buddhist (narratively and iconographically), Buddhists can worship exactly as they please there, and they have been able to build dozens of Buddhist temples and guesthouses in and around Bodh Gayā in recent years. The presence of the Pancapandav Mandir, a few brahmin priests, numerous Hindu pilgrims, and a joint Hindu-Buddhist Management Committee has not interfered with this. So while most foreign pilgrims and monks would prefer an all-Buddhist committee (especially if this could include foreign Buddhist members),[67] their basic attitude is: why make a fuss?

A third criticism leveled against this movement is that monks should not be involved in politics to this extent—a critique that is certainly not new. Several foreign Buddhist monks I spoke with were particularly critical of the practice of ordaining monks for the purpose of participating in agitations, and then referring to them as a "Dhammasena," or Buddhist Army. "This," contended one Theravāda monk, "dirties our Sangha, dirties our robes. It does great harm to the *sāsana* (Buddhist tradition), and should not be allowed."

The last reason that the Mahabodhi Liberation Movement has not received foreign sympathy revolves, I am told, around the rhetoric and tactics being used by the Dalits. Their more militant agitations have disrupted Buddha Purnima celebrations and resulted in the Temple being barricaded, curfew instituted, and shops and restaurants closed. Moreover, it should be remembered that the Dalits have lashed out against not only Hindus but foreign Buddhists. For instance, they have accused the head of the Mahabodhi Society of misappropriating temple funds,[68] and several monasteries of illegal activities (including "antinational manoeuvres" and "outright prostitution").[69] Moreover, they have denounced the Karmapa for desecrating the temple by wearing shoes inside the inner sanctum, Tibetans for seriously damaging the face of the temple with their burning candles, and the Dalai Lama for fraternizing with Hindu leaders during the Kumbha Mela in 2000, all the while not speaking a "single line on this (Mahabodhi) matter with His millions of followers."[70] Regardless of the veracity of these claims, or the legitimacy of the anger many Dalits feel at having been ignored by their "elite" Buddhist brethren, certainly none of this has endeared members of the Mahabodhi Liberation Committee to Buddhist pilgrims, leaders, or resident monks.

This, of course, is the risk of being militant, or (in Sally King's words) of forcefully denouncing what one sees as error, and taking up "an oppositional stance" vis-à-vis one's enemy.[71] Whether such oppositional, militant strategies and rhetoric will result in an internationalization of this movement seems highly unlikely. But one wonders: will they influence the social and political landscape of India, or effect changes in the 1949 Act? That remains to be seen.

NOTES

This chapter draws on research done primarily in 1991–1992, and more briefly in the fall of 1994 and the winter of 2002. I am grateful for research support from the American Institute of Indian Studies, Fulbright Hayes, and Emory University. I would also like to thank Christopher Queen, Eleanor Zelliot, and Laurie Patton for comments on earlier versions of this paper, and Bhante Surai Sasai, P. C. Roy, and other people I interviewed, both named and unnamed, for sharing their thoughts and time with me.

1. My description of this agitation derives from newspaper and magazine articles from this period, discussions with Bodh Gayā residents, and interviews with Gaya D. M. Rajbala Verma, and the agitation's leaders, Bhikkhu D. Sangharaks.it (Convener, Maharashtra Bhikkhu Sangh) and Rameshchandra Dhongre (Head, All-India Depressed and Minority Peoples' Action Committee).

2. "Buddha's Full Moon" usually occurs in May and, according to Theravāda Buddhists and Indians, commemorates Buddha's birthday, enlightenment, and death. While other Buddhists do not accept this tripartite assignation, they do celebrate it while in Bodh Gayā. In 1992, Buddha Purnima occurred May 6.

3. The Marathi word dalit, which literally means "broken," was chosen as a term of self-reference, sometime in the 1960s, by several groups of politicized ex-untouchables, including the Dalit Panthers. As Eleanor Zelliot points out, adoption of this word (as opposed to untouchables, scheduled castes, depressed castes, or harijan) represented "a new level of pride, militancy and sophisticated creativity" among these groups, in much the same way as "Black" did for Afro-Americans. See From Untouchable to Dalit (New Delhi: Manohar, 1992), p. 267. Although many who call themselves Dalits are Buddhist converts, this term has been adopted by politicized secular, Hindu, and Christian ex-untouchables as well.

4. In brief, these oaths comprise the rejection of Hindu gods, practices, beliefs, and social systems, the acceptance of Buddhist precepts and principles, and the adoption of such principles as equality, liberty, and fraternity.

5. Interviews, Pannarama Bhikkhu (head of Bodh Gaya Mahabodhi Society) and Kabir Saxena (director, Root Institute), May 1992. Also, "Buddhists Oppose Bodh Gaya Temple Act," *Indian Express*, Bombay (22 May 1992): 6.

6. Interviews, Narayan. Dube, Bodh Gaya, May 1992, and Bhikkhu D. Sangharaks.it and Rameshchandra Dhongre, Nagpur, Dec. 1992. Also, "Another 'Ayodhya type' Issue in the Offing," *Hindustan Times* (24 May 1992): 4, and Faizan Ahmad, "When Will They Ever Learn? Yet Another Disputed Shrine Sparks Off Communal Trouble," *Sunday* (31 May–6 June 1992): 80–81.

7. Interviews, D. M. Rajbala Verma (June 1992), Narayan. Dube (May 1992), Kabir Saxena (May 1992), and Rameshchandra Dhongre (December 1992).

8. Headlines are from *Hindustan Times* (May 24): 4; Arvind N. Das and Abdul Qadir, *Times of India* (May 29); and Faizan Ahmad, *Sunday* (31 May–6 June 1992): 80–81, respectively.

9. "Backward Castes" (primarily comprising Śūdras), while quite low in the caste hierarchy, are higher than "Scheduled Castes" (Dalits), which comprise untouchables and tribals. Yadavs, a Backward Caste, are numerous and politically powerful in northern India, with many aligned with the RJD. While the RJD attempts to champion both Backward and Scheduled Caste issues, there is often infighting along these lines. Thus, although Laloo has to some extent supported Sasai's movement, he has more frequently obstructed it. One reason is that most Backward Caste people are Hindu, including Yadavs, and would thus tend to be opposed to handing the Mahabodhi over to Buddhists. There is also regular, bloody conflict between Yadavs and Dalit groups in Bihar.

10. In all English references to this group—not only in media coverage but in the group's own publications—the term *andolan* is translated as "action." This, however, does not adequately reflect the more militant nature of this term, which literally means "agitation" or "struggle."

11. "Buddhists Launch Stir," *Times of India* (12 August 1992): 1.

12. Abdul Qadir, "Hindus vs. Buddhists: Peace Loses," *Times of India*, Patna (7 July 1992): 10.

13. Statement issued in Muzaffapur, Bihar, on May 26. Ranjiv Ranjan Lal, "Temple of Doom," *Illustrated Weekly of India* (27 June–3 July 1992): 34–35.

14. Statement by Prayag Yadav. Quoted in Ranjiv Ranjan Lal, "Temple of Doom," *Illustrated Weekly of India* (27 June–3 July 3 1992), p. 34.

15. "Lanka Told to Keep Out of Bodh Gaya," *Times of India* (30 June 1992): 10.

16. Ibid.

17. Important early works include Fred Eppsteiner's volume *The Path of Compassion: Writings on Socially Engaged Buddhism* (Berkeley: Parallax Press, 1988), Sulak Sivaraksha's *A Socially Engaged Buddhism* (Bangkok: Thai Inter-Religious Commission for Development, 1988), Ken Jones's *The Social Face of Buddhism: An Approach to Political and Social Activism* (London: Wisdom, 1989), Ken Kraft's edited volume *Inner Peace, World Peace: Essays on Buddhism and Nonviolence* (Albany: State University of New York Press, 1992), and numerous books by Thich Nhat Hanh.

18. Preface to Christopher Queen and Sally King, eds. *Engaged Buddhism: Buddhist Liberation Movements in Asia* (Albany: State University of New York Press, 1996), x. Emphasis added.

19. Ibid., x–xi.

20. Ibid., p. 430. Emphasis added.

21. In his introduction, Queen contends that "It is only in the late nineteenth-century revival of Buddhism in Sri Lanka . . . that we first recognize the spirit and substance of the religious activism we call 'socially engaged Buddhism.' And it is only in this context that we first meet the missing ingredient—. . . the influence of European and American religious and political thought." Ibid., p. 20. King reiterates Queen's contention in her conclusion. Ibid., p. 404.

22. In particular, Holt is referring to Obeyesekere's idea of "Protestant Buddhism" and Hallisey to contentions found in Philip Almond's *The British Discovery of Buddhism*. Their critiques, however, hold for a wider range of works. See John Holt, "Protestant Buddhism?" *Religious Studies Review* 17, no. 4 (October 1991), and Charles Hallisey, "Roads Taken and Not Taken in the Study of Theravāda Buddhism," in *Curators of the Buddha*, Donald Lopez, ed. (Chicago: University of Chicago Press, 1995), p. 32.

23. This account was related to me by Surai Sasai at his Nagpur temple, in December 1992.

24. Nichidatsu Fuji is most famous for erecting over fifty *stūpa*s, or "peace pagodas," an activity his followers have continued since his death in 1985. The majority of these are in Japan, but over a dozen exist in India, Sri Lanka, Austria, England, and the U.S.A.

25. Nichidatsu came to India in 1930 and began residing in Rajgir in 1936. As part of the Rajgir Reconstruction program initiated by Nehru, Fuji offered to build a *stūpa* on Ratnagiri, a hill adjacent to Vulture's Peak. The foundation was laid on 15 March 1965 by India's president, Dr. S. Radhakrishnan, while the 160-foot-tall, gold-topped *stūpa* was designed by Japanese architect Minoru Okoka and noted Indian artist, Upendra Maharathi. The *stūpa* was inaugurated 25 October 1969. D. C. Ahir, *Pioneers of Buddhist Revival In India* (Delhi: Sri Satguru Publications, 1989), pp. 50–54.

26. Chanting this *mantra*, "Homage to the Lotus Sutra," usually accompanied by a drum, is central to Nichiren practice.

27. Godbole organized Ambedkar's *dīkṣā* in Nagpur.

28. Dr. Bhau Lokhande, interview, Nagpur, January 1993.

29. For more on Dharmapala's campaign, see my forthcoming *Journeys to the Diamond Throne* (Boston: Wisdom Publications).

30. *Maha-Bodhi Society: Its Constitution, Rules and List of Officers*, p. 1.

31. *Maha Bodhi Journal* 1, no. 1 (May 1892): 1–2.

32. Dharmapala's pre-eminent place in this history is found in a variety of Dalit sources, including works by the Dalit's most famous author, D. C. Ahir (e.g., *Buddha Gaya Through the Ages*, pp. 109–121), articles by professor Bhau Lokande (e.g., "Buddha Gaya: Past and Present," *Lokmat Times*, 26 July 1992), and a one-rupee pamphlet sold at Mahabodhi agitations (Naresh Kumar's *Mahābodhi Mahāviāra Saṃkṣipta Itihāsa*), which includes a long section on Dharmapala entitled *"Mahāvihār Mukti Andolan."*

33. Recounted by both Surai Sasai and the movement's other major leader, Uttar Pradesh monk Bhante Anand.

34. P. C. Roy, personal communication, November 1994.

35. "The Great Conversion: Dr. Ambedkar and the Buddhist Revival," *Tricycle* (Spring 1993): 63.

36. Quoted in Eleanor Zelliot, "Religion and Legitimation in the Mahar Movement," in *Religion and Legitimation of Power in South Asia*, ed. Bardwell L. Smith (Leiden: E. J. Brill, 1978), p. 102.

37. During this period, Ambedkar did not turn his back on politics. He founded the Independent Labour Party, was elected to the Legislative Assembly, was appointed to the Defense Advisory Committee and, after independence, was made minister of law, whereupon he drafted the Indian Constitution. But throughout, Ambedkar remained a fierce critic of Congress, calling them "those Brahmin boys" who would simply replace one tyranny (colonialism) with another (caste-Hinduism).

38. *The Buddha and His Dhamma* (Bombay: Siddharth Publications, 1984 [1957]), p. 83.

39. Quoted in Zelliot, "Religion and Legitimation in the Mahar Movement," pp. 103–104.

40. For more, see Bhimrao Ambedkar, *The Untouchables: Who Were They? and Why They Became Untouchables* (New Delhi: Amrit Book Company, 1948), p. 43.

41. For Ambedkar's view on how Buddhism might best be spread in India, see his *Maha Bodhi* article, "The Buddha and the Future of His Religion" (April–May 1950), where he writes that three things are necessary: a Buddhist bible, changes in the organization and aims of the Bhikkhu Sangha, and the establishment of a World Buddhist Mission. Due to his untimely death, he was able to produce only the first item: his "bible," *The Buddha and His Dhamma*.

42. *The Buddha and His Dhamma*, p. 327.

43. For more, see Sarvepalli Gopal, ed., *Anatomy of a Confrontation: The Babri Masjid-Ramjanmabhumi*, (New Delhi: Penguin Books, 1990); Peter van der Veer, *Religious Nationalism* (Berkeley: University of California Press, 1994); and David Ludden, ed., *Contesting the Nation: Religion, Community, and the Politics of Democracy in India* (Philadelphia: University of Pennsylvania Press, 1996).

44. This idea of Dalits reclaiming their "rightful religious patrimony" comes from Owen Lynch's conference paper, "Our Culture Is Being Destroyed: Baba Sahab's Children and the Liberate the Bodh Gaya Movement," Columbia University Seminar on Tradition and Change in South Asia, 16 April 1996.

45. Richard Davis, "The Iconography of Rama's Chariot," in Ludden, ed., *Contesting the Nation*, pp. 27–28.

46. See, for instance, *Outside in the Teaching Machine* (New York: Routledge, 1993), pp. 3–4, where Spivak clarifies this term.

47. Visnulal Barik, personal communication, 18 June 1993.

48. See Anand Patwardhan's film *In the Name of God* (1990) for a chilling depiction of such songs and statements.

49. Such "majority-minority" issues are key to contemporary Indian politics; for Hindus can only be considered a "majority" as long as large numbers of the lower-

castes do not openly declare themselves outside that group. Following Ambedkar, Surai Sasai's ex-untouchable Buddhist followers declare just that.

50. That the Mahabodhi Liberation Committee's main demand has been Buddhist control of a temple visited by hundreds of thousands of Hindus yearly, has not gained them much popularity among pro-scheduled and backward-caste politicians and voters, the vast majority of whom are Hindu. Were the Mahabodhi Temple in Maharashtra, where millions of voters are Buddhist, the possibility of gaining control would be far greater. But this is not true in Bihar.

51. During the Dalits' 1992 *yātrā* demonstration, the D.M. ordered the resident Buddhist abbots to bar the Maharashtrians from their monasteries, and all shops and restaurants closed. She also stationed approximately 500 policemen and scores of plainclothesmen around the Mahabodhi Temple, barricaded the front entrance, and fenced off large sections of town. The Dalits were, however, allowed inside the temple compound, after passing through a metal detector, in groups of ten. Interviews, Gaya D. M. Rajabala Verma (December 1992) and Surai Sasai (January 1993).

52. *The Hindustan Times* (24 May 1992).

53. Information about these agitations comes from "Buddhists Hold Rally in Bodh Gaya," *Times of India* (6 May 1993), "Buddhist Monks Launch Agitation"; *The Hindu* (6 May 1993): 2; and P. C. Roy, interview (8 December 1994).

54. Information about this gathering comes from personal observation and interviews with the movement's leaders.

55. A significant presence at this event was a group of Agra women, dressed in white *saris* and sporting epaulets comprising the five colors of the Buddhist flag. Several made speeches, demanding the liberation of the temple and the further emancipation of women. For more on the participation of Agra Buddhists in this movement, see Lynch, "Our Culture Is Being Destroyed."

56. See n. 9.

57. "Monks on Fast over Mahabodhi Temple," *Times of India* (14 July 1995).

58. Rajesh Kumar, "Buddham Sharanam Gahchami?" *Rashtriya Sahara* (October 1995): 51.

59. Ibid.

60. Robert Pryor, personal communication, September 1995 and January 1998.

61. Not surprisingly, members of these groups fought back. The head of the local Mahabodhi Society, Bhante Vimalasara, countercharged the Dalits with misappropriating funds. In retaliation, Surai Sasai's people threatened to sue Vimalasara, contending that he was fraudulently raising large amounts of money by claiming that the society (not the committee) was maintaining the temple. They also asserted that these funds were being funneled into the war against the Tamil Tigers, an incendiary charge with potentially significant ramifications in the region. Amarnath Tewary, "Zen of Making Money: Acrimonious Buddhist Monks Squabble over Foreign Funds," *Outlook* (8 October 2000): 48–49.

62. Prajnasheel and his followers did not take this lying down. Just before Kalicharan took office an announcement appeared on the temple's website (http://www.mahabodhi.com) asking that foreign Buddhists not donate funds to the new Management Committee. Furthermore, Prajnasheel sent an e-mail letter to the official Dalit website (dalits@ambedkar.org) alleging that "the new nominated

Hindu Secretary [was] not only a politician but also an antisocial man," and that donations received from abroad were being used by Hindu members "for their own house and personal use [sic]." 8 August 2001.

63. New members are, with the first five Hindu and last four Buddhist: Sri Brijesh Mehrotra (Ex-officio Chairman), Sri Kalicharan Singh Yadav (Secretary), Mahanth Sudarshan Giri, Ramswarup Singh, Kamla Sinha, Bhante Surai Sasai, Bhadant Gyneshwar Mahathera, Sri Nangzey Dorjee, and Sri Mangal Subbha.

64. Abdul Qadir, "Laloo Will Have to Pay for His Sins, Says Betrayed Monk," *Times of India* (2 September 2001) and "Monks lock horns with RJD govt," *Times of India* (27 November 2001).

65. Given the sensitive nature of this topic, everyone I interviewed requested that his or her name be withheld.

66. "Lanka Told to Keep Out of Bodh Gaya," *Times of India* (30 June 1992): 10.

67. The 1949 Act stipulates that all members of the Mahabodhi Management Committee be Indian citizens.

68. Tewary, "Zen of Making Money," pp. 48–49.

69. Ibid., p. 49.

70. E-mail letter sent to dalits@ambedkar.org by Bhante Anand, general secretary, Mahabodhi Vihar Liberation Action Committee, February 2002, just after the Dalai Lama's Kalachakra initiation in Bodh Gayā was canceled.

71. Queen and King, *Engaged Buddhism: Buddhist Liberation Movements in Asia*, p. 430.

Index